BOATING
SKILLS &
SEAMANSHIP

TENTH EDITION
SECOND PRINTING

U.S. COAST GUARD AUXILIARY

1-88-10/2

Library of Congress Catalog Card Number: 74-164-688
ISBN 0-930028-03-1
Printed in the United States of America at no cost
to the United States Government or United States
Coast Guard.

Contents approved by the
National Association of
State Boating Law Administrators
and recognized by the
United States Coast Guard

THE COMMANDANT OF THE UNITED STATES COAST GUARD
WASHINGTON, D.C. 20593

FOREWORD

Experience has taught us that education is a key factor in the prevention of boating accidents. Too often, investigations of major boating mishaps reveal that the skippers had not attended a safe boating class of any kind. This text will introduce you to such lessons as basic piloting, navigation rules, seamanship and other subjects to help you enjoy your boating activities.

This text was prepared by the U. S. Coast Guard Auxiliary and serves as a nucleus of the Boating Skills and Seamanship Course. Presenting this course is one of the ways the Auxiliary helps boaters get more pleasure from their boating experiences. Completing the course will give you the basic skills and knowledge to help you make boating safer and more enjoyable.

As Commandant of the United States Coast Guard, I salute our Auxiliary for their concern and dedicated efforts in promoting safe boating, and for the development of this course. I heartily endorse it for all who use our country's waterways for recreational boating.

P. A. YOST
Admiral, U. S. Coast Guard

PREFACE

The 10th Edition of the BOATING SKILLS AND SEAMANSHIP student text is produced by the Department of Education of the United States Coast Guard Auxiliary. The purpose of the textbook and the course for which it is written is to promote safe boating through public boating safety education. The Coast Guard Auxiliary's Boating Skills and Seamanship public education course is recognized as the most comprehensive available today for pleasure boaters. This 10th edition of the course is up-to-date with the latest safety-oriented material related to the Navigation Rules and Aids to Navigation currently in use within U. S. waters. The course covers essential boating information for pleasure boaters. It is professionally written for adults in laymen's language, and liberally illustrated with photographs, drawings, and diagrams.

The text and course reflect the resources of the entire Coast Guard Auxiliary. Much of the contents are a measure of the Auxiliary's training, experience and capabilities in Search and Rescue, Aids to Navigation patrols, and our Courtesy Marine Examinations (CME). The CME consists of our check, without charge, and only at the owner's request, equipment on pleasure boats for state and federal requirements plus other minimum safety-related standards.

The material in the BOATING SKILLS AND SEAMANSHIP text and course materials has been reviewed and approved by the U. S. Coast Guard.

The course is presented by qualified and certified Auxiliary public education Instructors, your fellow boaters, who voluntarily give their time to share with you, their knowledge and experience in boating skills.

Many insurance companies discount premiums for their boat insurance to those graduating and holding certificates for this course.

Other public education courses are also offered by the U. S. Coast Guard Auxiliary. They include SAILING AND SEAMANSHIP (7-12 lessons), ADVANCED COASTAL NAVIGATION (12 or more lessons), and youth courses. We invite you to increase your boating skills and knowledge, and to promote safe operation of pleasure boats by taking these valuable public education courses.

William C. Harr
National Commodore
United States Coast Guard Auxiliary

CONTENTS

Introduction

Welcome Aboard!

Boating is one of the most popular recreational activities today, and it is growing. In 1986, the latest year for which complete statistics are available, Americans went "down to the sea" for pleasure in 16 1/2 million recreational boats. This is up 10 million from just 20 years ago.

Obviously, boating today bears little resemblance to the "yachting" of yesterday, although that still exists. But for most recreational boaters, "boating" means a fun way for the family and a few friends to pass a weekend or a summer afternoon.

Fig. I-1   The Basic Principles of Good Seamanship Apply...

Unfortunately, for thousands of Americans every year, what boating involves is injury, financial loss, and even death. In 1984 over one thousand people were reported killed in recreational boating accidents, and thousands more received serious injuries. The death and injury rates for that year are lower than they have been since these records have been kept. Yet, when you consider the number of casualties in light of the very small amount of time that each boater actually spends boating, the rate of death and injury exceeds that in many traditionally hazardous occupations!

The victim of these boating accidents is typically a man between the ages of 24 and 34, fishing in a quiet lake on a late Saturday afternoon. He doesn't think of himself as a "boater"; the boat is just another part of his "fishing outfit."

Maybe he makes a sudden move with a fish on the line, or maybe he stands up to relieve himself of some of the beer he has drunk that afternoon. For whatever reason, the small boat capsizes, and the man falls into the water.

Of course, the life jackets he kept carefully in the boat drift away from him as he estimates the distance to shore and starts to swim away from the capsized boat. The one thing that could have saved his life he didn't have on, either because it was "uncomfortable," or because he was a "good swimmer," or because it isn't "manly." For whatever reason, the extra effort he expends swimming without a life jacket soon exhausts him, and he slips beneath the surface.

Of course, not all boating accidents happen this way. Many involve collisions, either with other boats or with fixed objects (piers, breakwaters, etc.). A very high percentage of these accidents, in turn, were due at least in part to the fact that the judgment of some of those involved was impaired by alcohol, drugs, or excess fatigue.

The Coast Guard and the Coast Guard Auxiliary believe that many of these losses could be prevented, or the consequences reduced, if more boaters knew more about seamanship, navigation, and related topics. Experience is a hard teacher, and lessons may be very hard, indeed. Formal instruction and training can help, but few people have formal training. Education cannot make you accident-proof. But experience has shown that a good fundamental course in seamanship (such as this one) is the single most cost-effective means of reducing losses.

Had our fisherman described above taken this course, for instance, he would have known to buy and wear a well-fitted PFD (life jacket) whenever he was underway. He would also have known that, by far, it is best to stay with the boat if he fell in.

He would also have known how to load his boat for best trim and balance, and how not to exceed load limits.

He would also have learned the importance of keeping a lookout at all times, to avoid collisions.

And, finally, he would have known what alcohol and fatigue can do to impair balance and judgment.

Family Activity

By and large, recreational boating is a family activity. Something about boating will appeal to every member of the family. If you are a member of a boating family and the other members of your family are not also enrolled in this course, you should talk with your instructor about enrolling them as soon as possible.

Fig. I-2 **...Regardless of the Size of the Boat...**

This Course

The purpose of this course, then, is to help you become a better recreational boater by gaining knowledge and skills. This knowledge can help you avoid difficulties and enjoy your on-the-water activities more. In addition, we would like to raise your awareness of things that might happen, and thereby help you avoid them. Finally, we hope to help you to help yourself in case you have problems on the water, or to help you help others should the need arise.

Fig. I-3 **...or the Amount of Money It Cost.**

Your Instructors

This course is being taught by members of the United States Coast Guard Auxiliary. Your instructors are all volunteers, and most of them are recreational boaters who started out in just such a class as this one. They are here to share with you some of their experience and some of the benefits of the special training they have received from the United States Coast Guard, the "parent" of the Auxiliary.

The members of the Coast Guard Auxiliary are civilians. They have no military or law enforcement duties or powers. They are concerned individuals who give freely of their time and energies by being involved in public education activities such as this one, or in other Auxiliary programs supporting the Coast Guard. If you would like to know more about the Coast Guard, the Coast Guard Auxiliary, or any of its programs, one of your instructors will be happy to talk to you about it. In the meantime, be sure to read the "Invitation" on the inside front cover of this book for more information.

Fig. I-4   The Members of the Coast Guard Auxiliary are Concerned Civilian Volunteers.

Course Format

Depending on local needs and the resources of the Auxiliary unit offering the course, a variety of formats may be followed, ranging from as few as six to as many as thirteen lessons. Your instructor will tell you what format this course will take.

Whatever the format, the course will contain a core of specific lessons. Each lesson is outlined briefly here to give you a preview.

Chapter 1, Boat Construction and Nomenclature, describes some of the most

popular types of boats that exist, points out some of the advantages (and drawbacks) of each type, and discusses various techniques that are used to build them and what those techniques mean to you.

This lesson also introduces you to the language of boats. We do not intend to make you sound like an "old salt," or to overwhelm you with a strange vocabulary. Nevertheless, it is useful to be able to recognize (and use) some of the terms that you find in common use among boaters.

In Chapter 2, Boat Operations and Seamanship, practical, everyday considerations of good boat keeping and management are covered. Docking, undocking, anchoring, layup and storage, fueling and maintenance are discussed.

There are, of course, Safety and Legal Requirements. Chapter 3 lays out for you what you must have on your boat, and what your obligations are under the law. We also look at other equipment, not strictly required by law, that you should carry for your general safety and convenience.

Fig. I-5   Boaters Must Be Able To Rely On Their Equipment.

Chapter 4 on Navigation Rules is a vitally important one, since its sole purpose is to help you prevent the most common injury-producing accident, a collision. This chapter describes the internationally-enforced "rules of the road" that guide your movements in the presence of other boats.

Every mariner trusts and depends on Aids to Navigation. Chapter 5 describes the simple principles that underlie the bewildering complexity of shapes and colors that mark the sea lanes and channels.

Trailering, Chapter 10, introduces some of the techniques of trailering your boat, techniques that can expand your boating horizons. This lesson discusses the selection of a trailerable boat, the choice of a trailer, and the things that you have to consider in selecting an appropriate tow vehicle. Techniques for launching and retrieving your boat are also discussed, as well as highway driving tips to make your boating trips more enjoyable.

Several additional lessons may be offered, based on your needs and the available resources. These include the following:

Chapter 6, Piloting, introduces you to basic techniques of using charts and aids to find your position. It gives you the basic techniques you need to read a chart, keep track of your position by dead reckoning, and keep a deck log.

Chapter 7, Marine Engines, describes the elements of boat power plants, inboard or outboard. Basic maintenance and emergency repairs are included.

Chapter 8, Marlinspike Seamanship, covers the art and science of doing useful things with ropes and lines. You will learn the difference between a line and a rope, between a knot and a hitch. Afterwards, you will be able to tie the three knots (and one hitch) which you will need most often. You will learn to tie up your boat, and to care for your lines so they will give you better, longer service.

Chapter 9, Basic Sailing, introduces some of the mysteries of wind-powered boats. You will learn how a boat can sail into the wind. You will learn to understand some of the strange terms used by your sailing friends, and how to recognize various types of sailboat.

After the Weather lesson, Chapter 11, you will be able to recognize most common weather patterns and form your own short-term weather forecasts based on local conditions, trends, and official weather information. You will learn about better and more reliable sources of weather information that are available, and you will be able to make more sense of broadcast weather forecaster's charts and symbols.

Fig. I-6   An Understanding of the Elements of Weather Forecasting is Important to Good Seamanship.

Chapter 12, The Radiotelephone, introduces the marine radiotelephone. You will learn about licensing, how to use the radiotelephone to make necessary calls to marinas, locks, and bridges, to keep track of developing conditions that may affect your safety, and to summon help (or extend help to others) in times of distress.

Chapter 13, Inland Waterways, Locks and Dams, describes the thousands of miles of inland waterways (rivers, canals, and the Intracoastal Waterway). The lesson describes the particular cautions necessary in these waterways, and gives you many hints of things that can enhance your enjoyment of the unique pleasures these waterways afford.

Fig. I-7   The Inland Waterways Make Recreational Boating Available to Millions.

You may have noticed that the most frequently-used word in the past few paragraphs was "introduce." In a course as brief as this one it is not possible to do more than introduce you to the material. There is much, much more to learn. We hope that your experience in this course will stimulate your interest in further study. Your instructor will be glad to discuss further learning opportunities available in your area.

Additional Information

Even if certain lessons are not covered in the schedule of the course, you should feel free to read those chapters. If you have any questions, one of your instructors will be glad to discuss it with you and help you find answers.

In addition, there is supplemental material in appendices in the back of the book. This supplemental material is not part of the course, but is included for you to read and use, since it is material a responsible boater should know about. It includes useful information about hypothermia, drugs and alcohol.

The Responsible Skipper

"The skipper of a vessel is responsible for everything that happens on her or to her." This is certainly true in merchant vessels on the high seas, and in naval vessels. It is true of the officer in charge of a lifeboat, no matter what his rank. And it is true of the skipper of a small recreational boat. The skipper is responsible, no matter what. It's the law!

But responsibility is not just the right to get blamed if things go wrong. The responsible skipper has the authority (right) to expect that things be done properly on his boat. Along with that goes the assumption that he knows what the "proper" way is.

Crew Training

One of the first things that a responsible skipper does is to make sure that his crew (family as well as guests) understand what is expected of them and how they are to behave in an emergency. This begins even before anybody arrives at the boat. Common courtesy and common sense dictate that guests (especially inexperienced ones) should be given explicit guidance about such things as what clothing to bring, and what accommodations they can expect. You can imagine how you would feel if you showed up at a formal dinner in casual clothes! So shall your guests feel if they are invited for a day on your "yacht," and show up dressed for a 65-footer, only to learn that your "yacht" is a 17' open boat!

More is involved here than just embarrassment at wearing the wrong clothes. The wrong shoes can be deadly on a slippery deck, and a guest who appears for a weekend visit on a larger boat carrying hard-sided luggage can unknowingly create a dangerous condition below decks if the boat starts to pitch and such objects fly about the cabin.

Safety

The responsible skipper takes the time to show his guests where the emergency equipment is and how it works. This need not be handled like the preflight briefing on a commercial airliner (although that is not too bad an idea), but can be worked into the guided tour you will inevitably want to give your guests.

Make sure each crew member and guest has a personal flotation device ("life jacket") and knows how to wear it. Make sure everybody knows where the fire extinguishers are. (Also make sure there are enough of them, that they are located in appropriate places, and that they are all charged and in good condition.)

These items, and many more that are covered in Chapter 3, are part of your being a responsible skipper.

Health

Another aspect of the skipper's responsibility is monitoring, and if necessary controlling, behavior. You are the knowledgeable one on board; your guests may not appreciate as you do the effects of too much sun too soon, or of the effects of alcohol taken with a lot of fresh air, noise and sunshine. Do not permit your guests to "overdo." Keep an eye on their behavior, be alert for signs that they may not be functioning as they should. If they do not cooperate, or if they appear to be suffering ill effects, halt your boating activities and return to shore at once.

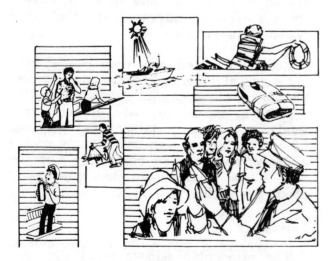

Fig. I-8 **Special Care May Be Needed for Very Young or Very Old to Protect Their Health.**

Above all, do not tolerate "substance abuse." Alcohol, drugs and boating are a deadly mixture, no less than in an automobile. You are the leader; be firm, be fair, and set a good example.

Be sensitive, too, to the needs of the very young and of the elderly. Either may be adversely affected by environmental effects that may not bother others at all. Hypothermia, heat exhaustion, sun stroke and dehydration are extremely dangerous life-threatening emergencies. Differences in clothing, diet, and general health can be critical in determining who is stricken. Be sensitive to the possibilities, and prevent or correct potentially dangerous situations, even if it may mean cutting your boating activities.

Special Considerations for Smaller Pleasure Craft

The smaller pleasure craft are very sensitive to speed, loading, balance, and rough water. For this reason special care should be taken when operating these types of boats.

When loading your boat, weight should be evenly distributed from bow (front) to stern (back) and athwartships (from side to side). The more weight you put into a boat, the deeper it sinks into the water, thus reducing the amount of freeboard. Freeboard is the vertical distance from the gunwale (pronounced gun'l), or top ends of the hull, to the water. The more you reduce the freeboard, the greater the tendency to swamp (fill with water) or capsize (turn over). An overloaded or improperly loaded boat is unstable and dangerous.

Whether you should carry the maximum weight recommended by the manufacturer (see pages 3-8 and 3-9 for discussion on capacity plates) depends on several factors.

First, consider the anticipated sea state, or water conditions. It is important to realize that if rough water is expected, less weight should be carried. A heavily laden boat will ship water more easily than one which is riding higher in the water. Watch your freeboard. Many small boats have swamped or capsized when they were loaded to the point where they had insufficient freeboard.

Second, consider the activity in which you expect to engage while underway. For instance, if you want to do some fishing, it's possible that persons will stand up occasionally in the boat. Standing up in a small boat is extremely dangerous, especially if it is done in choppy water conditions or if the boat is too heavily laden. By standing up you will change the center of gravity of the boat, and if the hull is being buffeted about appreciably, it could cause the boat to capsize, or for you to fall overboard.

Other factors to consider would be weight of the equipment, fuel, tools, food and other gear which will be carried. The more gear loaded aboard, the less passenger-carrying capacity you will have left.

Be wary of sea and wind conditions when you operate your boat. If you run too fast you can buffet your boat excessively and damage it. You also lose control if you buffet too much. You could flip if you caught a wave at too fast a speed, or even capsize if you took a curve too hard.

One other thing. Stay out of restricted areas, especially swimming areas and areas near (above or below) dams. Swimmers and power boats don't mix! Dam gates can open without warning, with the resulting water flow either pulling your boat over the dam (or through the gate) if you are behind the dam, or flooding you out should you be caught below it.

Boat Theft Prevention

Pleasure boats of all sizes, small outboard motors (less than 25 HP), radios, compasses, binoculars, and other boating gear are stolen every year. With a few

simple measures and some forethought, most of this theft could have been avoided. Some of these simple precautions include:

1. Permanently mark your Hull Identification Number (HIN)--for boats built after 1972--at some hidden location on your boat. Although the HIN is permanently stamped or engraved on the outboard, starboard side of the transom, or on the starboard, outboard side of the hull, aft, or on the aft crossbeam of catamarans and pontoon boats (see page 3-8), this number can be defaced or altered. A hidden HIN would provide positive identification when the boat is recovered, if the visible HIN is altered.

2. Mark all of your valuable equipment with an identification number. Operation Identification, supported by police and sheriff departments, provides identification numbers for this purpose. Your local police can provide you with an engraving tool with which you can scribe your ID number on the hard surfaces of your equipment. Soft materials, such as cloth covers, sleeping bags, blankets, tents, etc., can be marked with paint, indelible "magic markers," or invisible ink which shows up under special ultra-violet light. Visible identification numbers, boat name, and owner's name have been deterrents, discouraging thieves, and providing assistance to law enforcement authority in return to the owner after recovery.

3. Keep valuables out of sight! When you park your car, put your gear in the trunk, and lock the car. Leave your car in a well lighted area for personal safety as well as theft prevention if you expect to be gone after dark.

4. Remove valuable, portable equipment from your boat, such as binoculars, radios, compasses, depth finders, personal flotation devices (PFDs), signaling equipment, etc., and lock them in a safe place. Also take your keys and boat registration card when you are away from your boat.

5. If you trailer your boat, whether you keep it at home or in a storage area, you may prevent theft of the trailer and boat by securing the trailer to some immovable object, such as a fence post. A case-hardened steel bolt or eye-bolt can be set in concrete, and serve as a theft-deterrent anchor for a chain wrapped around the trailer axle or frame and locked tight to the anchor bolt. You can also jack up the trailer and remove a wheel, locking it in your trunk. If the trailer is not to be used for some time, such as during the winter, remove all of the wheels from your trailer, and store them in a safe place. This will not only prevent their theft, but save them from the elements.

6. Use a trailer hitch lock to keep the trailer from being removed from your car, or hitched to another if the trailer is left unattended.

7. If you have a small outboard motor, usually less than 25 HP, remove it from your boat when not in use, or fasten it with a motor lock or locked chain (across the clamps). On larger, less portable, permanently-mounted outboard motors, you can use special transom retainer bolts, which may only be removed with special sockets.

8. If you keep your boat at the dock or on a mooring buoy, secure it with a case-hardened lock and chain. You may also wish to remove portable fuel tanks and some vital engine component (such as a distributor rotor, ignition wire(s) or other difficult to replace part). A hidden cutoff switch, installed between the engine and ignition power, can also be a useful deterrent.

9. Work with your neighbors and fellow boaters in keeping watch for strangers or suspicious activity. Call your local law enforcement officials if you have any doubts whether someone is authorized to work on a boat or trailer. Write down a description of any suspicious individuals, and the license number of their vehicle or registration number and description of their boat.

To assist law enforcement officials in the recovery of any stolen property, and to document any losses for your insurance company, keep an up-to-date inventory of your boating and fishing equipment. Make sure you record the name of the equipment, its description, any serial numbers, and other means of identification. Color photographs or slides provide an excellent means of identifying and documenting the condition of your boat and its equipment.

Make sure that your insurance covers theft of your boat or equipment. Homeowner's policies may not provide adequate coverage of marine equipment. Marine coverage including your boat, trailer, outboard motor(s), and associated equipment, is usually worth the generally low premium.

Stolen vessels can be used for a number of illegal purposes, from simple—but dangerous—joy riding, to use in the illicit drug trade, or for resale to another unsuspecting victim. It's up to the boat owner to make sure that his or her property doesn't end up being used for a purpose they did not intend. Although not foolproof, the precautions discussed above can go a long way toward theft prevention.

Chapter 1

Boat Construction and Nomenclature

Every skilled activity has a language of its own, and boating is no exception. The language of the mariner has been developing for centuries, and it has a utility and an exactness that is remarkable, while at the same time it is often undecipherable to the uninitiated "landlubber."

Learning the language is a part of the fun of acquiring a new skill. And an understanding of the special meaning of certain words can be the key to understanding what you read in books and periodicals. In the case of the boater's language, too, you may be called on to react quickly in an emergency. If you do not know what the words mean, you may inadvertently make a bad situation worse.

The terms defined in this chapter should gradually become a part of your boating vocabulary. As your boating knowledge increases, you will find yourself using many of these terms to describe parts of your boat and its equipment. These terms may also be used when giving instructions to others aboard your boat. The first few times you use a nautical term, explain it carefully so that your crew members will know what it means.

Also in this chapter we will look at the various types of boats that exist and describe the features which distinguish one from the other, and the materials and construction methods used to build them.

Basic Terminology

Listed below are some of the nautical terms that you should learn now so that you may fully understand this chapter and those to follow. They are common, everyday terms as far as boating is concerned. Each has a specific meaning that will be understood by other boatmen.

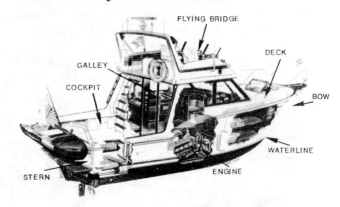

Fig. 1-1 The Parts of a Boat.

The following terms describe parts of a vessel:

HULL - The body of a vessel exclusive of superstructure such as the cabin, flying bridge, masts, etc.

BOW - The forward part of a vessel.

STERN - The after part of a vessel.

TRANSOM - The stern of a vessel, when it is cut off flat, at right angles to the boat's centerline.

BOTTOM - The surface of the hull below the waterline.

CHINE - On a flat or vee-bottom boat, the fore-and-aft line formed by the intersection of the side and the bottom.

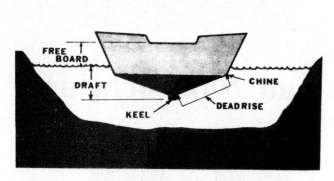

Fig. 1-2 The Underwater Parts of a Boat.

KEEL - The principal framing member of a vessel, running the entire length fore-and-aft and supporting the frames. It is the boat's "spine."

FRAMES (Ribs) - The curved framing members attached to the keel of a wooden boat. They form the "ribs" of the boat's "skeleton."

DECK - The floor of a vessel, resting upon the beams.

GUNWALE - ("Gun'l") The top edge of the hull.

TOPSIDES - The outer surface of the hull from the waterline to the gunwale.

BILGES - The lowest internal spaces within a vessel's hull.

NAUTICAL TERMINOLOGY

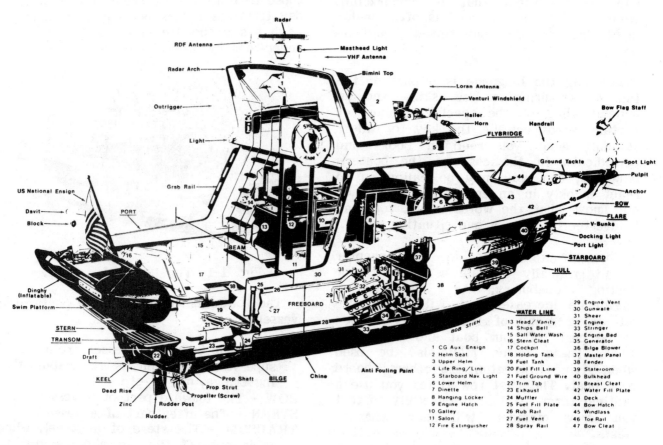

Fig. 1-3 The Interior Parts of a Boat.

PORTSIDE - Facing forward, the left hand side of a vessel.

STARBOARD SIDE - Facing forward, the right hand side of a vessel.

PORTHOLES OR PORTS - Openings in the vessel's sides for admission of light and air. Sealed openings (glass only) are also called "dead lights." Opening ports can also be called "port lights."

SCUPPERS - Overboard drain holes on the deck.

HATCH - An opening in the deck to afford entry to spaces below.

HEAD - The vessel's toilet compartment.

GALLEY - The area aboard a vessel where cooking is done.

LADDER - Stairs or steps aboard a vessel.

WINDWARD SIDE - The side of the vessel currently exposed to the wind.

LEEWARD SIDE ("Loo-ward") - The side of the vessel currently sheltered from the wind.

Terms that describe fittings and other equipment are:

LINE - Rope that has been put to use aboard a vessel.

CLEAT - An anvil-shaped deck fitting to which lines are secured.

CHOCK - A deck fitting through which lines are passed.

RUDDER - A vertical underwater blade which can be pivoted to steer the vessel.

HELM - The mechanism by which the vessel is steered, including the tiller, wheel, etc.

Fig. 1-4 Deck Fittings

FENDERS - Padded "bumpers" hung over the side of the vessel to protect it from chafing or other damage to the hull.

The dimensions of a vessel are expressed as:

BEAM - The breadth of a boat at its widest point.

DRAFT - The vertical distance from the waterline to the lowest part of the vessel beneath the water.

FREEBOARD - The minimum vertical distance from the waterline to the gunwale.

LENGTH - The distance from the bow to the stern, measured along the vessel's centerline, exclusive of bowsprits and other projections.

SHEER - The longitudinal upward or downward curve of the deck fore-and-aft.

The following terms describe directions or locations of items aboard the vessel or closely alongside:

ABAFT - Toward the stern.

AFT - Near the stern.

ALOFT - Above the deck.

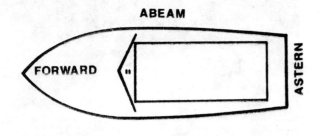

Fig. 1-5 Directions on a Boat.

AMIDSHIPS - The center of the boat - with reference to her length or to her breadth.

AHEAD - In the direction of the bow.

ASTERN - In the direction of the stern.

ATHWARTSHIPS - Across the line of the vessel's keel.

BELOW - Beneath or under the deck.

FORE-AND-AFT - Lengthwise with the vessel's keel. The opposite to athwartships.

CLOSE ABOARD - Alongside, close to the hull.

FORWARD - Near the bow.

INBOARD - Toward the centerline of a vessel.

OUTBOARD - Away from the centerline of a vessel.

WINDWARD - Toward the wind.

LEEWARD - The direction opposite that <u>from</u> which the wind blows; downwind.

The following terms describe relative directions as viewed <u>from</u> a vessel <u>toward</u> an object which is <u>not aboard</u> the vessel:

AHEAD (Dead Ahead) - In the direction of the vessel's fore-and-aft center line, forward of the bow.

ABEAM - In a direction at right angles to the vessel's keel, on either side.

BROAD ON THE BOW - In a direction half-way from ahead to abeam of the vessel, on either side.

ASTERN (Dead Astern) - In the direction of the vessel's fore-and-aft center line, behind the stern.

BROAD ON THE QUARTER - In a direction half-way from abeam to astern of the vessel, on either side.

Some of the fittings and equipment found on sailboats should be of interest. A few are mentioned here. Chapter 9, Basic Sailing, goes into much more detail.

MAST - A spar set upright from the deck to support rigging and sails.

SHROUDS - Wire lines on each side of a vessel, reaching from the masthead to the vessel's sides, to support the mast.

STAYS - Wire lines used to support masts, leading from the head of one mast to another, or to the deck. Those which lead forward are called forestays. Those which lead aft are called backstays.

HALYARDS - Lines used for hoisting and lowering sails, flags, dayshapes, etc.

BOOM - A spar used to extend the foot (bottom) of a sail.

BOWSPRIT - A spar extending forward from the bow of a vessel.

JIB - A triangular sail set on a stay, forward.

MAIN SAIL - The principal sail.

Types of Motorboats

If you are shopping for your first boat, you will find that there is a bewildering number of models and sizes on the market. Each has been developed to meet a specific need. Some are adapted to suit specific boating activities and are not suitable for others. So when you select a boat, be sure that it will suit your intended purposes.

Boat-building Materials

Boats are built from a variety of materials, some of them rather surprising. There is probably no such thing as the ideal boat-building material. All of the materials in use now or in the past have properties which afford some advantages and some disadvantages. The choice of material depends on those properties, availability, cost, and available technology.

Wood

Wood is an obvious boat-building material, and it was the material of choice for centuries. No doubt the fact that most wood will float by itself had something to do with man's very first ventures upon the water.

Wood is workable, and can be formed easily into useful shapes. It has intrinsic beauty. It is relatively inexpensive, and in times past it was plentiful in most parts of the world where seafarers lived and worked.

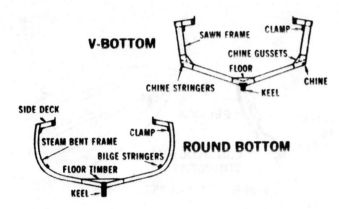

Fig. 1-6 Wooden Boat Construction.

Unfortunately, wooden boats and ships require a large amount of maintenance, and it is difficult to build very large structures of wood which are very strong without also being very heavy. This is no serious problem with buildings on land, but is critical in something which must be made to move through the water. These factors, along with the declining availability of quality boat-building lumber, have combined to make wooden boats more and more unusual today. But for some special purposes, and especially for the amateur builder, wood is still an excellent material.

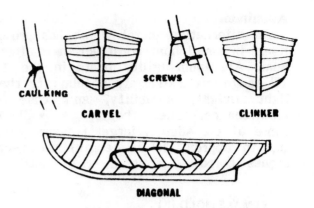

Fig. 1-7 Wood Plank Construction.

Steel

The discovery that the ability of a boat to float did not depend on the ability of the material to float by itself undoubtedly came very early in the development of boat-building, and ultimately paved the way for all manner of improbable building materials.

Perhaps the most improbable of these are iron and steel. The very epitome of materials which will sink if dropped in water, these metals nevertheless lend themselves to ship construction. Once the technology was developed and shipbuilders learned to shape and join plates of iron and steel (and eventually to protect them from the corrosive effects of seawater), they were able to build large ships which had enormous strength with reasonable weight. Thus they could begin to take advantage of some of the efficiencies of scale and make commerce even more profitable. The fact that the Great Eastern, the first large iron ship, was not only the largest ship of her day, but at that was roughly twice the size of her next-largest competitor, speaks volumes.

Unfortunately, the strength and weight advantages of steel and iron do not begin to come into play in small boats. In general, although exceptions exist, boats built of these materials under 30-35' in length are too heavy for economical operation. Even so, when speed is not a major issue and can be sacrificed for strength, steel is an excellent building material.

Aluminum

An alternative metal which has proven itself in small boat construction is aluminum. Aluminum utility boats in the 13-17' range are extremely popular for their light weight, durability, and ease of maintenance. These boats, as well as some of the slightly larger pleasure craft (up to approx. 30' in length) use techniques borrowed from aircraft construction, with a relatively thin skin of aluminum stiffened with ribs and bulkheads. Larger vessels (in some cases up to 100' and more) use welded plate construction with heavier gauges of metal, similar to what is done with steel ships.

The light weight of aluminum hulls contributes to operating economy, but some people feel that this very quality

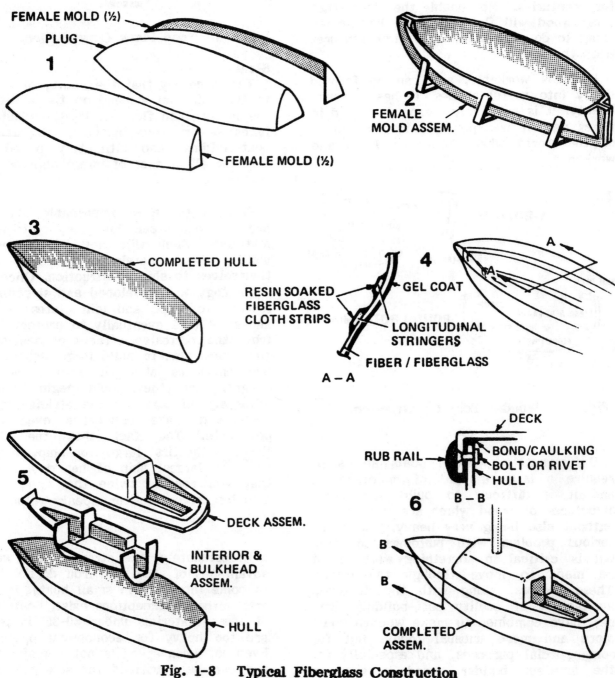

Fig. 1-8   Typical Fiberglass Construction Techniques.

tends to give aluminum hulls a more uncomfortable ride, and they are certainly more noisy unless steps are taken to deaden the sound of water striking the hull. On the other hand, aluminum is relatively easy to repair if damaged (although it is difficult to conceal the repairs), and with the exception of some early disastrous experiences with salt water corrosion which have been corrected through improved metallurgy, is as nearly maintenance-free as one could hope for in a small boat.

Fiberglass

Fiberglass, or more properly, fiberglass-reinforced plastic, has become the most popular single material used in small boats in recent years. This material is strong, lends itself well to various manufacturing techniques, can be formed easily into complex shapes, is relatively inexpensive, and requires very little maintenance effort. (See Fig. 1-8)

Fiberglass-reinforced plastic boats (hereafter referred to simply as "fiberglass") are properly constructed of several layers of glass fibers, often woven together into cloth for strength and ease of handling, embedded in a plastic material which is applied as a liquid and which sets as a solid. The result is an enormously strong, relatively light-weight structure, which can have the color and other elements (such as toe rails, non-skid deck surfaces, etc.) molded right in. Thus, much of the labor that would have gone into adding these elements piecemeal is saved. It is likely that this alone has contributed significantly to making pleasure boats available to a wide range of the buying public at a reasonable cost.

Fiberglass hulls can be repaired if damaged, often without loss of strength and without leaving any visible evidence of the repair. That technology is not generally available to the individual, however, and repair (and construction) of fiberglass boats may best be left to the professional. Needless to say, some regard this as a drawback.

Enormous increases in the cost of pe-

troleum (the source of the resins) have raised material costs somewhat over what they were some years back, but there has been no large-scale retreat from fiberglass as a favored construction material.

Other Materials

The materials listed above account for most of the boats in use today, but the list of other materials used for special applications is very long. New synthetic fibers have appeared on the market recently which can replace fiberglass in the resin bed. These fibers are lighter and stronger than glass, but for now are limited to some special applications (such as racing hulls) whose owners are willing to bear the high cost of these exotic fibers in return for the reduced weight and increased strength. But they remind us that new materials and technologies are always just around the corner, and the last word has not yet been spoken.

Some home boat-builders have had excellent success with the use of steel-reinforced concrete (ferrocement) in boat construction. Many of the weight and size considerations that apply to steel and iron construction apply as well to ferrocement, and cracking has been a problem in designs that were not well thought out. But this is true of boats built with traditional materials as well, and one should not reject any material out of hand just because it is non-standard. Material selection is always a compromise, and the builder and owner must decide which properties are most desired and which can be accepted as a cost of having the rest.

Hull Design

Boats can be classified as displacement hulls or planing hulls, depending on the way they ride in the water. Displacement boats move through the water, pushing it aside (displacing it) as they move along. Planing boats, on the other hand, move considerably faster and ride more nearly on top of the water.

Displacement Hulls

Of course, all boats at rest or moving

slowly are displacement boats, since the displacement of a mass of water equal to the mass of the vessel is the principle on which the boat floats. If the mass of the boat exceeds the mass of the water displaced, the boat sinks.

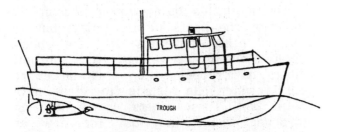

Fig. 1-9   Displacement Vessels Move Through the Water.

As a displacement hull is moved through the water it pushes the water aside. At low speeds, this is a relatively easy thing. But as speeds increase, it becomes more and more difficult to do, and more and more power is required. Finally, the additional power required to achieve any additional speed is simply prohibitive, so a virtual limit on the maximum speed that a displacement hull can achieve is reached. What this speed actually is depends primarily on the length of the hull and on its underwater shape, but for most small boats that speed does not exceed 7 - 8 knots or so.

Despite their speed limitation, displacement hulls have their attractions. Nearly all sailboats are displacement boats, for instance, as are trawlers, canoes and ocean liners. Displacement boats tend to be steady, comfortable, more capable of handling rough water, and economical to operate. If speed is not a prime consideration, a displacement hull may be the best choice.

Planing Hulls
Planing hulls are specially designed hulls which tend to ride up on the water as it moves through it faster and faster. A planing hull tends to "fly" over the surface, buoyed up by its own forward motion more than by the water it displaces. At speed, most of the energy produced by the engine is translated into

forward motion of the boat, not into lateral movement of water away from the hull.

Fig. 1-10   A Hydroplane is an Extreme Form of a Planing Hull. It Moves on Top of the Water.

Operators of planing boats often find that their boat passes through three distinct phases of movement as it gains or loses speed. At slow speed, starting off from a dead stop, it is a displacement hull. As more power is applied the boat moves forward faster.

As the boat accelerates, the stern may squat and the bow rise. The drag of the water increases rapidly, as indicated by the large wake, or disturbance following the boat, as the water fills in the "hole" made by the boat's passage through it. More and more power is required, as the boat literally digs a hole in the water and attempts to climb out of it. The boat may feel somewhat unstable in this condition, and fuel consumption is tremendous. Generally, too, forward visibility is reduced, as the bow is too high. This is an awkward, wasteful, and somewhat dangerous phase in the operation of a planing boat. Most boats should be run slower or faster than this transitional speed.

Eventually, as more and more speed is gained, the boat feels as though it has "climbed out of its hole," and it rides up "on plane." Both the bow and fuel consumption drop, speed goes up, the wake diminishes, and the boat once again feels stable and comfortable. The throttle can be set back considerably and still maintain the same rate of speed, dropping fuel consumption still further. The planing hull is in its natural element.

As the speed of the boat DECREASES, then, it passes through the same stages in reverse order. Typically, a planing hull will settle quickly once the power is reduced, and it will stop in a relatively short distance. In fact, the operator must use some caution slowing down quickly, since the following wake can overtake the boat and, in some cases, swamp it. This is called "pooping" (since the following wave crosses over the boat's transom ["poop"]), and is a particular safety problem with small outboards having cut-out transoms.

There are many types of planing hulls. Most are characterized by fairly extensive flat surfaces, although these may be angled to form a "V" shape in the water. Actually, hulls may be comprised of many complex shapes, and include steps and ramps and other structures which come into play at various speeds, in turns, and so on. There is no single, all-purpose, perfect hull design. Each design is a compromise, and the owner must make his choice based on his priorities and the kind of use the boat will receive.

Uses of Boats

Boats may also be classified by the use they are intended for, or by the type of propulsion used. Sail boats are further cataloged according to very elaborate distinctions made in the form and arrangement of their sails (their "sail plan"). (See diagram).

Power boats are classified as utility boats, runabouts, cruisers, or houseboats, depending on their use.

Utility Boats

Prams and Dinghies are among the smallest of the utility boats (8'-10' long) with wide beams relative to their length. They are usually intended for rowing, but may be fitted with small outboard motors or sailing gear. They are used principally as tenders and are often carried aboard larger boats.

Skiffs are utility boats. They are popular because of their simplicity and durability. Skiffs are flat-bottomed with either straight or slightly flared sides. A skiff is easy to row or may be fitted

with a small outboard engine. Because it is flat-bottomed, a skiff is ideal for a hunter or fisherman to operate on protected shallow water.

Utility Outboards are favored by boatmen who rely on outboard motors for power. They are specifically designed for outboard motors, and consequently may be difficult to row. Some utilities have a small decked-over area in the bow, although most are completely open.

Fig. 1-11   A Utility Outboard.

In 14' - 16' lengths, these boats are very popular as fishing boats in sheltered waters.

Runabouts are more sporty craft. Runabouts may have decked-over bows and are intended for general use such as day cruising, water skiing and fishing. They may have outboard, inboard or inboard/outboard (I/O) power. (See below.) They generally lack cooking, sleeping and sanitary facilities (a "head"), although runabouts exist with some or all of these features. Runabouts are as close as any to being the true "general purpose" recreational boat.

Fig. 1-12   Runabouts are Useful for a Variety of Activities on the Water.

Cruisers are built in a wide variety of shapes and sizes depending on their intended use. Small cruisers are designed for occasional overnight use; large cruisers are used by some as houseboats. The cruiser "type" is described by the configuration of the hull and superstructure - raised deck, flush deck, trunk cabin, sedan or flying bridge.

Fig. 1-13 **Cruisers Have More Room for Longer Trips.**

Cruisers are somewhat more seaworthy craft, generally, than the other categories, and usually afford some sort of living quarters, suitable for periods ranging from a weekend to a lifetime. They are designed to travel considerable distances, and are generally suitable for a wide variety of conditions. They range in size from small "day cruisers" with "cuddy cabins," having little more than sitting headroom and spartan sleeping accommodations for two, to world-girdling small ships with luxury accommodations for dozens of guests and crew.

A houseboat is a popular modification of the cruiser. Until the early Sixties the houseboat lacked dash and appeal, but today's modern houseboat can offer all the conveniences of home. Some have sufficient power and speed to tow water skiers.

Generally, houseboats afford the owner a lot of usable space per foot of boat, although at some cost. Often seakeeping ability is sacrificed for livability, and houseboats tend to be limited to relative-

ly sheltered waters, either by their hull design, or by the presence of large windows (which could be dangerous in rough water), or other features.

Fig. 1-14 **A Houseboat is Like a Floating Summer Home.**

Power Plants

Powered boats are generally classified according to the type and arrangement of their power plants. The first and most obvious characteristic is the location of the engine itself. If the engine is mounted inside the hull, the boat is termed an inboard-powered boat. If the engine is mounted outside the hull on the transom, it is outboard powered. (Until recently, outboard power implied small boat, perhaps less than 22'-25'. This no longer applies, however, as more and more medium-sized boats [30'-40'] are being designed to take advantage of improved outboard technology.)

Inboards

Inboard-mounted engines must somehow transmit their power to the water, so some part of the machinery must pass through the hull at some point. In the case of the traditional inboard, a straight shaft leads aft (backwards) from the engine (which is mounted near the mid-point of the hull) and passes through a special fitting in the bottom of the boat (see diagram). This fitting allows the shaft to rotate while keeping most of the water out. (Some small amount of water does manage to leak in, and actually serves to lubricate the fitting.) The shaft, in turn, turns the propeller, which drives the boat (see Chapter 2).

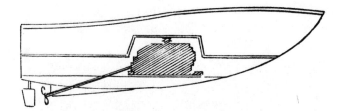

Fig. 1-15   A Single Inboard Engine Installation.

Inboard/Outboards

An alternative arrangement places the engine right aft against the transom. The power drive shaft then exits through a special fitting mounted on the transom. The rotary motion of the shaft is transmitted through a series of gears, couplings and shafts through a sealed unit to the propeller. A part of the external mechanism (the "lower unit"), including the propeller, can be swung from side to side to steer the boat. The motor itself remains fixed inside the hull. This arrangement is called an inboard/outboard, or I/O, arrangement. (See Diagram. See also Chapter 2 for further information about the impact of this arrangement on boat handling.)

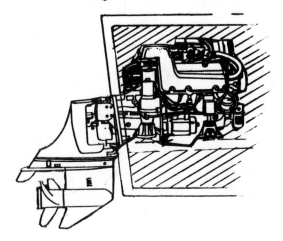

Fig. 1-16   The I/O Power Plant Offers Many Advantages to Its Owner.

Outboards

Outboard motorboats are the most numerous among small boat types. In this arrangement the motor is mounted on the transom, and both the motor and the lower unit pivot to steer the boat.

Fig. 1-17   Outboards Remain Extremely Popular with Recreational Boaters.

Outboard motors are generally lighter in weight than inboards of corresponding power, which gives them a performance edge. They often take up less space inside the boat, which is a major factor in many small boats. If it should become necessary to replace the motor, it is a relatively simple matter to attach a new outboard, while replacing an inboard engine is usually a major undertaking.

See Chapter 7 for more technical details about engine operations.

Chapter 2

Boat Handling

Introduction

Handling a boat, like driving an automobile or flying a plane, is a complex skill that is acquired through practice and experience. Handling a power boat is very similar to handling an automobile. Handling a sailboat, on the other hand, is different. There is often less familiarity for a beginner to build on, but there are likewise fewer bad habits that may have to be unlearned.

Whatever kind of boat is involved, a considerable amount of effort, pain, anxiety (and possible expense) can be avoided if you understand the basic principles of boat handling before you leave the dock. That is the purpose of this lesson.

Fig. 2-1   A Boatman is Judged By His Ability at Close-in Maneuvering.

After you learn the basic principles, however, you must practice the skills based on those principles. And you must relearn them with every new boat, for every boat has its own unique properties which vary with weight, hull shape, and type of power. Even two boats which are nominally identical to one another will handle differently. It is up to you, the skipper, to learn those differences, and if possible to turn those characteristics to your advantage.

The discussion of boat handling which follows in this chapter describes a "typical" recreational power boat. That is, it is powered by a single outboard motor or an inboard/outboard system, and is 16'-30' in length. There are special cases, of course (larger boats, inboard power plants, single and multiple propellers [screws], etc.) The effects of these differences will be discussed as they arise.

The Propeller

Almost all recreational power boats are propeller driven. Most propellers are designed to rotate in a clockwise direction (viewed from aft) to drive the boat forward. This design is called a <u>right-handed</u> propeller. Left-handed propellers also exist, and are almost always paired with a right-handed one on a twin-screw boat. They are also being seen on I/O boats up to 26 feet.

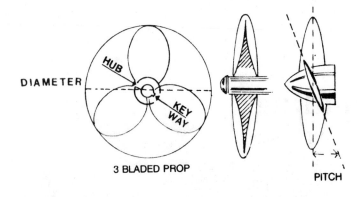

Fig. 2-2   A Three-Bladed Propeller.

Propellers are defined by their <u>diameter</u> (tip to tip) and their <u>pitch</u>. The pitch of a propeller is the distance its helical surfaces would screw themselves into the water on a single complete rotation if the water were a semi-solid material and there were no slippage. (In fact, of course, a real propeller will not move quite that far through real water, but the measurement remains a convenient one to use.) Thus a propeller might be designated "14 x 12", indicating a 14" diameter and a 12" pitch. This is a relatively "flat" propeller that might be found on a houseboat or a workboat, where speed is not the issue but efficient transmission of power is. A faster boat might have a "10 x 17" propeller, for instance, which would have a higher top speed but might have less torque, or low-speed "pulling power." The choice of a particular propeller depends in part on manufacturer's recommendations, in part on experience, and in part on experiment. A single-digit change in pitch, for instance, can make a tremendous difference in the performance characteristics of a particular boat, either improving it or degrading it.

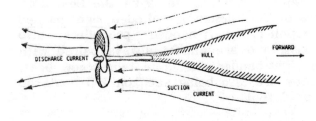

Fig. 2-3   The Propeller "Flies" Through the Water.

How a Propeller Works

The propeller is really a "lifting surface," similar to an airplane wing. Rather than advancing through the water like a screw through wood, a propeller is more properly thought of as flying through the water. As the wing-shaped propeller blade rotates through the water, lift is produced which forces the propeller forward. This forward thrust is transmitted through the shaft and power train of the boat to the engine or the "thrust bearing." From there the force is transmitted to the hull of the boat.

Fig. 2-4   Fluid (Air or Water) Moving Across a Curved Shape Creates Areas of Low Pressure, or "Lift."

Lift is produced in any foil section because the fluid in which it moves (air or water) is forced to move faster over one surface (the top of an airplane wing, the front surface of a propeller) than over the other. The slower-moving fluid exerts a greater pressure than the faster-moving portion, and the difference between the two pressures is "lift." (See Fig. 2-4.)

If too much pressure differential exists, the pressure in the fluid on the top (front) surface of the foil becomes lower and lower until the fluid is eventually disrupted, or torn apart. In the case of water, the pressure can be made so low that the water literally boils. This boiling creates bubbles of steam, which collapse immediately after the propeller blade passes and the pressure of the water returns. This rapid building and subsequent collapse of bubbles interferes with the action of the propeller, destroys lift, and can actually damage the metal of the propeller and supports. This phenomenon is called <u>cavitation</u>.

A cavitating propeller still produces enough lift to move the boat, although not as much as it would if there were no cavitation. There also exist specially-designed propellers ("super-cavitating" propellers) which allow high horsepower levels to be transmitted to the water without the damaging effects of cavitation on the machinery.

Thus, if the propeller is pivoted to the right, the <u>stern</u> moves to the <u>left</u>, forcing the bow to move to the <u>right</u>. This is the first major departure from what we learned about handling automobiles; in a boat, the steering is done from the <u>rear</u>.

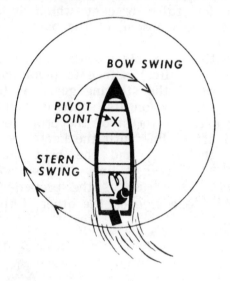

Fig. 2-6   A Turning Boat Pivots About a Point Somewhat Aft of the Bow.

Fig. 2-5   A Supercavitating Propeller.

The driving force of a boat, then, is applied to the after portion of the boat, where the propeller is. This is, in effect, identical with the traditional arrangement of the rear-wheel drive automobile, which is pushed down the road by its rear wheels.

The major differences between handling a boat and driving a car, however, comes with the matter of steering and stopping. With an outboard motor or an inboard/outboard power plant, steering is accomplished by rotating the propeller and the drive machinery about a vertical axis and causing the thrust generated by the propeller to be aimed off to one side or the other. This directed thrust then forces the after (stern) portion of the boat in the direction away from the propeller.

All boats have a pivot point somewhere forward of the midpoint. Exactly where it is depends on the underwater shape of the hull, the loading, the placement of the propeller, etc., but it is generally about 1/3 of the way back from where the stem of the boat enters the water.

This fact is of no particular concern when the vessel is being maneuvered in open water. But alongside a pier or another boat, it becomes critical. Obviously, any skipper who insists on operating his boat in that position the way he would his automobile is simply going to drive the stern of his boat sideways into the adjacent structure.

Of course, a boat also has no brakes, another important way in which boats differ from automobiles. In most situations, a boat's forward motion can be stopped quickly only through application of reverse power.

Outboard Motors

An <u>outboard</u> motor is one whose power head (assembly including the cylinders, crankshaft, etc.) is installed outside the confines of the hull. Almost always this means an engine bolted or clamped to the transom (or to a bracket which is attached to the transom) of the boat.

The entire assembly (power head, shaft, gears and propeller) is free to pivot under the control of the steering gear. As long as the propeller on its shaft is pointed directly aft, the thrust of the propeller is directed aft in line with the keel (center) line of the boat, and the boat moves forward in a straight line. As the motor is turned, the thrust of the propeller is directed to one side or the other, turning the boat.

Fig. 2-7   The Directed Thrust of an Outboard or Inboard/Outboard Moves the Stern of the Boat in a Turn.

The directed thrust of the outboard motor gives the whole vessel a great deal of maneuverability, even at low speeds. Indeed, it is possible to turn <u>too</u> sharply, causing the boat to turn over (capsize). Skippers are well-advised to be careful making sharp turns with an outboard motor, especially at high speeds.

A more detailed discussion of the construction, operation and maintenance of marine engines, including outboards, appears in Chapter 7, Marine Engines.

Inboards

A major feature of inboard motors and power trains is the long rigid shaft which carries the power aft to the propeller. Since the shaft cannot bend and flex to redirect the thrust of the propeller the way an outboard or an I/O can, some other indirect way must be used to turn the boat.

The Rudder

The answer is the rudder, which is a blade extending down into the water at the stern of the boat. In most power boats the rudder is located directly behind the propeller in the propeller wash.

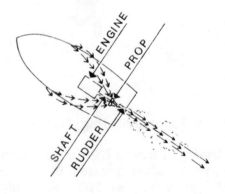

Fig. 2-8   The Discharge Current From the Screw Flows Over and Acts On the Rudder.

The rudder is connected by some mechanical linkage to the steering wheel, and can be rotated right and left to deflect water flow to one side or the other. This causes the stern of the boat to be pushed opposite to the direction of the deflection, thus steering the boat.

Some control of the boat's direction can be had by forcing water from the propeller over the rudder before the boat has gained any forward headway. (This is known as "kicking" the stern.) But most of the rudder's effect comes from water flowing past it as the boat moves through the water. (In fact, sailboats without engines have rudders, too, and there is absolutely no propeller current there to work on the rudder at all. The sailboat rudder is completely useless until the boat begins to move through the water.) The faster the boat moves through the water, the more control the rudder provides over direction.

Twin Screws

Some boats, especially larger ones, are equipped with two or more engines. This arrangement is considered by some to afford greater reliability, since it is unlikely that both engines will fail together. It may also be easier to design a boat around two smaller engines than around one very large one. But a major reason for installing twin engines is the added maneuverability that arrangement gives.

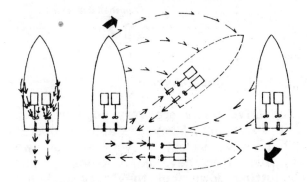

Fig. 2-9   A Twin-screw Inboard.

Twin propellers, shafts and rudders, mounted some distance apart on opposite sides of the keel, allow the operator to "twist" the boat by applying forward power to one propeller and a compensating reverse power to the opposite propeller, with the rudders set straight ahead. The result of this maneuver is that the entire vessel will turn away from the side with the forward engine. By careful management of the throttles (see Reverse, below) this can usually be done without moving the boat forward or backward, and most twin-screw boats can be turned

completely around in very little more than their own length.

Skilled operators can, by using various setting of the rudder along with the twisting of the boat, make a twin-screw boat move sideways. Such an ability has obvious benefit in docking and undocking, but it is far beyond the scope of this course. Suffice it to say that the twin-screw inboard is probably the most maneuverable boat on the water today.

Operating in Reverse

Boats are designed to move forward. The propeller, for instance, as discussed above, is designed to "fly" forward through the water. It is capable of working in reverse, but just as an airplane trying to fly backwards, it is not particularly efficient.

So, too, with the rudder of an inboard boat. When the boat is moving backwards, even under power, there is no propeller wash acting on the rudder to help control the direction of the boat. The boat must be moving backwards through the water with some speed for the rudder to have any effect at all.

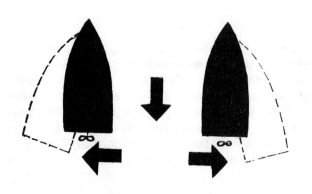

Fig. 2-10   Left-Hand Propeller and Right-Hand Propeller.

But in most instances, operating in reverse is a short-term affair, and is done at low speeds, so there is generally more than enough surplus power available to overcome the inefficiency of the propeller. And, in the case of outboards and I/O's, the principles of directed propeller thrust work equally well in reverse (even though there may not be quite as much of it per horsepower expended as there is in forward gear), so the shortcomings of the rudder are of no concern.

In the case of the single-screw inboard, however, there is one important phenomenon which should be recognized and dealt with about operating in reverse at slow speeds. Because of the incline angle of the shaft, due to the inboard mounting of the engine, the blades of the propeller attack the water at different angles, depending on whether on the starboard (descending) or port (ascending) side of the "wheel." The effect is that the starboard, descending, blades have a greater effective pitch, and take a deeper bite of the water than those on the port, ascending, side. That makes the RIGHT HANDED inboard mounted propeller push or pull more on the starboard side than on the port side. This is called UNEQUAL SIDE-BLADE PRESSURE. When BACKING DOWN at slow speeds (actually, when backing at slow speeds the rudder has no effect), the unequal side-blade pressure causes more thrust to appear on the starboard side, and pushes the boat's stern to port.

Twin-screw inboard boats (almost always equipped with one right-handed propeller and one left-handed one), as you would expect, can back straight, since the tendencies of one propeller to walk the stern in one direction are offset by the tendencies of the other propeller to walk it in the opposite direction.

Some few twin-screw boats are equipped with two like-handed propellers (as in the case of boats mounted with two standard outboard motors, or some WW-II landing ships, for instance). In these cases, the tendency to back to one side is even greater, and can cause some severe handling problems.

Jet Drives

There is yet one other sort of drive arrangement which we must mention, the jet drive. In essence, this is a special form of an I/O, since it has an inboard-mounted engine and uses directed thrust. But the jet boat has no propeller in the usual sense.

The engine of a jet boat drives a powerful water pump, which draws water in through the bottom of the boat and ejects it at great speed through a special nozzle in the transom. The nozzle can be directed to one side or the other to steer the boat.

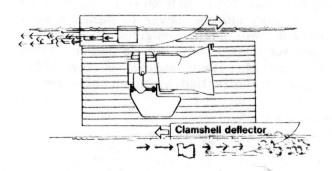

Fig. 2-11   Jet Drive.

Jet drive boats are very popular among some sportsmen. They are able to operate with relative safety in very shallow water, since they have no propeller or rudder jutting down (but they may suck mud or debris into the pump if they run too shallow). The lack of a propeller is also a safety feature which makes jet boats popular with water skiers, who would like to avoid the risk of injuring someone in the water by contact with sharp propeller blades.

Jet boats appear to handle reasonably well at higher speeds, but they are not especially maneuverable at low speeds.

Fuel Handling

No discussion of power boats would be complete without a discussion of fuel handling practices.

Taking on fuel is one of the most dangerous times in boating, because of the volatile nature of the fuel. Recently, the addition of alcohol to gasoline to improve performance has caused accelerated deterioration of hoses and gaskets, and may lead to other problems. It is likely that situations like this will only become more common as time goes by and supplies of good-quality oil become scarcer and refiners try in other ways to meet the need for fuel.

Fuel tanks in boats may be built in or they may be portable. Whatever their size or shape, it is critical that all fittings and hoses be checked regularly for leaks, and that the tanks themselves be checked regularly for signs of corrosion.

Some built-in fuel tanks may be inaccessible or surrounded by flotation foam. The operator should be sensitive to the possibility of leaks in places where they cannot be seen easily and investigate any suspicious gasoline odors carefully.

Since gasoline vapors are heavier than air and explosive, every effort should be made to avoid creating them, and when it is impossible to avoid creating them, to avoid trapping them where they can cause problems.

Portable tanks should be removed from the boat for filling if possible, and any spills should be cleaned up immediately. Rags used to clean up spills should be disposed of safely on shore, NOT kept on the boat.

If fuel tanks are built in and cannot be removed for filling, close off all compartments so gasoline vapors will not have any spaces to accumulate in. Close cabin doors, hatches, ports, etc. and turn OFF any ventilating fans. Turn off all electrical equipment that might cause a spark (including all automatic equipment, such as bilge pumps, generators, etc.). Shut off all stoves and open lights and extinguish all smoking materials.

The fuel filler must be located in such a position that any spills will be directed overboard, not back into the boat. But it is still the operator's responsibility to avoid spills, both for safety reasons and to avoid polluting the environment.

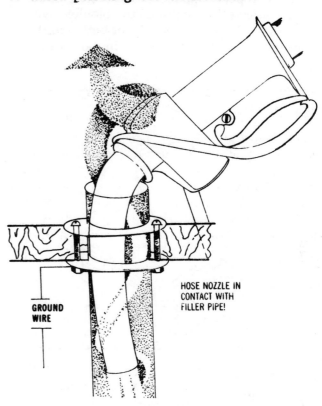

HOSE NOZZLE IN CONTACT WITH FILLER PIPE!

GROUND WIRE

Fig. 2-12 Filler Pipe Deck Flange with Hose Nozzle.

The fuel hose nozzle must be kept in direct metal-to-metal contact with the filler plate, which in turn must be connected securely to the boat's electrical grounding system. Under certain conditions static electric charges can be generated in fuel filler hoses. These charges can produce sparks and ignite vapors escaping from the fill spout of the fuel tank.

These charges can be dissipated through the ground system.

Built-in fuel tanks are equipped with an air vent. This vent, which is located on the outside of the hull, serves both to provide an outlet for gasoline vapors built up in the tank and to allow air to enter the tank as fuel is used up. Without this replacement of fuel by air, it would not be possible to draw off fuel to the engine without causing the fuel tank to collapse from outside air pressure. (Some cases of poor engine performance have been traced to fuel starvation caused by blocked air vents, sometimes caused by insects building nests in the vents and similar problems.)

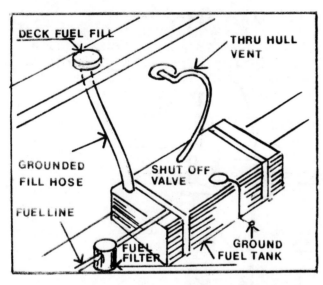

Fig. 2-13 **Fuel Filler Deck Plates and Air Vents Must Be Located Outside the Hull.**

After completing the refueling operation, be sure to open all closed compartments and ventilate them thoroughly before starting engines. Run the blower for at least 4-5 minutes, then check all compartment and engine spaces carefully by sniffing for gasoline vapors before starting the engine.

Check the engine and transmission dipsticks. Keep lubricating fluids at recommended levels, and carry spare supplies. But don't overfill, either.

Once the engine is started and warmed up enough to do so safely, cast off all lines and depart the fuel dock immediately. (Not only is the fuel dock a place of business that needs the dock space for other customers, but it is also a dangerous place. There may be other customers who do not know proper fueling procedures as well as you do!)

The Technique of Docking and Maneuvering

One of the best ways to judge the competence of a boatman is to observe the manner in which he gets his craft underway from a float or pier, and how he places his boat alongside the float when returning to his dock.

Before Getting Underway

Before getting underway, the prudent boatman will check all of the vessel's systems and gear, usually with the aid of a check list. He will measure the fuel in the tanks and determine engine oil level. He will check all lights, including running lights. He will check the whistle or horn and the condition of the bilges. He will break out hand lines, ready for use, and bend on the anchor, ready to let go. He will take personal flotation devices out of their lockers and place them in readily accessible places. He will turn on all electronic gear that will be used. Open all hatch covers to ventilate engine and fuel tank spaces and turn on bilge blowers. A heaving line and boat hook should be available for instant use. In short, he will determine that all equipment aboard is in satisfactory operating condition. Only then will he start the engine or engines.

Starting Engines

Even though the engine and fuel tank compartments have been thoroughly ventilated, test for gas vapors which may be present in these spaces. This is best done with the nose. The nose is generally far more sensitive than a device in detecting gasoline vapors, and it is more reliable. The nose should be satisfied that no vapors are present.

Once the engines are started, allow the temperature to come up some, to keep the engine from stalling. However, avoid excessive idling. At this point, it is also a good idea to check water flow through exhausts and check the manifold drain plugs, etc.

Getting Underway

With the engines started, and all gauges reflecting desired readings, it is time to get underway. Before casting off the mooring lines, make a careful inspection of the immediate surroundings. All hazards and obstructions and the direction and strength of the wind and current should be noted and kept in mind, along with their probable effect on the boat's motion.

This chapter describes typical situations which you may encounter while docking and getting underway. Before getting into this, however, you should remember that you should maintain a slow speed through crowded anchorage or marina areas. You are legally responsible for any damage caused to others by your vessel's wash (wake). Most marinas have a 5-knot speed limit, but this may be too fast if the wake doesn't flatten appreciably within a few feet from the stern.

Fig. 2-14   Marinas and Congested Areas are No-wake Areas.

Take in all fenders, mooring and hand lines, and secure all loose gear about the decks.

Leaving the Dock

The first and most important point to remember is that the stern is the only part of the boat that can be steered. As stated earlier in this chapter, the stern tends to move sideways and must always be watched. This is not to say that the bow must not also be watched, but all too many boatmen concentrate on the bow, and in this concentration slam the stern into the wharves and floats with damaging results.

Wind and Current

There are also other factors at work; however, if you are alert, you can make these forces work for you. These forces, which are almost always present, are wind and current. Most boatmen think of wind and current as hindrances. Both can be of considerable help in maneuvering if you know how to use them.

The way wind and current act on a boat depends on the characteristics of the boat. Deep draft boats, with comparatively low freeboard, are far less affected by the wind than by the current. This is because there is more underwater body for the current to work against on deep draft boats, while there is less topside area (and cabin structure) against which the wind can work. Most powerboats have high topsides and relatively large cabin areas, so are affected more by the wind than by the current. This is important to remember while underway, but it is most important to remember when maneuvering in close quarters.

Generally, the bow of a powerboat has higher freeboard than the stern and is considerably less heavy. Consequently, the bow will almost always be blown downwind at a faster rate than the stern. This accounts for the characteristic of most powerboats to turn their sterns into the wind if left to themselves. In some marina areas, where maneuvering is necessarily restricted to close quarters, it is not physically possible to get up enough way to bring the bow up into the wind. Under these conditions, the boatman has no choice but to go into reverse and cooperate with the wind instead of attempting to resist its effects.

Getting Under Way

Getting underway (undocking) can range from a very simple maneuver, if the wind and current are favorable and there are few other boats or other obstructions in the vicinity, or it can be much more complicated. Whatever the situation, however, a little thought given to the problem beforehand will undoubtedly suggest a way.

Wind/Current Off the Pier

Consider the simplest case first: wind and/or current directly away from the pier. All that is necessary in this case is to cast off all lines and let the wind or current carry the boat far enough away from the pier to allow safe maneuvering room. Under these conditions it is not necessary to do more. All that would be accomplished would be to speed up the undocking process, and it is seldom wise to rush such things.

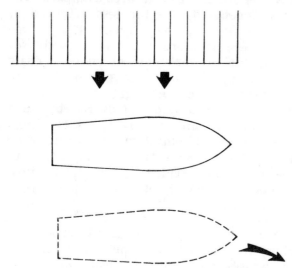

Fig. 2-15   Leaving a Dock, Wind Blowing Off the Pier.

Wind/Current On the Pier

In the opposite case, with the wind/current on the pier, a different approach is needed. Most outboards or I/O's are easiest to maneuver away in reverse. (Remember that the stern is where the control is.) With all lines cast off, set the wheel hard over in the direction AWAY from the pier, and put the engine slow astern.

Remember that the boat will pivot. It may be necessary to protect the bow with a fender as it swings in toward the pier as the stern moves out. When the boat is far enough away from the pier to allow maneuvering, put the engine in forward gear and turn toward the direction you want to go.

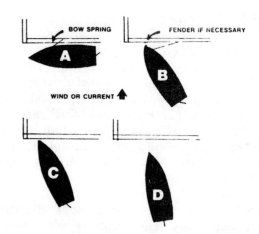

Fig. 2-16   Leaving a Dock, Wind Blowing Onto the Pier.

If the boat is an inboard there is less control of the stern, so a different approach may be required. If the boat has a single right-handed screw, and if the boat is docked with the starboard side toward the pier, the same maneuver described for the outboard (above) can be used, as the stern will tend to swing to port in reverse. If the port side is toward the pier, though, it may be necessary to use a SPRING LINE.

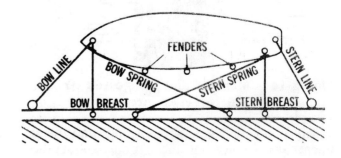

Fig. 2-17   Mooring Lines.

A line lead aft from the bow to the pier is called a <u>bow spring line</u>. With the spring line secured to a strong fitting on the boat and one on the pier, set the rudder hard over toward the pier, then "kick" the stern out with a brief application of power. Remember to tend the bow and protect it with sufficient fenders, as the boat will tend to move forward and into the pier, pivoting on the spring line.

Fig. 2-18   Using the Bow Spring Line.

With the stern swung out it should be possible to bring in the spring line (which has been doubled about the pier fitting and secured back on the boat for just that purpose) and continue backing away with the wheel set amidships. As the boat picks up speed in reverse the rudder will come into play and allow you to steer the stern to begin bringing the boat a-round to the direction you want to move.

Wind On the Stern

Cast off the stern line and hold an after bow spring line. Have fenders over the bow and tend the line carefully. Go ahead slowly with the wheel hard over <u>toward</u> the pier; the stern will swing away from the float. When the stern is sufficiently clear of all obstructions, place the wheel amidships, cast off the spring line and place the engine in slow astern. The boat will back into the wind. When clear, go ahead with a short burst of power to check sternway. Go ahead slowly, steering away from the pier.

In close quarters, where there is little room to maneuver, it is usually not practical to attempt to bring the bow into the wind. If the desired direction of travel is upwind, it may be simpler to travel backwards to a point where there is more space to maneuver.

Wind On the Bow

In this case, the wind can be of considerable help. Cast off the bow line and hold a forward quarter spring line (a line leading forward to the pier from the rear [quarter] of the boat). This will allow the bow to fall off on the wind, away from the float. It might be necessary to start this by a gentle push with a boat hook against the float. Watch the stern and use fenders as necessary, and when the bow has fallen off sufficiently to be clear of all obstructions, cast off the spring line and go ahead slowly.

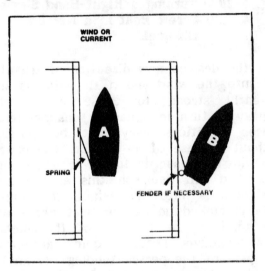

Fig. 2-19   Leaving a Dock-Wind on the Bow.

Turning In a Narrow Channel

In some cases it may be necessary to make a complete 180° turn in a channel that is too narrow when compared to the boat's minimum turning circle. A twin-screw boat, of course, will swing around in a very small area. If the boat is a single screw vessel with a right-hand-screw, start the turn as close to the left hand side of the channel as possible. Put the rudder over to hard right and LEAVE IT THERE. Alternately go ahead and reverse until the turn is complete. When the boat is properly aligned with the channel in the opposite direction, put the wheel amidships and proceed under slow speed ahead.

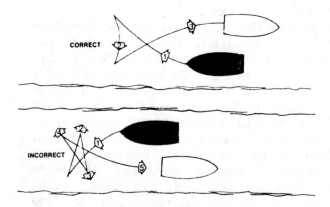

Fig. 2-20   Turning a Right-Hand Single-Screw Boat in a Narrow Channel.

If the desired new direction of travel is not into the wind and if the wind is sufficiently strong to cause considerable leeway, a turn in a narrow channel under these conditions may not be possible without the use of an anchor. The procedure in this case is to lower a bow anchor and fall back on this anchor until the bow is into the wind. The anchor rode is picked up as the boat heads into the wind to the position of the anchor. This maneuver requires quick action on the part of the person tending the anchor and is not recommended for the average boatman except in extreme cases.

Docking

Docking a boat can be a source of pride or embarrassment. Frequently, a would-be salt approaches a pier at breakneck speed, throws everything into reverse and if he doesn't plow through the pier, he gets alongside just in time for his own wake to pound his boat against the pilings.

Don't be a "hot rodder." Make the landing approach cautiously and slowly. All that is needed is enough speed for the boat to respond to the rudder. It may not look as spectacular, but it is certainly better seamanship, safer, and much cheaper. It is also good seamanship to have fenders, mooring lines, a heaving line and at least one long line ready well in advance of actual docking.

Because of the varied construction of piers and floats, you will not always have a choice of which side of the pier or float to approach. If you do have a choice and have a vessel with a right-handed screw, it is usually easier to get alongside port-side-to (port side toward the pier) than to get in starboard-side-to.

Whenever wind or current is a factor in the situation, the approach should, if possible, be made with the bow headed into the wind or current. Downwind landings are difficult and require more skill than landings into the wind, but there may be certain situations where this cannot be avoided.

All landings should be carefully planned in advance, but downwind landings require extra care and planning. A mistake under these conditions will usually cause the boat to slam into a wharf or into another boat with costly results. In any case, it is hard to make it stop when you want it to.

Docking With No Wind or Current

A landing is usually made by bringing the bow alongside the wharf or float un-

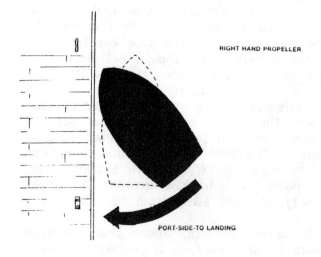

Fig. 2-21   Effect of Backing Propeller: Single Inboard, Right-Hand Screw.

der slow headway and reversing to stop the boat. If there is no wind or current, a single-screw boat with a right-hand screw should land portside to the wharf. When the port bow is put alongside and the boat is backed to check the headway, the natural tendency of the boat to back to port puts the stern alongside. In a starboard-side-to landing, the same propeller effect sends the stern away from the float. It is obvious then, that a starboard-side-to landing must be made at a very flat angle to the float and with as little headway as possible so that little or no backing is necessary. Most outboard, I/O, or twin-screw boats can dock nearly equally well to either side.

Wind Blowing Off the Float

Make the approach at a relatively sharp angle since the wind will tend to blow the bow downwind, away from the float. It will be necessary to hold a certain amount of rudder to maintain the correct heading. A fender should be rigged on the bow.

When close aboard, send the bow line ashore and put the rudder over to hard away from the pier. Go ahead on the bow line, which will act as an after bow spring. The stern will come alongside the float. Send the stern line ashore and secure the engine. Adjust mooring lines as necessary.

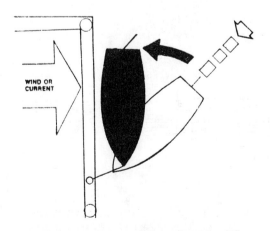

Fig. 2-22 Docking from Leeward.

Wind Blowing Onto the Float

The approach should be made at a flat angle, allowing the wind to blow the boat toward the float. Since the bow will fall off more than the stern, a certain amount of rudder must be held away from the dock to maintain the desired heading. Plenty of fenders should be rigged. When in the proper position, reverse the engine to check headway, and the boat will come alongside parallel to the float. This could be a hard landing, depending on the strength of the wind. DO NOT use arms or legs to fend off as the boat approaches the float. Many an arm and leg has been broken or crushed in this manner. When alongside, send mooring lines ashore and adjust as necessary.

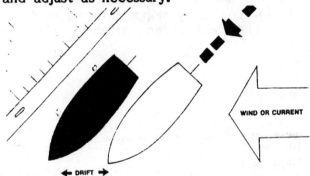

Fig. 2-23 Docking from Windward.

Twin Screws

The twin-screw boat has handling advantages. The effects of leeway caused by wind or current can be overcome without constantly holding a right or left rudder to maintain the desired heading by adjusting (increasing) the rpm's of the leeward engine. Increase the rpm's of the leeward engine a little at a time until the bow ceases to fall off. The boat will now maintain heading with little or no rudder correction necessary. This avoids the problem of added drag from the deviated rudder, but in some boats may result in uncomfortable or destructive vibrations.

If the rudder is damaged, the twin-screw boat can be steered by use of the throttles. Either the port or the starboard engine is set at a desired speed and the other is speeded up or slowed down to steer. Assuming that we set the port engine at a convenient speed, the boat can be turned to the left by speeding up the starboard engine, or turned to the right by decreasing the starboard engine's rpm's.

The boatman who "graduates" from a single-screw to a twin-screw boat often tends to become "lazy" in his maneuvering. This is due to the fact that less precision is required with the twin screw.

On the other hand, the twin-screw boat operator can make a mistake on his approach, stop, back down, and make another approach, since the twin-screw boat will back to port, to dead astern or to starboard. The best response to a failed landing approach is to back away and try again. Too many skippers trying to recover a botched docking attempt only make a bad situation worse.

Mooring to a Buoy

Mooring buoys are secured to permanent anchors sunk deeply into the bottom. Mooring buoys are usually found near a yacht club or in a harbor. (It should be noted that mooring buoys are established and maintained specifically for mooring purposes and that they are the only buoys to which pleasure boatmen may legally moor their vessels. Mooring to an aid to navigation is illegal, and if the aid is that of a public agency, it is a violation of public law.) Mooring buoys offer safe, convenient anchorages, eliminating the need for the boatman to use his own anchor. These buoys also have the effect of keeping many craft anchored in close proximity to each other in an orderly manner.

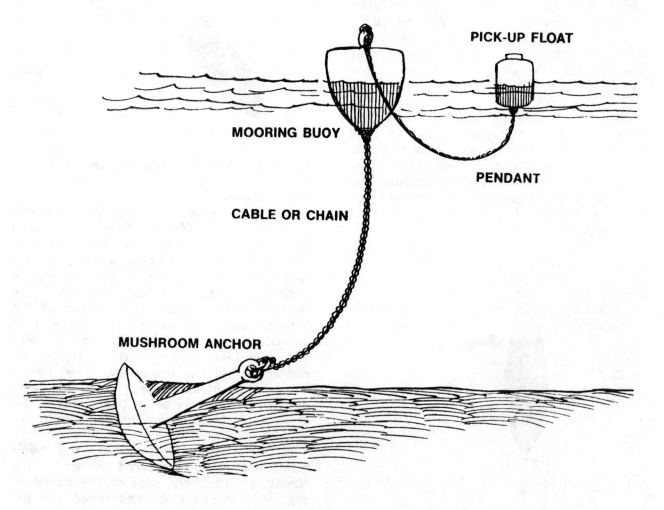

PICK-UP FLOAT

MOORING BUOY

PENDANT

CABLE OR CHAIN

MUSHROOM ANCHOR

Fig. 2-24 Typical Mooring Rig.

A mooring usually has four major parts. These are (1) an anchor (usually very heavy); (2) an anchor cable or chain leading from the anchor to the buoy on the surface; (3) a mooring pendant consisting of a wire cable or fiber line attached to the mooring buoy; and (4) a small pick-up float which is attached to the pendant. A boat is moored by securing the end of the pendant to a bitt or cleat on the bow of the vessel.

When picking up a mooring, approach the mooring buoy against the force of the wind or current, whichever is stronger. If other boats are moored in the vicinity, observe how they are heading. They will be heading into the wind or current and you can adjust your approach to roughly parallel them, proceeding upwind. (Remember-some boats are sensitive to current, some to wind.) Disengage the clutch when you see that you have enough forward motion to reach the buoy. Have a person on the bow pick up the pick-up float with a boat hook, bring the pendant aboard, and secure it to a bow bitt or cleat. Use your engine to maneuver as necessary. After the pendant is made fast, stop the engine and let the boat drift back on the anchor rode.

Leaving the mooring is a fairly simple operation. About the only difficulty you may have is the possibility of getting the pendant fouled in your rudder or propeller. When the pendant is let go, go astern slowly until you have enough room to maneuver without hitting the buoy or fouling the pendant.

Anchoring

The art of anchoring should be mastered by every boatman, if only for his own protection. Many recreational boatmen become very proficient in navigation and boat handling but neglect the important problem of anchoring once their destination has been reached.

Equipment

The general term applied to all equipment used for anchoring a vessel is ground tackle. A large percentage of recreational boats are poorly equipped in this respect. The selection of ground tackle must be made with due regard to a number of factors.

There are so many variables in the requirements for adequate ground tackle that it is not possible to establish a firm set of rules. Among the factors which must be considered are the type and weight of the vessel and the character of bottom found in the locality. The average depth of water in the anchorage area and the relative strength of the prevailing wind and current should also be considered. Unless the ground tackle can be depended upon to hold securely even while the boat is unattended, it is not adequate for the task.

Each boat should carry at least two anchors. One anchor may be of light weight and small size for easy handling. This anchor may be used in good weather when anchoring in protected areas for a relatively short time. The other anchor should be larger and heavier for use during bad weather conditions or when you intend to anchor overnight when there might be danger of dragging the anchor. For more serious cruising, experts recommend a third storm anchor for use in really heavy weather.

The size of the anchors will depend on the size of the boat on which they will be used. Do not trust your own judgment in selecting these anchors. Get expert advice or use the manufacturers' recommendations.

Types of Anchors

There are many types of anchors available on the market. Modern anchors may be known by the names of their manufacturers and usually have great holding power for their weight. The choice of one anchor over another may depend on bottom condition. The following types of anchors are available.

Yachtsman's Anchor

The yachtsman's anchor is an adaptation of the age-old kedge, redesigned to overcome some of the kedge's objectionable features. The plane of the stock is perpendicular to that of the arm and the stock is at the head. It has a sharp bill for good penetration of the bottom and the fluke is diamond-shaped to permit the cable to slip past it without fouling as the boat swings with changing current or shifting tide.

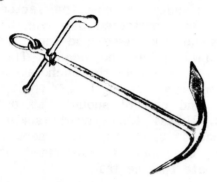

Fig. 2-25   The Yachtsman's Anchor.

The traditional yachtsman's anchor is heavy and expensive, and has a shape which makes it very awkward to stow. Some models are available which can be partially disassembled so that they can be stowed more easily, and these are often carried by long-range cruising yachtsmen as storm anchors.

Mushroom Anchor

The mushroom is stockless, with a cast iron bowl at the end of the shank. The mushroom anchor is used principally in large sizes for permanent moorings. This anchor will gradually sink deeply into the bottom and when so embedded, has tremendous holding power.

Fig. 2-26   Mushroom Anchors. Larger One Used for Permanent Mooring, Smaller One Used for Fisherman's Anchor.

Fisherman's Anchor

The fisherman's anchor is a small mushroom anchor which is sometimes used in protected waters to hold a boat in position briefly, or to slow down the rate of drift. It should not be considered for general-purpose use to hold a boat in position.

Grapnel

The grapnel has a straight shank with four or five curved claw-like arms and no stock. It is used mostly for recovering lost articles or objects. It is used as an anchor on bottoms of rock or coral, with the deliberate intention of hooking it under a rock or coral head. A trip line, attached to the crown, is a must for retrieving it.

Fig. 2-27   Grapnel.

Northill (R)

The Northill (R) anchor has a stock at the crown instead of at the head. The arm is at right angles to the shank and the broad flukes are set at an angle carefully designed to assure a quick bite and penetration. The sharp point on the bill causes the anchor to dig into the bottom as soon as a pull is placed on the cable.

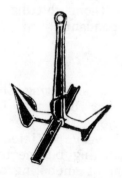

Fig. 2-28   NORTHILL (R) Anchor.

CQR Plow

This anchor is of British design and takes its name from the design of its fluke, which resembles a plow. This anchor is designed to lie on its side on the bottom. When a pull is placed on the cable, the fluke digs in quickly and deeply. The CQR (R) Plow is an efficient anchor but is clumsy to handle and stow. It is now manufactured in this country and is gradually gaining favor among boatmen.

Fig. 2-29   A Plow Anchor.

Danforth

The Danforth (R) anchor is a by-product of World War II. Many thousands of these anchors (up to 3,000 lbs.) were used to pull landing craft off the beachheads of the Pacific. The Danforth (R) anchor is lightweight and is characterized by long narrow twin flukes pivoted at one end of the relatively long shank. The stock is attached to the rear of the flukes. The flukes engage the bottom quickly and the anchor tends to bury completely under heavy strain.

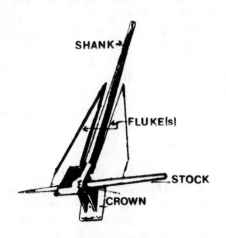

Fig. 2-30   A DANFORTH   Anchor.

Many copies of this anchor design exist under a variety of names. The design works very well under a wide variety of conditions, including mud and sand, but it does not work especially well on a rocky bottom.

Navy Stockless

The Navy-type anchor is found principally on large vessels. Because it is stockless, it stows conveniently in hawse pipes. The Navy anchor has a very high ratio of weight to holding power. Much of the holding power of this type of anchor is attributable to the weight of the anchor chain, rather than to the anchor itself. On small craft, a Navy anchor heavy enough to provide adequate holding power is a backbreaker to handle. If the weight is kept down to make it easier to handle, its holding power is highly questionable. Several adaptations of the Navy type are on the market today, designed specifically for small craft.

Fig. 2-31   Navy Stockless Type Anchor.

Rode and Scope

The rode is the anchor line and/or chain on which a boat is riding. Scope is the length of the anchor rode measured in units of water depth.

Anchors hold best when the pull of the rode on the shank of the anchor is as near to horizontal as possible. For this reason, the holding power of an anchor increases as the scope is increased. A scope of 7 to 1, (a length of line equal to seven times the depth of the water) is

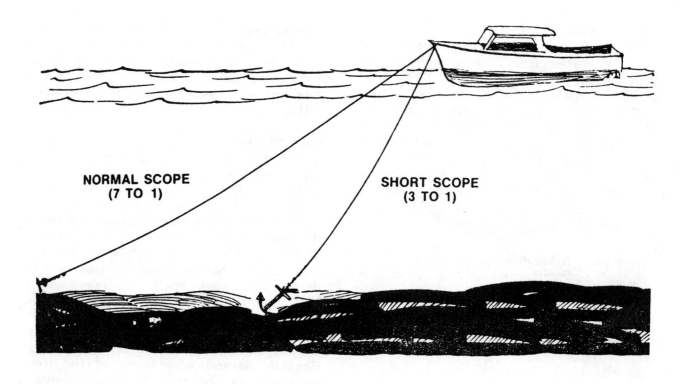

NORMAL SCOPE
(7 TO 1)

SHORT SCOPE
(3 TO 1)

Fig. 2-32   Proper Anchoring.

considered adequate for most anchoring purposes. A ratio of 5 to 1 is marginal, and 3 to 1 is poor unless the weather is excellent, the consistency of the bottom is also excellent, and the rise and fall of the tide is not excessive. A storm anchor is typically set with a scope of 10 to 1 or more, and an anchor watch is still a recommended precaution against dragging. Figure 2-32 illustrates this principle, though you should realize that the actual angle between the rode and the bottom will be much flatter than shown (i.e., the rode lies much flatter at the bottom.)

How to Anchor Your Boat

Head your boat into the wind or current. Reduce speed and make sure your anchor rode is ready for free running. Reverse the engine and when the boat starts to make a slight sternway through the water lower the anchor. Make sure that you are not standing on any part of the line as it goes over the side, and al-

ways be sure that the end of the anchor rode is secured to the boat. This end of the rode is known as the bitter end. (It is so named because it is the end of the line that is tied to the bitt.) The loss of an unsecured anchor and line has embarrassed more than one boatman.

When sufficient rode is out, usually five to seven times the depth of the water, stop the engine and make the rode fast to a forward cleat or bitt to make the anchor dig into the bottom. A hand on the rode can feel the anchor on the bottom. If it digs then skips, or just skips, pay out more rode until it is felt to dig in firmly. You should feel a definite halt in the drift of the boat as the anchor digs in.

It is wise at this time to take a sight on some stationary object on shore to make certain that your anchor is not dragging. If the anchor is not holding, it can usually be made to bite in by letting out more line.

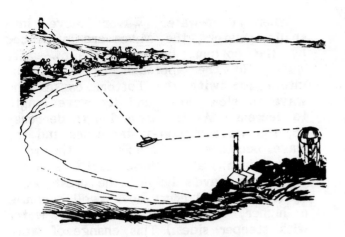

Fig. 2-33   After Anchoring, Check Position with Land Objects.

Bear in mind that an anchor will usually hold best in a mixture of mud and clay or in sandy mud. Hard sand is excellent with some anchors. Soft loose sand is very poor and soft mud may be almost useless. Rocks can give good holding power but may hold your anchor permanently.

It is always good practice to check the character of the bottom before anchoring. This can be done by either looking on your chart or lowering an armed lead. An armed lead is a weight which has a hollowed bottom and is armed with tallow, grease, wax, chewing gum or bedding compound to bring up a sample of the bottom.

Be sure to take adequate precaution not to let out so much rode that a changing wind will swing your boat into another boat, buoy, wharf, or onto the shore. If the wind or sea conditions deteriorate while at anchor, take frequent bearings to make sure that the anchor is not dragging. If it is dragging, let out more rode. If this is not practical for the reasons mentioned above, it might be prudent to weigh anchor and set it again in a better location. In heavy weather, it may be necessary to use engine power to relieve the strain on ground tackle.

Weighing Anchor

When you are ready to leave the anchorage, start the engine and be certain that it is operating properly. Then go ahead slowly to a position directly above the anchor. Have a person on the bow take up the slack in the rode as you proceed. Ordinarily, the anchor will break free of the bottom when the rode stands vertically. It can then be raised to the deck and stowed.

If the anchor does not break free easily, secure the line to a bitt and go ahead slowly. If the anchor still does not break free, it is probably fouled. One way to attempt to clear it is to make the line fast to a bitt, and then run the boat slowly in wide circles on a taut line. In those cases where the anchor will not break out under any circumstances, the boat should be run up as close as possible, the anchor rode cut and a marker float attached to mark the remaining end. This will make it possible to attempt to retrieve the anchor later.

Heavy Weather

Recreational boating is, by its nature, generally done in nice weather. However, sometimes you get caught or during extended cruises you may encounter adverse conditions of wind and sea. Some understanding of the principles of heavy weather seamanship is necessary to cope with these conditions.

Waves

Waves are caused principally by the wind. Other causes are submarine earthquakes, volcanic eruptions and the tides. Ripples form if a breeze of less than two knots blows across the surface of the water. If this breeze were to stop suddenly, the ripples would soon disappear. If the wind exceeds two knots, more stable waves are formed. These progress in the direction of the wind.

When the wind ceases to blow, energy is no longer transferred to the wave (now called a "swell") and its height begins to diminish. This reduction takes place quite slowly. If a wave is of sufficient strength, it will continue to travel until it reaches shore, perhaps thousands of miles away.

After the deep water waves are generated far out at sea, they move outward, away from their wind source, in ever-increasing curves, and become what is called SWELLS. The farther the swell moves from its source, the more uniform its characteristics become, as it travels in a series of waves, relatively equidistant, and moving at more or less constant speed. Swells generated from storms far out at sea can be distinguished by their smoothness and uniformity from those which are more coarse (peaked and irregular), which have recently originated nearby. The distant-generated swells have gentle slopes, rounded troughs and crests that are moderately sharp to rounded.

When deep-water waves move into shallow waters, the waves are influenced by the bottom, becoming shallow-water waves. In the approach to shore, the interaction with the bottom causes the wave to slow down and its wave length to decrease. As the wave length decreases, the wave steepness increases and the wave becomes less stable. As the wave moves into water whose depth is about twice the wave's height, the crest peaks up (the rounded crest of a swell becomes a higher, more pointed mass of water with steeper sides.) This change of wave form intensifies as the wave moves farther into shallow water. These changes in wave length and steepness occur before breaking. Finally, at a depth of water roughly equal to 1-1/3 times the wave height, the wave becomes unstable. This happens when not enough water is available in the shallow area ahead to complete the crest and the wave's symmetrical form. The top of the onrushing crest is left unsupported and collapses. The wave breaks, and we have surf.

Fig. 2-34 Deep Water Waves, or "Swell."

The distance between consecutive crests is called the wave length and the vertical distance between the crest and the trough is called the wave height.

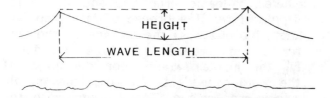

Fig. 2-35 Wave Length and Wave Height.

Small craft are generally quite comfortable in this type of sea as they move smoothly up and down without any violent motions.

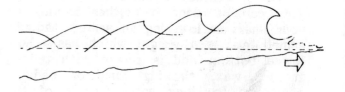

Fig. 2-36   The Character of Waves Changes as They Enter Shallow Water.

Except in very shallow waters. the horizontal flow of water caused by a wave is negligible. Wave motion at sea is energy moving through the water, not the water itself rushing along. This can best be visualized if you have ever seen the waves caused by wind in a field of wheat. Each stalk sways back and forth but the wheat does not pile up at the downwind end of the field. The motion of a given particle of water in a wave is quite similar to the action of the wheat. If this particle of water were on the surface, it would rise as the wave crest approached, with a slight forward motion. As the crest passed, it would descend, with a slight backward motion. The speed of this slight horizontal motion would increase at the crest and slow down in the trough. When added to the vertical motion of rising and falling, a given particle of water would roughly describe a circle (in a vertical plane) as each wave passed.

Because of the many independent wave systems in the sea at the same time, the surface acquires a complex and irregular pattern. Longer wave systems outrun shorter ones as the systems interfere with one another. This is the principal reason that successive wave crests are not the same height. This may be further accentuated by wave systems crossing each other at an angle. From time to time, two or more waves can combine to produce very large "rogue" waves. Such very large waves are unpredictable, dangerous, and blessedly rare.

In very heavy weather, waves with breaking crests may form well out to sea. This is an extremely dangerous condition for the small boat operator and should be avoided if at all possible. The boatman should get weather information before setting out.

Heavy Weather Precautions
At the first warning of heavy weather, whether by local observation or by radio warnings, you should rig for heavy weather. Secure all hatches and portholes and all loose gear. Rig life lines and make extra lines available. If you are in shallow water, be certain that the ground tackle is in condition to let go quickly. If in deeper water, break out the sea anchor and make it ready for use. If you are towing a dinghy, either bring it aboard or set it far back on a heavy tow line. Set the tow line so that the dinghy will ride in step with your boat. In extreme cases, cut the dinghy painter and abandon it.

Be sure the first aid kit is available and put on your personal flotation devices. Secure the galley and put out all fires. It might be a good idea to prepare sandwiches or other food rations against the time when they will be needed. Finally, just before the weather hits, get the best navigational fix that you can. In decreased visibility, you will not be able to see landmarks as well as you could in clear weather.

Heavy weather, in itself, does not place the small craft in danger. It is comforting to note that a well-found boat, manned by a knowledgeable skipper and an able crew, is usually equal to the task.

Running Into a Sea
As seas build up, the bow of a boat moving into the wind will be driven into the waves with increasing force instead of lifting over them as it would in calmer water. This causes the boat to take a tremendous pounding. Heavy objects could break loose and become battering rams, and violent motion of the hull could cause serious falls for people in the boat. Injuries are difficult to treat under these conditions. The propeller is alternately submerged and out of the water, causing the engine to be loaded one moment and racing wildly the next. The boat, her crew, and all the boat's gear are under extreme stress.

The first thing to do is slow down. Many inexperienced boatmen, caught in their first storm, are unable to resist the temptation to run for the nearest port. This would have been an excellent idea before the storm arrived, provided a safe harbor were near enough to reach in time. But now it is too late.

If the boat is slowed, to bow can lift with the waves. Take the seas slightly off the bow, preferably at an angle approaching 45 degrees. This will cause the boat to roll and pitch, but it is far easier on both boat and crew than the violent motions of pitching alone.

If you cannot make headway under

these conditions, it is advisable to lay to. Most power craft, if left to their own resources, turn their sterns into the wind. This can be dangerous, so it may be necessary to use enough power to keep the bow up into the wind, adjusting the speed so that you will be making neither headway nor sternway.

If the storm is of long duration, fuel may become a problem. If this causes concern, it might be best to fall back on a sea anchor. The sea anchor should be securely attached to the rode and the bitter end of the rode secured to a bow bitt or cleat before the sea anchor is set out. A trip line should be tied to the cone end of the sea anchor to help bring it back in. When the sea anchor is set out, the boat will fall back on the line, and the bow will be held into the wind. This may not be very comfortable, but it may be the best you can do under the circumstances. In any case, it is better than broaching or pitchpoling (see below). Depending on the size of the sea anchor, the drift will be reduced drastically. Try to keep the center of gravity as low as possible by keeping all persons down or near the bottom of the boat, and keep the bow up by concentrating the load nearer the stern. This will make the boat more stable and reduce the chance of capsizing.

Fig. 2-37   Use of a Sea Anchor.

Running in a beam sea or "in the trough," as it is commonly called, is an acceptable procedure only under conditions of comparative calm. In a beam sea, the waves are acting directly on the vessel's sides (coming from abeam) and, in

rough water, could roll some boats over on their side. It is especially hazardous if the timing of the waves matches or nearly matches the natural period of roll of the vessel. The boat's natural period of roll is the time it takes to complete one roll cycle without outside influences, as when you first step aboard at dockside on a calm day. If the next wave strikes just as the boat completes one roll and starts to roll back for the second cycle, the energy of the second wave will be added to that remaining from the first, and so on, until the boat takes on enough energy to roll over. If the required course is laid so that you are in the trough of the waves and the action of the boat becomes excessive, it might be best to change course slightly to take the seas off the bow or quarter. In order to make the desired landfall it may be necessary to run a "zig-zag" course, taking the seas off the bow for awhile, then off the quarter. The distance traveled over the water will be longer and your time of arrival will be later, but this change of plan is highly preferable to a change of plan occasioned by capsizing at sea with all hands ending up in the water.

Fig. 2-38   Zig-Zagging Through Heavy Seas.

Running Before the Sea

When a vessel sails in the same direction that the seas are running, it is running before the sea or running in a following sea. In deep water, a following sea is usually no more than a nuisance. Precise attention to the rudder is required, as the turning action of the hull appears to be more lively and difficult to control. Inexperienced boatmen in their first following sea tend to overcontrol, with the result that they find themselves wandering all over the ocean.

In shallow bays and large shallow lakes, following seas often build up to the point where they become extremely dangerous for small craft. This danger is confined principally to power craft, which usually have large transom areas. Sailing vessels and craft with "double ender" hulls generally experience little difficulty in following seas because of their streamlined underwater shape. The force of the water, acting on the relatively large non-streamlined transom of a power cruiser can cause the boat to yaw wildly from side to side. On some boats, the rudder and propeller can be lifted clear of the water as the stern is picked up by an approaching wave. If the boat is yawing at the time the stern is lifted clear of the water, the boat is completely out of control and could be thrown broadside into the trough and rolled over by the next wave. This is known as "broaching" and should be avoided at all costs.

Fig. 2-39 Broaching.

The secret of avoiding a broach is to keep yawing under control at all times. It is important to keep sideways motion to a minimum. This can be accomplished only when the rudder is in the water. The rudder can be kept "wet" by slowing down

as the wave approaches the stern and allowing the wave to pass under. Engine power is then increased slightly until the next wave approaches the stern. Power is again reduced long enough to let the next following wave pass under. By using the throttle and the rudder carefully, you can keep yawing to a minimum. It is important to remember that a yaw can quickly become a broach, and once the broach has started it is almost impossible to stop.

At this point, you might conclude that running before the sea is a lot of hard work. The fact is that it is a lot of hard work. Both the throttle and the rudder must be tended constantly. Under extreme conditions, a heavy line or small sea anchor trailed far astern will help to "nail the stern down" and make the yawing tendency easier to control.

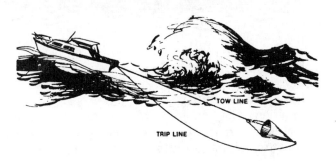

Fig. 2-40 Drogue Used with Following Seas.

Control of the engine rpm's in a heavy following sea cannot be over-emphasized. Unless the boat is slowed down appreciably as the wave approaches the stern, the vessel will be picked up by the wave and may find itself racing down the forward face of the wave at a greatly increased speed. While this might seem exciting, it could become too exciting as the boat races forward and plows into the trough, burying the bow well under in the process. The following wave might well pick up the stern and, with the bow deeply set in the water, flip the boat end over end. This is known as pitchpoling and is extremely dangerous. It is a sad fact that either a broach or a pitchpole has an air of finality about it. The usual result of either is loss of life and property. Needless to say, either can happen instantly in a strong following sea and makes running before heavy seas potentially the most dangerous point of heavy weather boat handling.

Fig. 2-41   Pitchpoling.

Impaired Visibility

When the subject of impaired or restricted visibility is brought up, most boatmen immediately think of fog. While it is true that fog is the most common impairment to visibility, other conditions such as heavy rain, sleet, hail and snow also fall within this category. The techniques for cruising in impaired visibility are common to all of these conditions.

The first and most obvious rule for safe boat operation in conditions of impaired visibility is not to go out on the water in the first place. If it's too foggy to see, it follows that is too foggy to cruise. Fog has a habit of burning off eventually and the boatman is well advised to be patient until the visibility improves a bit. The inexperienced boatman, caught out on the water when these conditions close in, will find himself in a whole new world.

Visibility never changes instantaneously and without warning. You should always

be sensitive to changing conditions and use the time before visibility fails to determine the vessel's position. In the section on Piloting we will learn how to do this, but at this time we emphasize the need for determining a position as accurately as possible.

Also, if a cruise log has not been maintained up to this point, it is an excellent idea to start one now. If you don't have a log book, the back of an envelope or the back page of your engine manual will do. Record the compass heading, the speed (as accurately as possible) and the <u>time</u>. Unless you know where you were at the time the fog closed in, you will have absolutely no idea where you are at any later time. Further, unless you know what direction you are heading in and how fast you are cruising, you will have absolutely no idea where you are going or when you might get there.

With your position determined and the log entered you are as ready for the fog as you will ever be. As soon as things close in, slow down. Your speed should be determined by the visible distance. The Navigation Rules require you to be able to avoid collision, and to travel at a "safe speed." It is the skipper's responsibility to determine what is a "safe speed," a decision that must take all factors into account, not only visibility. A large vessel moving too slowly to maintain adequate control may be a greater hazard to itself and to other vessels than one moving faster and maintaining adequate visual and radar lookout.

Regardless of weather conditions, the law requires that you maintain an efficient watch at all times when you are underway. This becomes more important than ever in a fog. A lookout should be posted on the bow, or as far forward as possible. The bow lookout should be as far removed from the engine noise as possible so that he will be able to hear other sounds around him. Since the fog has deprived all hands of the use of their eyes in navigating the vessel, the ears become more important. In extreme cases, it may become necessary to stop the engine frequently to allow all hands silent listing periods.

The behavior of sound traveling through fog can be deceptive and unpredictable. In heavy fog, sound has been known to travel long distances and "skip" large areas in the process. A bell or horn, for instance, has been heard clearly a mile away and not heard at all at a distance of 100 yards. Further, when the sound is heard, it can often be interpreted as coming from more than one direction. If the sound is faint, it could appear to come successively from all points of the compass.

According to law, you must sound proper fog signals on the whistle (horn). (See Chapter 4.) Vessels under 16 feet must sound fog signals even though the law does not specify that a whistle must be carried aboard. Accordingly, if your boating area is plagued by foggy seasons you should have a whistle (and a bell, as we shall see later), even if your craft is less than 16 feet long. Your whistle signals warn others of your presence. Since all craft are similarly bound to sound fog signals, their signals should warn you of their presence. Upon hearing the fog signal of another vessel, stop immediately and do not start again until you have determined to your full satisfaction that it is safe to proceed. Other sounds that may be heard are fog horns of sailboats, fog horns of lighthouses, bells, sirens, diaphragm horns, the sounds of breakers and other land sounds. Identification of the sound is important as it could possibly be related to an object found on your chart. (See Chapter 6, Piloting.)

Depending on the depth of the water and the configuration of the shore, an anchor could be lowered from the bow and allowed to hang straight down with sufficient cable out to engage the bottom before the boat runs up on the shore. If you have a radio direction finder aboard it can help determine your position and in "homing in" on a radio signal. A word of

caution to those using this "homing in" technique. Be sure to <u>stop</u> before you arrive at the transmitter. Many radio beacons are situated on the ends of breakwaters or piers and many hapless boatmen have "homed in" on these aids with such precision that they smashed right into the pier or ended up holed on a rocky breakwater.

If possible, the best thing to do in a heavy fog is to get clear of channels and shipping lanes and anchor. When you anchor, you are not underway. However, you are required to sound proper anchor signals when anchored in a fog. (See Chapter 4.)

Running Narrow Inlets

No text on the art of seamanship and safety would be complete without a few words on the running of narrow inlets. Many rivers and coves are connected to the sea by narrow inlets. While no two inlets are alike, they have a lot in common. Shoaling is not gradual as it is along most coasts. At the mouth of most narrow inlets shoaling is quite rapid and it is usually complicated by bottom irregularities such as sand bars with deeper pools in between.

Fig. 2-42   Running an Inlet is Serious Business.

As waves approach narrow inlets, their height increases rapidly and breakers form over the shallowest areas, indicating the location and (to some extent) the size of the sand bars. Further, these sand bars are constantly shifting, making it difficult to mark the channel with buoys. Every narrow inlet has its own peculiarities and it is here more than anywhere else that local knowledge and intimate familiarity with existing conditions come into play.

It is not possible to learn the techniques of running narrow or breaking inlets from the printed page. Narrow inlets come in all shapes and sizes. Some are reserved only for experts even under the best of conditions. Others present only minimum difficulty at best and require a high degree of skill only under the worst of sea conditions. In all narrow inlets, the water is confused and irregular and no prudent boatman would attempt his first run in an unfamiliar inlet without having a "native" aboard to point out known hazards and indicate the areas where the safe channel could most probably be found.

One point to remember when running a narrow inlet is that you may be required to use bursts of high power. This automatically rules out sailboats (even sailing auxiliaries) and low powered displacement-hull power craft. These types of vessels do not have the necessary quick response to run anything but the mildest form of narrow inlet.

While standing off the inlet, prepare a sea anchor or drogue. In use, this will slow down the boat so that power can be used to steer without running down the face of the wave. Use a heavy line for the drogue and be certain that a smaller trip line is attached to the narrow opening of the drogue. Determine the cadence of the waves by observation, select a small one and run up onto its back surface. Stream the drogue astern by the trip line, ready for use. As the wave moves forward maintain your position exactly on the back of the wave. Set the drogue by letting out the trip line if you feel the boat moving toward the crest of the wave. Use bursts of power if you feel the boat sliding backward into the trough. Maintain your position on the wave until

it eventually breaks ahead of your boat. Trip the drogue (if it is still set) and apply full power as you enter the turbulent water. Caution: tripping and resetting the drogue as desired may be difficult or impossible. Don't place too much dependence on success here if you can avoid it. As you reach calmer water, slow down and haul in the drogue by the trip line.

Sometimes the air in the turbulent water at an inlet can render rudders and propellers completely useless. A boat in these conditions is at the mercy of the waves.

Do not attempt to tow a dinghy astern of your boat while entering a breaking inlet. It can only cause trouble. If possible, bring the dinghy aboard and secure it. If this is not possible it might be better to abandon the dinghy and try to get it back later.

Conclusion

In conclusion, use good common sense when it comes to deciding whether or not you should use your boat when the wind is high and seas are increasing. If there is the least doubt in your mind, decide against it. Strangely enough, the more a man goes to sea, the greater respect he has for it. Don't tempt fate. Don't take chances on becoming another statistic. The sea has always seemed mysterious. Let the professional seaman seek out its mysteries - he is far better equipped for it. On the other hand, if you confine all of your boating activities to perfect conditions, you will be totally unprepared when you do get caught in unexpected bad conditions.

Chapter 3

Safety and Legal Requirements

Introduction

The Congress of the United States has recognized the need for safety in boating, and in August of 1971 major federal legislation, PL 92-75 or the Federal Boat Safety Act of 1971 was signed into law. Through this law Congress gave the U. S. Coast Guard a mandate to improve recreational boating safety. In addition, there are numerous state and local regulations which go beyond federal requirements. As in all other areas of our society, ignorance of the law does not exempt you from prosecution if you violate it. You as skipper, owner or crew must be aware of your responsibilities on the water and equip your craft according to federal and state requirements.

Some of the items covered by law are vital to safe operation; others are purely administrative in nature.

This chapter describes the federal laws and regulations applicable to boats and boatmen. State and local requirements vary so much across the country that it is impossible to cover them here. You can obtain information concerning these from the nearest state or local boating law enforcement agency responsible for your boating area.

Numbering of Vessels

Power boats operated on (federally-controlled) navigable waters of the United States must be numbered, regardless of length. In general, the term "navigable waters of the United States" refers to waters which provide a "road" for transportation between two or more states or to the sea.

This numbering requirement excludes boats used exclusively for racing in organized and sanctioned regattas and vessels documented as yachts. Other exceptions include public vessels, state and municipal vessels and ships lifeboats. Vessels that have a valid temporary certificate may operate without displaying the registration number on the bow while awaiting issuance of a permanent certificate.

Under the Federal Boating Act of 1958, most states have assumed this numbering function. Their systems are compatible with the Federal system. If you intend to operate principally on waters in a state which has received federal approval of its numbering system you must determine that particular state's requirements. For information regarding individual states with approved systems, consult your marine dealer, the Coast Guard, the Coast Guard Auxiliary, or the State Boating Law Administration.

If your boat must be numbered, the place of application depends upon the waters of principal use. Where these waters are within a state that has a Federally approved numbering system, application is made in accordance with that state's instructions. If you live in one state but operate your boat principally in another state, your boat should be registered in the state where it is operated.

When a boat is used principally on the ocean or waters of the Gulf of Mexico or on similar bodies of water, the place where it is normally moored becomes the determining factor in where the application is made. If the state where the boat is moored has a federally approved system, application is made to that state. When the state system has not been federally approved, application is made to the appropriate District Commander (see Appendix C). However, most states have enacted numbering laws approved by the Federal government.

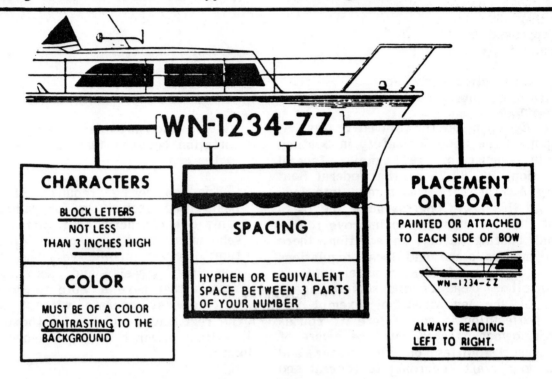

Fig. 3-1 Proper Number Placement

The number assigned by the certificate is to be painted on or attached to each side of the forward half of the vessel (the bow), and no other numbers there. Numbers are to read from left to right, are to be vertical plain block numbers that must be of contrasting color to the background and not less than three inches high. Between the prefix, the numerals, and the suffix, there must be a hyphen or space equal to the width of any letter or number except "I" or "l" (about 3").

The number shall not be placed on the obscured underside of a flared bow where the angle is such that the number cannot be easily read. When the vessel configuration is such that the number cannot be so placed on the bow, it will be placed on the forward half of the hull or on the permanent superstructure located on the forward half of the hull, as nearly vertical as possible, and where easily seen. If all of these methods are impossible or do not result in clear, readable numbers, the number may be mounted on a bracket or fixture firmly attached to the forward half of the vessel.

Sales and Transfers

Boat numbers and Certificates of Numbers are not transferable from person to person, nor from boat to boat. This number stays with the boat unless the state of principal use is changed, in which case it must be renumbered in the new state.

When numbered by the Coast Guard, a new application with a fee must be filed by each owner for every boat (except dealers) with the appropriate District Commander (see Appendix C).

Sales to Aliens

Federal law restricts the sale or lease of certain types of boats to aliens. If the sale or lease involves a vessel powered by more than 600 hp, it must be specifically approved by the Maritime Administration.

The same stipulation applies to the sale, transfer, mortgage, or lease (to an alien) of any vessel presently documented or last documented or numbered in the United States, regardless of its length or specified horsepower.

Specific advance approval of the Maritime Administration is also necessary for the sale of any vessel to a citizen or resident of certain Communist-controlled countries.

For approvals or further information, communicate with the Division of Ship Disposals and Foreign Transfers, Department of Transportation, Washington, D.C. 20593.

Documenting of Vessels

Under navigation laws administered by the U. S. Coast Guard, a vessel of 5 net tons or over owned by a citizen of the United States and used exclusively for pleasure may be documented as a yacht. If your yacht is documented, you may have the privilege of recording and retaining copies of mortgages, bills of sale, and other instruments of title with the U. S. Coast Guard. Mortgages which are so recorded may, upon compliance with the applicable requirements, become preferred mortgages, thus giving additional security to the mortgagee. You may also properly fly the yacht ensign, and you may find some advantages in clearing customs on returning to the U. S. from cruises in foreign waters.

Length of Motorboats

The law specifies minimum equipment for various classes of boat, categorized by length. (See Figures 3-3 thru 3-6.) Manufacturers may specify length in any of a variety of ways, but the official length of a boat is the end-to-end length of the boat over the deck, parallel to the keel line, excluding bow sprits, boomkins, rudders, brackets, outboard motors or outdrives, or other such attachments. (See Fig. 3-2.)

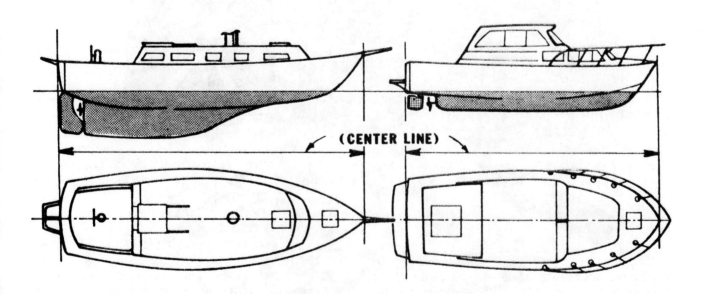

Fig. 3-2 Measuring the Boat

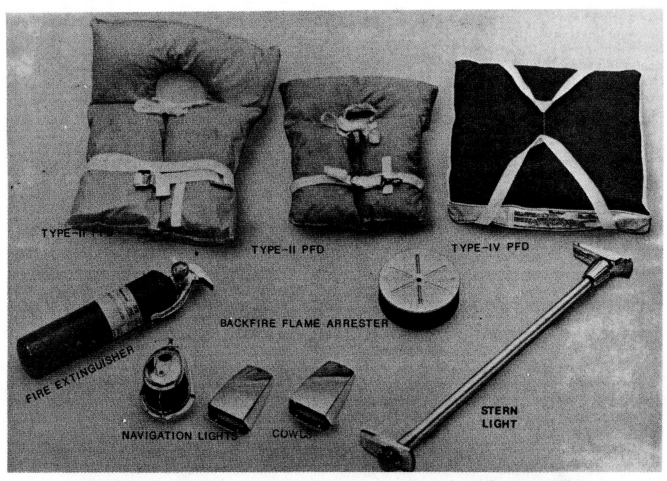

Fig. 3-3 Types of equipment for boats less than 16 feet in length.

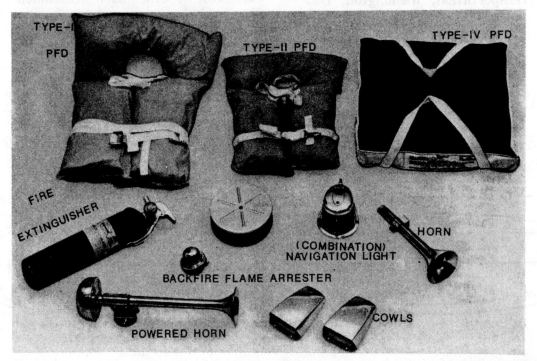

Fig. 3-4 Types of equipment for boats 16 feet to less than 26 feet in length.

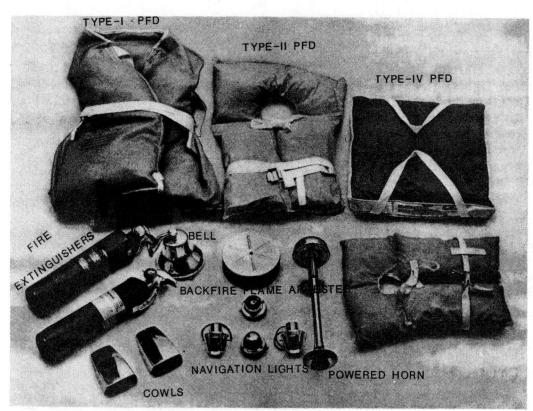

Fig. 3-5 Types of equipment for boats 26 feet to less than 40 feet in length.

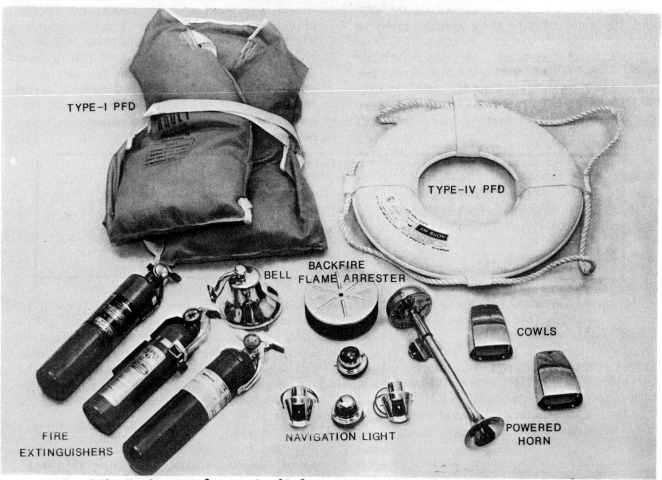

Fig. 3-6   Equipment for boats 40 feet to not more than 65 feet in length.

All motorboats (including sailboats either temporarily or permanently equipped with a motor) may be required to carry up to eight different items of equipment: navigation lights, fire extinguishers, personal flotation devices, flame arresters, ventilation devices, bells, whistles, and visual distress signals. Additional equipment may be required by state or local law or ordinance, or by good judgment and the requirements of good seamanship. (See Figs. 3-3, 3-4, 3-5 & 3-6)

Lights

By day, a vessel's movements are fairly obvious. By night, practically nothing can be determined about another vessel unless the vessel is lighted according to the Navigation Rules. As with the rules for maneuvering, the provisions for lights vary according to the place, the size of the vessel and her use. Lights for vessels will be discussed in Chapter 4.

Fire Extinguishers

Fire extinguishers are classified by size and the type of fire they are designed to put out. Motorboats are required to have either hand portable or semi-portable units capable of extinguishing fires involving flammable liquids and grease (class "B" fires). Table 3-I makes it easy to understand the classifications you will use:

prior to 1 January 1965, do not have the Coast Guard approval number of the nameplate. When a fire extinguisher does not show the Coast Guard approval number, the nameplate should be checked against the listing in COMDTINST M16714.3, Equipment Lists at Coast Guard Marine Inspection Offices, or Underwriters' Laboratories, Inc., Fire Protection Equipment List. To be acceptable by the Coast Guard for use, they must be in good and serviceable condition.

If there is a doubt about the approval status of any fire extinguisher, you should contact the nearest Coast Guard Marine Safety Office, Marine Inspection Office or Marine Safety Detachment.

You should make frequent checks to be sure your extinguishers are in their proper stowage brackets and undamaged. Cracked or broken hose should be replaced and nozzles should be kept free of obstructions. (In some areas, insects such as wasps, etc., often nest inside the nozzle, blocking it and rendering the extinguisher useless. They should be checked frequently.) Extinguishers having pressure gauges should show pressure within the designated limits. Locking pins and sealing wires should be checked to assure that the extinguisher has not been used since last recharge.

Class B Fire Extinguishers				
Classification (type-size)	Foam	Carbon Dioxide	Dry Chemical	"Freon" "(Halon)"
B-I	1-1/4 gals.	4 lbs.	2 lbs.	2-1/2 lbs.
B-II	2-1/2 gals.	15 lbs.	10 lbs.	--
B-III	12 gals.	35 lbs.	20 lbs.	--

TABLE 3-I

To meet Federal equipment requirements, portable fire extinguishers must be Coast Guard approved.

For current listings of marine type portable fire extinguishers, consult the Fire Protection Equipment List published by the Underwriters' Laboratories, Inc., 207 East Ohio Street, Chicago, Illinois.

Most fire extinguishers manufactured

Extinguishers should never be tried merely to see if they are in proper operating condition. The valves will not reseat properly and the remaining propellent gas will leak out within a short time, leaving an extinguisher with nearly a full charge of extinguishing material and no way to deliver it to a fire.

If you must use a fire extinguisher, use all of it. Do not try to "hold some back" for later. The fire may flare up again if you do not smother it completely and any that you might save by "holding back" will be useless in a few minutes when the propellant pressure has leaked away.

A discharged extinguisher should be recharged at the first opportunity.

FOAM   CARBON DIOXIDE   FREON (HALON)   DRY CHEMICAL

Fig. 3-7 Typical Fire Extinguishers

The following tests and inspections should be made by qualified persons:

Foam

Once a year discharge the extinguisher. Clean the hose and inside of the extinguisher thoroughly. Recharge and attach a tag indicating the date of servicing.

Carbon Dioxide or Freon (Halon)

Twice a year weigh the cylinder and recharge if the weight loss exceeds 10% of the weight of the charge. Inspect hose and nozzle to be sure they are clear. Inspect the lead seals on the operating levers to insure they are not broken. Attach a tag to indicate when the extinguisher was serviced or inspected.

Dry Chemical

With visual pressure indicator:

Regularly check the pressure indicator to insure the extinguisher has the proper amount of pressure. Check the nozzle to insure that there is no powder in it; if there is, weigh the extinguisher to insure that it has a full charge. Check the seals to insure that they are intact. Occasionally invert the extinguisher and hit the base with the palm of your hand to insure that the powder has not packed and caked due to vibration. Opinion among experts is divided as to whether or not this does any good. It is a known fact, however, that caking of dry extinguisher agent is a major cause of failure of dry chemical fire extinguishers. This would argue for spares over the minimum requirement. Also—one large is better than two small.

Without indicator:

Once every six months the extinguisher must be taken ashore to be checked and weighed. If the weight is 1/4 ounce less than that stamped on the container it must be serviced. The seals indicating that it has not been tampered with must be intact. If there is any indication of tampering or leakage such as powder in the nozzle, the extinguisher must be serviced. All servicing must be indicated by the servicing station on an attached tag.

Fire Extinguisher Requirements

Outboard motorboats less than 26 feet in length which are so constructed that entrapment of flammable vapors cannot occur are not required to carry fire

MINIMUM NUMBER OF HAND PORTABLE FIRE EXTINGUISHERS REQUIRED		
Length of Vessel	No fixed system in machinery space	Fixed fire extinguishing system in machinery space
Less than 16'	1 B-I	None
16' to less than 26'	1 B-I	None
26' to less than 40'	2 B-I or 1 B-II	1 B-I
40' through 65'	3 B-I or 1 B-II and 1 B-I	2 B-I or 1 B-II

TABLE 3-II

extinguishers but they are recommended. All other motorboats must be equipped with fire extinguishers according to Table 3-II.

The construction arrangements listed below are considered to permit entrapment of flammable vapors and no boat having one or more of them may be exempted from the requirement to carry fire extinguishers.

1. Closed compartments under the thwarts and seats wherein portable tanks may be stored.
2. Double bottoms not sealed to the hull or which are not completely filled with flotation material.
3. Closed living spaces.
4. Closed stowage compartments in which combustible or flammable materials are stowed.
5. Permanently installed fuel tanks.

Conditions which, by themselves, would not require fire extinguishers to be carried on outboard motorboats less than 26 feet in length include:

1. Bait wells.
2. Glove compartments.
3. Buoyant flotation material.
4. Open slatted flooring.
5. Ice chests.

Hull Identification Number

Boats manufactured between 1 November 1972, and 31 July 1984, were required to use a hull identification number such as those shown in Fig. 3-8. The letter "M" in Fig. 3-8(b) indicates the optional method for displaying the date of certification. The last three characters of Fig. 3-8(b) indicate the Month and Model Year. Note that under this method the model year begins in August.

Effective 1 August 1984, all boats must use a new Hull Identification format, such as shown in Fig. 3-8c. The 9th character indicates the month of certification or manufacture. Character #10 indicates the last digit of the year of manufacture. Characters #11 and #12 indicate the Model year.

Two identical hull identification numbers are required to be displayed on each boat hull.

The primary number must be affixed:

1. On boats with transoms to the starboard side of the transom within two inches of the top of the transom, gunwale, or hull/deck joint, whichever is lowest.

2. On boats without transoms or on boats on which it would be impractical to use the transom, to the starboard outboard side of the hull, aft, within one foot of the stern and within two inches of the top of the hull side, gunwale or hull/deck joint, whichever is lowest.

3. On catamarans and pontoon boats which have readily replaceable hulls, to the aft crossbeam within one foot of the starboard hull attachment.

The duplicate hull identification number must be affixed in an unexposed location on the interior of the boat or beneath a fitting or item of hardware.

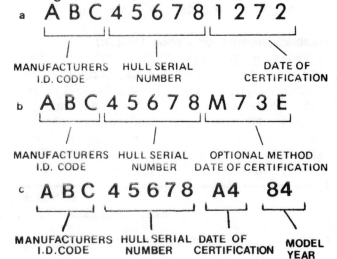

Fig. 3-8 Hull Identification Number

Display of Capacity Information

All monohull recreational boats less than 20 feet in length the construction of which began after October 31, 1972, except sailboats, canoes, kayaks, and inflatable boats, must have a legible capacity marking permanently displayed where it is clearly visible to the operator when he is getting the boat underway. The information required to be marked must be displayed as illustrated in Figures 3-9 and 3-10.

Manufacturer's Certification of Compliance

A certification of compliance must be affixed to any vessel for which a Coast Guard Standard applies. Each label must contain (1) the name and address of the manufacturer who certifies the boat or associated equipment and (2) the words: "This ('Boat' or 'Equipment') complies with U. S. Coast Guard Safety Standards in effect on the Date of Certification. Letters and numbers must be no less than one-eighth of an inch in height. The certificate of compliance label may be affixed at any easily accessible location on the boat or associated equipment. This label may, at the manufacturer's option, be combined with the capacity plate. Examples of the Manufacturer's Certificate of Compliance are illustrated in Figures 3-11 and 3-12.

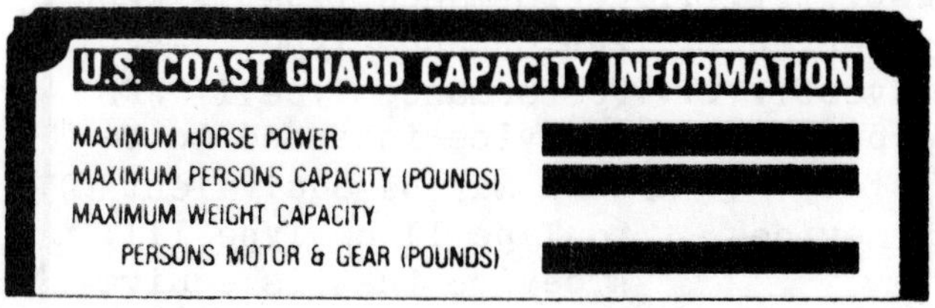

THIS BOAT COMPLIES WITH U.S. COAST GUARD SAFETY STANDARDS IN EFFECT ON THE DATE OF CERTIFICATION

MODEL NO. ░░░░░░░░░░   SERIAL NO. ░░░░░░░░░

MFD BY

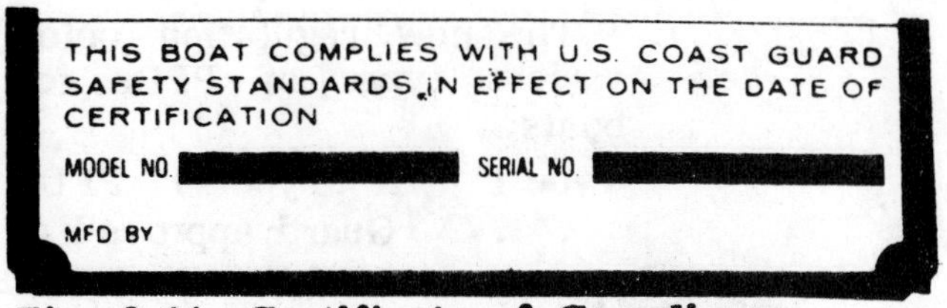

Fig. 3-11 Certificate of Compliance

U.S. COAST GUARD CAPACITY INFORMATION

MAXIMUM HORSE POWER ░░░░░░

MAXIMUM PERSONS CAPACITY (POUNDS) ░░░░░░

MAXIMUM WEIGHT CAPACITY
PERSONS MOTOR & GEAR (POUNDS) ░░░░░░

THIS BOAT COMPLIES WITH U.S. COAST GUARD SAFETY STANDARDS IN EFFECT ON THE DATE OF CERTIFICATION

MODEL NO. ░░░░░░░   SERIAL NO. ░░░░░░░

MFD BY

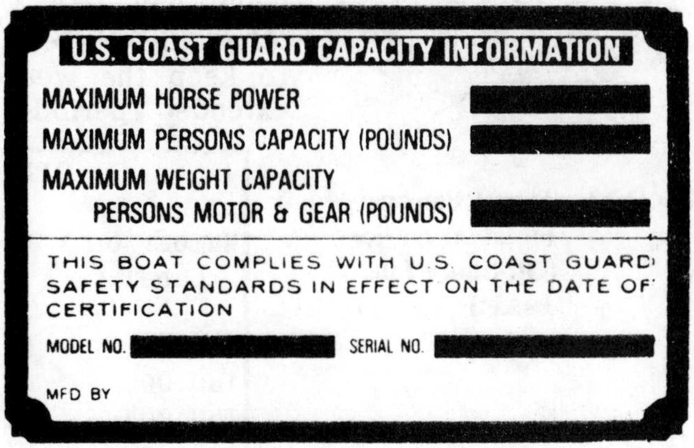

Fig. 3-12 Combination Capacity Plate and Certificate of Compliance

U.S. COAST GUARD CAPACITY INFORMATION

MAXIMUM HORSE POWER ░░░░░░

MAXIMUM PERSONS CAPACITY (POUNDS) ░░░░░░

MAXIMUM WEIGHT CAPACITY
PERSONS MOTOR & GEAR (POUNDS) ░░░░░░

Fig. 3-9 Capacity Plate for Outboards

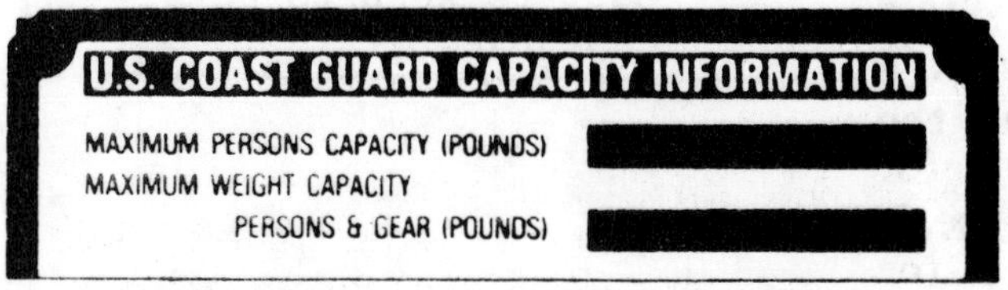

U.S. COAST GUARD CAPACITY INFORMATION

MAXIMUM PERSONS CAPACITY (POUNDS) ░░░░░░

MAXIMUM WEIGHT CAPACITY
PERSONS & GEAR (POUNDS) ░░░░░░

Fig. 3-10 Capacity Plate for Inboards, etc.

Personal Flotation Devices

The law requires that (1) all recreational boats less than sixteen (16) feet in length, including sailboats and rowboats, and all kayaks and canoes, carry at least one Type I, II, III or IV PFD for each person on board, and (2) all recreational boats sixteen (16) feet or over in length, including sailboats and rowboats, carry at least one Type I, II, or III (wearable) PFD for each person on board and one Type IV (throwable) PFD in each boat.

The new regulation below defines the various types of PFDs for recreational boats:

Type I - A Type I PFD is a Coast Guard approved device designed to turn an unconscious person in the water from a face downward position to a vertical or slightly backward position, and to have more than 20 pounds of buoyancy. This is the familiar collar-type life jacket, bulky and less wearable than other PFD types, but designed to keep the wearer afloat for extended periods of time.

Fig. 3-13 Type I Personal Flotation Device (Off-Shore Life Jacket)

TABLE 3-III

APPROVED PERSONAL FLOTATION DEVICES		
Number on Label	Devices Marked	are Equivalent to
160.002	Life preserver.....	Performance Type I PFD
160.003	Life preserver.....	Performance Type I PFD
160.004	Life preserver.....	Performance Type I PFD
160.005	Life preserver.....	Performance Type I PFD
160.009	Ring life buoy.....	Performance Type IV PFD
160.047	Buoyant vest.......	Performance Type II PFD
160.048	Buoyant cushion....	Performance Type IV PFD
160.049	Buoyant cushion....	Performance Type IV PFD
160.050	Ring life buoy.....	Performance Type IV PFD
160.052	Buoyant vest.......	Performance Type II PFD
160.053	Work Vest.........	Performance Type V PFD
160.055	Life preserver.....	Performance Type I PFD
160.060	Buoyant vest.......	Performance Type II PFD
160.064	Special purpose.... water safety buoyant devices	A device intended to be worn may be equivalent to Type II or Type III. A device that is equivalent to Type III is marked "Type III Device-may not turn unconscious wearer." A device intended to be grasped is equivalent to Type IV. Performance Type V PFD Must be worn to be acceptable.
160.077	Hybrid	

Type II

A Type II PFD is a Coast Guard approved device designed to turn an unconscious person in the water from a face downward position to a vertical or slightly backward position, and to have at least 15.5 pounds of buoyancy. This is a more wearable device than the Type I and is recommended for closer, inshore cruising. Type II PFDs are also acceptable for all size boats.

3-14 Type II Personal Flotation Device (Near-Shore Life Vest)

Type III   Type III PFD is a Coast Guard approved device designed to keep a conscious person in a vertical or slightly backward position. Like the Type II PFD, Type III must have at least 15.5 pounds of buoyancy. However, it has a lesser turning ability than either Type I or Type II. Type III PFDs are recommended for in-water sports, or on lakes, impoundments, and close in-shore operation. They are acceptable for all size boats.

Fig. 3-15 Type III Personal Flotation Device (Flotation Aid)

Type IV   A Type IV PFD is a Coast Guard approved device designed to be thrown to a person in the water and not worn. It must have at least 16.5 pounds of buoyancy. Type IV PFDs are acceptable for boats less than 16 feet in length and canoes and kayaks, and at least one Type IV PFD is required for boats 16 feet and over in length.

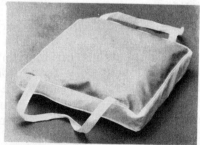

Fig. 3-16 Type IV PFD (Buoyant Cushion)

All Coast Guard approved personal flotation devices bear markings indicating the manufacturer, the type, and an approval number. However, since the above type designations were adopted in 1973, there are many kinds of Coast Guard approved PFDs in existence which are not marked as "Type I, II, III, IV, or V." Table 3-III gives equivalent "type" information for previously existing devices.

Personal flotation devices can have excellent flotation materials, be expertly manufactured and be in serviceable condition without being a good personal flotation device. The proper use of any personal flotation device requires the wearer to know how it will perform. The only way to gain this knowledge is through personal experience. Every person going out on the water in a boat should first understand how to properly fit and wear the personal flotation device intended for his use. He should then understand how the device will react when the wearer and device are in the water. Only then can he be sure he and the device are ready for an emergency which would cause him to leave the boat. Children, especially, require this practice. Any wearable PFD shall be of an appropriate size for the person who intends to wear it. Child size devices are acceptable only for persons weighing less than 90 pounds.

It is recommended that all PFDs be marked indelibly with the vessel's name and number and hailing port. This can be important in a search and rescue effort, and could help concentrate effort where it can do the most good.

Life Preservers (Type I PFDs)

Life preservers will last for many years if they are given reasonable care. They should be dried thoroughly before being put away and should be stowed in a dry, well-ventilated place. Do not stow in the bottom of lockers or deck storage boxes where moisture might accumulate. Frequent airing and drying in the sun is also recommended. Life preservers should not be tossed about haphazardly, used as fenders or cushions, or otherwise roughly treated.

Life preservers are most often of the kapok type, although buoyant fibrous glass, cork, balsa wood, and unicellular plastic foam are used. They are either jacket or bib design.

The jacket type is constructed with pads of buoyant materials inserted in a cloth covering. This covering is fitted with the necessary straps and ties.

Bib type life preservers are constructed of unicellular plastic foam with a vinyl-dip surface or cloth cover. They are fitted with an adjustable strap. Adult and child sizes are available. All Coast Guard approved life preservers (Type I) are required to be Indian Orange colored.

The jacket type life preserver should be put on the same as a coat with all ties and fasteners secured to obtain a snug fit. When the bib type is worn the body strap should be drawn snugly.

All life preservers are required to be ready for use and readily accessible. This means they should be ready to be worn without adjustments as well as being within reach. The straps should be adjusted for the person for whom it is intended and the fasteners unhooked to eliminate that step when time is most critical.

When underway in a small open boat, life preservers should be worn by children and non-swimmers. When rough weather is encountered on any type of boat, or when in hazardous waters, life preservers should be worn by everyone. As a matter of good seamanship and common sense, all unsatisfactory lifesaving equipment should be left ashore. Its replacement should be Coast Guard approved equipment. An emergency is no time to conduct an inspection to determine whether or not the equipment is serviceable.

Buoyant Vests (Type II PFDs)

Coast Guard approved buoyant vests are manufactured in several designs. They can be constructed of pads of kapok, fibrous glass or unicellular plastic with cloth covering, with straps and ties attached. The kapok and fibrous glass pads are enclosed in plastic bags. Other models of buoyant vests are made of unicellular plastic foam which has a vinyl-dip coating. They are made in three sizes: adult, child (medium) and child (small), and may be any color.

Buoyant vests are identified by a Coast Guard approval number and the model number which are contained on a label attached to the vest. Vests must be in good and serviceable condition.

As with life preservers, buoyant vests have a variety of adjustable straps which should be adjusted to fit before leaving the mooring. Be sure to make children's adjustments for proper fit, too. Vests should be worn snugly with all ties and fasteners pulled tight and worn by children and non-swimmers when underway in small boats or open construction type craft. They should be dried thoroughly before being put away, and when stowed on board should be in a readily accessible location which is dry, cool, and well ventilated. Buoyant vests should not be tossed about haphazardly, used as fenders or cushions, or otherwise roughly treated.

Buoyant Cushions (Type IV PFDs)

Buoyant cushions approved by the Coast Guard contain kapok, fibrous glass or unicellular plastic foam, come in a variety of sizes and shapes, may be any color, and are fitted with grab straps. Some unicellular plastic foam buoyant cushions are vinyl-dip coated.

Buoyant cushions are generally more readily accessible since they are sometimes used as seat cushions. However, the kapok or fibrous glass cushions used as seats become unserviceable rather rapidly because the inner plastic envelope may be punctured.

Cushions are usually available in time of emergency. However, they are difficult to hang on to in the water and do not afford as great a degree of protection as a life preserver or buoyant vest. For this reason, buoyant cushions are not recommended for use by children or non-swimmers. The straps on buoyant cushions are put there primarily for holding-on purposes. However, they may also be used in throwing the cushion. Cushions should never be worn on a person's back since this tends to force the wearer's face down in the water.

Approved buoyant cushions are marked on the side (gusset), showing the Coast

Guard approval number and other information concerning the cushion and its use.

Ring Life Buoys (Type IV PFDs)

These personal flotation devices can be made of cork, balsa wood or unicellular plastic foam, and are available in 30, 24, 20, and 18-inch sizes. Their covering is either canvas or specially-surfaced plastic foam. All buoys are fitted with a grab line and may be colored either white or orange.

It is desirable to attach approximately 60 feet of line to the grab rope on the ring buoy. When throwing a ring buoy, care should be taken not to hit the person in the water. Ring buoys should be stowed in brackets topside, readily accessible for emergencies.

Cork and balsa wood ring buoys must bear two markings, the manufacturer's stamp and the Coast Guard inspector's stamp. Plastic foam ring buoys bear only one marking, a nameplate attached to the buoy.

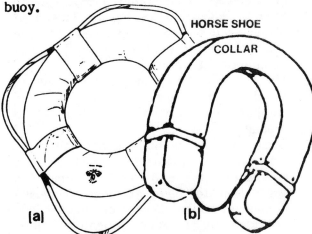

Fig. 3-17 Type IV PFD (Ring Buoy)

Special Purpose Water Safety Buoyant Devices

Type III PFDs

Approved special purpose water safety buoyant devices are manufactured in many designs depending on the intended special purpose. These include water ski jump vests, hunters' vests, motorboat racing vests, flotation jackets, and others.

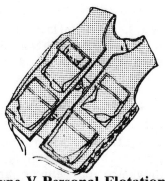

Fig. 3-18 Type V Personal Flotation Device (Special Use Device)

Additional strength is added where needed for the intended purpose of the device

Devices are made for either wearing or grasping and devices intended to be worn are available in adult and child sizes. Their markings include the Coast Guard approval number, indication of the purpose for which the device is intended, instructions for use and maintenance, and other necessary information, such as: "Warning-Do not wear on Back" for device intended to be grasped and not worn.

Type V PFDs

There are two groups of Type V PFDs. The first group consists of "special purposes" PFDs, such as light-weight jackets for kayak racers, exposure suits, and some types of "float coat." The second group within Type V consists of so-called "hybrid PFDs."

Special purpose PFDs are, as their name implies, designed and intended for particular application. In general, they are not suitable (or approved) for general use aboard a recreational boat.

Hybrid PFDs, on the other hand, are designed to meet a need for a comfortable, easy-to-wear PFD for recreational boaters. They are called "hybrid" because they have some inherent buoyancy (closed-cell plastic foam, etc.), but depend on inflatable chambers for additional support in the water.

Hybrid PFDs are designed to keep you afloat should you fall into the water, but they do not provide as much buoyancy as other types. The inflatable chambers or bladders may be inflated by a built-in compressed gas cylinder or by mouth to provide additional buoyancy.

Some manufacturers provide a mechanism that will inflate the flotation bladders automatically when the jacket and wearer enter the water. Such mechanisms, while they are convenient and may provide an extra margin of safety should the wearer be injured or unconscious and unable to inflate the chambers when he/she falls into the water, they do require careful maintenance to keep them workable.

Type V PFDs meet the legal requirements for wearable PFDs on board a vessel only if they are actually being worn at the time. On the other hand, they are designed to be comfortable enough that wearing them at all times when you are on the water should be no problem. The Type V PFD may be substituted on a pleasure craft for a Type I, II or III device — if worn.

Ventilation System

While ventilation is required on most power boats, there is no such thing as a ventilation system "approved" by the Coast Guard. A variety of systems exist, depending which designs and conformity of individual boats, for the purpose of conveying fresh air into each engine and fuel tank compartment and dangerous vapors out of the vessel. To create a flow through the ducting system, at least when underway or when there is a wind, cowls (scoops) or other fittings of equivalent effectiveness are needed on all ducts. A wind-actuated rotary exhauster or mechanical blower is considered equivalent and preferred to a cowl on the exhaust duct.

To scavenge gases from ventilated spaces and avoid undesirable turbulence within the spaces, at least one inlet duct must be installed to extend to a point at least midway to the bilge, or at least below the level of the carburetor air intake.

At least one exhaust duct must extend from the open atmosphere to the lower portion of the bilge. Ducts should not be installed so low in the bilge that they may become obstructed by normal accumulation of bilge water.

The minimum size of the duct must be 2 inches in diameter or have a cross-sectional area of at least 3 square inches.

Open Boats

The use of gasoline in boats will always present a safety hazard because the vapors are heavier than air and may find their way into the bilges from which there is no escape except through the ventilation systems. In an open boat these vapors may be dissipated through the scouring effect of exposure to the open atmosphere. Open boats are, therefore, exempted from the above ventilation requirements. All three of the following conditions should be met in order to consider a boat "open":

1. Engine and fuel tank compartments have a minimum 15 square inches of open area directly exposed to the atmosphere for each cubic foot of net compartment volume.
2. There are no long or narrow unventilated spaces accessible from such compartments in which a flame could propagate.
3. Long, narrow compartments (such as side panels), if joining engine or fuel compartments and not serving as ducts thereto, have at least 15 square inches of open area per cubic foot provided by frequent openings along the full length of the compartment formed.

Technical Details

Intake (Air Supply)

There must be one or more intake ducts in each fuel and engine compartment, fitted with a cowl (scoop), extending from the open atmosphere to a level midway to the bilge (fuel compartment) or at least below the level of the carburetor (engine compartment).

Exhaust

There must be one or more exhaust ducts from the lower portion of the bilge of each fuel and engine compartment to the free atmosphere, fitted with a cowl or an equivalent such as a wind actuated rotary exhauster or a power exhaust blower.

Ducting Materials

Depending on the design, vent cowls could be a major source of bilge water from rain, washdown, breaking seas. Also, periodic inspection is desirable - plastic ducting may break, fall down, etc.

Positioning of Cowls

Normally, the intake cowl will face forward in an area of free underway airflow, and the exhaust cowl will face aft. They should be located with respect to each other so as to prevent the return of displaced vapors to any enclosed space, or to avoid the pick up of vapors from fuel filling stations.

Carburetion Air

Openings in engine compartment for entry of air to the carburetor are additional to the ventilation system requirements.

General Precautions

Ventilation systems are not designed to remove vapors caused by breaks in fuel lines or leaking tanks. If gas odors are detected repairs are generally indicated. Prior to each starting of the engine, the engine compartment should be opened to dissipate vapors which may be present. The smaller the compartment the quicker an explosive mixture of gasoline vapors can be expected to develop.

Play it Safe—Keep Your Boat Free of Explosive Vapors!

Note: Vessels which are intended for carrying more than six passengers for hire are subject to special regulations. Owners should contact the nearest Coast Guard Marine Safety Office, Marine Inspection Office or Marine Safety Detachment for inspection requirements.

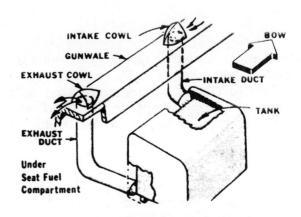

Fig. 3-19 Ventilation (Boats Built Before July 31, 1980)

Ventilation Systems — Boats Built Before July 31, 1980

Both (1) powered and (2) natural ventilation requirements are in effect after July 31, 1980, for boats built after that date. Some boat builders have been in compliance since July 31, 1978. If you are building a boat, check with the Coast Guard for details.

1. Any compartment on a boat containing a permanently installed gasoline engine with a "cranking motor" (e.g., starter) must have a power ventilation system and a label close to the ignition switch and in plain view of the operator: WARNING - GASOLINE VAPORS CAN EXPLODE. BEFORE STARTING ENGINE OPERATE BLOWER FOR 4 MINUTES AND CHECK ENGINE COMPARTMENT BILGE FOR GASOLINE VAPORS.

2. Other engine and/or fuel compartments may require natural ventilation.

All ventilation regulations, as in the past, require the operator to maintain them.

Backfire Flame Arresters

Gasoline engines (other than outboard engines) that have been installed since April 25, 1940, must have an acceptable means of backfire flame control. The usual method is by installation of a Coast Guard approved flame arrester. Alternate methods are a special Coast Guard approved reed valve system or a closed metallic duct system which would carry all backfire flames outside the vessel in a manner to permit dispersion without endangering the vessel, persons on board, or nearby vessels or structures.

Fig. 3-20 Backfire Flame Arrester

SOUND PRODUCING DEVICES

Fig. 3-22 Bell

Bell

Bell signals are required when a vessel is at anchor under conditions of restricted visibility. Under both the International and Inland Navigation Rules (see Chapter 4)

• All boats 39.4 feet (12 meters) or longer must also carry a bell, in operating condition, with a minimum diameter at the mouth of at least 7 7/8" (200mm).

Whistle or Horn

Whistle signals are required to be given by all boats under certain circumstances. Equipment requirements vary according to the length of the boat.

• For compliance with "Navigation Rules" and for distress signaling purposes, all boats must carry some type of sound producing device capable of a 4 second blast audible for 1/2 mile. Athletic whistles are not acceptable on boats over 12 meters.

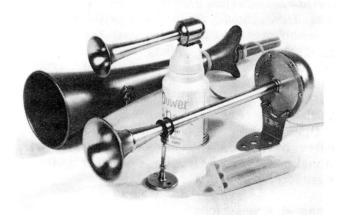

Fig. 3-21 Whistle and Horns

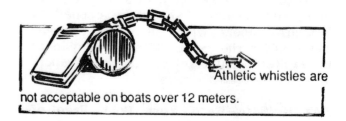

Athletic whistles are not acceptable on boats over 12 meters.

Visual Distress Signals

All recreational boats 16 feet or more are required to be equipped with visual distress signaling devices at all times when operating on coastal waters as of 1 January 1981. Also, boats less than 16 feet are required to carry visual distress signals when operating on coastal waters at night. Coastal waters are defined as (1) The ocean (territorial sea) (2) The Great Lakes (3) Bays or sounds that empty into those waters, and (4) Rivers over two miles across at the mouth, upstream to a point where they narrow to two miles. Completely open sailboats, less than 26 feet, without engines are excepted in the daytime, as are boats propelled manually. Also excepted are boats in organized races, regattas, parades, etc. Visual Distress Signals must be Coast Guard approved, readily accessible, serviceable, and, for those applicable, bearing a legible, unexpired date.

All vessels that operate in U. S. coastal waters or the Great Lakes are required to carry Coast Guard-approved visual distress signals (VDS's). In addition, vessels operating in inland lakes and rivers are strongly urged to carry them.

VDS's have been found to be extremely effective in attracting attention and in guiding rescuers in a search and rescue situation. The wrong type of signal, or one that is not used to best advantage, can be of no help at all, and can even be dangerous to you or to your vessel.

Vessels that are required to carry VDS's must carry types appropriate for day use and night use.

Types of VDS

VDS's may be of several possible types. The simplest is a bright orange flag bearing a black square and a black circle. This signal is, of course, usable only during the day, but it has the advantage of being constantly on display.

Another signal that is usable only in daylight is orange smoke. A smoke flare is particularly effective in attracting attention from aircraft. They have the disadvantage, however, of not lasting very long, and they are much less effective in conditions of poor visibility or in high wind.

A signal that can be used at night is an electric flashing light. This device, in order to meet Coast Guard approval standards, must be able to blink SOS (... --- ...) automatically.

Some VDS's are usable in either day or night conditions. These include a variety of aerial flares and handheld flares.

One serious disadvantage of flares of either sort is that they last for only a short time, possibly only seconds, after they are ignited. An aerial VDS, depending on the type it is and the conditions under which it is used, may not go very high. These facts should suggest that VDS's are best saved for use ONLY when other vessels ARE IN SIGHT. If you cannot see another vessel, the chances are that they will not see your signal.

Coast Guard approved flares have an expiration date stamped on them. Be careful when you buy flares. It is possible that some VDS flares sold in stores or by mail order may be very near the end of their shelf life. Devices that have expired do not meet the legal requirement. They may still work, but they should not be counted on to save your life in an emergency. If you carry flares to meet the VDS requirement, you must have at least three on board in good condition and bearing current dates. Of course, it is recommended that you carry more than the minimum number.

Even flares that are within their legal "lifespan" may fail to work if they have been damaged or abused. They are designed to withstand most "normal" onboard conditions, but they can be damaged, especially if they are allowed to get wet.

It is recommended that you keep outdated flares after you have replaced them with new, current-dated ones. They do not meet the legal requirement, but there is no penalty for carrying outdated spares. In an emergency, use the oldest devices first. There is no way to test either handheld or aerial flares, and it may be dangerous or illegal to discharge them unless a genuine emergency exists.

If you do use a VDS in an emergency, do so carefully. They are designed to be as safe as possible, but there are some hazards that cannot be avoided. (Hazardous as they are, approved flares are significantly LESS hazardous to handle in a marine environment than non-approved types. Road hazard flares, for instance, can easily start fires on boats, while approved marine types are carefully designed and manufactured to minimize this risk, even if it cannot be eliminated altogether.) Aerial flares should be given the same respect as firearms, which, of course, they are. (Note that some states regulate aerial flare launchers as firearms. Check with local law enforcement officials in your area for information about local enforcement policies regarding such devices.)

NEVER point a flare pistol at another person. Never allow children to play with or around them. If you discharge a flare pistol, check for overhead obstructions (sails, rigging, etc.) that may be damaged by the flare or deflect it to where it can cause damage.

Of course, in an emergency you can use any means at your disposal to attract attention. Probably the most effective means of summoning help, if you have it available, is the marine VHF radiotelephone. Your crew and guests should all be checked out on emergency procedures with the radiotelephone, since there is seldom time to learn effective operating during an emergency. See Chapter 12 for more information about the radiotelephone.

There are a large number of other means of signaling distress that have been developed and more or less recognized over the years, some more effective or widely recognized than others. On large vessels, for instance, it may be possible to build a large smoky fire on board in such a way that it will not endanger the ship. Smoke and flames will obviously attract attention, but it is equally obvious that it is difficult to build a "safe" fire on most small boats! In general, this is NOT a recommended distress signal for recreational boaters.

A mirror can be used to good advantage on sunny days to attract attention from great distances. It cannot reach searchers over the horizon, but the horizon for an observer in an aircraft can be many miles away. Not only is this an effective signaling device, but it needs no batteries, it always works as long as the sun is shining, and any shiny object can be used.

In most recreational boating situations the best distress signal to use when another boat is in sight may be waving the arms up and down slowly. This gesture is simple, seldom misunderstood, and requires no equipment.

Other "traditional" distress signals, such as flying the American flag upside down, probably have little impact. In an emergency, your efforts would probably better be put into more effective signaling methods.

Marine Sanitation Devices (MSDs)

Each vessel with an installed toilet must have attached to it either: (1) a marine sanitation device (MSD) certified by the Coast Guard; or (2) a holding tank. Operating a boat with a non-approved MSD is illegal in the navigable waters of the U.S., including the "territorial sea" ("three mile limit"). In addition, certain bodies of fresh-water have been declared no-discharge areas. To comply, all installed toilets must be certified by the Coast Guard or designed to retain waste onboard for pumpout at a land site. All non-approved overboard discharge toilets must be removed or permanently disabled, but there is no requirement to install toilet facilities on vessels not currently having them. These regulations do not affect portable toilets on vessels.

Your Responsibility as a Boatman

You are responsible for any damage your boat may cause other craft or for any injuries suffered by your passengers or others. For instance, if you pass close to a cruiser at high speed and your wake rocks this vessel so that the dishes in the galley are broken, you may be held responsible. If this should happen when hot foods are being prepared or served on board the cruiser and someone suffers serious burns as a result of the violent rocking caused by your wake, you may be held liable. You could be summoned into court and equitable civil damages assessed against you. In addition, you might also be cited for negligent or grossly negligent operation.

Water Pollution and Discharge of Oil

The recreational boatman has an important stake in the effort to keep the nation's waters free from pollution and to maintain the purity of water supplies and the environment of wildlife. You must help to provide and protect clean water not only for your own recreation but also for the enjoyment of sport fishermen, divers, swimmers, and all who appreciate a beautiful and bountiful natural resource. An important part of the responsibility to protect the marine environment is observing the Federal water pollution laws.

The law prohibits the throwing, discharging, or depositing of any refuse matter of any kind (including trash, garbage, oil, and other liquid pollutants) into the waters of the United States to a distance of three miles from the coastline. The Federal Water Pollution Control Act prohibits the discharge of oil or hazardous substances into the waters of the United States to twelve miles offshore. You must immediately notify the U. S. Coast Guard if your vessel or facility discharges oil or hazardous substances into the water.

Federal water pollution controls are rigidly enforced and provide penalties for individuals who violate them, even accidentally.

Federal regulations issued under the Federal Water Pollution Control Act require:

1. All vessels under 100 gross tons must have a fixed or portable means to discharge oily bilge slops to a reception facility. A bucket or bailer is considered a portable means.

2. Vessels 26 feet in length and over must have posted a placard at least 5 by 8 inches, made of durable material, fixed in a conspicuous place in the machinery spaces, or at the bilge and ballast pump control station, stating the following:

DISCHARGE OF OIL PROHIBITED

The Federal Water Pollution Control Act prohibits the discharge of oil or oily waste into or upon the navigable waters and contiguous zone of the United States if such discharge causes a film or sheen upon, or discoloration of, the surface of the water, or causes a sludge or emulsion beneath the surface of the water. Violators are subject to a penalty of $5,000.

3. No person may drain the sumps of oil lubricated machinery or the contents of oil filters, strainers, or purifiers into the bilge of any U.S. vessel.

You must also help to ensure that others obey the law. You are encouraged to report polluting discharges which you observe to the nearest U.S. Coast Guard office. Report the following information:

    a. location,
    b. source,
    c. size,
    d. color,
    e. substance,
    f. time observed.

Do not attempt to take samples of any chemical discharge. If you are uncertain as to the identity of any discharge, avoid flame, physical contact, or inhalation of vapors.

Boating Accident Reports

The operator of any vessel involved in an on-the-water accident must stop, render assistance to those in danger and offer identification. If a person disappears from a vessel or a death occurs as a result of a boating accident, local authorities must be notified immediately. A written boating accident report is required within 48 hours if, as a result of the accident a person dies, disappears from a vessel, or is injured and requires treatment beyond first aid. In addition, a written boating accident report must be submitted within 10 days if a vessel is lost or damage to the vessel or other property exceeds $200.

Boating accident report forms can be obtained from, and should be returned to the state authorities having jurisdiction over the waters on which the accident occurred. If an accident occurs on the waters of the state of New Hampshire which does not have an approved numbering system, the Accident Report Form (CG-3865) can be obtained from the nearest Coast Guard Marine Safety Office, Marine Inspection Office or Marine Safety Detachment. Accident reports are used to compile accident prevention data and the information contained in the individual reports are not made public.

Law Enforcement – Penalties

Coast Guard boarding vessels will be identified by the Coast Guard ensign and personnel will be in uniform. A vessel underway, upon being hailed by a Coast Guard vessel or patrol boat, is required to stop immediately and lay to or maneuver in such a way as to permit the boarding officer to come aboard. Failure to stop to permit boarding may subject the operator to a penalty.

The owner or operator of a vessel which is not numbered as required or who fails to file notice of transfer, destruction or abandonment of a vessel or fails to report a change of address, is liable to penalty which could be as much as $500.

A civil penalty may be imposed by the Coast Guard for negligent or grossly negligent operation, for failure to obey the Navigation Rules or failure to comply with regulations.

The law also provides for a fine of up to $1,000 and imprisonment of not more than 1 year for the criminal offense of reckless or negligent operation of a vessel which endangers the life or property of any person.

The law also authorizes a Coast Guard Boarding Officer, when in his judgment continued unsafe use of a boat creates an especially hazardous condition, to direct the operator to correct the hazardous condition immediately or return to a mooring and to remain there until the situation creating the hazard is corrected or ended. Reasons for using the authority could be insufficient personal flotation devices or firefighting equipment aboard, or overloading. Failure to comply with the orders of the Boarding Officer subject the offender to penalties provided for under the law.

Additionally the law authorizes any Coast Guard District Commander to issue regulations for a specific boat designating that boat unsafe for a specific voyage on a specific body of water when he has determined that such a voyage would be manifestly unsafe.

Courtesy Marine Examination

As a courtesy to pleasure boat owners and operators, members of the Coast Guard Auxiliary check thousands of boats each year for safety requirements. These members are qualified as Courtesy Examiners under strict requirements set by the Coast Guard and are very knowledgeable in their field. The examinations are performed as a courtesy, and only with the consent of the pleasure boat owner. To pass the examination, a vessel must satisfy not only federal equipment requirements but also certain additional safety requirements recommended by the Auxiliary. If the boat passes the examination it is awarded a safety decal which is placed conspicuously on the vessel.

UNITED STATES COAST GUARD AUXILIARY

COURTESY

U.S. COAST GUARD AUXILIARY

EXAMINATION

No. _____
CG-2902 (Rev.   )

SEAL OF SAFETY CHECK LIST
(To Be Completed by Your
Auxiliary Courtesy Examiner)

	YES	NO	NOT APPL
1. NUMBERING			
2. REGISTRATION/ DOCUMENTATION			▒
3. NAVIGATION LIGHTS			▒
4. SOUND PRODUCING DEVICES ○ BELL - BOATS 12M (39.4 ft) OR LONGER			▒
5. PERSONAL FLOTATION DEVICES			▒
6. FIRE EXTINGUISHERS			▒
7. VISUAL DISTRESS SIGNALS ○ INLAND ○ INTERNATIONAL			▒
8. VENTILATION			
9. BACKFIRE FLAME ARRESTER			
10. FUEL SYSTEMS			
11. ANCHOR AND ANCHOR LINE			▒
12. ALTERNATE PROPULSION			
13. DEWATERING DEVICE			
14. GENERAL CONDITIONS ○ SEAWORTHINESS ○ ELECTRICAL ○ GALLEY			▒
15. STATE REQUIREMENTS			▒

The following items are not a requirement for the CME decal. These additional items are required by Federal and State laws. The Courtesy Examiner has checked these items to assist the boater in determining if the vessel is within the requirements of these laws.

1. CG CAPACITY PLATE			
2. CERTIFICATE OF COMPLIANCE LABEL			
3. HULL IDENTIFICATION NUMBER			
4. MARINE SANITATION DEVICE ○ BOATER INFORMED			
5. POLLUTION PLACARD			
6. NAVIGATION RULES			

ADDITIONAL COMMENTS:

Fig. 3–23 Legal Requirements and Requirements For the Seal of Safety Decal

Chapter 4

Navigation Rules

History and Background

The danger of collision at sea has existed ever since the world's second boat was built. The Navigation Rules, or the "Rules of the Road" as they were formerly called, exist for one reason -- to prevent collisions between vessels. Just as we need driving rules to govern how we drive our cars on the highway, we need "driving rules" to govern how we maneuver our vessels on the waterways.

The Navigation Rules serve that purpose. They establish responsibility for actions, a priority or precedence among vessels, specific actions to be taken in specific situations, and mechanisms for communicating needs and intentions.

During the late 1800's, the Congress of the United States enacted special rules "relating to the navigation of any harbors, rivers, or inland waters." In the years since that time the rules have grown in complexity. Most recently, the United States has adopted the International Regulations for Preventing Collisions at Sea, 1972. These are commonly called the International Rules or the 72 COLREGS.

The Inland Navigational Rules Act of 1980 became effective in most applicable waters on Dec. 24, 1981. This new set of Inland Rules supersedes the old Inland Rules, the Western Rivers Rules, the Great Lakes Rules and parts of the Motorboat Act of 1940.

Navigation Rules, International -- Inland (COMDTINST M16672.2), published by the U. S. Government Printing Office for purchase, contains both sets of rules, including annexes, which are additional sections containing various technical details.

This chapter is a summary overview of the Navigation Rules. While it is believed to be accurate and to contain practically everything a recreational boater should know, it is not a substitute for the actual rules. You should get a copy of those rules and study them thoroughly, and keep it available for further reference.

Why are there two sets of rules? Just as most states have general traffic codes with special regulations for local conditions, so it is with the two sets of navigation rules. The International Rules (72 COLREGS) are designed for use on the high seas and similar bodies of water. The Inland Rules provide special regulations for crowded waterways, rivers, Vessel Traffic Services, lakes and busy harbors and other areas where the International Rules do not apply.

The Commandant of the U. S. Coast Guard establishes demarcation lines which mark the boundaries between waters which are governed by the International Rules and those waters which are governed by the Inland Rules. Demarcation lines are printed on charts and are also included in "Navigation Rules, International -- Inland."

Organization of the Navigation Rules

The International and Inland Rules parallel one another, but there are important differences. In this chapter, the Rules are presented as though they were one. When there are substantial differences, they will be pointed out.

The Navigation Rules are divided into 5 major sections: (A) General; (B) Steering and Sailing Rules; (C) Lights and Shapes; (D) Sound and Light Signals; and (E) Exemptions.

The Steering and Sailing Rules govern conduct when vessels are approaching each other so as to involve risk of collision. This section comprises the "driving rules."

Lights and Shapes and Sound and Light Signals describe lights and shapes used to mark vessels and indicate special conditions, and maneuvering signals. These sections constitute a "nautical communication system."

In this chapter we will discuss the "driving rules" and the "nautical communication system" together — vessel action first, and then communications.

General Principles

The purpose of the Navigation Rules is to prevent collisions at sea. The Navigation Rules apply to all vessels, with the Steering and Sailing Rules coming into play when vessels approach each other so as to involve risk of collision.

It is necessary to understand the following definitions in order to understand the Navigation Rules.

A power driven vessel means any vessel propelled by machinery.

A sailing vessel means any vessel under sail, provided that propelling machinery, if fitted, is not being used. A sailboat is a "power-driven vessel" if the engine is in use. All rules for power-driven vessels (maneuvering, sound signals, lights) apply to sailboats using their engines.

Underway means that a vessel is not at anchor, made fast to the shore or a pier, or aground. A vessel which is stopped (adrift) and not making way is still considered to be underway.

Restricted visibility means any condition in which visibility is restricted by fog, mist, falling snow, heavy rainstorms, sandstorms or other similar causes.

Conduct in Any Condition of Visibility

Every vessel must maintain a proper lookout and always proceed at a safe speed so that she can take proper and effective action to avoid collision. To determine safe speed, consider such things as the state of visibility; traffic density, including concentration of fishing vessels, etc.; background lights (at night); the state of wind, sea and current; the proximity of navigational hazards; the vessel's draft in relation to the available depth of water; and any other factors that may apply (availability of radar, etc.).

Every vessel must use all available means to determine if risk of collision exists. Such a risk exists if the relative bearing of an approaching vessel does not change appreciably. Therefore, if the direction to an approaching vessel stays the same, or nearly so, as the vessel gets closer, there will be a collision unless someone takes positive action. For example, if you sight a vessel directly over a cleat or in line with a radio antenna on your boat, and the vessel's position with respect to the cleat or antenna doesn't change, but the vessel keeps getting closer, it is in danger of collision with your vessel. Mariners call this a "constant bearing and decreasing range," and recognize it as critical to their vessels' safety.

When you take action to avoid collision, any alteration of course or speed you make should be large enough (at least a 60° change in course) to be readily apparent to another vessel. Avoid small alterations of course and speed; it is difficult to detect them from a distance and the other skipper might misunderstand, a situation which is dangerous.

International and Inland Rules differ slightly on the subject of Narrow Channels (overtaking sound signals, and downbound right-of-way — Inland). Both sets of rules state that vessels proceeding along a narrow channel or fairway must keep to the starboard side of the channel. Vessels of less than 20 meters in length or sailing vessels, which might otherwise have the "right-of-way", must not impede the passage of a vessel which can safely navigate only within a narrow channel or fairway. No vessel may cross a narrow channel or fairway if doing so impedes the passage of a vessel which can safely navigate only within that channel or fairway. All vessels must avoid anchoring in narrow channels, if circumstances permit.

Another difference between Inland and International Rules has to do with vessels operating in a current. Under the Inland Rules a power-driven vessel on the Great Lakes, Western Rivers, or other specified waters and proceeding downbound with the current has the "right-of-way" over a vessel traveling against the current. This is because downbound vessels are carried along by the current and have less control than vessels which are making their way against the current. The downbound vessel shall propose the manner of passage and must initiate the exchange of whistle signals prescribed by the Navigation Rules.

Traffic Separation Schemes

Traffic Separation schemes are covered under Rule 10 of the 72 COLREGS. A vessel of less than 20 meters in length or a sailing vessel must not impede the safe passage of a power-driven vessel following a traffic lane.

Vessel Traffic Services

Vessel Traffic Services (VTS) have been established in the ports of New York, New Orleans, Houston/Galveston, San Francisco, Valdez, and in Puget Sound and its approaches. Some Canadian waters used frequently by American yachts also operate VTS's, most notably on the St. Lawrence River and in Vancouver, B.C.

Other Vessel Traffic Services are located at St. Mary's River, Michigan; Berwick Bay, Louisiana; and Louisville, Kentucky.

Vessel Traffic Services have been established by the Coast Guard to reduce danger of collision in certain areas where ship traffic is heavy. VTS consists of one or more of three distinct components, depending on the area: (1) all have a Vessel Movement Reporting System (communications); (2) some have a Traffic Separation Scheme (TSS); and (3) some have Radar and/or Closed Circuit Television (CCTV) Monitoring (surveillance) of selected areas.

"Each vessel required by regulation to participate in a vessel traffic service shall comply with the applicable regulations," says Rule 10 in the first statement ever in any rule dealing with vessel traffic services. It would be unusual to find pleasure craft participating in a vessel traffic service; it is most important, however, to understand the Coast Guard's system for monitoring ship traffic.

If you are sailing in waters where there is a VTS you must learn its location and be able to recognize the buoys marking a traffic separation scheme, if any. You should never travel the "wrong way" in any one-way lane or anchor in a traffic lane. If you must cross a lane, do so at right angles to it. Realize that you are sailing where a ship is most likely to pass.

It is a good idea to listen to the radio communications between ships in the system and the Coast Guard's Vessel Traffic Communications Center for information about any ship in your proximity. VTS does not normally invite radio communications from pleasure boats except in cases of distress or emergency. **Any contact with the Coast Guard is normally made on Channel 16.** (See Chapter 12, Radiotelephone.)

TABLE 4-I.   VTS COMMUNICATIONS CHANNELS

VTS LOCATION	VHF CHANNELS									
	5	6	11	12	13*	14	16	18	22	67*
HOUSTON/GALVESTON ⓐ			♦	♦	●		●			
NEW ORLEANS ⓑ			♦	♦		♦	●			●
NEW YORK				♦	●	♦	●			
SAN FRANCISCO ⓒ				♦	♦		●			
PUGET SOUND					●	♦	●			
VALDEZ					♦		●			

*Channel 13 is the Bridge-to-Bridge frequency in all areas except New Orleans and the Intracoastal Waterway, which use Channel 67.

Notes: ⓐ Houston, Channel 11, Galveston, Channel 12, boundary of separation, Exxon Baytown.

ⓑ Channel 12: Southwest Pass to mile 75.5, Above Head of Pass (AHP); Mississippi River Gulf Outlet (MRGO) to mile 50.7 MRGO; and mile 113.0 AHP to mile 159.5 AHP. Channel 11: mile 75.5 AHP to mile 113.0 AHP; and light "114" to mile 60.0 MRGO and westerly along GIWW and IHNC. Channel 14: mile 159.5 AHP to mile 242.4 AHP.

LEGEND

♦ = VTS WORKING FREQUENCY
● = VTS-MONITORED FREQUENCY

ⓒ Channel 12: Offshore approaches to Large Navigational Buoy. Channel 13: Remainder of VTS area.

Conduct of Vessels in Sight of One Another — Sound and Light Signals

There are three situations which involve risk of collision: overtaking, meeting head-on, and crossing. The rules for head-on and crossing situations are different for power-driven vessels and sailing vessels, as will be discussed later. Two important definitions must now be understood. In the above situations, one vessel will be the "stand-on" vessel; and one will be the "give-way" vessel. The rules point out which is the stand-on vessel and which is the give-way vessel in each encounter.

When one of two vessels is to keep out of the way, the other, the stand-on vessel, must maintain course and speed; but the stand-on vessel must take avoiding action as soon as it becomes apparent that the vessel required to give way is not taking appropriate action. All vessels are required to take whatever action is necessary to avoid collision.

If the give-way vessel does not take appropriate action, however, the stand-on vessel must take avoiding action as soon as it becomes apparent that the vessel required to give way is not doing so.

The give-way vessel must, under the rules, take whatever action necessary to keep well clear, and do so early and obviously. If a collision occurs, it is not enough to say that you followed the rule, for the rule requires that you take whatever action necessary to avoid a collision. This means that if the give-way vessel fails to act appropriately, the stand-on vessel may actually be required to violate the rules, if that is what it takes to avoid a collision.

Inland and International Rules for Sailing Vessels

When two sailing vessels are approaching one another so as to involve risk of collision, one of them shall keep out of the way of the other as follows:
1. When each has the wind on a different side, the vessel which has the wind on the port side shall keep out of the way of the other. (See Fig. 4-2.)
2. When both have the wind on the same side, the vessel which is to windward

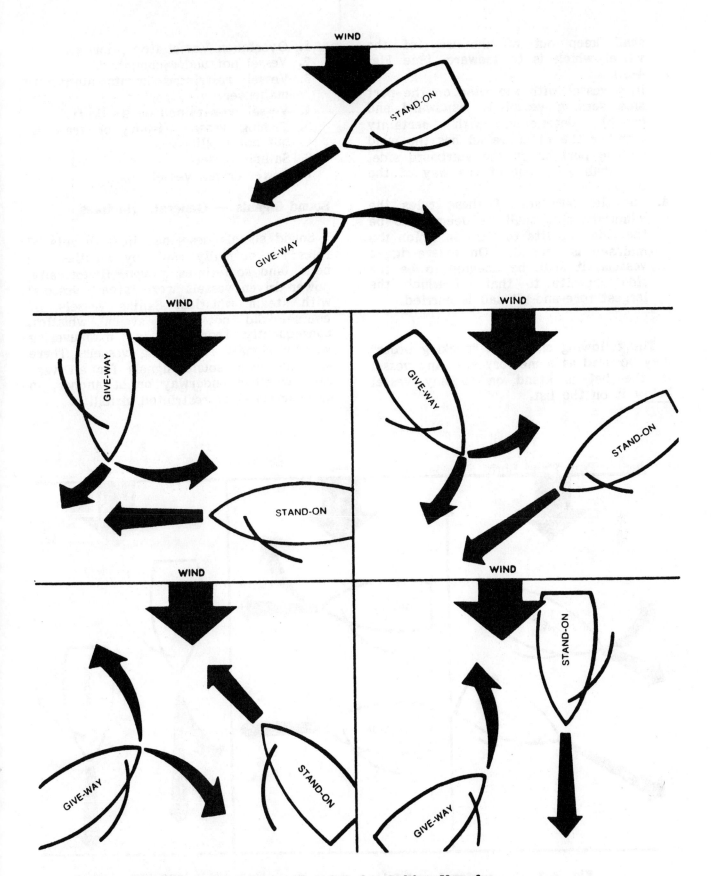

Fig. 4-2 International and Inland Rules for Sailing Vessels
(Wind on Different Sides – Boat with Wind on Port Side Gives Way)

shall keep out of the way of the vessel which is to leeward. (See Fig. 4-3.)

3. If a vessel with the wind on the port side sees a vessel to windward and cannot determine with certainty whether the other vessel has the wind on the port or on the starboard side, she shall keep out of the way of the other.

4. For the purposes of these rules the windward side shall be deemed to be the side opposite to that on which the mainsail is carried. On square-rigged vessels, it shall be deemed to be the side opposite to that on which the largest fore-and-aft sail is carried.

The following simplified "pecking order" may be used as a memory aid. Any vessel in the list is stand on to any vessel <u>below</u> it on the list.

1. Overtaken Vessel (top priority).
2. Vessel not under command.
3. Vessel restricted in its ability to maneuver.
4. Vessel constrained by its draft.
5. Fishing vessel (fishing or trawling, but not trolling).
6. Sailing vessel.
7. Power-driven vessel.

Sound Signals — General Principles

Sound signals described in both sets of rules are normally made by whistles and bells (and sometimes gongs). Historically, power-driven vessels were "steam vessels" with steam whistles. Sailing vessels, of course, did not have steam whistles, consequently there are no maneuvering whistle signals for sailing vessels. There are, however, sound signals for all vessels, whether underway or at anchor, in or near areas of restricted visibility.

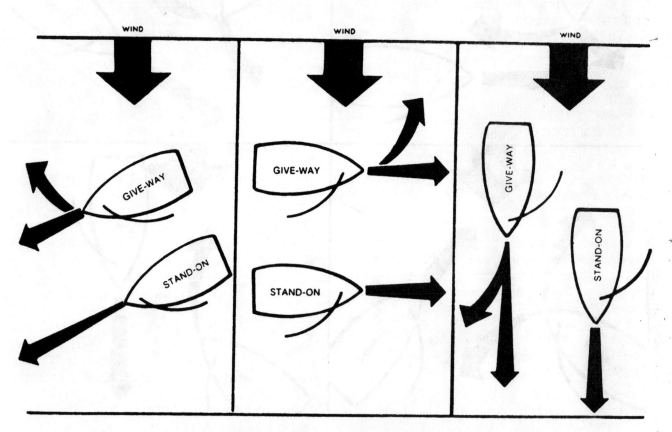

Fig. 4-3 International and Inland Rules for Sailing Vessels
(Wind on Same Side - Windward Gives Way to Leeward)

The term short blast means a blast of one second duration.

The term prolonged blast means a blast of 4 to 6 seconds.

A vessel 12 meters or more in length must be provided with a whistle and a bell, and a vessel of 100 meters or more in length shall, in addition, be provided with a gong. A vessel of less than 12 meters in length is not obliged to carry such sound signaling appliances but must be provided with some other means of making an efficient sound signal. [Note that these are requirements of the Navigation Rules and that other rules may apply. Vessels under 12 meters in length are required to have a whistle (horn) under Federal equipment requirements. (See Chapter 3.)]

Rules governing sound signals for maneuvering are different under each set of rules. Sound signals under the 72 COLREGS for head-on, crossing and overtaking (except in narrow channels) situations are signals of action. Only the vessel actually altering course sounds a signal and the vessel not altering course does not answer. Sound signals under the Inland Rules for head-on, crossing and overtaking situations are signals of intent; one vessel signals intended action and the other responds.

Maneuvering and Warning Signals — Danger/Doubt Signal — Both International and Inland Rules

When vessels in sight of one another are approaching each other and for any reason either vessel fails to understand the intentions or actions of the other, the vessel in doubt must immediately signal his doubt by giving five or more short and rapid blasts on the whistle. The doubt signal is sometimes called the danger signal, and it may be used to announce danger whenever necessary.

Maneuvering and Warning Signals Under the International Rules:
- one short blast means, "I am altering my course to starboard."
- two short blasts mean, "I am altering

my course to port."
- three short blasts mean, "I am operating astern propulsion."
These signals are sounded only when the action is being taken.

Maneuvering and Warning Signals Under the Inland Rules:
- one short blast means, "I intend to leave you on my port side."
- two short blasts mean, "I intend to leave you on my starboard side."
- three short blasts mean, "I am operating astern propulsion."

Under the Inland Rules, the vessel hearing the signal of the other vessel must, if in agreement, sound the same whistle signal and take steps to effect a safe passing. "Cross signals" are not permitted under the rules. (Two blasts are never answered with one blast, for example.) If in disagreement or doubt, the only allowed response is the doubt signal (5 or more short and rapid blasts).

The Overtaking Situation

Any vessel overtaking any other must keep out of the way of the vessel being overtaken. (Notice that this includes sailboats which are overtaking.) (See Fig. 4-4.)

A vessel is deemed to be overtaking when coming up with another vessel from a direction more than 22.5 degrees abaft (behind) her beam. At night only the sternlight of a vessel being overtaken would be visible and neither of the sidelights would be seen. If in doubt about whether it is an overtaking situation, the vessel should assume that it is and act accordingly.

The International Rules, in effect, give consideration to two types of overtaking, according to whether (1) maneuvering in a narrow channel or fairway (as explained below); or (2) maneuvering elsewhere (when the usual signals of action explained above are used).

Under the International Rules vessels in

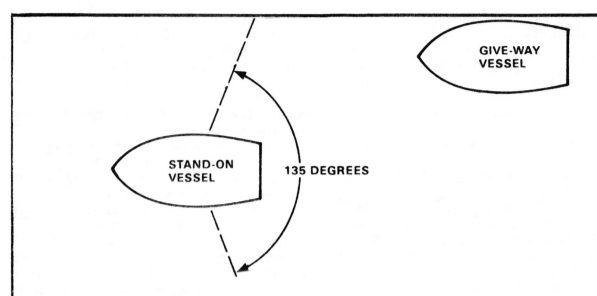

Fig. 4-4 Overtaking Situation Under International Rules (All Vessels)

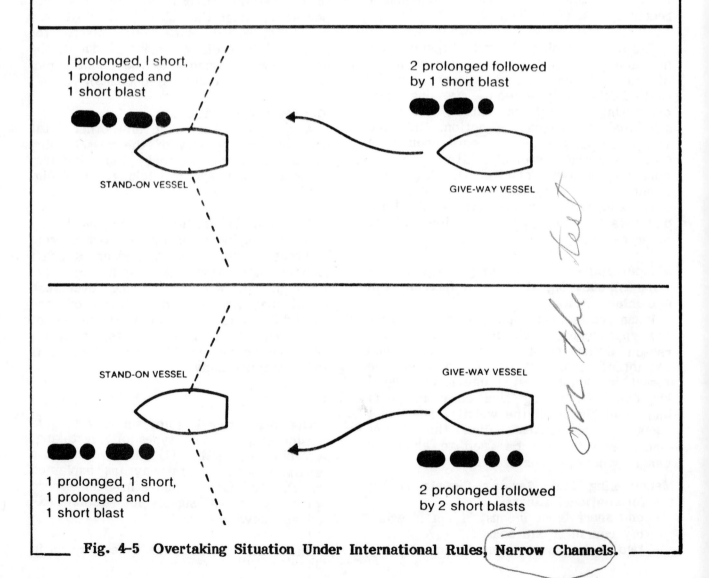

Fig. 4-5 Overtaking Situation Under International Rules, Narrow Channels.

sight of one another in a narrow channel or fairway must use these signals in the overtaking situation whenever the vessel ahead must take action to permit safe passing. (See Fig. 4-5.)

A vessel overtaking indicates intention by the following whistle signals:
- two prolonged blasts followed by one short blast to mean, "I intend to overtake you on your starboard side."
- two prolonged blasts followed by two short blasts to mean, "I intend to overtake you on your port side."

The two prolonged blasts, in both cases, serve as a preliminary "wake-up" signal to the vessel being overtaken.

The vessel about to be overtaken indicates agreement by:

one prolonged, one short, one prolonged and one short blast, in that order (Morse code "C").

When either vessel fails to understand the intentions of the other, or doubts whether sufficient action is being taken by the other to avoid collision, or the overtaken vessel deems the overtaking action to be unsafe, the vessel in doubt must give the doubt (danger) signal.

Under the Inland Rules, a power-driven vessel intending to overtake another power-driven vessel indicates intention by whistle signals (see Fig. 4-6):
- one short blast means, "I intend to overtake you on your starboard side."
- two short blasts mean, "I intend to overtake you on your port side."

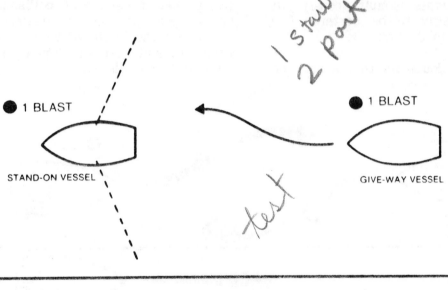

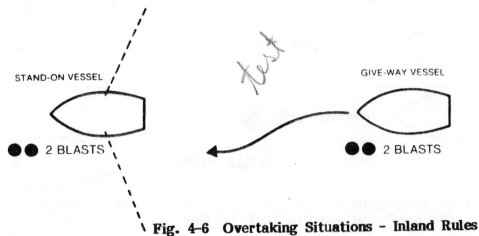

Fig. 4-6 Overtaking Situations - Inland Rules

The power-driven vessel about to be overtaken shall, if in agreement, sound a similar signal or, if in doubt, sound the danger signal (at least five short and rapid blasts on the whistle).

Vessels being overtaken may be passed on either side, as long as all concerned understand what is being planned and agree to it.

The Head-on (Meeting) Situation

Vessels which approach one another on a reciprocal (opposite) or near-reciprocal course are said to be meeting, or head-on. At night it is considered to be a head-on situation when a vessel sees the other vessel's (white) masthead lights in a line or nearly in a line or sees both (red and green) sidelights simultaneously. It may not be so easy to be certain of a reciprocal course in daylight.

If there is any doubt whether a head-on situation exists, assume that it does exist and act accordingly.

A small vessel running in a heavy chop or ground swell will often yaw (move from side to side, off course). Occasionally its red light will be visible; then both red and green will be seen; and then only the green light will be seen. When you observe this sequence of light changes you must assume you have a head-on situation.

The International and Inland Rules for maneuvering in a meeting situation are identical in wording, but the whistle signals are different. See Figures 4-7 and 4-8.

Each vessel in a meeting situation must alter course to starboard so that each will pass on the port side of the other. (Note that if danger of collision exists, a port-to-port passage is required.) Neither vessel has the "right-of-way" in a meeting situation, and both are equally responsible for avoiding collision.

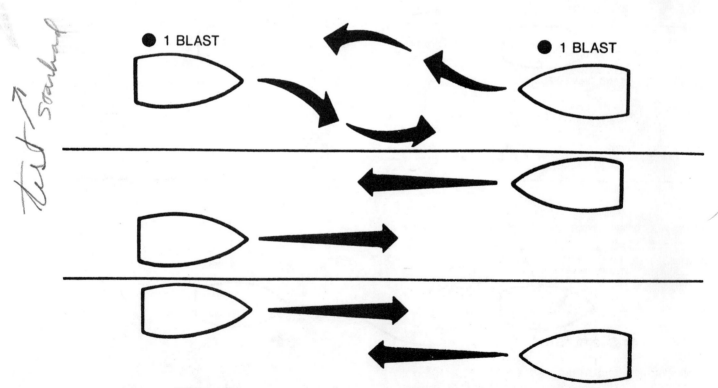

● 1 BLAST   **● 1 BLAST**

Fig. 4-7 Meeting Under International Rules (Power-driven Vessels)
Neither Vessel Has The Right-Of-Way

4-10

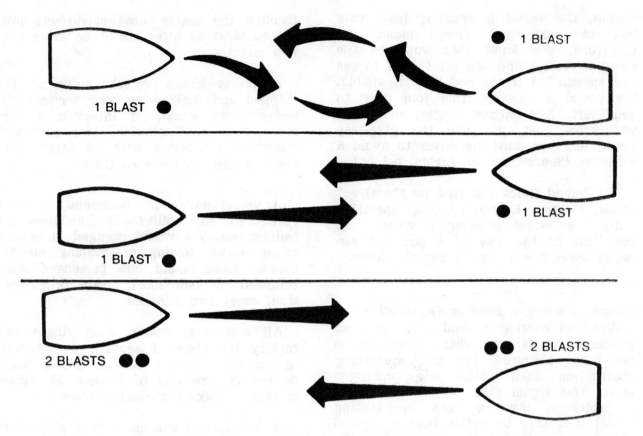

Fig. 4-8 Meeting Sound Signals for Power-driven Vessels Under Inland Rules

The Crossing Situation

Both International and Inland Rules state that when two power-driven vessels are crossing so as to involve risk of collision, the vessel which has the other on her starboard side must keep out of the way and, if circumstances permit, cross behind the other vessel. See Fig. 4-9.

At times there may be some doubt whether the situation is a crossing or a head-on meeting. In case of doubt, you should assume that it is a <u>meeting</u> situation, in which neither vessel has a clear-cut "right-of-way", and each must act to avoid the other.

At night when it is difficult to see vessels and know their speed and direction, their lights convey important information. It is a crossing situation when only one of the other vessel's colored lights is visible. If the green light is

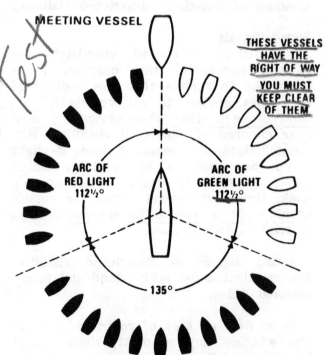

Fig. 4-9 Stand-on and Give-way in a Crossing Situation (Power-driven Vessels)

visible, the vessel is crossing from your left to your right. Green means go; therefore, you know that you are the stand-on vessel and you must hold course and speed. But if the red light is visible, the vessel is crossing from your right to your left. Red means danger; therefore, you know that you are the give-way vessel and you must maneuver to avoid a collision. (See section on Lights, below.)

The Inland Rules add that on the Great Lakes, Western Rivers, or other specified waters, a vessel crossing a river must keep out of the way of a power-driven vessel ascending or descending the river.

Vessels Nearing a Bend or Obstruction

A vessel nearing a bend or an area of a channel or fairway where other vessels may be obscured by an intervening obstruction shall sound one _prolonged_ blast. This signal shall be answered with a _prolonged_ blast by any approaching vessel that may be within hearing around the bend or behind the intervening obstruction. (International and Inland Rules)

Conduct of Vessels in Restricted Visibility

Sound Signals

The term "restricted visibility" was defined earlier in this chapter. It is important to realize that this section of the rules applies to all vessels <u>not in sight of each other</u> when navigating <u>in or near</u> an area of restricted visibility. Why "near"? Because a vessel in broad daylight could be surprised by a large ship's emerging suddenly from a nearby fog bank. Note - the sound signals for vessels <u>within sight of each other</u> are <u>not</u> used in restricted visibility.

Sound Signals in Restricted Visibility are identical under both Inland and International Rules.

In or near an area of restricted visibility, whether day or night, signals must be used as follows:

A power-driven vessel making way

through the water must sound one prolonged blast at intervals of no more than two minutes.

A power-driven vessel underway but stopped and making no way through the water must sound, at intervals of not more than two minutes, two prolonged blasts in succession with an interval of about 2 seconds between them.

A vessel not under command, a vessel restricted in ability to maneuver, a sailing vessel, a vessel engaged in fishing, or a vessel towing or pushing another vessel, must sound one prolonged blast followed by two short blasts in succession, every two minutes.

All vessels at anchor must ring a bell rapidly for about 5 seconds at intervals of not more than 1 minute. (Inland Rules do not require this of vessels 20 meters or less in special anchoring areas.)

It is helpful for a small boat skipper to know that a vessel of 100 meters or more in length sounds a bell in the forepart of the vessel and, immediately following this, sounds a gong in the after part of the vessel.

A vessel at anchor may, in addition, sound one short, one prolonged and one short blast in succession to give warning to an approaching vessel of her position and of the possibility of collision.

A vessel aground must give the bell signal (and, if required, the gong signal) given by a vessel at anchor, and in addition, give three separate and distinct strokes on the bell immediately before and after the rapid ringing of the bell.

A vessel of less than 12 meters in length is not obliged to give the above-mentioned signals but, if she does not give them, she is obliged to make some other efficient sound signal at intervals of not more than 2 minutes.

It's important to understand the signals which are used when visibility is restrict-

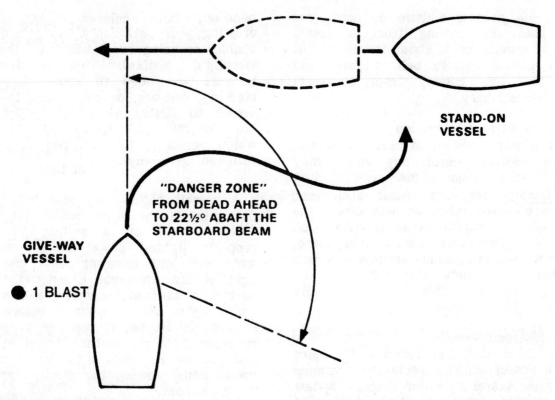

Fig. 4-10 Crossing Situation Under International Rules (Power-driven Vessels)

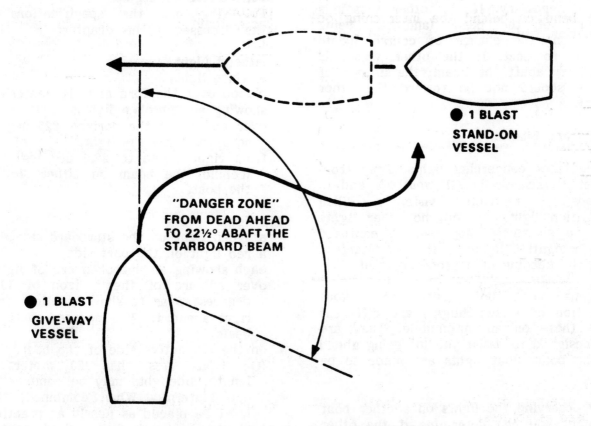

**Fig. 4-11 Crossing Situation Under Inland Rules
(Power-driven Vessels Passing Port To Port)**

ed. If you hear a whistle or horn, you know that it's coming from a vessel which is moving or is about to move. But if you hear a vessel's bell or gong, you know that it's coming from a vessel which is stationary.

Signals to Attract Attention

If it is necessary to attract the attention of another vessel, any vessel may make light or sound signals that <u>cannot</u> <u>be mistaken</u> for any signal authorized elsewhere in the rules, or may direct the beam of her searchlight in the direction of the danger. One should take care, however, not to blind another vessel's operator by shining the light at the steering station. This is specifically prohibited by the rules.

Radar-equipped Vessels

There is a special provision in the rules for the vessel which detects the presence of another vessel by radar alone. The law requires this vessel to take action in ample time if a change of course becomes necessary. If the other vessel is forward of the beam (and not being overtaken) the change of course should not be to port. If the other vessel is abeam or abaft the beam, the change of course should not be toward the other vessel.

Lights and Shapes

The rules concerning lights apply from sunset to sunrise in all weathers and in periods of restricted visibility. When navigation lights are on, no other lights may be shown if they can be confused with navigation lights or if they interfere with the keeping of a proper lookout.

Lights on a boat (with the obvious exception of a searchlight) are different from those on an automobile. They are not designed to assist you in seeing ahead of the boat. Boat lights are made to be seen.

By observing the lights on another boat at night you can determine if the other boat is headed directly for you (meeting head-on, both colored lights visible), crossing your path (only one colored light visible) or being overtaken (only the white sternlight visible). This is important because you need to know if you are meeting, crossing or overtaking the other vessel to determine which vessel is to hold course and speed (stand-on) and which vessel is to maneuver to avoid a collision (give-way).

A vessel's lights may also help you to determine if the other vessel is a power-driven vessel or a sailing vessel. A properly lighted power-driven vessel or motorboat will have at least one white light visible whenever a colored light is visible. A sailboat, however, will have no white lights visible when a colored light is also visible. So, if you see a red light or green light on another vessel at night, and you see no white light, and it's not a vessel being towed, the chances are that it's a sailboat.

Specifications of Lights

Following are the specifications of lights discussed in this chapter:

Masthead Light
a white light,
placed over the fore and aft centerline,
showing an unbroken light,
over an arc of the horizon 225 degrees so as to show the light,
from right ahead to 22.5 degrees abaft (behind) the beam on either side of the boat.

Sidelights
a green light on the starboard side,
a red light on the port side,
each showing an unbroken arc of light,
over an arc of the horizon of 112.5 degrees so as to show the light from right ahead to 22.5 degrees abaft the beam,
on the respective side of the boat.
(On boats less than 20 meters in length, sidelights may be combined in one lantern. When combined, they must be placed as nearly as practicable to the boat's fore and aft centerline.)

Sternlight

a white light,
at the stern,
showing an unbroken light,
over an arc of the horizon of (135) degrees,
so as to show the light 67.5 degrees from right aft on each side of the boat.

Towing light

a yellow light with the same characteristics as the sternlight.

All-round light

a white light showing in an unbroken arc of 360 degrees.

Flashing light

a light flashing at regular intervals of 120 or more flashes per minute.

Special flashing light (Inland Rules)

a yellow light,
flashing at regular intervals,
of 50 to 70 flashes per minute,
placed forward on the fore and aft centerline of a tow,
showing an unbroken arc of the horizon of not less than 180 nor more than 225 degrees,
to show from right ahead,
to abeam and no more than 22.5 degrees abaft the beam,
on either side of the vessel.

The positioning and technical details of lights and shapes are in Annex I of each set of Rules. Technical data are not within the scope of this course.

The intensity of prescribed lights must be such that they be visible from the minimum distances in nautical miles as shown in Fig. 4-12.

Lights must be exhibited from sunset to sunrise and otherwise in restricted visibility.

LIGHT TYPE	VISIBILITY MIN DISTANCE — MILES			
	1	2	3	5
MASTHEAD		●	▲	◆
SIDE	●	▲◆		
STERN		●▲◆		
ALL-ROUND		●▲◆		
TOWING		●▲◆		
SPECIAL FLASHING (Inland Rules Only)		●▲◆		

VESSEL LENGTH
● Less than 12 Meters
▲ 12 Meters but Less than 20 Meters
◆ 20 Meters but Less than 50 Meters

Fig. 4-12 Light Visibility Required

Lights for Sailing Vessels Under Sail Only and Vessels Under Oars

Lights for sailing vessels are the same under both sets of rules.

A sailing vessel must exhibit sidelights and a sternlight.

However, a sailing vessel less than 20 meters in length may combine the sidelights and sternlight in one lantern carried at or near the top of the mast where it can best be seen. This light cannot be used under power or sail and power; regular sidelights and forward-looking white lights must be fitted for use in such circumstances.

A sailing vessel underway may, in addition to the sidelights and sternlight, exhibit at or near the top of the mast, where best seen, two all-round lights in a vertical line, the upper red, the lower green; these may not be used in conjunction with the combined three-color lantern described in the preceding paragraph.

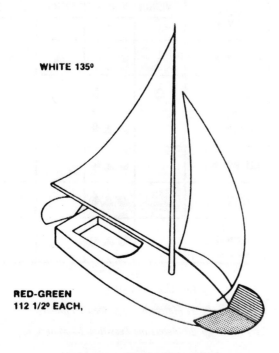

Fig. 4-13   Sailing Vessel Under 20 Meters in Length, Inland and International Rules (Option 1)

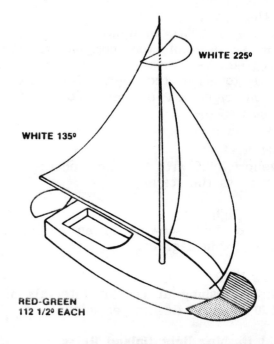

Fig. 4-15   Auxiliaries Under 20 Meters in Length Using Both Sail and Power, Inland and International Rules (Option 1)

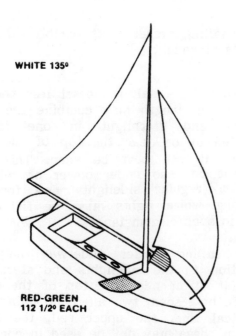

Fig. 4-14   Sailing Vessel Under 20 Meters in Length, Inland and International Rules (Option 2)

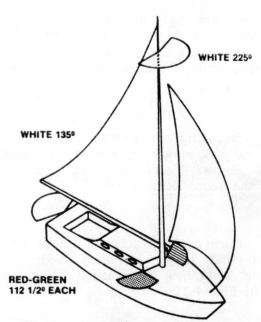

Fig. 4-16   Auxiliaries Under 20 Meters in Length Using Both Sail and Power, Inland and International Rules (Option 2)

A sailing vessel less than 7 meters in length must, if practicable, exhibit sidelights and a sternlight, but if she does not, must have ready at hand an electric torch or lighted lantern showing a white light to be exhibited soon enough to prevent collision.

A vessel under oars may exhibit the lights described for sailing vessels.

A reminder — sailboats with propulsion machinery in use must comply with the requirements for power-driven vessels.

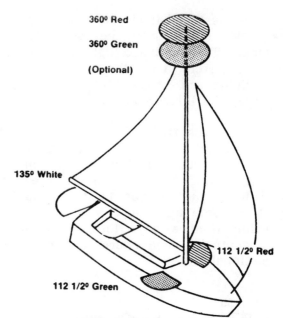

Fig. 4-18   Optional Sailboat Light Configuration, Inland and International Rules. Side Lights may be combined if desired.

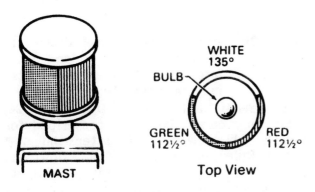

Fig. 4-17   Combination Tri-Color Light for Sailboats Under 20 Meters, Inland and International Rules

Lights for Power-Driven Vessels Underway

The lighting configuration on a power-driven vessel depends on its length, its area of operation, and, in some cases, its date of construction.

Lighting configurations described in the International Rules differ slightly from those described in the Inland Rules. However, lights in accordance with the International Rules are acceptable in all waters of the United States.

Navigation lights may appear to be complex because of the many different configurations used. However, you will find that only one or two of the possible configurations are applicable to your vessel.

Lights for power-driven vessels less than 20 meters in length, operating under the International Rules:

When operating under the International Rules, a power-driven vessel less than 20 meters in length must carry side lights, a masthead light and a stern light. The side lights may be separate or combined. If the vessel is 12 meters or more in length, its masthead light must be at least 2.5 meters above the gunwale. If the vessel is less than 12 meters in length, its masthead light must be at least one meter above the side lights.

A vessel less than 12 meters in length may carry an all-round light instead of the masthead light and the stern light. (This all-round light would best be placed in the after part of the vessel.)

Lights for power-driven vessels, less than 20 meters in length, operating under the Inland Rules:

Power-driven vessels less than 20 meters in length built on or after December 24, 1980, and operating under the Inland Navigational Rules must carry side lights, a masthead light and a stern light. The side lights may be separate or combined. The masthead light must be at least 2.5 meters above the gunwale. Note: These lights are acceptable when operating under the International Rules.

A vessel less than 12 meters in length may carry an all-round light in the after part of the vessel instead of the masthead light and the stern light. The all-round light must be at least one meter above the side lights and may be off the centerline if necessary. Note: These lights are acceptable when operating under the International Rules.

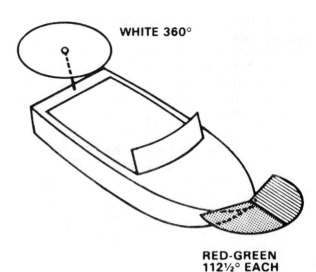

Fig. 4-21   Power-driven Vessel Under 12 Meters in Length, Inland and International Rules. Sidelights may be Separate if Desired

A vessel built before December 24, 1980, may carry the lights prescribed for vessels which were built after the new Inland Rules came into effect. However, if it does not, it may carry side lights and an all-round light which is located in the after part of the vessel. The side lights may be separate or combined. Please note, however, that the use of side lights and an all-round light on a vessel 12 meters or more in length is not acceptable under the International Rules.

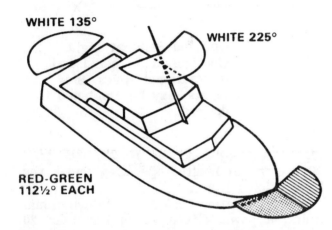

Fig. 4-19   Power-driven Vessel Under 20 Meters in Length, Inland and International Rules (Option 1)

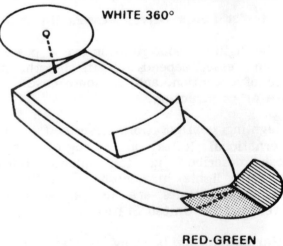

Fig. 4-22   Power-driven Vessel Under 20 Meters in Length and Built Before Dec. 24, 1980. Inland Rules (Option 1)

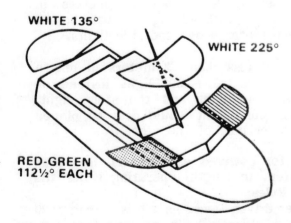

Fig. 4-20   Power-driven Vessel Under 20 Meters in Length, Inland and International Rules (Option 2)

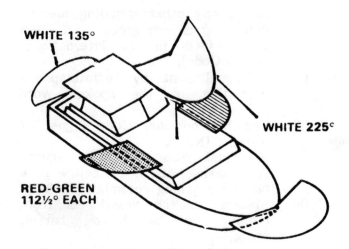

WHITE 135°

WHITE 225°

RED-GREEN 112½° EACH

Fig. 4-23   Power-driven Vessel Under 20 Meters in Length Inland Rules (Option 2)

The use of a masthead light forward and an all-round light aft is permitted only on the Great Lakes. Therefore, those vessels from 26 feet to 65 feet in length which display lights acceptable under the old Motorboat Act (sidelights, 225-degree white bow lights and all-round white lights), must extinguish their bow lights or convert their all-round lights to sternlights in order to comply with the new rules. However, no changes are necessary if the vessels are operating on the Great Lakes.

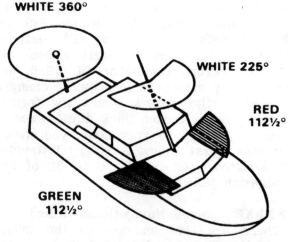

WHITE 360°

WHITE 225°

RED 112½°

GREEN 112½°

Fig. 4-24   Power-driven Vessel, Inland Rules Optional on Great Lakes only.

Fishing Vessels — Lights and Shapes

A fishing vessel underway must display (in addition to the side lights and stern light for sailing and power-driven vessels described above):

Fishing vessel trawling (dragging): 2 all-round lights in a vertical line, upper green, lower white.

Fishing vessel other than trawling (but not trolling): 2 all-round lights in a vertical line, upper red, lower white.

A fishing vessel within the meaning of the Navigation Rules must display, in addition to the lights prescribed in the Rules, a shape consisting of two black cones in a vertical line, one above the other, point to point. A vessel of less than 20 meters may display a basket instead. (International and Inland Rules.)

Other Lights — Special Vessels

Here are some other lights you should recognize. These lights are shown in addition to the sidelights and sternlight for sailing and power-driven vessels described above if underway:

Power driven vessel towing astern: 2 masthead lights (in a vertical line) instead of one (3 if tow exceeds 200 meters), plus a yellow towing light above the sternlight.

Vessel restricted in its ability to maneuver: 3 lights vertically, red-white-red, plus masthead light or anchor light as appropriate.

Vessel not under command: 2 all-round red lights in a vertical line.

Vessel constrained by her draft (72 COLREGS only): 3 all-round red lights in a vertical line.

Pilot vessel (pilot aboard): a white all-round light over a red all-round light, displayed in a vertical line.

Law enforcement vessel engaged in necessary duties: a flashing blue light.

Anchor Lights, Inland and International Rules

An anchored vessel less than 50 meters in length must display one all-round light where it can best be seen. In daytime, a black ball must be displayed instead.

A vessel less than 7 meters in length at anchor, not in or near a narrow channel, fairway, anchorage, or where other vessels normally navigate, is not required to display anchor lights.

Under the Inland Rules, a vessel less than 20 meters in length anchored in a specially designated anchorage area is not required to display an anchor light. A list of specially designated anchorage areas appears in Title 33, Code of Federal Regulations, Part 110.

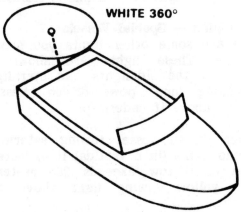

WHITE 360°

Fig. 4-25   Vessel at Anchor

Distress Signals

When a vessel is in distress and requires assistance, signals to be used or exhibited are listed in the Annex IV of each set of Rules.

These signals include:

(a) A gun or other explosive signal fired at intervals of about a minute;

(b) A continuous sounding with any fog-signaling apparatus;

(c) Rockets or shells, throwing red stars one at a time at short intervals;

(d) A signal made by radiotelegraphy or by any other signaling method consisting of the group . . . – – – . . . (SOS in the International Morse Code);

(e) A signal sent by radiotelephony consisting of the spoken word "Mayday";

(f) The International Code Signal of distress (N.C.);

(g) A signal consisting of a square flag having above or below it a ball or anything resembling a ball;

(h) Flames on the vessel (as from burning tar barrel, oil barrel, etc.);

(i) A rocket parachute flare or a hand flare showing a red light;

(j) A smoke signal giving off orange-colored smoke;

(k) Slowly and repeatedly raising and lowering arms outstretched to each side;

(l) The radiotelegraph alarm signal;

(m) The radiotelephone alarm signal;

(n) Signals transmitted by emergency position-indicating radio beacons;

(o) A high intensity white light flashing at regular intervals from 50 to 70 times per minute (Inland Rules only).

Exemptions (Inland Rules)

Many boats carry lights in conformity with the Rules which were superseded by the Inland Navigational Rules Act of 1980. Therefore, many (not all) boats of less than 20 meters in length whose keel was laid before December 24, 1980, are permanently exempted from being changed if used in the waters where the former rules applied. If you think these exemptions may apply to your boat, you should ask your Coast Guard Auxiliary Instructor for assistance or consult Rule 38 of the Navigation Rules.

ANNEXES (Inland Navigational Rules)

There are five annexes to the Inland Navigational Rules Act of 1980. Annexes I through III contain technical information. Annex IV and Annex V contain new requirements as follows:

ANNEX IV adds to the list of DIS-TRESS SIGNALS a high intensity white light flashing at intervals from 50 to 70 times per minute.

ANNEX V (Pilot Rules) requires the operator of each self-propelled vessel 12 meters or more in length to carry on board and maintain for ready reference a copy of the Inland Navigational Rules.

PENALTIES (Inland Navigational Rules)

Whoever operates a vessel in violation of the Inland Navigational Rules Act of 1980 is liable to a civil penalty of not more than $5000 for each violation. (Notice that the operator, not the owner, is named responsible if they are not one and the same. It follows that an operator chartering a boat is held liable under the law, not the chartering firm which owns the boat.)

International Rules' Requirements Legal Where Inland Rules Apply

All vessels complying with the construction and equipment requirements of the International Regulations are considered to be in compliance with the Inland Rules.

A Final Note

Certain things should be noted because they are not mentioned in the Rules. Nothing in the Rules ever imposes a requirement to place your own vessel in danger. If any action called for under the Rules seems to do so, remember that the Responsibility Rule provides for a departure from the Rules to avoid immediate danger. In such circumstances you would have to decide whether the danger/doubt signal and/or a course change would be appropriate.

Chapter 5

Aids To Navigation

Introduction

When man first went to sea he rarely left sight of land, and his only navigational aids were familiar landmarks. Today, our dependence on visible reference points is still great; however there are many more sophisticated means of determining our position.

An aid to navigation is any device external to a vessel intended to assist a navigator to determine his position or safe course, or to warn him of dangers or obstructions to safe navigation. Short range aids to navigation are buoys, daybeacons, lighthouses, and fog signals. Electronic aids to navigation include radiobeacons and LORAN-C to assist us

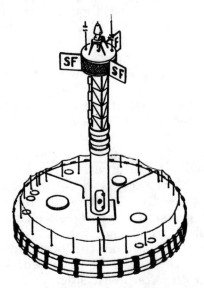

Fig. 5-1   A Large Navigational Buoy.

in finding our position on the water. As all aids to navigation serve the same general purpose, structural differences, markings, and other aid characteristics are solely for the purpose of meeting the conditions and requirements of the particular location at which the aid is established.

Although not Aids to Navigation, prominent landmarks, both natural, such as mountain peaks and promontories, and man-made objects, such as church spires, water tanks and radio towers can be useful to the navigator, but they must be visible from the water, and be shown on the applicable chart for the area. The chart symbols for these objects are covered in Chapter 6.

Buoy System

The principal system of buoyage in the United States has been the Lateral System; however, in April of 1982, the United States agreed to conform to the International Association of Lighthouse Authorities (IALA) system B, or IALA-B.

The IALA maritime buoyage System B applies to buoys and beacons that indicate the lateral limits of navigable channels, obstructions, dangers such as wrecks, and other areas or features of importance to the mariner. This system provides five types of marks: lateral marks, safe water marks, special marks, isolated danger marks, and cardinal marks. Cardinal marks are not used in the United States. Each type of mark is differentiated from other types by distinctive colors, shapes, and light rhythms.

The change to IALA-B is in process, and involves an interim stage, known as the Modified U. S. Aid System. This involves changing all black painted, odd-numbered marks (aids) to green; changing all existing white lights on lateral aids (with one exception) to either red or green, to match the mark color. The exception is the "safe water" mark, marking a fairway or mid-channel. This mark will always have a white light. The specific light characteristics for all marks will be covered in a later section of this chapter.

This book covers both the old system and the new system.

In the lateral buoyage system, marks indicate sides of a navigable channel, and also mark channel junctions, and indicate the safe side of a hazard for the navigator to use. In addition, some marks indicate the centerline of a particular channel. Buoyage systems differ among nations, and boaters navigating abroad should become familiar with other systems.

The navigator must be able to identify all aids to navigation accurately, quickly and easily in order to make the best use of them for safe navigation. Therefore, all marks are identified in various ways, and this identification is displayed on charts, along with the appropriate chart symbol for that mark. Knowing the color and number of an ATON (Aid to Navigation) will be of little use without the appropriate chart to tell the navigator the mark's position in that water area.

Aids to navigation will all have one or more of the following identifying marks: color significance (including specific combinations of more than one color in either horizontal bands or vertical stripes); number and/or letter significance; daymark significance; light significance; and sound significance.

Both our present Lateral System and the IALA-B System use odd numbers with all black or green marks and use even numbers with all red marks. On all navigable waterways returning from the sea, the black or green odd-numbered marks are on the port (left) side of the channel, and the red even-numbered marks are on the starboard (right) side of the channel. An easy memory phrase is "RED RIGHT RETURNING!" (Note this is not always true, which will be covered later in this chapter.)

For the sea buoys that delineate channels off the coast of the United States, and for the Intracoastal Waterway (ICW) red is on the right when proceeding in a clockwise direction (looking at a map of the U.S.). Therefore, red is on the right when proceeding south along the East Coast, either at sea or in the ICW, proceeding north along the West Coast of Florida, proceeding west and southwest along the Gulf Coast, and proceeding north along the West Coast in the Pacific Ocean.

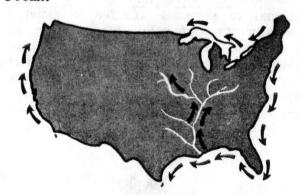

Fig. 5-2   Conventions About Directions of Travel in Coastal Waters.

For the Great Lakes, the outlet ends are defined as the seaward ends.

Marks with horizontal red and green bands indicate bifurcations or junctions in a channel, or wrecks or obstructions that can be passed on either side. If the upper band is green, the preferred channel when proceeding from the sea is followed by keeping the mark on the port side of the vessel; if the upper band is red, keep the mark on the starboard side.

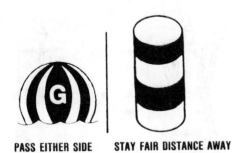

PASS EITHER SIDE   STAY FAIR DISTANCE AWAY

Fig. 5-3   Vertically-striped and
Horizontally-banded Buoys.

Marks with vertical red and white stripes are "safe water marks" indicating the mid-channel or fairway. Such marks may also be used at the beginning of a vessel Traffic Separation Scheme.

Both the junction or obstruction marks and the safe water marks will not be numbered, but may have letters for identification if necessary.

Characteristics of Aids to Navigation

Depending upon the location and needs of identification, aids have many shapes and characteristics. Generally they fall into six categories; 1) buoys, 2) daybeacons, 3) lights, 4) sound (fog signals), 5) ranges, and 6) radio and radar beacons.

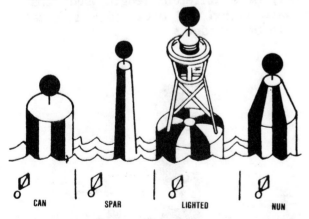

CAN   SPAR   LIGHTED   NUN

Fig. 5-4   Vertically-striped Buoys Mark
the Fairway or Mid-channel.

Buoys

Buoys are floating aids that warn the mariner of some danger, some obstruction, or change in the contours of the sea bottom, or to delineate channels so that he may avoid dangers and continue his course safely. Such features as size, shape, color, numbering (or other markings), and signaling equipment of buoys are for the purpose of identification and also telling the navigator what the aid stands for. For example, under System B, a spherical buoy with vertical red and white stripes indicates "safe water" or "mid-channel."

However, a word of caution should be included concerning buoys. They are at anchor. Just like a vessel, they will drift around the anchor position with wind or current or may even drag anchor such that they may be out of their charted position. The chart symbol for a buoy is a diamond shape with a small circle at the bottom indicating an approximate position.

Navigators should not rely completely upon the position of floating aids, but should use bearings toward fixed aids or objects onshore where possible. The lights on lighted buoys may be extinguished, or sound-producing devices on sound buoys may not function. Buoys fitted with bells, gongs, or whistles are normally activated by wave action and do not produce sounds at regular intervals, making positive identification near impossible without visual observation.

Fig. 5-5   A Nun Buoy.

Buoy Types

The spar buoy is similar in shape to a section of telephone pole and can be red, even numbered, or green, odd numbered. They can also be used with horizontal bands for junction buoys.

The nun buoy has the topmost section conical in shape, is painted red and even numbered, and normally marks the starboard hand side of the preferred channel entering from seaward.

The can buoy is cylindrical in shape, black or green, odd numbered, and normally marks the port hand side of the preferred channel. It also can be used to signify junctions or mid-channels with appropriate bands or stripes.

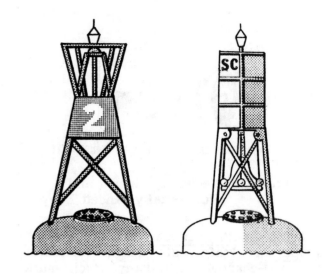

Fig. 5-7   A Lighted Buoy.

Fig. 5-6   A Can Buoy.

The spherical buoy (ball-shaped) is used for a mid-channel marker in the IALA-B System, with vertical red and white stripes. If the buoy is not spherical, it will have a red spherical top mark, instead.

A lighted buoy consists of a float on which is mounted a short structural or skeleton tower with a battery powered light mounted at the top. The batteries, or other power source, are placed in the body of the buoy. Under the older system, the light would be either white or green for black aids, and white or red for red aids. Under the new system, the light is either green or red, depending upon the basic color of the mark. Also, the light color will match the top band color on horizontally banded lighted marks.

A bell buoy is a similar float and tower structure in which is hung a bell with usually four clappers suspended externally to the bell such that the clappers strike the bell as wave action rocks the buoy.

A gong buoy is similar to a bell buoy, but with usually four gongs mounted in the tower, in a vertical stack, each of a different tone. Each gong has its own clapper, of a different length, such that the wave action will cause four different tones to be sounded.

Fig. 5-8   A Lighted Bell Buoy With Radar Reflectors.

A whistle buoy is constructed similarly to the bell or gong buoy, but with a low-pitched whistle, actuated by trapped air as the buoy moves up and down in the wave action. A horn buoy is similar, but the horn is powered from electric batteries.

Combination buoys are those with a light combined with a sound source; a lighted bell or gong buoy, etc.

The navigator should be aware fog and very calm water often go together. In a flat calm, there may not be enough motion to activate sound buoys.

As stated previously, most marks will be numbered, lettered, or a combination, depending upon their use. All solid color marks will be numbered, odd numbers for green marks, and even numbers for red marks. They will be numbered sequentially from seaward, the outermost mark being 1 or 2, depending upon its color.

Some numbers may be omitted along a channel when only one side is buoyed for some distance. For example, green marks numbered 1 through 5 might be installed on the port hand side, whereas only two red marks might be required on the starboard hand side, numbered 2 and 6, accordingly. Marks may also be added to a channel at a later date, in which case letters will be added. This could mean mark 7A added between numbers 7 and 8. Some numbered channel marks may also have letter abbreviations added to further identify their purpose, as 8 "CS." The number is in the usual sequence, but the "CS" would stand for Capri Shoal.

Daybeacons

Daybeacons are marks which are normally restricted to shore or shallow water use as they are fixed rather than floating, and less expensive to maintain. They are generally constructed of plywood signboards, called daymarks, painted, and affixed with a reflective border of the proper color and shape and an identifying number or letter (also of reflective mate-

rial). They are mounted on single piles or multiple pile structures (dolphins).

Fig. 5-9 Daymark On a Piling.

Daymark shape and color identifies the purpose for the mark. To be specific:

1. Triangular shape, red, and even numbered indicate a mark that should be kept on the starboard hand when returning from sea.

2. Square shape, green (or black), and odd numbered daymarks should be left on the port hand under the same conditions.

Ranges

Ranges are pairs of ATON's placed a suitable distance apart, with the far daymark mounted higher than the near daymark. When the two are aligned, one above the other, they will also be aligned with the center of a straight channel. The daymarks usually have lights attached at the top for guiding the mariner along a mid-channel route at night. The mariner must keep the pair of daymarks or lights in line for safe passage.

Fig. 5-10 Open Range - Not in Center of Channel.

Fig. 5-11   Closed Range - In Center of Channel.

Lighted Aids

Many of our buoys and daybeacons are fitted with lights to aid the mariner. A lighted daybeacon is one type of <u>minor light</u>. Minor lights are automatic unmanned lights on fixed structures such as a single pile, dolphins (multiple piles cabled together), or skeletal steel towers of varying heights. Minor lights are established in harbors, along channels, rivers and isolated locations. The skeletal tower is often found fixed to the end of a breakwater at a harbor entrance. It can also be fixed to a concrete foundation in shallower water, marking the side of a channel. Their lights are usually of low to moderate intensity. They are usually part of the Lateral System, with the same numbering, coloring, light and sound characteristics.

Fig. 5-12   A 'Texas Tower' Offshore Light Structure.

The characteristics of the lights (termed <u>light rhythms</u>) are designated on charts adjacent to the aid's symbol as well as in the applicable "Light List," published by the United States Coast Guard. Different rhythms use lights of various colors, <u>fixed</u> lights that shine continuously, <u>flashing</u> lights (off more time than on) and <u>occulting</u> lights (on more time than off). The standard colors are red, green, white, and yellow.

The lighted aid displaying a steady light, ("fixed"), marks a waterway which has no background lights to cause confusion. For coastal cruising mariners or anyone cruising in waters where background lights could cause confusion, flashing lights are used. The rhythm of the flashing light must be identified by the navigator and then referred to the local chart for determining position.

The <u>flashing</u> light blinks on at a rate of less than 50 flashes per minute with the duration of light shorter than that of darkness (it is off more than on). The flashing light draws attention, and nearby flashing aids have different flash rates or different colors for easy identification. The mariner must have a means of determining the flash period (the time difference between the beginning of one flash to the beginning of the next flash). An <u>occulting</u> light is one that is <u>on</u> more than it is <u>off</u>. It will also have a charted period.

The period of a flashing aid will be shown on the chart, adjacent to the aid symbol, as "10 sec" or "10s." This means the light will flash briefly, possibly 1 second, and then be off for 9 seconds, and continuously repeat. Obviously, this also means this example would only flash 6 times in one minute. Many lights will have a period of 2 or 3 seconds, or flash 20 to 30 times in one minute. A navigator must very carefully observe the characteristics of the navigation aid lights, because except for the specific light rhythms, many of such lights in a given area are very similar, and difficult to tell apart. By careful observation, during both day and night, the novice will gain valuable experience and learn to distinguish between the various lighted aids, regardless of their similarities.

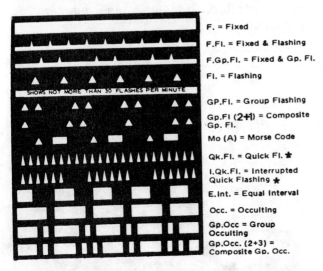

F. = Fixed

F.Fl. = Fixed & Flashing

F.Gp.Fl. = Fixed & Gp. Fl.

Fl. = Flashing

GP.Fl. = Group Flashing

Gp.Fl (2+1) = Composite Gp. Fl.

Mo (A) = Morse Code

Qk.Fl. = Quick Fl. ✱

I.Qk.Fl. = Interrupted Quick Flashing ✱

E.Int. = Equal Interval

Occ. = Occulting

Gp.Occ = Group Occulting

Gp.Occ. (2+3) = Composite Gp. Occ.

✱ Will no longer be used after 1989.

Fig. 5-13 Light Rhythms.

Some flashing aids have group flashing, in which a group of flashes, specified in number, is regularly repeated. The period is measured from the beginning of a group of flashes to the beginning of the next group. Major waterways often utilize this characteristic for rapid identification.

Where there is a need to indicate that special caution is required such as at sharp turns, sudden constrictions, or for marking wrecks or obstructions to be passed on one side only, a quick flashing light will be displayed. It will blink on similar to the flashing light, but the rate will be more than 50 flashes per minute but less than 80 flashes per minute.

For channel junctions and obstructions, for the "old" system, the Interrupted Quick Flashing was used. It is a quick-flashing light in which the sequence of flashes is interrupted by regularly repeated eclipses of constant and long duration. A typical example would be 5 seconds of quick flashes followed by 5 seconds of darkness. After 1989, the Interrupted

Quick Flashing characteristic will be discontinued.

Under the Modified Aid System, for junction and obstruction aids which can be passed on either side, composite group-flashing (2 + 1) lights are used. On these red and green horizontally banded aids, the light color matches the color of the top band on the structure.

Mid-channel markers (also known as safe water or fairway marks) display a white light. To distinguish them further, they emit a dot-dash (short-long) light characteristic indicating the International Morse Code (A). As the name implies, they should be passed on the appropriate side to help separate incoming from outgoing traffic and eliminate collisions.

Directional Lights

The directional light is used when it is not practicable for some reason to install a pair of range lights. This light is installed at one end of the straight section of a channel, high enough to be seen the full length of the channel section. This single light projects a high-intensity, narrow width beam of white light. On either side, through separate lenses, will be a broader red sector and green sector. The red and green sectors will be on the same respective sides of the channel as the red and green buoys. The arcs covered by each sector will be shown on the chart. A vessel in the center of the channel will only see the white light.

Articulated Lights

The articulated light is a recent addition to available aids to navigation. It is a combination of a minor light and a lighted buoy. It consists of a sealed hollow cylinder, up to 50, or more, feet in length. The lower end is attached by a swivel to a normal buoy "sinker" or anchor, and the cylinder will float in a vertical position. Sometimes, an additional buoyancy chamber is attached to the upper end, somewhat below the water surface.

The length of the cylinder will be equal

to the normal water depth, plus tidal range, plus some 10-15 feet above the surface. Mounted at the top is a typical light and corresponding daymarks. These are to be used when a more precise marking of a position is required, but the water is too deep to make a normal pile or dolphin structure practicable. Since no anchor chain scope is involved, the aid is always directly over the sinker, with only a relatively small swinging circle.

Special Purpose Marks

A departure from our old system of yellow buoys indicating Quarantine areas is that special marks will be established which will be yellow in color; and, if lighted, will show amber (yellow) lights. These special marks will indicate the following areas:

Ocean Data Acquisition Systems (ODAS),
Traffic Separation Schemes where conventional channel marking would be confusing,
Fish Net Areas,
Spoil Grounds,
Military Exercise Zones,
Anchorage Areas.

Light Structures

Lighted aids to navigation vary from the simple battery powered lantern on a wooden pile in a small creek to the tallest lighthouse on the coast with millions of candlepower. Their basic function is still the same as a buoy; however, they are established in positions where they perform more suitably than buoys. Also, with the exception of lighthouses, they have the same numbering, coloring, light, and sound characteristics of buoys.

There are Short Range Aids (SRA) which are not part of the buoyage system. Lighthouses are normally in this category, and are placed where they will be of most use; on prominent headlands, at channel entrances, on isolated dangers (although this will soon have a separate aid), or at other points where it is necessary that mariners be warned or guided. Their primary purpose is to support a

light at a considerable height above the water displaying appropriate light characteristics. In many instances, automatic fog signals and/or radiobeacon equipment are installed, as well as quarters for personnel.

Fig. 5-14 A Lighthouse.

Lighthouse structures vary considerably, depending upon the desired height, and on the location and available foundation at that location. However, the Light List briefly describes their structure, such as "gray conical tower covered way to dwelling," or "white cylindrical granite tower connected to dwelling." Cylindrical or conical towers may have distinctive color combinations painted on them, such as the black and white spirals on the Cape Hatteras Light. The structure itself, together with any distinctive colors, make up a lighthouse "daymark" to help the navigator identify them during the day. During bright daylight, the light is normally turned off.

A major factor in both location and height above the water for the light are the differences in how far they need to be seen, for safety, from the sea. The higher the light is above the water and the more brilliant (greater candlepower) the light, the farther away it can be seen at night.

Lights are given classifications. These are primary seacoast light, secondary light, river or harbor light (also minor lights, normally part of a buoyage system) and these terms indicate, in a general way, lighted ATON's that are "fixed" rather than "floating." They are described in the Light List by:

a. Name and Light rhythm,
b. Location, including latitude and longitude,
c. Nominal Range,
d. Height above the water,
e. Structure, including height above ground and daymark,
f. Characteristics of sound devices present and year built.

Lighthouse light rhythms may encompass more than the light characteristics previously discussed. Sectors and alternating colors are also used.

A light sector is provided when sections of colored glass are placed in the lantern to warn the navigator of shoals or nearby land in that sector. Sectors are angular portions of the 360° circle around the light. When the light is cut off by a land mass or structure adjoining it, or by deliberately obscuring it toward its landward side, an obscured sector is also created. Both types of sectors are shown on the chart by broken lines that extend from the light on each side of the sector. These lines will be labeled with the true bearing in degrees, from the vessel to the light, and an arc between them will indicate the color. Any such sectors will also be described in the Light List.

When a navigator is heading toward a light, and finds he is in the red sector, he is definitely heading into danger. If a navigator sees a red sector light when crossing such a sector, he may or may not be heading into danger. For example, heading into South River from the Chesapeake Bay requires a navigator to cross a red sector from Thomas Point light, even though a safe passage is available if the navigator is paying attention to his chart and the South River channel buoyage.

The lightship has disappeared from the North American coast. At one time these vessels could be found at the entrances of many major seaports. All of them have been replaced by offshore light towers resembling oil drilling structures, or by large navigational buoys. These structures are equipped with lights, fog signals, and radiobeacons, and take the place of lighthouses which would be impractical to build in that location.

Light Structure Sound Signals

A significant sound producing aid to navigation is the fog horn. Most lighthouses and major aids and some minor light structures are equipped with fog horns to aid the mariner during periods of low visibility. These signals are operated by either mechanical or electrical means and may be recognized by the timing of the signal, its silent period, and its tone. Where the number of blasts and the total time for a signal to complete a cycle is not sufficient for positive identification, reference may be made to details in the Light List regarding the exact length of each blast and silent interval.

In boating areas there might be several fog horns with different periods and tones being heard at the same time. The mariner needs to recognize them for safe passage.

An important electronic aid to navigation is the radiobeacon. The navigator must be equipped with, 1) a Radio Direction Finder (RDF) adjustable throughout the marine frequencies in use, 2) a chart showing the location, frequency, and International Morse Code characteristics of such aids, 3) some experience tuning in and recognizing these radio signals, and 4) a deviation curve for the receiver in the location for which it is to be operated. (Radio signals are affected similar to deviation of a compass, discussed in Chapter 6.)

These radiobeacons can be used in two ways. Using an RDF, a relative bearing from the vessel to the radiobeacon can be obtained, converted to a true bearing, plotted on the chart from the vessel to the radiobeacon (chart symbol "R Bn"). Two or more bearings will provide the navigator with an "RDF fix," although the precision of such bearings is nowhere near the quality of a visual one. A vessel can also home in on a radiobeacon. After the signal is found with the RDF, the vessel is steered directly toward the radiobeacon. This takes place when the vessel's heading is such that the RDF relative bearing is 000°.

Great caution must be observed when homing because the vessel is obviously heading toward the land where the antenna is mounted on a tower, or possibly toward a lighthouse mounted on a steel structure out in the water, surrounded by riprap. The navigator should be taking depth soundings, and attempting to determine his position more accurately by other means. In a fog or other reduced visibility, the prudent decision might be to anchor until other ATON's can be seen.

Visibility of Lights

The nominal visibility of lights on light structures is printed, along with the height of the light, on the chart, i. e. 10M = 10 nautical miles.

Bridges

Bridges across navigable waters are often encountered and have fixed light combinations. Of special importance is vertical clearance, which can be determined from the local chart. Additional aids are also provided for the mariner's safe passage.

Red lights mark piers and other parts of the bridge or to show that a drawbridge is in the closed position. Green lights are used to mark the centerline of navigable channels through fixed bridges or for indicating a drawbridge in the open position. For major bridges where there is more than one safe passage, the preferred channel will be marked by three white lights in a vertical line above the green light.

Intracoastal Waterway Aids

The Intracoastal Waterway route runs parallel to the Atlantic and Gulf Coasts from Manasquan Inlet on the New Jersey shore to the Mexican border. Marks for this route are very similar to those of the old Lateral System and the new Modified U. S. System. There are some differences in aid markings between the Intracoastal Waterway and open ocean waterways.

Aids marking the Intracoastal Waterway have some portion of them marked with yellow. Otherwise, the coloring and numbering of buoys and beacons follow a lateral system similar to that used in other U. S. waterways, with red on the right side of the channel clockwise around the United States.

In order that vessels may readily follow the Intracoastal Waterway route where it coincides with another marked waterway, such as an important river, special markings are employed. These special markings are applied to the buoys or other aids that already mark the river or waterway for other traffic. These aids are then referred to as "dual purpose" aids.

The mark consists of a yellow square or a yellow triangle, placed on a conspicuous part of the dual purpose aid. The yellow square, in outline similar to a can buoy, indicates that the aid on which it is placed should be left on the left hand side when following the Intracoastal Waterway clockwise around the United States. The yellow triangle has the same meaning as a nun; it should be kept on the right hand side when proceeding clockwise around the United States. When such dual purpose aid marking is employed, the mariner following the Intracoastal Waterway should disregard the shape and color of the aid and be guided solely by the yellow mark.

Uniform State Waterway Marking System

The Uniform State Waterway Marking System (USWMS) includes a system of marks to supplement the federal system in marking of state waters and a system of regulatory markers to warn a vessel operator of dangers or to provide general information and directions.

For the supplemental portion where standard federal aids are inappropriate, much smaller buoys of a cylindrical shape are generally utilized although the shape has no significance in itself. Channel marks are cylindrical, all black (or green) or all red, numbered odd or even, respectively, with red on the right when heading upstream.

Fig. 5-15   A dangerous area is indicated by an open diamond shape, as shown above.

Fig. 5-16   A prohibited area is marked by a diamond with a cross inside, as shown above.

Fig. 5-17   A controlled area, such as one which excludes water skiing or fishing, is indicated by a circle, as shown above.

Fig. 5-18   General information and directions are shown on a square or rectangular marker, as shown above.

Other marks are normally white in color with a topmost color of green or red indicating safe passage areas similar to federal aids. Mooring buoys are also of the same shape and color except that a blue horizontal band located near mid-buoy marks their intended function.

The important difference between the USWMS and the standard federal system is that of regulatory marks. They are colored white with international orange horizontal bands completely around the buoy. One band is at the top of the mark, and the other is just above the waterline so that both orange bands are clearly visible to approaching vessels. With these marks, there are four different purposes and four different markings to indicate the purpose. Two of these markings indicate dangerous conditions, one indicates caution and one is for information.

Of the two types of danger markings, both have an international orange diamond located between the horizontal bands. The diamond with an internal cross means "boats keep out" whereas the standard danger marking without the cross may have additional information inside the diamond to indicate the nature of the danger (e.g. rocks, shoal, etc.).

The controlled area marker, as its name implies, provides instruction to the boater. The basic recognition factor is that there will be an international orange circle between the horizontal bands and within that circle may be such regulatory information as speed limits, no fishing, no anchoring, no wake, etc.

Navigation Publications

The most important publication to be kept on the boat is a current chart of the boating area. Since the location, characteristics, and maintenance status of aids to navigation may change from time to time, an obsolete chart can be dangerous. While there are a number of sources of charts, the charts produced by NOAA are the most up-to-date and complete. They can be obtained at marinas, boat stores, and other designated chart dealers.

To keep your charts current, and to get news of all matters of interest in your boating area, the Coast Guard publishes Local Notice to Mariners, which may be obtained for free from your Coast Guard District.

A copy of the Light List will help you identify aids to navigation. Published by the Coast Guard, it is available in several volumes:

Volume I, Atlantic Coast, describes aids to navigation in United States waters from St. Croix River, Maine to Ocean City Inlet, Maryland.

Volume II, Atlantic Coast, describes aids to navigation in United States waters from Ocean City, Maryland to Little River, South Carolina.

Volume III, Atlantic and Gulf Coast, describes aids to navigation in United States waters from Little River, South Carolina to Econfina River, Florida and the Greater Antilles.

Volume IV, Gulf Coast, describing aids to navigation in United States waters from Econfina River, Florida to Rio Grande River, Texas.

Volume V, Mississippi River System, describes aids to navigation on the Mississippi and Ohio Rivers and navigable tributaries.

Volume VI, Pacific Coast and Pacific Islands, describes aids to navigation in United States waters on the Pacific Coast and Pacific Islands. For the convenience of mariners, there is also included some of the lighted aids on the coast of British Columbia, maintained by Canada.

Volume VII, Great Lakes, describes aids to navigation maintained under the authority of the U. S. Coast Guard, and some aids maintained by Canada, on the Great Lakes and on the St. Lawrence river above the St. Regis river.

Light Lists are sold to the public by the Superintendent of Documents, Government Printing Office, Washington, D. C. 20402, from Government Printing Office Branch Bookstores, located in many cities, and by sales agents located in most major ports. A list of sales agents is published yearly in the Notice to Mariners, and also in a pamphlet available free of charge from the National Ocean Survey (C-44), Washington, D. C. 20840.

Chapter 6

Piloting

Introduction

Navigation is the science of knowing where you are on the Earth and knowing how to get to where you want to be. Piloting is navigation in coastal waters, usually within sight of land. While some piloting makes use of electronic aids that operate at a distance, most piloting is done using visual sightings of natural or man-made landmarks.

In a basic course such as this one, we can only introduce you to some of the many facets of piloting. We can, however, give you a "leg up" on your study of this fascinating and important subject, and give you some tools and techniques that you will find useful in your recreational boating.

If you have any serious interest in advancing your skills as a pilot, and you really should if you take boating seriously, we recommend that you follow up this course with Advanced Coastal Navigation taught by the Coast Guard Auxiliary, or a similar course. See your instructor for details.

Tools

The tools required for piloting are minimal. You can spend a great deal of money on them, however, you are advised to keep your investment small and limit yourself to only the basic tools until you have a good understanding of what is really needed.

Your basic piloting tool kit should include:

- Charts of the area of interest,

- A good-quality magnetic compass,

- Parallel rulers or course protractor,

- Dividers and drafting compass,

- Fine-lead mechanical pencil, medium-soft,

- Good-quality eraser, preferably vinyl.

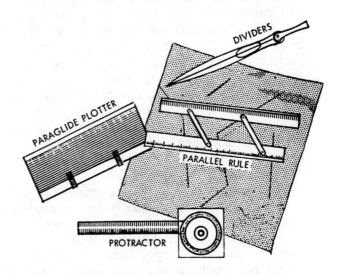

Fig. 6-1 Basic Piloting Tools.

Additional piloting implements could include a good binocular (7x50), some means of measuring water depth (calibrated pole, lead line, or electronic depth sounder ["sonar"]), and a hand bearing compass.

As your skills increase, or as your circumstances require and permit, you may want to add electronic tools, such as a radio direction finder (RDF), satellite navigation equipment, or LORAN-C. But no matter how sophisticated your piloting equipment may become, there are times when it still comes down to chart, compass, pencil and straight edge.

The Nautical Chart

Maps are what make serious navigation possible. A "map" is a graphical representation of a portion of the surface of the earth, generally on paper. Usually a map is drawn "to scale." That is, the sizes of objects in the drawing are proportional to the sizes of those objects on the earth.

In general, the word "map" applies to drawings of land areas. More properly, drawings of areas of water, especially those drawn specifically to aid piloting and navigation, are called "charts."

Charts are not restricted to showing water areas. Remember that piloting is navigating near the coast, using landmarks as aids. Nautical charts show areas of land near the water, and may actually include a great deal of detail about objects on the land, if those objects are useful to finding position (the shape of the coastline, landmarks visible from the sea, man-made aids to navigation) or for providing services for mariners (marinas, harbors, etc.)

Today's chart is a technological marvel. If the same information were converted into words and written down, the contents of a single nautical chart would probably require several large books. And they would be much harder to read and interpret.

This compact presentation of information is possible in part through the use of symbols. These symbols stand for various objects that cannot be represented to

scale in their true shapes. We will discuss the symbols used on a chart later in this chapter.

Sources of Charts

Charts of U.S. waters are prepared and published by the National Ocean Service (NOS), and free catalogs are available directly from that organization. These catalogs are also provided by authorized chart sales outlets, including map stores, navigational instrument sales and service facilities, boat yards and marine service businesses.

Charts are only as good as the information on them, and because that information changes with time, you should be sure to buy and use up-to-date charts. To help you be certain of having the most recent version, charts are dated.

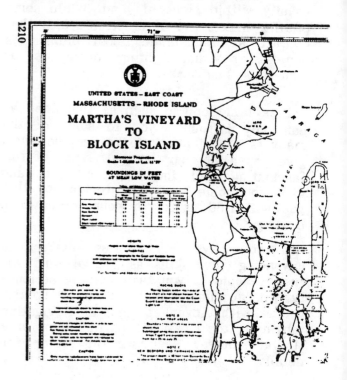

Fig. 6-2   Portion of a Nautical Chart.

The "Notice to Mariners," published monthly by the local Coast Guard District, gives information on changes that are needed to charts between formal updates. Changes always occur faster than charts can be updated, printed and distributed. Even newly-purchased copies of the latest editions of charts probably require some correction.

Projection

The surface of the earth is curved. Most maps and charts, on the other hand, are flat. It is just not possible to represent a curved surface on a flat piece of paper accurately without some distortion. If the area is small enough, the distortion may be small enough to ignore, but it will always be there.

The process of mapping a curved surface onto a flat one is called projection. It is a fairly complex mathematical process in execution, but the concept is simple.

There are several projection techniques. The one most commonly used in navigational charts is the Mercator projection. This projection works well for most purposes, but shapes and distances are increasingly distorted as you move into extreme northern and southern areas. The distortion makes these charts nearly unusable in polar and near-polar areas, but this is no serious problem for most of the areas where recreational boating occurs.

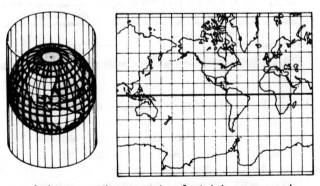

- Angles are correctly represented • Great circle appears curved
- Rhumb line appears as straight line
- Distortion in BOTH directions

Fig. 6-3   Mercator Projection.

Another common projection, used for charts of the Great Lakes, for example, is the polyconic projection. This projection gives less distortion in high northern and southern areas.

Scale

Charts are classified according to scale. A harbor chart, for instance, may have a scale of 1:20,000. That is, the drawing of the object as it appears on the chart is 1/20,000 the size of the actual object. A harbor entrance that is 1" wide on the chart is actually 20,000" wide, or about 3/10 of a mile.

If the chart's scale were 1:40,000 the same 1" drawing would represent an object just twice that size, or about 3/5 of a mile. Conversely, the 3/10-mile wide harbor entrance would only appear 1/2" wide on the chart.

Harbor charts sometimes are drawn in scales of 1:10,000. These charts can show an enormous amount of detail, but they cannot cover a very large area. Coastal charts, on the other hand, are typically 1:80,000. They show much larger areas, with correspondingly less detail.

Even smaller scales (1:100,000; 1:1,000,000; etc.) are used for special purposes, such as planning ocean passages. Some charts show an entire ocean on one sheet of paper. In general, you should select charts to give the amount of detail you need for each portion of your cruise; small-scale, large-area charts for overall planning; large-scale, detailed charts for maneuvering within harbors; and so on.

Most nautical charts are printed on large sheets of heavy, good-quality paper. They are designed to be used with a large flat table, such as might be found on the bridge of a ship. They are difficult to work with on a small boat, however, so special folio-style charts, known as Small Craft Charts, are published for areas that have a lot of small boat traffic. These charts, generally in 1:40,000 scale, are specially designed in a format with fold-out segments to be used in the cramped quarters of a small boat. Their covers also carry other useful information, such as tidal data, descriptions of facilities available in the area, etc.

Fig. 6-4   Small Craft Chart.

If you have an open boat, you may want to protect your chart by encasing it in a transparent plastic cover that will allow you to spread it out flat without worry of its being damaged by rain or spray.

Datum and Sea Level

Datum is the technical term for the base line from which a chart's vertical measurements are made - heights of land or landmarks, or depths of water. Most landsmen's maps use sea level as datum, and that is quite good enough for most purposes.

But in coastal areas with tides, depths are constantly changing. Since depth is a primary concern of the mariner, a more sophisticated datum is required.

The marine datum used for heights of objects on land is mean high water, the average (mean) level of all high tide levels (excluding unusual conditions, such as severe storms, etc.)

The figures for water depths, on the other hand, are based on a more conservative datum, mean low water (MLW). In the Pacific, there are two tides per day, generally unequal. The datum used on the West Coast is the average of the lower of the two low waters, called the mean lower low water (MLLW). On the Gulf of Mexico, the datum is the Gulf Coast Low Water Datum, and a similar low water datum is used in the Great Lakes.

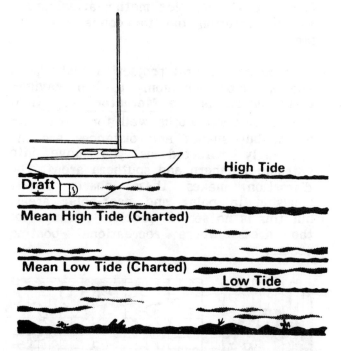

Fig. 6-5   Datum – Depths of Water.

Note that the depth of water that appears on a chart is based on datum. The actual depth of water at any given time will depend on many factors and may differ considerably from what the chart shows.

Units of Measurement

Depths of water ("soundings") are usually given in feet on U.S. charts, but may also be given in fathoms (1 fathom = 6 feet) or <u>meters</u>. The units of depth measurement, the scale, and the datum are among the important data prominently displayed on the <u>title block</u> of the chart. (See Fig. 6-2.)

Other Charted Information

Besides heights and depths, charts also describe the type of bottom material, using special abbreviations. This information is especially useful if you are trying to select a place to set an anchor. Soft mud is not generally suitable holding ground, whereas sand or hard mud is usually excellent for anchoring. (See Chapter 2.)

1		Ground
2	S	Sand
3	M	Mud; Muddy
4	Oz	Ooze
5	Ml	Marl
6	Cl	Clay
7	G	Gravel
8	Sn	Shingle
9	P	Pebbles
10	St	Stones

Fig. 6-6   Types of Bottoms

Obstructions and other hazards in the water are also charted. Symbols tell the mariner what to be ready for and what to avoid. It is worth bearing in mind that a wreck, even one that is largely exposed, soon ceases to look like the ship it once was, and may be difficult to recognize.

Shallow water is tinted light blue on a chart, while deeper water is shown in white. This gives a ready visual reference without having to look at the numbers. (As a rule of thumb, moving into the blue is generally time to switch to a larger-scale chart.)

Shore Details

Charted details ashore include prominent structures, especially those that stand out because of their distinctive shape (churches, water towers). Land contours are frequently charted. Bridges of all types are described in detail.

The shoreline contour is one of the chart's most important features. It is usually tinted gold, or light green if it is swampy or if it covers and uncovers with changes in water level.

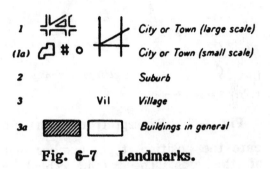

1		City or Town (large scale)
(1a)		City or Town (small scale)
2		Suburb
3	Vil	Village
3a		Buildings in general

Fig. 6-7   Landmarks.

(You should keep in mind that structures that were once prominent enough to warrant appearing on the chart may have been torn down, or may be screened by larger buildings that were built later. The process of keeping charts up-to-date is a continuous one, and depends on cooperation from chart users, such as you. Your instructors can tell you how you can participate in the cooperative chart updating program.)

Aids to Navigation

Man-made structures, both fixed and floating, serve as signposts, beacons, direction signals, and warnings of danger to the mariner. These aids to navigation, placed and serviced by the U. S. Coast Guard, are described in detail in Chapter 5.

Obviously, aids to navigation -- except for major lighthouses -- are far too small to appear on the chart in their true shape. Instead, symbols are used to indi-

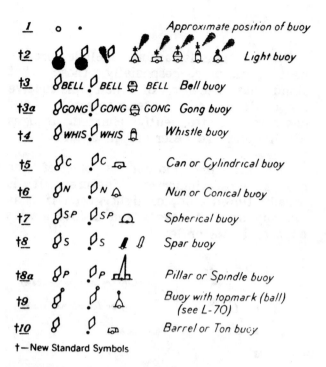

_1_	o •		Approximate position of buoy
†2			Light buoy
†3	⊗BELL ○ BELL ⊡ BELL		Bell buoy
†3a	⊗GONG ○GONG ⊡ GONG		Gong buoy
†4	⊗WHIS ○WHIS		Whistle buoy
†5	⊗C ○C ⊡		Can or Cylindrical buoy
†6	⊗N ○N △		Nun or Conical buoy
†7	⊗SP ○SP ⌂		Spherical buoy
†8	⊗S ○S		Spar buoy
†8a	⊗P ○P		Pillar or Spindle buoy
†9			Buoy with topmark (ball) (see L-70)
†10			Barrel or Ton buoy

†—New Standard Symbols

Fig. 6-8 Excerpt from Chart No. 1.

cate the position, type, number and color of the aids. These (and other) symbols used on nautical charts are shown in **Chart No. 1**, a sample of which is shown in Fig. 6-8.

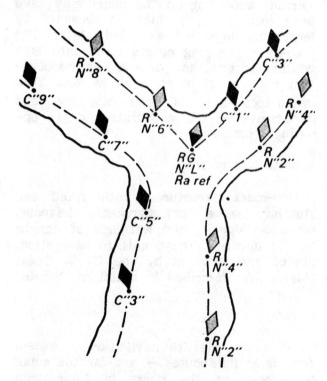

Fig. 6-9 Channel Markers.

The actual location of a buoy is the small circle at one end of the diamond symbol. A fixed aid is marked with a small, isolated circle. Lighted buoys are distinguished by light purple (magenta) circles printed around the position circle. Lighted fixed aids have a purple (magenta) "exclamation mark" with its sharp end pointing toward the position circle.

In practical piloting, it should be remembered that buoys are anchored in place, and at low tide they may move off their charted positions. They may even end up outside the channel they mark. They may be sunk, or be displaced by ice or debris.

They may be damaged by vandals or accident. Fixed aids, on the other hand, usually stay put. Even if their lights are extinguished, they are usually recognizable.

The Magnetic Compass

Many centuries ago, mariners oriented themselves by the sun's place or rising and setting, or by the direction of the prevailing winds. This was less than precise, especially on windless or cloudy days. The magnetic compass, perfected slowly over years of experimentation, trial and scientific endeavor, became the sailor's most common and most reliable direction-indicating aid.

In principle, the magnetic compass remains as simple as it was when it was invented in medieval times. It is a magnet, balanced so it can pivot freely in a horizontal plane. The magnet -- as any magnet will, given the opportunity — aligns itself with the earth's magnetic field. A pointer attached to the magnet will point the way toward the north magnetic pole.

The north magnetic pole is near, but not the same as, the earth's true north pole, or axis of spin. The magnetic pole wanders somewhat over many years, and is located in far northern Canada.

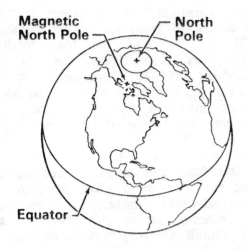

Fig. 6-10 Relative Position of Poles.

The difference between the location of the north magnetic pole and the true north pole has important effects on the way we use the magnetic compass. This effect, and the way we handle it, are discussed below.

Selecting a Compass

A magnetic compass should be selected carefully to suit the boat it will be used on. Power boats should be equipped with a compass designed and built to withstand the vibrations and pounding of a power boat moving at high speeds, while a sailboat compass needs to be able to operate satisfactorily when it is heeled over at an angle.

(A major achievement in the design of compasses for the Royal Navy was building one that would be accurate enough to use for navigation while not jumping off the pivot with the shock of guns being fired on board!)

In general, since large compasses tend to be more stable and more finely calibrated than small compasses, all other things being equal, the compass should be as large as practical under the situation. Most small boats have small compasses, while larger, steadier boats have larger compasses, when it should probably be the other way around. On the other hand, larger boats are used on longer passages, where greater accuracy is needed.

Whatever the size of the compass chosen, it must be installed with care. Try to locate the instrument so that it can be sighted over in all directions. But even more important, it must be easily visible to the helmsman.

Marine compasses are filled with an oily or alcohol-based liquid to help damp out vibrations and oscillations. Good quality compasses have bellows chambers to allow for expansion and contraction of this fluid with changing temperatures. All compasses should be protected from excess heat and direct sunlight, but you may find an inexpensive compass leaking fluid from a ruptured seal if it is allowed to overheat. Such a compass must be repaired or replaced, since without the fluid it is virtually useless on a boat.

Make certain that the fore-and-aft marks on the compass — the center pivot and the lubber's line — are parallel with the keel.

A good compass almost always has internal adjusters, small magnets that allow the instrument to be adjusted for local magnetic influences that contribute error. It is also useful to have a light (preferably red) installed so the compass can be read at night.

Fig. 6-11 Small Boat Magnetic Compass.

The compass should be located at least three feet in every direction from radios, other electronic instruments, or masses of ferrous metal. This may be difficult in a small boat, but do the best you can.

When you have installed the compass in the best possible location, choose a calm day and move into an area with several charted landmarks or fixed aids to navigation. Point the boat toward each landmark in turn and check that the compass reads appropriately for each landmark.

You may wish to have your compass adjusted by a professional. The techniques for doing so are not complex, but they are tedious and not especially convenient for most recreational boaters. On the other hand, you may find, as many do, that your compass is as accurate as you can read, just as you installed it.

Latitude and Longitude

A coordinate grid pattern gives a reference framework to describe locations and to make it possible to perform some of the operations necessary for careful navigation. This grid pattern is provided by parallels of latitude and meridians of longitude.

The parallels are numbered north (N) and south (S) from 0° at the Equator to 90°N and 90°S at the true north and south poles, respectively. Each degree is subdivided into 60 equal segments called minutes ('), and each minute can be subdivided into 60 seconds ("), or, alternatively, into tenths of minutes (00.0').

On most charts, true north is located at the top, and parallels are indicated along the side margins by divisions in the black-and-white border, as well as by lines running across the chart at intervals. (Small Craft Charts are sometimes printed to show a maximum stretch of shoreline per sheet. When this is the case, the top edge of the chart may not be north.)

It is handy to remember that one minute of LATITUDE (but not of longitude) equals one nautical mile, or 6076 feet. This is useful in measuring distances on the chart. Each chart also includes at least one printed scale, giving distances in nautical miles, statute miles, kilometers, and/or yards. (See Fig. 6-13.)

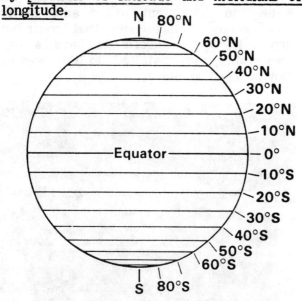

Fig. 6-12 Parallels of Latitude.

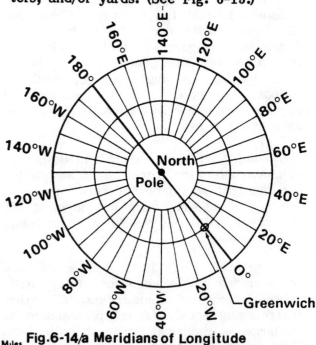

Fig. 6-14/a Meridians of Longitude

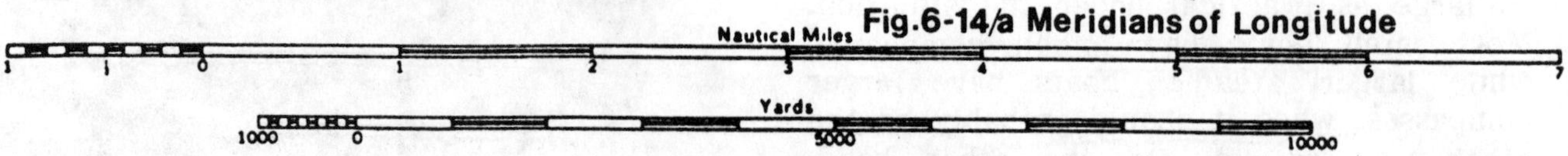

Fig. 6-13 Distance Scale.

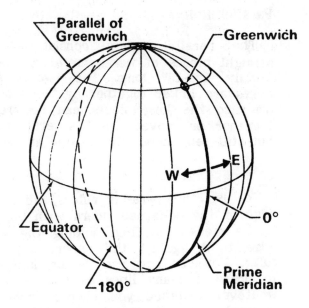

Fig. 6-14b Meridians of Longitude

Meridians of longitude run north (N) and south (S) between the true poles. By convention, meridians are numbered east (E) and west (W) from the Prime Meridian (000°), the one passing through the Royal Observatory in Greenwich, just outside London, England. West and east longitude meet at 180° in the Pacific Ocean. (See Fig. 6-14 [a] & [b].)

Almost the entire United States is thus in west longitude -- from about 60°W on the East Coast to about 130°W in California or 150°W in Hawaii. (Several islands in the Aleutian Chain in Alaska are over the 180th meridian and in east longitude.)

Latitude and longitude always include north or south, east or west, in their designation, but they give a unique representation of position. If a boat's position is given as 45° 30.1'N, 73° 20.4'W, there is only one place on earth it can be.

Course Plotting

Navigational charts are constructed so that if you draw a line on the chart connecting the point representing your present location with the point representing the position you want to go to, the

angle that the (course) line makes with any meridian is the angle with true north, or direction, that you need to travel to get to your destination. Furthermore, the length of the line is a measure of the distance that you have to travel to get there.

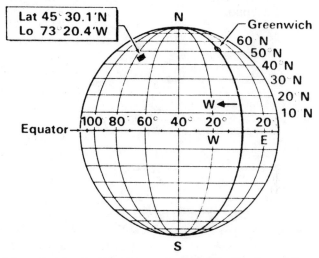

Fig. 6-15 Latitude and Longitude Provide a Coordinate Grid System.

To "plot" or "chart" a course, the first step in piloting, first draw the course line. Extend it if necessary so that it crosses a meridian (one of the north-south lines). Use a protractor to measure the angle that the course line makes with the meridian. Always measure the number of degrees moving from the meridian around to the right.

Note that direction measured in degrees is a number between 0 and 360. To avoid confusion with other numbers we will be using later, course directions are always written as three digits. Thus 0 degrees is written 000, 25 degrees is written 025, and so on.

Compass Rose

The use of the course protractor is made a little bit easier on marine navigation charts, since one is provided directly on the chart, usually in more than one place. This printed protractor is called the <u>compass rose</u>. (See Fig. 6-16.)

All that is necessary to use the compass rose is to move a course line parallel to itself so that it passes through the exact center of the rose. The course angle can then be read directly where the course line cuts through the margin of the rose.

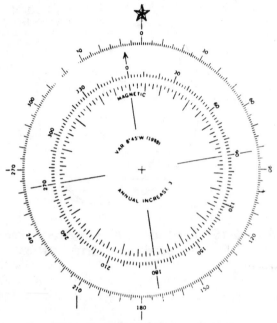

Fig. 6-16 Compass Rose.

Moving the course line parallel to itself is not especially difficult, and several tools exist specifically to do that. These range from the traditional parallel rulers through a number of other patent devices, all the way up to drafting machines costing hundreds of dollars. Very simple devices, used carefully, work very well, indeed.

Fig. 6-17 Parallel Rulers.

Parallel Rulers

The parallel rulers consist of two straight pieces of wood, metal or plastic, usually 12"-15" long. The two straight edges are linked together by two movable arms so the long pieces can be brought together or moved apart several inches, but still remain parallel to one another.

To use the parallel rulers, align one edge of the collapsed rulers with the line to be measured. Then holding the other edge tight against the paper, open the ruler. You can now use the original edge to draw as many lines as you want, at whatever distance you choose from the original line, all exactly parallel to one another and to the original line, as long as the fixed straightedge does not slip.

It may be necessary to "walk" the rulers, moving one edge, then the other, avoiding slips, to get to the nearest compass rose. It may take some practice to get comfortable with the procedure, and it is always good practice to "walk" the line back again to the original course line to make sure you haven't slipped a little bit.

You should also avoid the temptation to place the lower edge along the course line and measure with the upper edge. The two edges are not guaranteed to be parallel to one another (although they should be), but only that either edge can be moved parallel to itself.

Naming Courses

A course straight north will not cross any meridian. Another way of saying that is that it forms an angle of 0 degrees with a meridian, or the course is 000. The same line, traveled in the opposite direction (due south) forms a 180 degree line with the meridian, measured from the meridian around to the right. This is spoken of as "course 180."

Similarly, a course to the east crosses a meridian (a north-south line) at right angles (course 090), while the same course line followed to the west is course 270.

It is easy to become confused and read the "reciprocal course" (same course line, opposite direction of travel), but it is equally easy to avoid the confusion. The course direction must fall between the appropriate limits. Thus a course to the northeast (045°) falls between north (000°) and east (090°). The same course line, followed in the opposite direction (towards the southwest) must fall between south (180°) and west (270°), as indeed 225° does.

Sources of Error

As mentioned above, the magnetic north pole is located several hundred miles away from the true north pole. The magnetic compass points toward the magnetic pole, and unless you happen to live in one of those few parts of the world where the magnetic north pole just happens to lie in the same direction as the true north pole, this creates some practical problems for the navigator. The task of actually following the plotted course depends on following a compass indicator, so it is necessary to correct the compass reading or correct the course followed to get where you really want to go.

Variation

The amount by which the magnetic compass points away from true north is called variation. The amount of variation that exists varies, depending on where you are on the globe. If you cruise off the East Coast the magnetic north pole is west of true north, and the error is called westerly variation. On the West Coast, the compass points east of true north, and the error is easterly variation. And there are some areas in the Midwest that actually are fortunate enough to have no variation at all, as the two poles are in line with one another.

The amount of variation that applies in any given area is printed on the chart as a notation in the center of the compass rose. Note that if more than one compass rose appears on the chart, you should use the variation in the rose nearest your position, since variation can differ slightly from place to place.

Also note that the compass rose has two protractor scales. The outer scale is oriented so that 000 on the protractor is pointed toward true north. The inner scale, on the other hand, is oriented to the magnetic north pole. It is possible to measure the magnetic course between two points directly from that inner scale.

Remember: Variation is the same for all vessels in a particular area.

Correcting the Course

It is not practical to correct the magnetic compass to compensate for variation because the variation changes with the vessel's location. It is practical, on the other hand, to correct the course line. Adding westerly variation (or subtracting easterly variation) to the plotted course yields a magnetic course that compensates for the effects of variation.

For example, if the desired course is 072° (somewhat east of northeast) and the local variation is 9°W, the desired magnetic course is 072° + 9°W = 081°M.

Deviation

Another important influence on the boat's magnetic compass is magnetic material in and on the boat itself. The engine, steering gear, radio loudspeakers, even electric currents in dashboard instruments, all cause the compass to deviate from an accurate reading. Furthermore, since this deviation is caused by the unique magnetic elements on that particular boat, the deviation pattern is different for each vessel.

Since deviation is the result of an interaction between the magnetic compass, the earth's magnetic field, and other magnetic influences on the vessel, it stands to reason that moving these elements around with respect to one another will change the effect that they have on one another. In practical terms, this means that the amount of deviation experienced by a compass depends on the direction, or heading, of the vessel.

On the other hand, since the vessel carries its magnetic environment along with it, the deviation pattern for a given small craft is, essentially not a function of its location.

It may be necessary to develop a deviation table for the vessel that shows the amount and direction of error for each heading. Generally for modern small craft, the errors are small (less than a few degrees), and a correction for deviation is unnecessary. On the other hand, if the compass deviations are large (over 3-5°), it may be necessary to make a table of these deviations (Deviation Table) and apply these corrections when converting from compass to magnetic directions and vice versa.

It may also be necessary to develop a new deviation table each time major magnetic items (radios, etc.) are added or changed. Unfortunately, construction of a deviation table is beyond the scope of this course. The subject, however, is covered thoroughly in the Advanced Coastal Navigation course.

Positioning

It is important to be able to establish the position of the boat frequently, in order to know where you are in the event of an emergency, in case the visibility becomes restricted (i.e., fog), or simply so you can determine if you have enough fuel to get you where you want to go. A Line of Position (LOP) is a line established on a chart that can be drawn through the known position of the vessel. By itself, an LOP is insufficient to establish the position of the vessel. But, the intersection of two, or more, LOPs definitely establishes the position of the vessel.

The simplest form of LOP is the Range. Recall from Chapter 5, the discussion of Range Marks, which establish whether the vessel is on the centerline of the channel. When the two range marks align, a Range LOP is established. If that line is drawn on the chart, and the vessel is on the range, then the vessel is known to be on that line. Although this single LOP is insufficient to establish the vessel's exact position, it clearly indicates where the vessel is not.

If two LOPs observed at the same time can be drawn on the chart then the position is established. This position is established at the intersection of the two LOPs, and is termed a FIX. LOPs can be determined using the vessel's magnetic compass.

Given a reasonably accurate compass, you can use it and measurements you make with it to determine your position. Select two or more identifiable landmarks (or preferably navigational aids). The more evenly they are distributed around the horizon, the better. If you use only two marks, the angle between the lines from your vessel to each of the two objects should be as near 90° as possible. Locate the marks on the chart.

Head the vessel directly toward one mark and note the compass heading. As soon as you have recorded the compass heading, head toward the other mark and note its compass heading.

These two readings are called bearings and they will be used to draw LOPs. Since they are measured in terms of compass readings, they are called compass bearings, and they must be corrected to give true directions. Before the compass direction can be plotted on a chart as a true direction, corrections must be made for both deviation and variation.

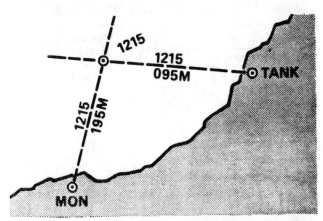

Fig. 6-18 Positioning by Crossed Bearings on Two Landmarks.

The process of converting from compass bearings to true bearings is the reverse of the process of converting from true directions read from the chart to a compass direction to be followed. Westerly errors, either deviation or variation, must be subtracted, and easterly errors must be added when correcting, to get a true direction.

For example, suppose the first compass bearing is 095°C, and the second is 195°C ("C" for compass). Variation shown on the chart for the area is 12°E. (This would seem to imply that our example is taking place somewhere in the western part of the United States.)

For the purposes of illustration, we assume that our compass has a deviation of 3°W for a compass heading of 095°C, and a deviation of 3°E for a compass heading of 195°C. (These values for deviation would have been obtained from a deviation table constructed specifically for our compass. The table would be entered with the compass heading or the magnetic heading to obtain the respective deviation error.)

We must correct our compass bearings to true bearings in order to plot them on the chart. (Remember, the directions on the chart are true directions, relative to true north, not compass directions.) First, we correct for the deviation error. For the compass bearing of 095°C, our deviation of 3°W must be subtracted (095°C −

3°W = 092°M). Our magnetic bearing is 092°M. Now, correcting for 12°E variation, we add this <u>easterly</u> error to our 092°M to obtain our true bearing (092°M + 12°E = 104°). (Note that it is unnecessary to add the designator "T" to indicate true, since the chart's directions are true.) Thus, our 095°C compass bearing becomes our 104° true bearing.

Applying the same procedure to the 195°C compass bearing, we correct for the deviation on that heading of 3°E, by adding, to get 198°M, the magnetic bearing. Again, adding the 12° variation, we get a true bearing of 210°. Our two true bearings of 104° and 210° may now be plotted on the chart. These are our LOPs.

Your next task is to draw the first LOP through the first mark at a true angle of 104°, and the second LOP through the second mark at an angle of 210°. Extend the lines back (in the <u>reciprocal direction</u>) as needed until they pass through the area where you are likely to be. The point where these two LOPs cross is your position. A position determined in this fashion is known as a <u>fix</u>.

Ideally, if you conduct the same operation with three marks, the three resulting LOPs should cross at a single point. In most real situations, however, this seldom happens. The triangle that is formed by the near-intersection of three LOPs — known as a "cocked hat" — is a measure of your care in taking and recording bearings, the accuracy of your deviation table, and a multitude of other factors. The smaller the triangle, the better. With practice, and good observing conditions, you should be able routinely to get triangles so small that they can almost be disregarded and considered to be one point.

Taking visual bearings on landmarks is only one of many possible ways of obtaining LOPs. You are encouraged to continue your study of piloting and investigate the many other techniques available to you.

Speed-Time-Distance

When you set a course, it is important to know how long it will take to reach your destination.

Unfortunately, measuring speed over the water is never very simple. Speedometers for small boats exist, but they are not especially accurate. The mechanisms used in most such instruments are not sensitive at slow speeds, but in any case, they only measure speed through the water.

Fig. 6-19 Tachometer

What is really needed is speed over the bottom. The readings you get from any speed instrument will be influenced by currents, as well as any intrinsic inaccuracy in the instrument. Part of the "art" of piloting is involved in estimating the effects of those currents and other factors and judging the true speed over the bottom.

Most inboard engines have tachometers, instruments that indicate the speed of the engine. A good indicator of a boat's speed is the reading of the tachometer, coupled with a suitable conversion table or chart relating that engine speed to speed through the water.

Speed Trial Tabulation Over Measured Mile

RPM	N-S		S-N		Average Speed	Current
	Time	Speed	Time	Speed		
800	6m 47s	8.85	8m 32s	7.03	7.94	.91
1000	5m 46s	10.41	7m 31s	7.98	9.18	1.23
1200	5m 01s	11.96	6m 46s	8.87	10.41	1.55
1400	4m 28s	13.43	6m 13s	9.65	11.54	1.89
1600	4m 03s	14.82	5m 47s	10.38	12.6	2.22
1800	3m 42s	16.22	5m 01s	11.96	14.09	2.13
2000	3m 31s	17.06	4m 53s	12.29	14.67	2.39
2200	3m 24s	17.64	4m 41s	12.81	15.22	2.42

Fig. 6-20 Speed Table.

It is necessary to construct a speed curve for your boat, in which you relate the engine speed (as indicated by the tachometer) to your measured speed between known points. Use a stopwatch to time the trip between buoys at various engine speeds.

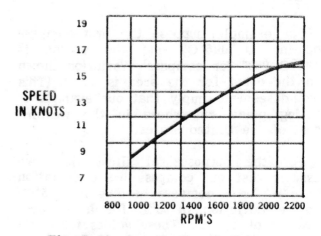

Fig. 6-21 Sample Speed Curve.

Run the course in both directions to cancel out the effects of any current that may be present. Calculate the speed by the formula S(peed) = 60 x D(istance) / T(ime), in minutes. Calculate the speed for each run, then average the runs made at the same engine speed but in different directions together to get the speed table entry for that engine speed. Do not make the mistake of averaging times to compute the speed.

Fig. 6-22 Measuring Distance.

Distance on a Mercator chart is usually measured on the latitude scale. This is the scale that appears on the right and left edges of the chart. One nautical mile, remember, equals one minute (1') of latitude.

One important characteristic of a Mercator projection is that the size of areas is distorted. Because of this distortion, one minute of latitude will appear to get larger as you move away from the equator. On large-scale charts (1:80,000 or larger) this distortion makes very little practical difference, although it is measurable. However, with smaller-scale charts, the difference in the length of one minute of latitude from the top to the bottom of the chart is significant. For that reason, you should always choose latitude markings near the level (mid-latitude) of the line being measured as your scale of distance.

Plotting

In almost any piloting situation, the answers to be determined concern either establishing a course line or determining position. The determination of position may be the whole problem, but most of the time position is only a point necessary to the fixing of a course line to another destination.

Time

Time is noted on a chart using the 24-hour system, and it is always written in four digits. (Courses, remember, are always written in three digits.) The first two digits tell the hours since the previous midnight, and the last two digits tell the minutes. No punctuation marks are used.

Midnight is written 2400, 9:45 a.m. is written 0945, while 9:45 p.m. is written 2145. Mariners never use the word "hours" following a time designation.

Plotting Symbols

There are several terms and symbols that are used in piloting. You need to be completely familiar with them.

A line of position (LOP) is a line passing through a known position along which a vessel is presumed to be located. LOP's may be obtained from bearings on a charted object (as in our example, above), from a measured distance from a charted object, from the depth of the water, two charted objects in line, or any of several other means.

An LOP is labeled with the time (in 24 hour notation) and the true bearing (in degrees). Bearings are always noted as directions from the vessel toward the object.

A true bearing at 9:30 a.m. on an object directly east of the vessel would be recorded as:

$$\frac{0930}{090}$$

If the LOP is derived from a range (two charted objects in a line), only the time is noted.

A fix is an accurate position obtained by the crossing of two or more LOP's, or by passing close aboard a charted object (such as a lighthouse or harbor entrance). It is indicated by a circle around the position dot (the <u>dot</u> marks the <u>exact</u> position on the chart) with the time parallel to the top or bottom margins of the chart.

A <u>DR position</u> is a position determined by applying the vessel's course and speed, and all changes in either, to the last known accurate position.

A DR position is marked with the time and a half circle around the position dot. The time is written at an angle to the charted course line.

An <u>estimated position</u> (EP) is the most probable position for a vessel, given all considerations that apply. It is often a DR position modified by additional information, such as currents and wind drift ("leeway").

An estimated position is marked with the time and a square around the position dot.

The Dead Reckoning Plot

If a cruise is to be any appreciable length (an hour or more), it is customary practice to set up a DR plot. This is a scale drawing on the chart of the course we intend to follow, marked with hourly estimates of our position. These positions are based solely on the courses (directions) sailed and the speed, based on the speed (RPM) curve, log, or speedometer.

It is helpful if there are landmarks along the course from which good LOP's can be obtained. Again, it is accepted practice to plot fixes whenever possible and compare those known positions with the DR position for the same time. This gives valuable information about leeway that can then be applied to refine our EP as we move along the track.

Note that in nearly every case, we begin a new DR plot with every fix.

Plotting DR Position

Outside most harbors there is a buoy or other landmark that marks the entrance to the harbor, and from which we take departure, the final fix anchoring one end of a DR plot. There will be another such marker at our destination.

If there are no obstructions between these two marks, we can simply draw a straight line between them, then sail it as best we can. More often, however, it will be necessary to travel an irregular course to avoid hazards such as intervening land, shallows, etc. If possible, select at each turning point some suitable landmark, such as another buoy, etc.

Using your plotting tools, draw in your intended course as a series of straight lines between the turning points. Measure and label the course to follow on each leg. Remember to plot only true directions. You will want to convert them to <u>magnetic</u> and <u>compass</u> courses for your own use later, and when you do so, they should be correctly labeled.

When you label your course, write the course numbers along the line, <u>above</u> the line and precede the number with the letter "C," for <u>course</u>. The fact that it is a three-digit number and <u>above</u> the line tells you immediately that it is a course, not a bearing.

Follow the numbers with "M" (for "magnetic"), or "C" (for "compass"). We don't have to label the line with a "T" for <u>true</u>, since all normal directions on a chart are <u>true</u>, and the additional label would be redundant.

Your compass course line, then, might look like this:

C047C

Make all measurements and calculations as carefully as possible. In piloting as in school, neatness and accuracy count.

Now use your dividers and the latitude scale to measure the lengths of the course legs. Measure carefully to the nearest 1/10 of a nautical mile.

Finally, estimate the speed that you intend to use on each leg. Write the number below the course line, preceded by a notation "S."

Calculate the amount of time that should be required to get from your departure to your first turning point at your projected speed. Use the formula T(ime) = 60 x D(istance) / S(peed), where time is measured in minutes, distance in nautical miles, and speed is measured in knots, or nautical miles per hour. (Never say "knots per hour." It is a sure sign of a person who does not know the first thing about piloting.)

(If you are operating on the Great Lakes, the rivers, or on other bodies of water where charted distances are in statute miles the speed will be noted in miles per hour. This is perfectly acceptable as long as units are not mixed.)

After you have calculated the time that should elapse between your departure and your arrival at the first turning point, add it to the departure time and note the expected time of arrival (ETA) at the turning point. This is now a DR position, so it should be marked with a dot and a half-circle and labeled with the time.

If the trip to the first turn will include the start of a new hour on the clock, calculate where you should be at that time and plot that position on your course line.

To do this, you must alter your Time-Speed-Distance calculations. You now must calculate the distance you will travel in a given time, so the formula becomes D= S x T/60.

Thus, if you depart at 0930 and you do not expect to reach your first turning point until 1015, you must calculate how far down your track you should be 30 minutes after you depart. At a speed of 6 knots, traveling for 30 minutes you should cover D = 6 x 30/60 = 3 nautical miles. Measure off 3 miles (3 minutes of latitude) along the track from the departure point and mark it with a dot and half-circle and the time (1000) at an angle to the course line.

In addition to the course and speed changes and the whole hours, you should compute a DR position whenever you obtain a fix or calculate an EP. In the end, you should have a plot on your chart that resembles Fig. 6-23.

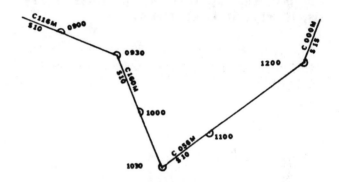

Fig. 6-23 Typical Plot.

If the channel is narrow, or the conditions particularly hazardous, you should plan on more frequent DR positions and fixes. Large ships moving into and out of harbors take a constant series of fixes to be sure of their position. You in a small boat cannot do that, but you also have more maneuverability, so you should adjust your practice accordingly.

Summary

As we noted above, the navigation of the average small boat can appear to be a "seat-of-the-pants" procedure. Having mastered the basic techniques described in this chapter, however, you will be in a much better position to get where you want to go or figure out where you are, provided you practice what you have learned and hone your skills.

Even Sir Francis Chichester, arguably the greatest small boat navigator of modern times, felt the need to practice his piloting techniques if he did not actually use them for a few days at a stretch.

Another important concept is that of a "buddy system." Whenever you move into unfamiliar waters, it is always advisable to travel with a companion vessel piloted by someone who is familiar with the area. Not only will you feel more comfortable until you, too, learn the area, but you will probably have more fun in the process, and that, in the final analysis, is what it is all about.

Chapter 7

Marine Engines

Introduction

In past times, "power boat" meant steam or naphtha engines, or even electric motors. Today, however, the most common source of power in boats by far is some sort of internal combustion engine, either gasoline or diesel.

Engines may be either INBOARD, with the engine itself installed inside the hull, or OUTBOARD, with the engine somehow installed outside the hull usually mounted on the transom. We have already discussed (Chapter 2) the various types of drive train that transmit the power of the engine to the propeller to drive the boat forward.

In this chapter we shall concentrate on the engine itself, its care and routine maintenance, and some elementary trouble-shooting techniques for those times when things don't work as they should.

Inboard Engines

The general category of inboard-mounted engines includes both traditional "straight" inboards and inboard/outboard (I/O) engines. While they differ in the way they transmit power and steer, the engines themselves are identical.

Fig. 7-1   Outboard Motors Are a Popular Form of Power For Small Boats.

Fig. 7-2   Most Inboard-Mounted Engines Are Automobile Engines Modified for Marine Use.

Some engines are designed from the very beginning for marine use, but most marine engines in use today are derived from automotive and industrial engines.

Very Large numbers of automotive engines are built each year. Because of mass production, each engine can be relatively inexpensive, and parts are generally available. Repair services are also readily available.

Perhaps the most basic distinction between types of engine is in the choice of fuel. Most burn gasoline, while a smaller number use diesel fuel.

Relative Merits of Gasoline and Diesel

Gasoline has the advantage of being widely available at a reasonable cost. It provides a good amount of energy in a very condensed (compact) form at reasonable weight.

On the other hand, gasoline has some hazards associated with it. The property of forming an explosive mixture with air, the very thing that makes it useful as a fuel, also makes it dangerous to handle, especially within the confines of a boat's hull. Any maintenance work on marine engines that can cause any leak of gasoline, even the smallest quantities, must be done very carefully.

Diesel fuel is much safer than gasoline to handle, since it is far less flammable than gasoline.

Diesel engines are most expensive to purchase and are heavier than equivalent gasoline engines. The initial cost can be offset by savings in maintenance, however. Diesel engines have a well-deserved reputation for reliability and long-term economy of operation.

Unfortunately, recreational boaters rarely use an engine enough to get the benefit of a diesel's longevity. It is up to the purchaser to decide if the safety edge and greater reliability provided by a diesel engine is worth the weight expense.

Some may choose gasoline engines simply because they are more familiar with them.

The following descriptions of engine workings are stated in terms of four-stroke gasoline engines. Many of the same principles apply to diesel and two-stroke engines, both of which are described later in this section.

Gasoline Engines

Virtually all inboard gasoline engines derive power from the burning of an air-fuel mixture inside a closed cylinder. (There are engines that burn fuel within a non-cylindrical chamber to drive a rotor. These are seldom used in boats, and we will not discuss them here.)

The basic mechanism of an internal combustion engine is the cylinder and piston. The cylinder is closed on one end and the other end is plugged by a movable piston, which is connected to a crankshaft. As the crankshaft turns, its

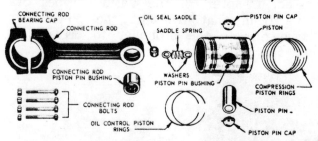

Fig. 7-3 **The Piston is the Basic Element of an Internal Combustion Engine.**

rotary motion is converted into an in-and-out motion of the piston inside the cylinder. An engine can have one or more cylinders, all with their pistons connected to a common crankshaft. The actions inside a single cylinder are repeated in turn in all of the other cylinders.

The Four-Stroke Engine

Most inboard engines are "four-stroke" engines. That is to say, the working cycle involves four strokes of the piston.

The first stroke begins with the piston pushed as far inside the cylinder as it will go, leaving a very small space within the cylinder. As the piston begins to move outward a valve in the closed end of the cylinder opens and a fuel-air mixture from the carburetor (see below) is allowed to fill the expanding space on the cylinder, following the piston.

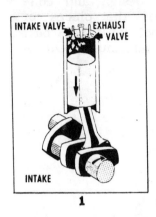

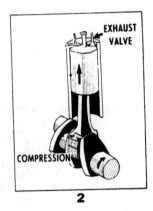

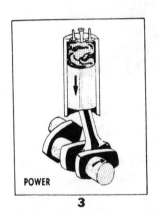

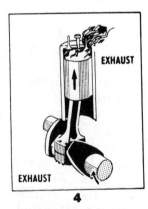

Fig. 7-4 The Four Stroke Gasoline Engine.

As the piston reaches the farthest point of its travel the continuing rotation of the crankshaft (aided by the momentum built up by a flywheel connected to the crankshaft) reverses the movement of the piston, and it begins to move inward once

again. As the piston begins its second, inward stroke, the valve in the end of the cylinder closes and shuts off the flow of the fuel-air mixture.

As the piston continues to move inward, forcing the space inside the cylinder smaller and smaller, the trapped fuel-air mixture is compressed more and more. Finally, at the end of this second stroke when the fuel-air mixture is compressed as much as it can be, a spark plug in the end of the cylinder fires, igniting the mixture. This explosion marks the beginning of the third, or power, stroke.

The hot expanding gases from the explosion of the fuel-air mixture force the piston outward. The energy released on this stroke drives the crankshaft driving the other cylinders (if any) of the engine and whatever other devices are connected to it, including the propeller.

The fourth and final stroke begins with the piston once again reversing its direction of travel and beginning to move back inward. At the beginning of this fourth, or exhaust, stroke, another valve opens in the end of the cylinder, allowing the spent gases to be exhausted from the cylinder, clearing the stage for the cycle to repeat with the drawing in of a fresh charge of fuel and air.

Induction System

The fuel-air mixture is created by the carburetor, and is piped to the intake valves through the intake manifold. Fuel is pumped to the carburetor by a fuel pump, driven by power taken from the engine itself.

The carburetor is a delicate and complicated piece of equipment, but is essentially a continuous atomizer that sprays gasoline into an air stream where it is converted to a vapor. The proportion of gasoline vapor in the air is critical. Too much ("too rich") or too little ("too lean") and the engine will not run. Too, the ideal proportions

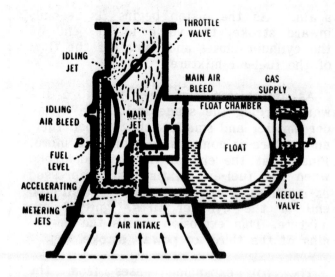

THROTTLE VALVE

IDLING JET

MAIN AIR BLEED

GAS SUPPLY

IDLING AIR BLEED

MAIN JET

FLOAT CHAMBER

FLOAT

FUEL LEVEL

P

ACCELERATING WELL

METERING JETS

AIR INTAKE

NEEDLE VALVE

P

Fig. 7-5 The Carburetor is an Atomizer That Creates a Measured Amount of Fuel Vapor On Demand.

are not the same at all engine speeds. A very simple idea (the atomizer) can become complicated as all of these subtle adjustments are engineered in to a real carburetor. You may not wish to attempt carburetor overhauls or adjustments at first without expert guidance, but an understanding of the principles involved can still be enormously helpful in solving problems.

Flame Arrester

Sitting atop the carburetor is a device that resembles an automotive air cleaner, but is not. It is a flame arrester, an important piece of safety equipment.

A "backfire" is a small explosion through the carburetor back into the engine space. If there are gasoline vapors in the bilge or engine space, they can be ignited by a backfire and explode.

(A backfire usually occurs when the air-fuel mixture in a cylinder ignites prematurely while the intake valve is still open. This, in turn, generally indicates carbon buildup in the cylinder or ignition mistiming.)

The flame arrester has thin metal fins or screens that cool the hot gases from the backfire to the point that they will not ignite stray gasoline vapors.

It is important that the flame arrester be in place, tight, clean and undamaged. The flame arrester is so important that the Coast Guard has established stringent standards for its design and construction. It is one of the pieces of equipment on a boat that must be Coast Guard approved and that must bear a proper approval number.

Backfire Flame Arrester

Fig. 7-6 A Flame Arrester Can Prevent An Accidental Explosion.

The paragraphs above describe the operation of traditional automotive-type gasoline engines most commonly found in inboard and inboard/outboard installations on boats. There are two important variations, both having to do with the way that the fuel-air mixture is introduced into the engine, that deserve some separate attention.

Fuel Injection

The first of these is FUEL INJECTION. In some gasoline engines a carburetor is not used to create the fuel-air mixture. The induction system carries only air, and the fuel is injected (sprayed) under pressure into the cylinder at the precise moment it is needed for most efficient combustion.

Fuel injection systems can get higher performance out of a given size of engine than carbureted systems, and can be more fuel-efficient. But fuel injector pumps are quite complicated, and can be delicate things, especially sensitive to dirt and water in the fuel.

Supercharging

The second variation is the use of SUPERCHARGING. Some engines, especially high-output engines, use air compressors or pumps to force air into the induction system under pressure. The more fuel-and-air mixture that can be forced into a cylinder on a given power cycle, the greater the power output of the engine.

Superchargers draw power from the engine, either by a belt drive or a crank attached to the crankshaft, or through a turbine powered by exhaust gas (in which case they are generally called turbochargers). In either case, they consume a portion of the power they help generate, but the net increase in engine output is significant.

Nothing is entirely free of cost, however, and superchargers, like fuel injection, extracts a cost in increased engine complexity, cost, and ultimately, wear. (There are only so many horsepower-hours in an engine. The faster you take them out, the faster the engine wears out and has to be rebuilt or replaced.)

This is the basic functioning of a four-stroke gasoline engine. In order for it to do these things, however, it must have the aid of a number of other systems.

Supporting Functions and Equipment

Starter

The first motion of the crankshaft and piston that starts the engine running is provided by a starter motor. The starter motor is usually electric, although it can be powered by compressed air or even by hand. However it is powered, the initial starting turns are applied to the flywheel, and if an electrical or air-powered motor is used, it is connected through a device that immediately disconnects the starter motor from the flywheel once the engine has started running under its own power.

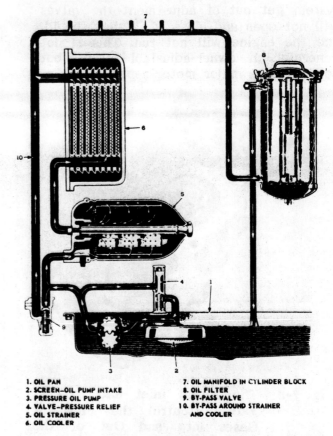

Fig. 7-7   The Lubrication System of an Inboard Engine

1. OIL PAN
2. SCREEN—OIL PUMP INTAKE
3. PRESSURE OIL PUMP
4. VALVE—PRESSURE RELIEF
5. OIL STRAINER
6. OIL COOLER
7. OIL MANIFOLD IN CYLINDER BLOCK
8. OIL FILTER
9. BY-PASS VALVE
10. BY-PASS AROUND STRAINER AND COOLER

Lubrication

Oil for lubricating moving parts in a four-cycle engine is held in a sump, or well, inside the engine and is distributed to wear points through oil channels and by being splashed about inside the engine by the movement of the crankshaft and other rotating parts.

Oil also serves to help cool the engine by distributing heat more uniformly.

Camshaft and Valves

The valves (intake, for the fuel-air mixture; exhaust, for the spent exhaust gases) are operated by a rotating camshaft, which controls the timing of the opening and closing of the valves. The camshaft itself is driven by the crankshaft through gears or a chain-and-sprocket or belt-and-sprocket mechanism (the "timing chain"). Should this drive system get out of adjustment the valves will not open and close when they should, and the engine will not run. This is not generally an owner-adjustable item, but constitutes a major motor repair.

Fig. 7-8   The Round Inlet and Exhaust Valves Control the Flow of Gases Into and Out of the Cylinders.

Electrical System

Several systems of a four-cycle gasoline engine are electrical. The motor that starts the rotation of the crankshaft before the first power stroke is usually electric. The spark that ignites the fuel-air mixture to start the power stroke is created from high-voltage electricity, timed to occur at exactly the right instant in the cycle by the distributor.

Electrical power for these and other functions on a boat (lights, radios, etc.) is produced by a generator or alternator,

driven by power drawn from the engine, usually by a belt-and-pulley arrangement. There are differences between the ways alternators and generators produce electrical power, but their purpose is the same.

Also included with the electrical system is a battery to store electricity for use during periods when the engine is not running.

Battery

The battery in a boat can be the source of considerable hard-to-locate trouble, and deserves special attention and care. The terminals must be kept tight and free of corrosion. Loose terminals can cause a battery to fail to charge properly, and can cause loss of energy just when it is most needed to start a balky engine. In the worst case, they can cause sparking that can trigger an explosion if there happen to be gasoline vapors in the bilge or engine compartment.

The battery should be kept charged, especially during long periods of disuse, even if it means removing the battery from the boat and connecting it to a suitable battery charger.

Fig. 7-9   Test the Condition of Each Cell of the Battery With a Hydrometer Regularly.

Make certain the electrolyte is at the proper level. Engine heat or overcharging can result in loss of electrolyte, which reduces battery capacity and can cause outright failure.

Always bear in mind that a storage battery is a complex chemical reactor. It is filled with a corrosive acid, and when it charges the chemical reactions that take place within it release considerable quantities of hydrogen gas. Hydrogen is very explosive when mixed with air, and you should always take special precautions to prevent gas buildup and sparks.

Short circuits across a battery can cause extremely rapid internal heating, even to the point of boiling the acid and exploding the battery case. Many injuries have been caused by battery explosions during charging operations, "jumping" dead batteries, or by accidental short circuits produced by tools dropped across terminals, etc.

Batteries with terminals on the side can pose special problems, especially if they are not properly secured and/or covered. Batteries that are free to move about inside the hull, or that are located where portable gasoline tanks can touch the contacts, can cause fires or explosions, with potentially tragic results. At the very least, an unsecured battery can do considerable damage as it slides about inside the hull, and can conceivably batter a hole in the hull itself.

Keep battery terminals covered against accidental short circuits, and if it is necessary to work on a battery, wear eye protection.

Finally, batteries are heavy, and are usually located in awkward places. Take care when you move or lift batteries, to avoid injuries to yourself or to others.

Ignition System

Gasoline engines need an electric spark to ignite the fuel-air mixture in the cylinder. High voltage is needed to make a suitable spark, but boat electrical systems normally supply only low voltages (6-32 volts, direct current). Special equipment is needed to produce the necessary high voltages.

In a battery ignition system, a coil, a switch ("breaker points") and a condenser are used to convert low voltage DC into brief bursts of very high voltage, as much as 60,000 volts.

In other systems (commonly small engines, such as small outboards) a magneto is used to produce high voltage pulses directly. A magneto moves a permanent magnet rapidly past a coil of wire, inducing (generating) a brief, high voltage.

However it is generated, the high voltage in an ignition system can be hazardous. If you come in contact with spark current and avoid injury from the current itself, you could still be injured in a fall or hard contact with sharp objects from the startle reaction.

Cooling System

Much of the heat energy released inside the engine is converted into motion, which is, of course, the primary function of the engine. Most of the heat, however, is excess, or waste heat, and is often concentrated in places where it can do a great deal of harm. This waste heat must be dissipated and removed from the engine before it causes irreparable damage.

In most marine engines the cylinders and other high-heat areas are jacketed by water channels. The water in these channels carries the excess heat away to a heat exchanger of some sort where it can be dissipated safely. In most automobile engines this is a closed system, and includes a radiator that dumps the excess heat to the air. In boats operated in fresh water, cool water can be drawn in and exhausted to the environment after one pass through the engine, carrying the waste heat with it.

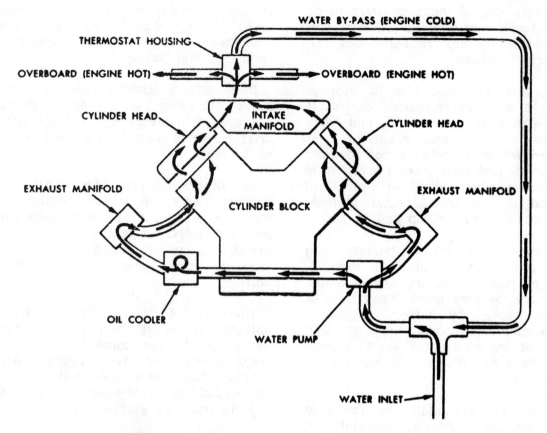

Fig. 7-10 The Inboard Cooling System

Water intakes for the engine, transmission and other equipment (generators, etc.) are potential weak points in the hull, subject to leaks and failure. They should be fitted with shutoff valves, they should be inspected regularly, and plugs should be kept readily available for emergency use.

It is not desirable to have salt water inside the engine where it can cause corrosion or block passageways. A closed cooling system similar to that found in automobiles is commonly used in salt water operations, except that the waste heat is dumped through the "radiator" (heat exchanger), often a "keel cooler," and into the water, not air. The closed cooling system is filled with fresh water or a water-antifreeze mixture.

The coolant is circulated through the engine by a water pump, usually driven from the same belt-and-pulley arrange-

ment that drives the generator or alternator. In some engines a two-stage pump may be used, or a separate pump may be provided to "prime" the main pump and/or to pump cooling water into the exhaust system.

Some small engines (e.g. lawn mower, chain saw, small outboards) and larger engines where weight is a special problem (e.g. airplane engines) do not use liquid to remove waste heat. Instead, they use air. Since air-cooled motors depend so on the free flow of air around them, it is especially important that they be kept free of dirt and grease, and that nothing be done to interfere with or change the pattern of air flow around the engine.

Two-Stroke Engines

Most outboard engines use a different plan, reducing the number of strokes in each power cycle to two. Every down-

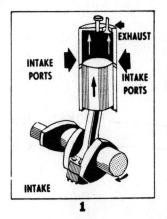

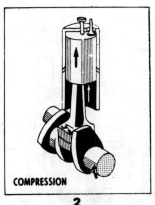

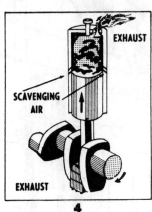

Fig. 7-11 The Two-Stroke Engine.

As the piston moves into the cylinder a partial vacuum is created in the crankcase. The fuel-air mixture from the carburetor moves into the crankcase to fill that vacuum. At the same time, the charge of fuel and air from the previous induction cycle is being compressed in the cylinder, then ignited by the spark plug. As the piston is forced out of the cylinder by the expanding gases, the mixture now trapped in the crankcase is compressed (since the one-way valve will not allow it to escape).

As the piston nears the outer-most limits of its travel, its skirt clears ports in the cylinder wall that allow the spent gases to be exhausted and the new charge, still compressed from the just-completed outward stroke of the piston, to flow into the cylinder.

The piston now begins an inward stroke once again, driven by the momentum of the flywheel, and begins the cycle all over.

ward stroke is a power stroke, but some efficiency is lost on the intake/exhaust cycle.

The two-stroke gasoline engine has two working chambers. One is the cylinder, similar to that described above; that is the upper chamber. The crankcase below the piston is the lower chamber. It acts as a pump, delivering the fuel-air mixture from the carburetor to the upper chamber, the cylinder.

The lower chamber is connected directly to the induction system through a one-way spring or reed valve that allows the fuel-air mixture to be drawn into the chamber, but not to be pushed back.

If the two stroke engine has more that one cylinder, the crankcases are sealed from one another, each working with its own cylinder, or upper chamber.

Two-stroke gasoline engines do not have oil sumps for lubricant. Instead, lubricating oil is added directly to the fuel. It is drawn into the cylinder through the crankcase, where some of the oil "settles out" on moving parts and lubricates them.

It is important that oil be added to the fuel in the proper proportions, according to the manufacturer's recommendations. Too much oil fouls sparkplugs; too little results in excessive wear. On the other hand, the lubricant in the crankcase is always being replaced with fresh, unused oil. As a result, with reasonable care, two-stroke motors can have very long life expectancies.

Outboard Engines

We began our discussion of marine engines with inboard engines, primarily because of their greater familiarity. Now

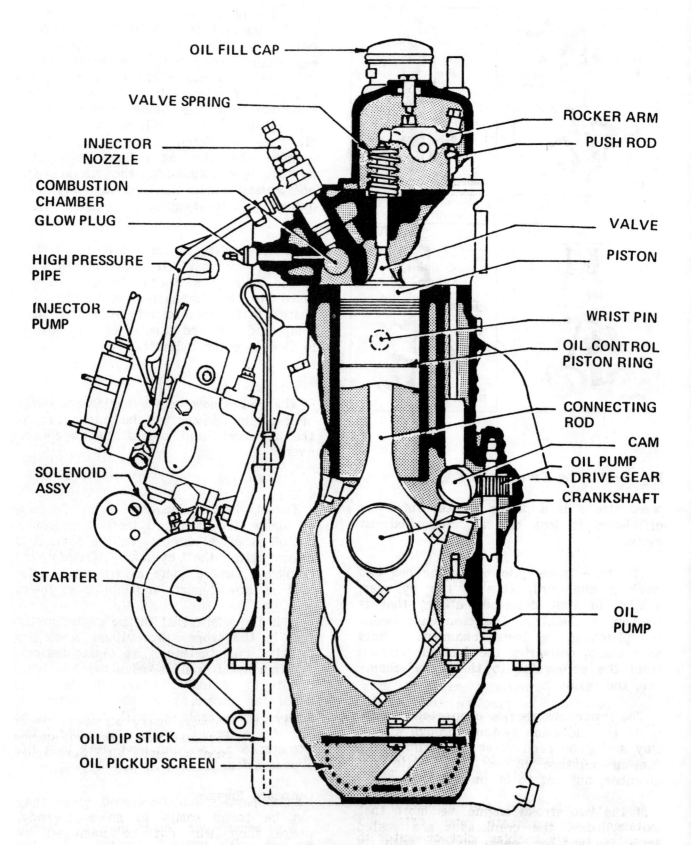

OIL FILL CAP

VALVE SPRING

INJECTOR NOZZLE

COMBUSTION CHAMBER

GLOW PLUG

HIGH PRESSURE PIPE

INJECTOR PUMP

SOLENOID ASSY

STARTER

OIL DIP STICK

OIL PICKUP SCREEN

ROCKER ARM

PUSH ROD

VALVE

PISTON

WRIST PIN

OIL CONTROL PISTON RING

CONNECTING ROD

CAM

OIL PUMP DRIVE GEAR

CRANKSHAFT

OIL PUMP

Fig. 7-12 The Components of the Diesel Engine

let us consider the most common kind of marine engine, the outboard.

In times past the term, "outboard motor," was synonymous with "small." Now, however, outboard motors cover the range from fractional parts of a horse-power to over 300 horsepower. Larger and larger boats are being designed and built to use outboards, sometimes in multiple installations.

The operating principles of outboard motors are identical to those described above. Some outboards are four-stroke gasoline engines, but most are two-stroke gasoline engines.

As described above, outboard engines should have very long life spans, given reasonable maintenance. They are, how-ever, generally mounted in an exposed position on the transom of a boat, and usually used only intermittently, both conditions that make life difficult for engines of any kind, and that make good maintenance practices essential.

Diesel Engines

Diesel engines differ from gasoline engines in one or two significant ways. First, diesel engines are fuel injection engines (see above). Second, there is no external ignition source to trigger the explosion of the fuel-air mixture. Instead, the fuel-air mix is ignited by the heat produced when it is compressed in the cylinder.

So it is that diesel engines lack two systems that potentially cause a great many problems in gasoline engines, the ignition system and the carburetor.

Diesels are subject to other problems, of course, so the trade is not an unmixed blessing. The pumps and nozzles used to inject the fuel into the cylinders, for instance, are delicate and extremely sensitive to air bubbles, dirt or water in the fuel.

General Maintenance

A part of good engine maintenance is keeping a clean engine compartment and bilges. This is relatively easy, since marine engines are not typically exposed to the same dirty environment as engines in automotive, agricultural or industrial applications.

Keeping an engine compartment clean is not just a matter of taste, however, but is a safety consideration. Oily rags pose a fire hazard, and oil in the bilges can lead to environmental pollution that can result in substantial fines and embar-rassment.

Spare Parts and Tools

A careful seaman will be sure to have tools and spare parts to be able to make necessary repairs. In addition to standard hand tools, be sure to carry any special tools that may be needed to work on your boat.

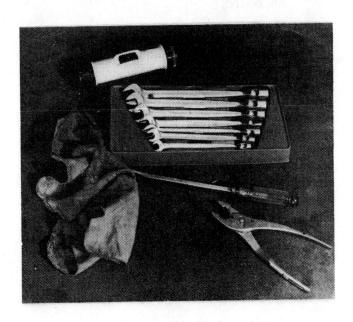

Fig. 7-13 "Always carry all spare parts you may need for emergency repairs and all the tools necessary to install them."

Spare parts should be stored where they can be found easily in an emergency, where they will not be damaged by moisture, etc.

At the minimum, a set of spares should include:

- a propeller;

- any fittings (special nuts, washers, pins, etc.) needed to install it;

- spark plugs;

- ignition breaker points;

- condenser and coil (if used);

- distributor cap and rotor;

- fuel filter elements;

- at least two of every type of fuse used on board;

- spare light bulbs of every type used on board;

- replacement fuel pump;

- belts;

- oil; and

- hydraulic fluid (if used).

A recommended kit of basic tools should include at least the following:

- standard and Phillips screwdrivers (various sizes);

- Allen wrenches;

- 6" or 8" open-end adjustable wrench;

- slip-joint pliers;

- electricians's pliers;

- spark plug wrench;

- hammer;

- utility knife;

- ignition tools;

- feeler gauges;

- hydrometer;

- DC test lamp.

Optional tools that you may find useful in addition to this basic set include:

- open-end and box wrench sets;

- ratchet drive and socket set;

- file;

- electrical test meter.

Outboard Maintenance – Pre-Season

Ignition System

Clean, regap or replace pitted or worn spark plugs. (Routine replacement is a good policy.) Check the battery charge (with a hydrometer). Clean, inspect and tighten battery cables. (Check polarity.) Clean and lubricate starter drive mechanisms.

Lubrication System

Check oil level in lower unit and replenish if necessary. Replace if dirty. Check seals for signs of leaks.

Fuel System

Change or replace fuel filter elements. Check all fuel hoses for cracks or leaks, fuel tanks for corrosion.

General

Check for general cleanliness, signs of weakening of metal parts due to corrosion. Check condition of sacrificial anodes ("zincs"). Check for signs of moisture in inappropriate places.

Outboard Maintenance – Post-Season

Fuel System

Run engine in fresh water. With engine at fast idle, pour clean motor oil into carburetor air intakes until engine smokes heavily, then stop motor. Drain carburetor float chamber, filter bowl. Clean/replace filter elements. Check condition of all gaskets and seals. Empty and clean portable fuel tanks, or top off permanent tanks with fresh fuel.

Ignition System

Remove spark plugs. Push throttle to the "stop" position and rotate the flywheel by hand to pump out any remaining cooling water. Clean and lubricate starter motor, drive assembly. Replace or file and regap worn or pitted breaker points.

Battery

Remove the battery from the boat and store it indoors in a secure, warm area. Check charge monthly and recharge as needed. (Connecting a battery over a long term to a "trickle charger" is NOT recommended.)

Lubrication

Drain the lower unit gear case and refill with fresh lubricant. Follow the manufacturer's recommended procedures carefully.

General

Wipe all metal surfaces with a lightly oiled rag. Remove the propeller and lubricate the propeller shaft. Examine the propeller for damage and have repaired, if necessary.

Inboard Maintenance - Pre-Season

Electrical Systems

Check condition of all electrical circuits. Check light bulb bases (especially those in the navigation lights) for corrosion. Clean or replace, as needed. Check spare bulbs, fuses.

Ignition System

Check condition of breaker points, clean or replace, as needed. (Replace condenser at the same time.) Clean and regap (or replace) spark plugs.

Carburetor

Lubricate carburetor linkages. Check for signs of gum and fuel residue from previous season. Clean and readjust if needed.

Engine Mounts

Check condition of engine mounting brackets, engine bed stringers, etc. Check condition of propeller shaft flange couplings, stuffing boxes, etc.

Flame Arrester

Clean and inspect flame arrester. Check that it fits tightly on the carburetor inlet, and that there are no gaps or visible dirt or damage.

Belts

Check the condition of all drive belts. Replace as needed, and tighten to the manufacturer's recommendations.

Cooling System

Inspect all cooling system hoses carefully. Replace any hoses that appear to be cracked or that feel too hard or too soft. Check for leaks. Turn the water pump by hand to free the impeller, if it is accessible. Check the coolant level in a closed system. Replace all drain plugs in engine manifolds.

Battery

Check the specific gravity with a hydrometer to ensure that it has an adequate charge. Check polarity, then clean terminals and connect and tighten cables. Cover terminals and cable ends with a light coating of grease to retard corrosion.

Lubrication System

Check the oil level. If the oil was not changed at the end of the previous season, drain and replace with fresh oil of the type recommended by the engine manufacturer. Check transmission gear case for proper lubricant level, and perform all other lubrication checks recommended by the manufacturer.

General

REPLACE THE BILGE **DRAIN PLUG** !

Inboard Maintenance - Post-Season

Lubrication System

Allow the engine to warm up, then drain and replace engine oil. Replace the oil filter. Run the engine at fast idle and pour clean motor oil slowly down the carburetor inlet until the engine stalls. Lubricate carburetor linkages, other points, as recommended by the engine manufacturer.

Cooling System

Drain the cooling system, including engine manifolds, exhaust channels. If it is a closed system, refill with an appropriate water/antifreeze mixture. If it is a raw-water (once-through) cooling system, flush thoroughly with fresh water and drain. Loosen water pump drive belt(s).

Ignition System

Remove spark plugs, squirt a teaspoon full of oil in each cylinder, then replace plugs. Tighten them finger-tight only. Lubricate the distributor, generator, etc., as recommended by the manufacturer. Remove the battery and store as recommended for an outboard battery. Loosen generator or alternator belts.

Fuel System

Drain all fuel from the carburetor bowl, filters, and fuel lines. Top off the fuel tanks with fresh fuel.

General

Wipe all exposed metal surfaces with a lightly-oiled rag. Check sacrificial anodes and all underwater metal parts for signs of corrosion.

Routine Checks

Before you leave the dock, before you cast off the mooring lines, check the engine and its systems to make sure everything is working as it should. Check the oil pressure gauge to make certain it is within the manufacturer's recommended limits. Check the engine temperature gauge, if one exists. The engine should be allowed to warm up at least until the temperature gauge shows a reading before getting under way.

Make certain water is flowing through the exhaust system. Most inboard and I/O exhaust systems include parts made of rubber, and a few minutes of operation without cooling water can produce considerable damage, not to mention the risk of fire.

While you are waiting for the engine to warm up, check the following:

- Fuel Level. Never begin a day of cruising without topping off the fuel tank(s). You can never anticipate your fuel needs exactly; don't run out of fuel at sea.

- Belts. Check condition of belts. Replace frayed, broken or glazed belts. Tighten loose belts, but do not overtighten.

- Coolant Level. Check closed cooling systems for proper coolant level.

- Batteries. Check electrolyte level. Top off low cells with distilled water if necessary.

- Ventilation. Operate bilge blower(s) for at least five minutes, then sniff the bilges and engine compartments for fuel vapors.

- Alarm Systems. Check all alarm systems and confirm proper operation.

- Fuel Pump. Check the "sight glass" if present for signs of fuel. If fuel is present in the glass, repair or replace fuel pump before continuing boating activity.

Chapter 8

Marlinspike Seamanship

Introduction

Marlinspike seamanship is the art of handling and working all kinds of fiber, synthetic and wire rope. It includes every variety of knotting, splicing, worming, parceling, serving and fancywork. The term originates from the name of a tapered metal tool, a marlinspike, that is used in working rope, especially for splicing. In this chapter the term marlinspike seamanship is expanded to include not only handling and working rope, but also the composition, use, care and selection of various types of rope for specific uses, and the hardware associated with those uses.

The term "rope" is seldom used on a boat. Mariners generally refer to rope as "line," although in many cases rope is named for its specific use. For example, a stay is a rope (usually wire) that supports a mast; a sheet is a rope that controls a sail; an anchor line of any material is called a rode; and the line securing a dinghy is a painter. There are a few exceptions when a rope is still called a rope, such as bell ropes, boltropes and manropes, among others. However, to call a mariner's mooring lines "ropes" is to brand yourself as a landlubber.

Rope Material

Natural fibers used may be of many types, such as Manila, sisal, hemp, jute, cotton or flax. Of the natural fibers, the best for all around use is Manila. It can be used for mooring lines, anchor lines and running rigging such as sheets to control sails and halyards to raise and lower sails. Manila is noted for its strength and durability with a minimum of stretch. Sisal is less expensive than Manila; so it is sometimes used as a substitute, although it is inferior in many ways. The other natural fibers are used mostly for small lines such as lead lines and flag halyards.

Unfortunately, all common natural fiber lines shrink when they get wet and will rot if stowed wet. They are also weaker, size for size, than rope manufactured from synthetic materials.

Today, most boat owners prefer rope made from synthetic materials that have good strength, both wet and dry, and resist water, mildew and rot. Nylon rope is the strongest, size for size, of the synthetic fiber ropes. It also resists chafe or rubbing very well. Nylon stretches more than other synthetic or natural fiber ropes without permanent damage to its fibers or construction. This feature can make nylon rope dangerous if it breaks under strain. Nylon rope can also shrink up to 10% of its length under some circumstances, but it does not shrink when wet, like Manila. It is best suited for use where stretch is a help. For example, the stretch in a nylon anchor rode will absorb surges that may otherwise pull the anchor loose. Nylon is also suitable for dock lines which do not need to be pulled taut.

Polyester fiber rope, sold under trade names such as Dacron or Terylene, is about 10% weaker than nylon rope, but not nearly as stretchy. It is acid and alkali resistant. Nylon and polyester lines look somewhat alike but polyester is easier and smoother to handle than nylon. Polyester line costs more than nylon. It is used for running rigging such as sheets and halyards which should not stretch under changing conditions. A polyester line under tension chafes easily and must be protected.

Polypropylene rope is the least costly of the common synthetic ropes. Its major advantage is that it floats. However, it deteriorates rapidly from sunlight and, under a load, its hard texture allows it to slip on cleats and to cut a person's hands. Polypropylene rope is most suited for use where its buoyancy is a major factor, such as for water-ski tow ropes. It is suitable as a dinghy painter, the line attached to a dinghy's bow, because it will not sink and foul the propeller of the boat towing the dinghy.

bing holds knots so well, it is frequently used as sail stops, which are ties used to hold a lowered sail to its boom.

How Rope is Made and Measured

In the manufacture of fiber rope, fibers are twisted together in one direction to form yarns, and the yarns are twisted together in the opposite direction to form strands. The strands are then twisted together in the original direction to form the finished rope. The direction in which the strands are twisted is known as the lay of the rope. Rope is described as either right-laid or left-laid. Most laid line used on boats is made of three strands twisted clockwise in a right-hand lay as shown in Fig. 8-1.

Rope may also be braided, with the fibers interwoven individually or in three or four strands. Braided rope is smooth like clothesline and is easier on the hands

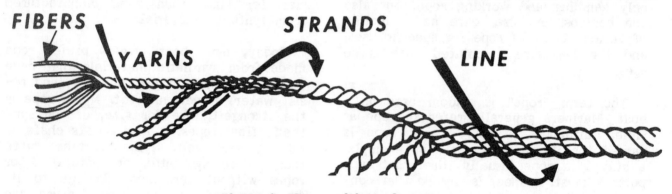

Fig. 8-1 Composition of a Line

Other forms of flexible materials are also used on boats to serve the same purposes as rope. These include Shock cord, a multi-strand rubber line with a synthetic cover that can stretch up to twice its own length. It is used to hold things in place and to prevent halyards from slapping against the mast of a moored boat. Shock cord is often sold with hooks or eyes at each end to facilitate connections. It cannot be spliced. Webbing of woven nylon or polyester is very strong. It can be either single or double (two flat layers with a hollow center). Webbing can be used to tie down a dinghy on a larger boat or hold down a boat on a trailer. Because web-

than laid rope. Small sizes of single braided rope, up to 1/4 inch, are used for sail bag ties, flag halyards and similar special purposes. However, most synthetic braided rope used on boats is double-braid or two-in-one line. It is formed of an outer braided cover and a separate inner braided core as shown in Fig. 8-2. Double-braided rope is stronger than laid rope of the same size, in part because of the friction between the two layers. Single-braided rope is comparable in strength to the same size laid rope, but is more costly to make.

Fiber rope is correctly measured by its circumference (the distance around the rope). However, most marine suppliers measure it by its diameter, especially in smaller sizes. Most sailors also follow this practice. Small diameter fiber rope is known as small stuff and is designated by size according to the number of yarns it contains. Yarns are called threads when referring to small stuff. For example, six-thread small stuff is made up of six yarns of fiber twisted together. Small stuff is frequently used for whipping or wrapping the end of a larger piece of rope to prevent it from fraying.

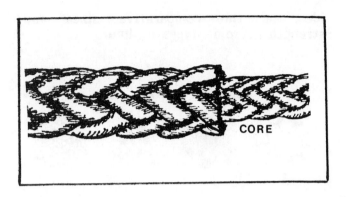

Fig. 8-2 Braided Line.

YACHTING ROPES — WEIGHT AND STRENGTH
COMPARISON

SIZE Diameter	NYLON (lbs) Weight per 100 ft	lbs Breaking Strength	"DACRON" (lbs) Weight per 100 ft	Lbs Breaking Strength	MANILA (lbs) Weight per 100 ft	Lbs Breaking Strength
¼ "	1.7	1,750	2.2	1,300	2.0	600
⅜ "	3.5	3,200	4.5	2,850	4.0	1,350
½ "	6.6	6,600	7.6	4,900	6.1	2,650
⅝ "	10.5	10,200	12.4	7,800	13.1	4,400
¾ "	15.0	13,500	19.3	10,780	16.3	5,400
⅞ "	20.5	18,500	23.5	14,000	22.0	7,700
1"	27.0	24,000	31.3	17,500	26.5	9,000
1⅛ "	34.5	32,000	40.4	23,500	35.2	12,000

Table 8-1

Steel wire is used where maximum strength and minimum stretch are vital, such as for standing or permanent rigging and halyards for hoisting sails. Wire for standing rigging is called 1x19 (spoken as "one by nineteen"), which means that it consists of 19 equal elements wound a-round each other. It is strong, but not particularly flexible. Wire rope for running rigging such as halyards is called 7x19 (seven elements, each composed of 19 individual strands) or 7x7 (seven strands, seven elements each). Running rigging wire rope is slightly weaker than standing rigging of the same diameter, but it is a great deal more flexible. Nearly all wire rope used on boats is made from stainless steel.

Rope Selection
You should purchase each line for its specific purpose. Strength; stretch; resistance to chafing, slipping and sunlight; buoyancy; handling ease and storage conditions are all considerations. Small lines may be suitable for securing small items,

but most people have trouble holding on to a loaded line smaller than about 3/8 inch diameter. You should choose larger-size lines for sheets, halyards and anchor lines for any but the smallest boats.

Other benefits from choosing a larger line include less stretch for an equal load and fewer turns required around a winch. Winches are used to supply a mechanical advantage for tightening running rigging and hauling in anchor lines. Larger lines offer more friction per turn around a winch.

Sailing gloves, which have palms but no fingers, are useful if you have to handle a rough line and have soft hands.

The disadvantage of a larger line is the cost, not only of the line itself, but also of the blocks or pulleys and cleats associated with the larger-line diameter. One way to determine the proper match between a fiber line and a block is to measure the block itself. The diameter of the sheave (pronounced "shiv") or pulley wheel, should be about twice the circumference of the line. The diameter of the block itself, measured along its longest axis, should be about three times the circumference of the line. For example, the circumference of 1/2-inch diameter fiber rope is 1-1/2 inches; therefore, the sheave diameter should be about 3 inches and the block diameter about 4-1/2 inches. If you want to replace an existing line that has been lost, you can reverse the procedure to find the size fiber line you should buy. Table 8-1 will give some idea of the comparative sizes and strength of some types of line.

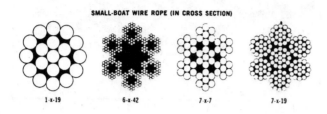

SMALL-BOAT WIRE ROPE (IN CROSS SECTION)

1·x·19   6·x·42   7 x 7   7·x·19

Fig. 8-3 Wire Rope Has an Important Place in the Marine World.

Care of Fiber Line

Your efforts in caring for fiber line aboard your boat will be repaid in greater safety and longer line life. Proper care begins as soon as the rope is purchased. If a coil of new rope is opened without care, it can easily tangle and kink, forming "hockles." This makes handling the rope more difficult and can possibly weaken the fiber. There is a procedure you can follow that will avoid making kinks in the rope. If the rope is coiled, place the coil upright so that the end of the rope inside the hole in the coil is at the bottom of the hole. Take the end up through the hole and draw off the desired quantity of rope. Normally, synthetic rope is received on a reel and should be rolled off, not uncoiled. If these procedures are

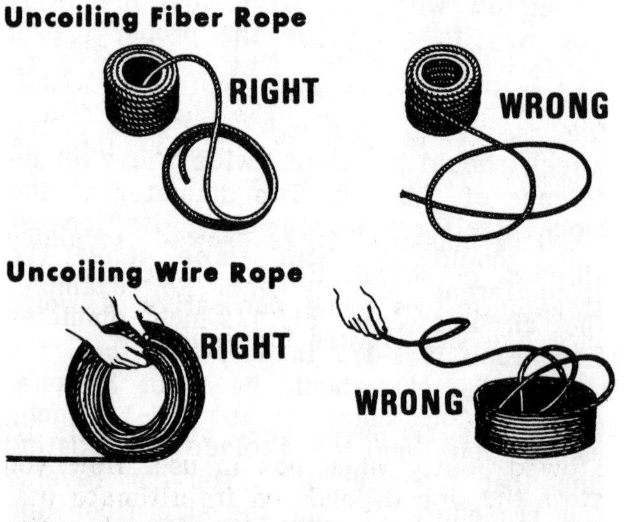

Uncoiling Fiber Rope

RIGHT   WRONG

Uncoiling Wire Rope

RIGHT   WRONG

Fig. 8-4 Uncoiling Rope.

not followed, there will be a kink in the rope for each turn taken off the coil or reel. Kinks should always be taken out of a rope whenever they occur. By putting a strain on the rope, a kink can be made to disappear but the rope will be badly weakened by the breaking down of the fibers at the point where the kink occurred.

For easy, seaman-like handling, each length of rope should be taped temporarily at both ends with marine tape when cut from the original coil or reel and more permanently whipped at the earliest opportunity.Rope that is not being used should be stowed in a dry, well-ventilated place to prevent accumulation of moisture and resultant rot. Lines should be stowed on shelves or gratings off the deck and other material should not be stowed on top of them. Natural fiber lines are most susceptible to damage from moisture. Manila line, for instance, should be washed off with fresh water after salt-water use and thoroughly dried before being stowed. Synthetic fiber lines such as nylon may be stowed when wet, but this practice introduces unpleasant dampness below. All lines should be kept away from exhaust pipes (and other sources of heat) and battery acids.

A fiber line should never be overworked or overstrained. Although it may not show it, the line may be seriously weakened because of breakdown of the fibers. A good way of checking for deterioration of a line is to look at the inside of the line. If there is a noticeable accumulation of grayish, powdery material, the line should be replaced. Another indication is a decrease in the diameter of a weakened line.

Natural fiber lines will contract if they become wet or damp. A line secured at both ends will become taut during rainy weather and may become badly overstrained unless the line is loosened. This is particularly true of mooring lines and flag halyards, which should be slacked off if they become taut because of rain or dampness.

It is good practice to wrap your mooring lines with canvas chafing gear where they pass through chocks. Anchor line, too, should be protected from chafing and rubbing.

To obtain the maximum use of a line and at the same time maintain safety, it is a good idea to turn a line end-for-end periodically. Anchor rodes or boat falls, used to haul small boats out of the water, where one end of the line usually has all the strain put on it, are good examples of lines which should be reversed from time to time.

Never leave the end of a line dangling loose without a whipping to prevent it from unlaying. Unless protected, it will begin to unlay of its own accord. To prevent fraying, a temporary plain whipping can be put on with anything, even a rope yarn or a piece of friction tape.

Whipping and Finishing
Some of the most unattractive and unseamanlike things visible on many boats are the tattered, frayed ends of line with overhand knots tied in the ends to keep further unlaying at bay. The end of every line aboard your boat should be neatly finished off, both to preserve the line itself and to make it easier for the rope to run through tight places like chocks and blocks.

There are several ways to finish the end of a nylon or Dacron line, but the easiest with lines of 3/8" diameter or less

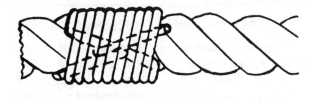

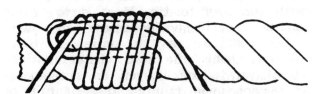

Fig. 8-5 Temporary Whipping

is simply to hold a match to the end until the fibers melt and fuse. Use a freshly-cut end for a neat job.

For a temporary end, simply take four to five tight turns of waterproof tape, or buy one of the many commercial products and treat the end - usually by dipping into a plastic liquid that hardens.

Another temporary whipping using small stuff is shown in Fig. 8-5. For a more permanent and dependable whipping, the method shown in Fig. 8-6 may be used.

Fig. 8-6 Whipping

With Dacron or nylon thread, lay a series of tight turns around the end of the main rope, about half or three-eighths of an inch from the very end of the fibers.

When the whipping turns form a lashing about equal in length to the diameter of the main rope, sew through the strands. Lay the thread in the spiral groove formed by the strands of laid line, or diagonally along braid.

After making three sewed retaining threads, as shown, tie off the end of the thread. Besides being decorative, a whipping like this is very functional.

Making Up Line
All line on board your boat should be stowed neatly when not in use. How you stow the line depends on its ultimate use. There are three methods of making up

line - <u>coiling</u>, <u>faking</u> and <u>flemishing</u>. Line that is to be stowed in a compartment or locker should be coiled and made up, or stopped off with small stuff. Right-laid rope should be coiled right-handed (clockwise) and left-laid rope should be coiled left-handed (counter-clockwise).

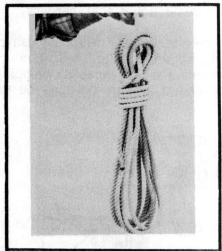

Fig. 8-7 Line Ready for Stowing

Lines that are made up for a fast run-off, such as mooring lines, heaving lines, and running rigging, may be faked down if there is sufficient room. Faking down consists of laying the line in coils either in a figure eight fashion or with each fake lying clear of the next. Faking down leaves the line in the most advantageous position for running out without fouling or kinking.

Some boatmen like to leave their line on the deck when not in use. To give it a neat, ornamental look, it can be flemished. The line is laid on the deck like a spring, each coil circling the one preceding it. Right-laid line should be coiled clockwise, and left-laid line should be coiled counterclockwise. To tighten the coils when you are finished, lay both hands flat on the line at the center and twist in the direction the coils are laid, thus forming a tight mat. It should be noted here that a beautifully flemished line should not be left on a varnished surface for any length of time, especially overnight. The trapped moisture will spoil a good varnished finish.

Knots, Bends and Hitches

A line by itself is of very little use on a boat. Line is used for pulling, holding, lifting and lowering, but it must be fastened to something before it can serve those purposes. The way you fasten a line depends on purpose you have in mind. Among sailors, the landsman's all-inclusive term <u>knot</u> is broken down into more specific terms. The proper use of the term <u>knot</u> on a boat is limited to those alterations to the line that do not include any other object. A line is tied to itself with a knot. The term <u>bend</u> is used to describe methods of fastening one line to another, or to an object while the term <u>hitch</u> describes methods of attaching a line to another object, usually with the implication that it can be undone easily. Regardless of the terminology, all knots depend on friction created by turns in the line. This friction weakens the line. Splices also weaken a line because they depend on friction. Therefore a splice can be considered a variation of a knot when its impact on a rope's strength is tabulated as in Fig. 8-8.

How Knots and Splices reduce strength of rope

		%EFF
	Normal rope	100%
KNOTS	Anchor or Fisherman's bend	76
	Timber hitch	70-65
	Round turn	70-65
	Two half-hitches	70-65
	Bowline	60
	Clove hitch	60
	Sheet bend or Weaver's knot	55
	Square or Reef knot	45
SPLICES	Eye splice (over thimble)	95-90
	Long splice	87
	Short splice	85

Fig. 8-8 Strength of Different Knots·

To meet your needs a good knot (bend, hitch) must display certain characteristics. It must hold well without slipping. It must be used for a practical purpose rather than serve as an ornament. It should be easy to tie. If it is to be a superior knot it should possess these advantages and be easy to untie, as well. However, none of these characteristics are of any value if you do not know which knot, bend or hitch to use and how to tie it.

Before you can learn to tie knots, it is helpful to know some terminology. The <u>standing part</u> is that section of the line between you and the other end of the line; it is the main part of the line. A <u>bight</u> is a U-section that you make in the standing part of the line, and a <u>loop</u> is a small circle in the standing part. It is possible to use these terms to describe scores of knots, bends and hitches, but by far the best way to learn knots is to be shown by someone who knows how to tie them.

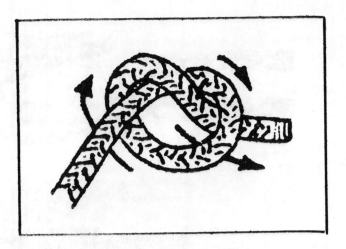

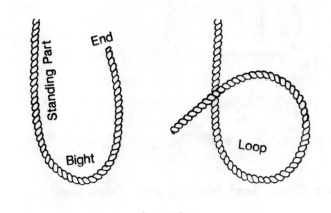

Fig. 8-9 Parts of a Line.

However, it is far better to have a good knowledge of a few commonly used knots for the normal operation of your boat than to have a superficial knowledge of a great number of seldom-used knots. The knots, bends and hitches illustrated here are functional, will serve almost every purpose, and, except as noted, are as easy to untie as they are to tie. Synthetic line is "slick" and some knots can and do pull out unless you leave an extra amount of line projecting and pull the knot tight.

<u>Overhand Knot</u> (Fig. 8-10). This knot is used for temporarily preventing a freshly cut rope from unlaying or unraveling. It can be used as a stopper which prevents a line from running all the way through a block or pulley. It will jam under tension and becomes very difficult to untie. It is tied by passing the bitter end through a loop in the standing part of the line.

Fig 8-10 Overhand Knot

<u>Figure Eight Knot</u> (Fig. 8-11). This knot is used as a stopper when heavy loads may occur. It is far superior to an overhand knot because it can be untied after being jammed. These knots should be used on every line on a sailboat except spinnaker sheets, which should always be free to run in an emergency. The knot is tied by forming a loop and passing the end around the standing part before putting it back through the loop.

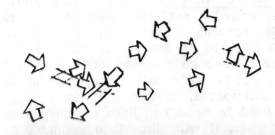

Fig. 8-11 Figure Eight Knot

Fig. 8-12 Square Knot

Fig. 8-13 Sheet Bend or Becket Bend, Double Sheet Bend and Slippery Sheet Bend.

Square Knot (Fig. 8-12). This knot is also called a reef knot because it is used when securing a reefed sail to a boom. It can be used to fasten two lines of equal size or two ends of the same line. However, it is useful only when no great load is anticipated, such as in tying packages. If used to bend two lines of unequal size together, it will slip. When jammed, it is very difficult to untie. If unequal tension is applied, such as a jerk on one side, the knot is apt to turn into two half hitches. It is tied by first passing the left-hand end over and under the right-hand standing part and then returning the same end back over and under the other end. It should look like Fig. 8-12 with both ends on the same side or you have tied a "thief's knot," which will slip under tension.

Sheet Bend or Becket Bend (Fig. 8-13[a]). This bend is used to tie equal-sized or different-sized lines together. It is comparatively easy to untie even after being subjected to heavy strain for long periods of time. When used on a tow line, the ends should be tied down with small stuff for maximum security. It is tied by forming a bight in the bigger line and passing the smaller line's end up from under the bight, around behind the bigger line, and back under itself.

The double sheet bend (Fig. 8-13[b]) offers more security when one line is considerably larger than the other. It is tied by first forming a bight in the bigger line and passing the smaller line's end up from under the bight, then passing the smaller line around behind that bight and under itself twice. The slippery sheet bend (Fig. 8-13[c]) is a variation of the single sheet bend that is easier to untie. (The term "slippery" is applied to any knot when one of the ends is returned as a loop to make the knot easier to untie under tension.)

Clove Hitch (Fig. 8-14). This hitch is used to tie a line to a piling or to tie a fender to a railing. It is easy to adjust

DROP OVER BITT

Fig. 8-14   Clove Hitch

the length of the standing part of a line tied with a clove hitch but the knot will slip if it is not under constant tension. While this feature makes a clove hitch easy to untie when it is not under tension, it can lead to trouble if the hitch comes untied by itself; so a clove hitch is considered a temporary knot. A clove hitch jams under a load; therefore, it is very difficult to untie if the load cannot be relieved. It is tied by looping the end of the line around the object twice in the same direction, once below, and once above, the standing part. The second loop is finished by passing the end between the second loop and the standing part.

A clove hitch can also be tied by making two loops in a row in the standing part, each with the end passing under the standing part. The loop nearest the end is then placed on top of the second loop before placing both loops over the

top of a piling. The clove hitch can be made more secure after it is pulled tight if the end is carried around the standing part and under itself, forming a knot called a half hitch.

Fig. 8-15   Two Half Hitches

Two Half Hitches (Fig. 8-15). This hitch is really a clove hitch tied around the standing part of a line after first forming a loop. It is used to tie a line to a ring, spar, pile, post or a grommet in the corner of an awning. It is a slip knot in the sense that the loop tightens under tension. Two half hitches are easier to untie than a clove hitch under tension and are considered a more permanent knot than a clove hitch. The knot is tied by first passing the end around the object and under the standing part. The end is then passed around the standing part and under itself. This forms the first half hitch. The second hitch is formed in exactly the same way, under the standing part from the same side, around the standing part and back under itself.

Anchor Bend or Fisherman's Bend (Fig. 8-16). This bend is one of the most secure knots for bending a line to an object. It develops considerable internal friction, reduces line chafe and weakens the line less than comparable knots. It can be difficult but not impossible to untie. As its name implies, it is often used to attach a fiber anchor rode to an anchor fitting or a fishing line or leader to the eye of a fishhook. The knot is begun by passing the end around the object twice. The end is then passed around the standing part and through the two loops previously made around the object.

ANCHOR BEND   ANCHOR BOWLINE

Fig. 8-16 Anchor Bend

The end is again passed by the same side of the standing part in the same direction, around the standing part and between the standing part and itself. The end is often tied to the standing part of a completed anchor bend with twine as added insurance that the knot will not work loose.

Rolling Hitch (Fig. 8-17). This hitch is used to tie one line to the middle of another so that it will not slip under strain. It can be used to hold a jib sheet while riding turns are removed from a winch or a block is relocated. When used to form a loop, it is adjustable, sliding easily to increase the loop size and retaining that loop size when tension is applied. It can be used to adjust fender lines and awning tie-downs. It must be tied with the double roll in the direction from which the standing part will be tensioned. The double roll must therefore be toward the inside of a loop for the knot to work. The knot is tied by passing the end around the line once, crossing over the loop and making a second turn with the end again passing the standing part on the same side, then making a third turn around the line on the other side of the standing part. The end is then passed between the standing part and the third turn to form a half hitch.

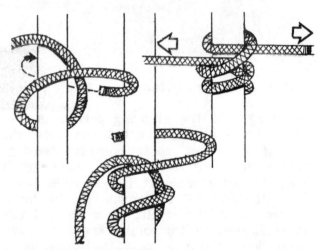

Fig. 8-17 Rolling Hitch

Bowline (Fig. 8-18). This knot is used to form a temporary but fixed size loop at the end of a line. It is often called the "King of Knots" because of its many everyday uses on a boat. Bowlines are easy to untie even after being under a load by pushing against the small bight around the standing part. They are used to tie jib sheets to the clew of the jib, to tie lines to fittings, to tie lines of equal or unequal size together and to attach a rode to an anchor. The knot is

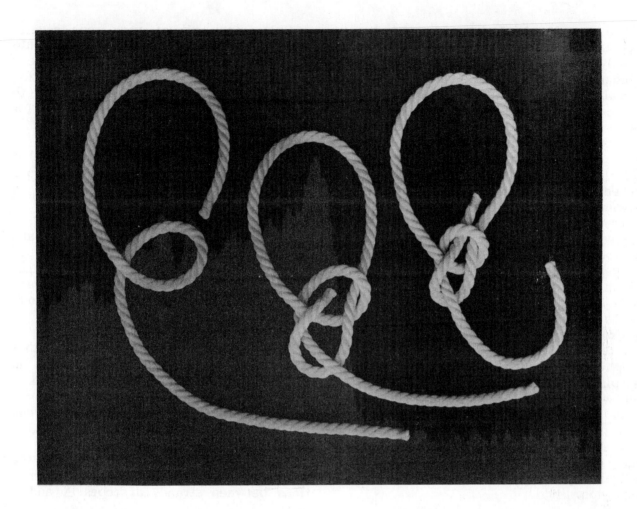

Fig. 8-18 Bowline

begun by forming a loop in the standing part with the end side of the loop on top. The end is then passed up through the loop, around behind the standing part and back down through the loop.

Splices

Splices are used when you want to join two sections of the same size line together permanently. An <u>eye splice</u> is used to form a permanent loop in a line. Either a <u>short splice</u> or a <u>long splice</u> can be used to join two pieces of laid line together (Fig. 8-20). Only a long splice will pass through a block or pulley. A <u>back splice</u> is used to prevent a fiber stranded line from unraveling.

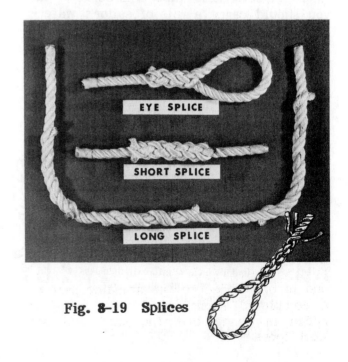

Fig. 8-19 Splices

The average boat owner usually buys docking lines and anchor rode that are already spliced. Sail makers or marine equipment suppliers usually provide sheets or halyards with custom splices. Splicing double braided line requires more time and practice than the average boat owner has to dedicate to such a seldom-needed skill. However the principle of splicing laid line is simple: three strands are tucked over and under so that they interweave with three other strands. If you understand the rudiments of splicing laid line you will be a wiser customer and you will be able to make emergency repairs. Many boating enthusiasts find great pleasure in knowing how to splice and find it an enjoyable off-season pastime. The ability to splice line is usually taken as a sign of a competent seaman.

Splicing Fundamentals. When learning to splice, it's a good idea to equip yourself with a length or two of Manila line about 3/8" in diameter. Manila is stiffer than nylon or Dacron and holds its construction better during the twists and pulls of splicing. As you become more skillful, try the same thing with Dacron and nylon.

You'll also need some waterproof tape - electrician's tape will serve - but you should carry a roll of sailor's waterproof tape in your ditty bag as well. If you're working with new, stiff rope, a fid (a sailor's tool for separating strands of rope similar to a marlinspike, but generally made of wood or plastic) will also be handy. Now you're ready to make a short splice.

Unlay one end of your rope several inches. This means undoing the line into its three component strands. Tape the end of each strand to keep it from untwisting and tape the point at which you want to stop the unlaying. Now do the same for the other end of the rope.

"Marry" the two untwisted ends so that one strand of rope A alternates with one of rope B. Tape one set of strands in place.

Now take one of the loose strands and lead it over the taped neck of the opposite rope. Open a space between strands of the opposite rope and push the strand through as far as it will go - but don't pull it tight just yet.

Now do the same thing with the other two strands, working each one through an adjoining opening and pulling it through.

Pull all three tucked strands tight, one by one.

Make a second set of tucks like the first. Be sure that you keep the alternations between strands of ropes A and B even.

Make a third set of tucks and pull them tight.

Untape the free set of strands and perform the same three-tuck operation with them.

When you're done, cut off the ends of the strands to within about a quarter-inch

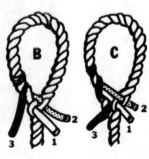

A.—First step is to unlay the end of the rope for a short distance. Form the desired size loop. Take middle strand of unlayed end "1" and tuck through any strand of the "standing" part of the rope.

B.—Take adjacent strand marked "2" in picture. Pass over strand under which "1" is tucked, then pass under adjacent strand of the "standing" part.

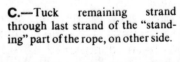

C.—Tuck remaining strand through last strand of the "standing" part of the rope, on other side.

D.—Tuck each strand alternately over and under, working against the lay of the rope. Taper off by halving the yarns on the last two tucks.

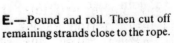
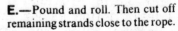

E.—Pound and roll. Then cut off remaining strands close to the rope.

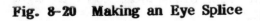

Fig. 8-20 Making an Eye Splice

of the main rope. Roll the completed splice between your palms or under your foot.

With practice, you'll find you can achieve great neatness and speed, but it does take time.

The eye splice is basically the same idea as a short splice, except you're making the tucks back into the standing part of the original rope. Unlay and tape the line as before. Now form the eye to the size you'll want (usually just large enough to be pulled over a cleat one arm at a time) and lay the unlaid end along the standing part with one of the strands arbitrarily chosen to be the first tuck.

Open the strands of the standing part (a fid may be useful here, or use your fingers) and insert the first strand, pulling it through.

Take the next strand to the right of the first, as shown, and insert that under the next strand to the right of the one you tucked the first strand under, pulling it through.

Turn the whole splice over - this is very important - and lead the remaining strand between the only two standing part- strands left. When you have completed the first series of tucks the ends of the strands will be tucked evenly around the standing part, ready to begin the second series of tucks.

Now continue with the next set of tucks by carrying any one of the loose strands over the next strand of the standing part and under the second. Repeat that process for the other strand. After you have completed three or four sets of tucks, you are ready to trim the ends of the strand, tuck them in or seize them (see below), and use your new eye splice.

When you splice artificial fiber line, which has less friction among the strands than does natural fiber line, you should take five full series of tucks instead of

three. This makes a somewhat lumpy-looking splice, but one with maximum strength, which is, of course, the most important thing.

Fig. 8-21 An Eye Splice Should be Sized To Just Fit the Cleat.

Seizing. As you can tell from reading these instructions and looking at the illustrations, this kind of splice can be made only in laid line. To splice braided line, one substitutes core for core and cover for cover. It's not really necessary, however, as one may form a semi-permanent loop by the technique of seizing (binding or lashing) the two parts of the line together.

To do this, you need a sailmaker's palm - a kind of super-thimble - large needle and thread of the same material as the line you are seizing.

Form the loop to the size desired. Now lay a series of tight, even turns of thread, lashing the two parts of the line together.

When the turns of thread have formed a lashing about equal in length to the diameter of the rope being used, sew the thread through the two parts of the line two or three times.

Now make a second series of turns with the thread between the two parts of the main rope. Draw these turns as tight as possible.

Sew through the main part of the rope, tie a figure eight in the end of the thread and cut it off.

Although not quite so neat as a splice, a seizing is very strong and can be unmade. It can also be done with laid line.

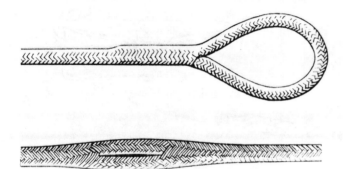

Fig. 8-22 Braided Lines Can Also be Spliced.

"Whipping" can also be used with laid line to finish the ends where a figure 8 knot is too bulky or tape will not hold, or to secure the loose strand ends of a splice. Begin by making a loop of small stuff and placing it alongside the end of the line to be seized. Hold the doubled portion of the loop in place and wrap the remainder tightly around the line. When a length of line approximately equal to its diameter has been wrapped, pull on both loose ends at once to tighten the wraps, then cut off the loose ends.

Securing Lines

There are many special fittings or pieces of hardware that can be used for securing lines on a boat. Typically, sailboats have a variety of special-purpose fittings, power boats have a more basic set of deck hardware.

A shackle, which is a "U" shaped connector with a pin or bolt across the open end, can be used to attach line to many types of equipment, including anchors.

Other than shackles, hardware for securing lines to your boat are attached to its hull or spars. All deck fittings should

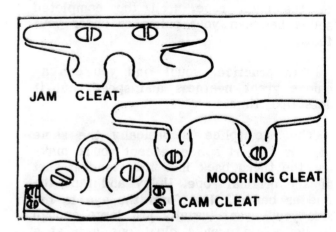

Fig. 8-23 Typical Hardware for Attaching Lines.

be bolted through the deck rather than screwed to it since you are going to rely on this hardware to protect your investment. On all but the smallest boats, the under side of the bolts should go through a backing plate rather than washers to prevent the bolts from pulling through the deck under heavy use. Remember that it is easier to replace a line than to patch a deck after a fitting has been pulled out of it.

A turnbuckle is a threaded fitting that pulls two eyes together. It is used on sailboats to attach the wire rigging or stays that support the mast. It is threaded so that you can put the proper amount of tension on the shroud or stay. After you adjust the tension, you should put cotter pins or ring clips through the holes in the threaded pins in the turnbuckle so that the adjustment will not change.

A horn cleat, which is an anvil-shaped fitting, may be provided for anchor rodes, mooring or docking lines, tow lines, halyards and sheets. Cleats are the most common fittings for lines on small boats.

There are two methods for securing lines to horn cleats. The first is considered as temporary and is used when a boat is underway. In such situations, it may be necessary to remove the line from the cleat in a hurry to prevent a mishap so no hitches are taken. First, take a complete turn around the cleat,

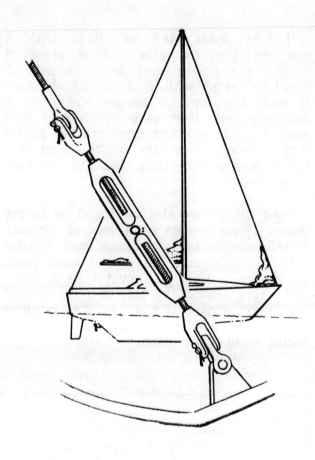

Fig. 8-24 A Turnbuckle.

making sure that the standing end of the line leads to the end of the cleat opposite the direction of pull so that the tension will not jam the turn later. Next, lead the line over the top of the cleat and around the horn or projection to form a figure eight. Make one more figure eight and pull the line tight so that it will not slip.

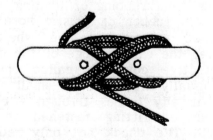

Fig. 8-25 Belaying to a Cleat.

When a line is to be belayed or tied to a horn cleat and your boat is going to be left unattended, the connection needs to be more secure. The best method is to lead the line in one round turn around the base of the cleat and then form at least one figure eight around the horns of the cleat. Finally, secure the line with a half-hitch over one of the cleat's horns. The result is really a clove hitch around the two horns of the cleat. It is important to take a full turn at the beginning, which allows you to undo the hitch while the cleated line is still under a load. One caution - be sure to have the line continue to form a figure eight when the half-hitch is made. Do not make the error of having the last loop come along the side of the cleat instead of crossing over or the knot will not develop as much friction.

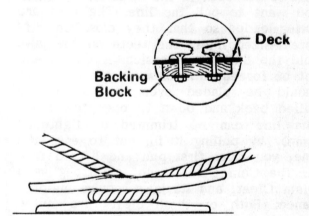

Fig. 8-26 A Jam Cleat

A jam cleat is similar to a standard cleat with one important difference. One of the horns forms a tapered slot into which the line is "jammed." This allows you to both secure and let go of the line more quickly since less than one full turn is required. Jam cleats are usually used on sailboats to secure the sheets or ropes that control the sails, and they are sometimes used to secure the centerboard pendant which controls the position or depth of the centerboard. A jam cleat must be installed so that the tapered slot is in the same direction as the standing part of the line; thus, when the line is first led around the base of the cleat, it will not bind. While oversized horn cleats are suitable for many purposes, a jam cleat must be sized to accommodate a specific line if it is to function properly.

Two other types of quick-action cleats are frequently found on sailboats. One is a Clam Cleat, which is a trademark name for a notched channel made of aluminum or hardened plastic into which a line is dropped. The notches grip the side of the line to hold it in place. To trim or haul in the line, simply pull back on it. To let the line go, or to free it, pull it in slightly while lifting it out of the cleat. A Clam Cleat works only with one specific size line.

The second is a Cam Cleat which has two moving, serrated cam-shaped jaws that rotate open in the direction in which you want to pull the line. The jaws are spring-loaded so that they close on different-sized lines. The teeth on the jaws hold the line under tension. A line should not be forced down between the cams but should be placed over the teeth and pulled back and down to open the cleat. The line can be trimmed or tightened simply by pulling it in; but to ease the line, you must first pull and lift to free it. The Cam Cleat is not as strong as a Clam Cleat, and its jaws require maintenance. Both of these cleats are suited only for small sailboats. They must be installed in the correct direction since they work only one way. They are hard to release when there is a heavy load on the line, the time you may most want to let the line go.

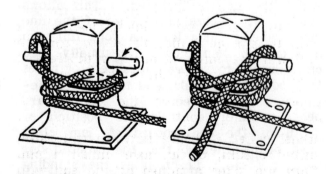

Fig. 8-27 A Sampson Post

Larger boats may be fitted with a sampson post in place of a standard cleat. A sampson post is a column of wood or metal with a pin or bar through it near the top. To secure a line to a sampson post, first take a complete turn around its base, then form several figure eights around the pins of the post and finish with a half-hitch, just like securing to a cleat.

Bow bitts may also be found on larger boats. These consist of a pair of circular metal columns on a common base, usually with a lip around the top of each post. To secure a line, you must take a complete turn around the bitt or post nearest the standing part of the line. The hitch is finished by making a number of figure eights around both bitts.

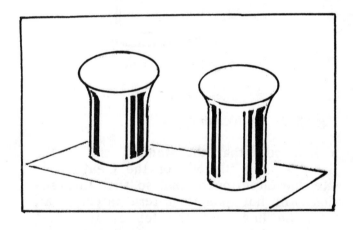

Fig. 8-28 Bow Bitts.

Mooring and towing lines that are attached to cleats undergo considerable movement and wear. In order to protect these lines from rubbing or chafing, canvas, leather, rubber or plastic hose can be fastened around the line where it passes over the rail or edge of the deck. This protective covering, called chafing gear, is usually tied on with small stuff. The line usually passes through a chock or "U" shaped fitting fastened to the boat's hull. The chock not only reduces line chafing, but also prevents hull or rail chafing as well as limiting the direction of the pull on the cleat.

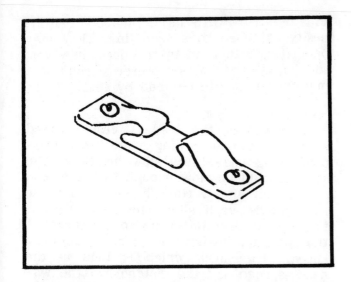

Fig. 8-29   Chocks Protect Both Boat and Line.

Other Hardware Items

A <u>winch</u> provides mechanical assistance in pulling in on a loaded line such as anchor rode, sheet or halyard. It consists of a metal drum fastened to a secure base, and has a series of gears inside. An anchor winch, called a <u>windlass</u>, may be powered by an electric motor, but sailboat winches are turned by means of a winch handle. Winch drums rotate clockwise; so you must wrap the line clockwise around the drum for the winch to work. The number of wraps depends on the load on the line since the winch transmits pull by friction. Four turns are usually the most that will be required for synthetic line, while wire rope may require six. Some winches provide two gearing ranges to provide even more pulling power.

Turning the winch handle on these devices clockwise provides normal power while turning the handle counterclockwise "changes gears" and increases the pulling capability. (The drum always continues in a clockwise direction no matter which way the handle is turned when a two-speed winch is used.)

Sometimes two people are required to operate a winch on a sailboat. One person cranks the winch handle while the second collects the tail end of the line as it feeds off the winch and secures it to a cleat when the line is properly trimmed. A <u>self-tailing winch</u> solves the problem of two people working in a confined space. The top of the drum contains a notched channel which holds the line as it feeds off the winch drum, eliminating the need of a tailer and the necessity of cleating the tail. A "U" shaped fitting guides the line into the channel.

Line is always wrapped around a winch drum from the bottom up. You must be careful to see that the turns do not overlap each other and jam. Such jams are called "riding turns." You should always pull the line in by hand until it has some tension on it even if the turns are put on first. Otherwise the winch drum won't function since there will be no friction between the line and the drum. If you are using a self-tailing winch, you must be careful that the tail does not snag on anything that will pull it out of the channel while you are tightening the line. When you need two hands to operate the winch handle of a self-tailing winch, another person may have to tension the tail to keep it in the channel. Otherwise you must pause occasionally to pull the tail into the channel yourself.

To slack off on a line wound around a self-tailing winch, you must first remove the line from the channel. You then permit the line to slip out two or three inches at a time by simultaneously easing on the tail with one hand and braking the line by squeezing on the loops around the drum with the palm of your other hand. With regular winches, you first uncleat the tail and then ease it out as described. If you wish to completely release the line on the drum rather than ease it out, you merely pull the loops up and out, using the hand which is holding the tail. It is a good idea to check that the tail will not catch on anything before you throw the wraps off the winch drum.

Pulleys are called <u>blocks</u> on a boat. They are constructed by connecting a wheel called a sheave between two sides, called cheeks, on an axle called a pin. They are often attached at one end with a shackle. You should be familiar with the names given to different types of blocks that are used on sailboats. A single block has a single sheave and is used primarily to change the direction of a line. A double block has two sheaves, side by side, and a triple block has three side-by-side sheaves. A becket block has one, two or three sheaves side-by-side and an eye or becket at the end opposite the shackle connection. The becket permits you to tie the end of a line to the block. A snatch block has a hinged cheek so that you can insert the standing part of a line rather than feed it through from the end. A foot block is a single or double block with one side screwed or bolted to the deck of a sailboat. It is used to change the direction of the lines that control the sails. When the same block is screwed or bolted to a spar, it is called a cheek block. Sheaves built into the top of a mast also function as pulleys to change the direction of the halyards, but since the mast itself replaces the cheeks, the pulley is known as a halyard sheave.

Special Lines

Among specific lines on a sail boat are wire stays to hold a mast in place, sheets to control the set of the sails and halyards to raise and lower the sails. Halyards quite frequently are made up of a combination of wire and fiber rope. Sometimes there is a fitting on the top of the mast under which you may hook the eye on the wire section. This fitting allows your sails to remain fully raised even when a strong wind is blowing because the wire section of the halyard will not stretch as much as the fiber halyard section under a heavy load.

A lead line is sometimes used on boats, both sail and power. It is a line which has been marked in such a manner that it can be used to measure the depth of the water. The line is weighted with a "lead." This generally weighs at least five pounds, and can be used for depths of up to 100 feet. Ideally, the line should be braided cotton, 150 to 200 feet long. It can be marked by strips of tape or leather or by knots to indicate the depth.

Plastic strips with large numbers can be easily attached to a lead line. They may be difficult to read in the dark, however, so many mariners prefer traditional markings that can be read by feel.

In practice, the lead is cast forward with an underhand swing while the boat is proceeding under very slow headway. The speed should be slow enough that the lead will reach the bottom by the time the line stands vertically. The vertical distance from the waterline to the hand of the person casting the lead should be known. The mark which is held in the hand is read and the distance to the water is deducted from this figure.

Fig. 8-30 Sounding With a Lead Line.

Some leads have a hollowed-out portion on the bottom of the lead which can be "armed" with a quantity of sticky material (tallow or bedding compound) to collect a small sample of the bottom. In most cases the character of the bottom is shown on your chart. By having a sample of the bottom, you may be able to further identify your position, especially in conditions of reduced visibility when no landmarks are in sight.

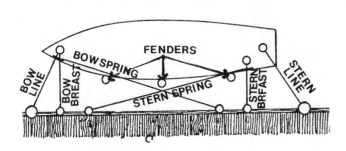

Fig. 8-31 Special Attention is Required When Tying Up in Tidal Waters

Other lines are <u>docking lines</u> or <u>mooring lines</u>. The most often used mooring lines are the bow line and the stern line. These are simple to employ and are usually sufficient, provided that fenders are suspended from the hull at strategic points to keep the hull from chafing against the float.

If the boat is to be left alongside a pier or float for a long time, as with a permanent mooring, or if conditions are rough, the use of <u>breast lines</u> and <u>spring lines</u> should be considered. Breast lines prevent sideways movement and spring lines limit the fore-and-aft movement of the boat. Spring lines are also extremely useful in reducing motion of a moored boat in rough conditions. If moored to a pier or wharf in tidal areas, it is important to leave sufficient slack in all lines to accommodate the rise and fall of the tide.

Spring lines may also be used in close quarters to help the boat into or out of a slip or to facilitate maneuvers alongside a wharf. If the spring line is to be handled by those aboard the boat, both ends of the line should be aboard, with the bight around a pile or a cleat on the wharf. The spring line is let go by hauling in on one end of the line. If used under these conditions, a spring line must be tended carefully to be certain that it does not become fouled on the rudder or propeller. Under no conditions should a spring line, which is being used to assist a maneuver, be tied off to a cleat or bitt aboard the boat. A half turn around the bitt or cleat is usually all that is required. The spring line should be able to be adjusted as necessary and cast off quickly when no longer needed.

Sometimes at busy docks, two lines with eye splices must be placed over one piling. If the two eyes are simply dropped over the top of the pile, it may be impossible to remove the first line before the second one has been taken off. To avoid this problem, you can follow a technique called "<u>dipping the eye</u>." Simply bring the end of the eye of the second line up through the eye of the first line and then drop it over the piling. Then either line may be removed first with no problem developing.

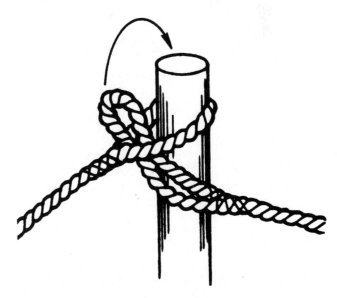

Fig. 8-32 Dipping the Eye.

Chapter 9

Basic Sailing

Introduction

Large or small, old or new, simple or complicated—all sailboats respond in the same basic ways to the forces of wind and water. If you learn the principles of sailing, you can take a giant step toward handling any sailboat with skill and safety. The information presented here is, however, only an introduction to the sport of sailing: having mastered it, you'll still be a beginning sailor. If you are primarily a power boater, this chapter should give you an appreciation of some of the problems faced by a large segment of the recreational boating public, the sailors with whom you share the waters.

A sailboat skipper is rather more at the mercy of outside forces than a comparably experienced powerboat skipper. If the wind fails, or is too strong, or blows from the wrong direction, he could lose his motive force.

By the same token, unskilled handling of the sails (boom, sheets, etc.) can cause injury or vessel damage. So it pays to act with caution, and advance the learning process in reasonable steps.

Following these simple rules will help you get the most fun from sailing:

1. Always check the weather before setting out: get a <u>marine</u> weather forecast that's up to date. If bad or even unsettled weather is predicted, don't go—there'll be another day.

2. Never sail alone: like skindiving solo, sailing single-handed exposes you to extra hazards and difficulties. If possible, crew for a more experienced sailor; don't be afraid to ask him or her what's going on, if you don't understand. If you sail with another beginner, take turns steering and handling the sails.

Fig. 9-1   Offshore Cruiser-racers

Fig. 9-2   Catamaran

3. Select a proper boat: you can learn to sail in virtually any kind of craft, but some boats are better for learning than others. The ideal boat for most beginners is a single-masted vessel of 16-20 feet in length (assuming a crew of two or three). It should have a place to stow safety and other gear (often under the forward deck), and it should be equipped with built-in flotation, so that in case of capsizing or swamping it'll stay afloat and support the crew as well.

4. Make sure your boat is properly equipped, with at least the minimum equipment required under the law. See Chapter 3 for a more detailed discussion of equipment requirements. At the very least, your sailboat should carry a Coast Guard-approved personal flotation device for each person aboard (a buoyant vest will do, but if you're serious about your sailing, consider one of the specially designed vests for sailors, which allow more freedom of movement than the standard model, while providing just as much buoyancy); paddles or oars, in case the wind doesn't blow; bucket and/or pump for bailing (a sponge for getting up the last drops is a good extra); waterproof packet of distress signals--orange smoke, night flares, distress flag; anchor; and line.

Finally, make sure you do your practice sailing out of the main channels, away from waterskiers and fishermen. Others will appreciate your courtesy, and you'll have a better time.

Parts of the Sailboat

The most important element in any boat is the hull, the container that supports the crew and their gear. While most small sailboat hulls don't have the added necessity of holding up a large engine and fuel system, they do need to provide relative stability against the heeling (tipping) forces imposed by the wind on mast and sails. There are three main ways of achieving hull stability:

Fig. 9-3 Wide, Vee-bottomed Sailboat.

1. Hull shape: A wide, flat- or vee-bottomed hull has what's called initial stability--its tendency is to stay on an even keel, because of its shape. To keep it from slipping sideways (called "making leeway") a fin-shaped keel is attached to the bottom. If the keel is retractable, it's called a centerboard or daggerboard. If the fin is hung on the side of the boat, it is called a leeboard.

2. Keel ballast: Some boats counter the weight of the masts and sails, and the force of the wind on the sails, by a heavily weighted keel in the water below the hull. The weight of the keel can be a significant fraction (1/3 to 1/2) of the total weight of the boat. It is usually made from some heavy metal (lead or iron), and can be encased in the hull material or exposed directly to the water.

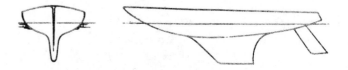

Fig. 9-4 Ballast Keel Hull

Ballasted keels are more effective if the weight is as far below the surface as possible. That is, the longer the lever arm that the ballast weight can work on, the more force it can exert to keep the hull upright.

Ballast keel boats tend to be rounded in cross-section, since the flat-bottomed shape is not needed to maintain stability, and a rounded shape is easier to drive through the water.

3. Live ballast: In smaller boats, the crew shifts from side to side to supplement or replace ballast and/or hull shape support. Most boats sail best when heeled

only slightly, and the crew hikes out (hangs over the windward gunwale) to a greater or lesser degree to keep the boat on her feet. When not hiking out, the crew sits in the cockpit, a recess in the deck with a raised edge (the coaming) that keeps out spray.

Fig. 9-5   Daysailer

The cockpit in a small sailboat isn't very roomy, and often the crew must share it with the centerboard or dagger-board trunk--the watertight casing in which the board rests when raised. A centerboard is pivoted, as in the illustration, at its forward end, while the simpler daggerboard is raised up and down in its slot. Obviously, a boat with either type of board can operate in much shallower water than can a boat with a fixed keel—but with the board all the way up, a boat under sail tends to slide downwind almost out of control.

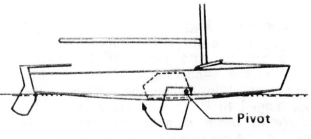

Fig. 9-6   Centerboard

Most small sailboats are steered by a simple tiller-rudder combination. The rudder is hinged to the boat's transom (in smaller craft), and the tiller is just a lever to increase the power of the helmsman's muscles. In some boats, where the helmsman hikes out, there's a tiller extender to add inches to his reach.

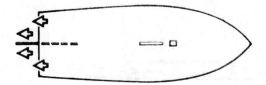

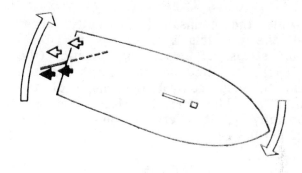

Fig. 9-7   Tiller Action and Boat Heading

The tiller works as shown in Fig. 9-7. All you need to remember is that pushing the tiller to the boat's port side makes the bow swing to starboard, and vice versa: move the tiller away from the direction in which you want the boat to go. After an hour or two, it becomes second nature.

The Sails

A vessel can operate efficiently with anywhere from one to a couple of dozen sails.   Most beginners' boats, however, have either one or two sails, the mainsail and the jib. Each, as you can see, is triangular in shape, and the main parts of each have the same names. Many sailors find it helpful to stencil head and clew on the appropriate corner of their sails.

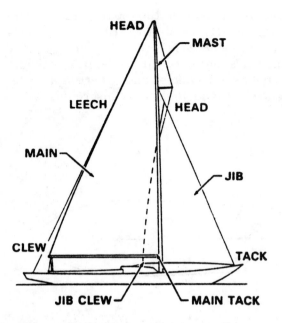

Fig. 9-8   Corners of Main and Jib

While the mainsail is normally larger than the jib, this isn't always the case. Also, strips of wood or plastic (the battens) are used in the leech of the main to help control the shape of the sail. The jib normally lacks battens, especially if it overlaps the mast (see Fig. 9-10).

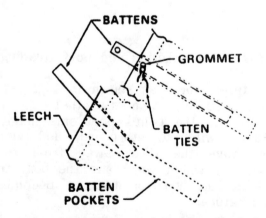

Fig. 9-9   Two Types of Batten Pockets

Both sails are raised by lines called halyards that run through pulleys and back down to cleats on deck. The mainsail, once raised, is controlled by another line called the mainsheet, usually made fast near the sail's clew. The jib has two sheets, one on each side of the mast, leading aft to cleats alongside the cockpit.

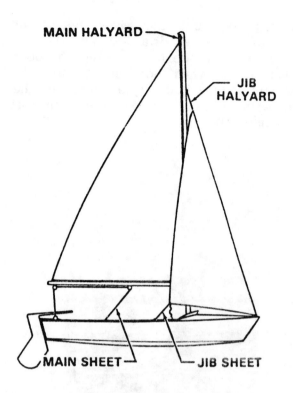

Fig. 9-10   Sheets and Halyards

Lines that are used to control the sails (halyards, sheets) are called, collectively, running rigging.

Most sails today are made of a synthetic material which is very light yet strong, and resists stretch and rot. Yet even modern synthetic materials require some maintenance and should be cleaned as needed, checked carefully for worn places, and protected from unnecessary exposure to sunlight. Tears must be mended immediately before they develop into larger flaws.

The Spars and Rigging

Obviously, cloth sails need a rigid framework to hold them up and extend them to the wind. Light wood or metal spars form this frame—the vertical mast and, hinged to it by a universal joint, the horizontal boom combine to extend two sides of the mainsail. While the sail itself may be fastened just at head, tack and clew, its foot and luff are usually set into grooves in the boom and mast respectively.

The jib is not usually attached to any spar, although a boom may be used on some boats. The jib is more typically attached ("hanked on") to the forestay, one of the supports which help keep the mast from falling or bending backward.

Other stainless steel wires support the mast in other directions—a backstay (not always found in smaller boats) counteracts the pull of the forestay. Shrouds run from the masthead to the sides of the boat, where they are made fast to chainplates, which distribute the load to the sides of the boat.

All these wires—the stays and shrouds—are known collectively as standing rigging. Their purpose is to keep the mast standing against the many stresses imposed upon it. In complex boats, there may be many pieces of standing rigging, and in the very simplest sailing surfboards, there is no standing rigging at all—the mast is set into a reinforced hole in the deck, and is strong enough to keep upright without stays or shrouds.

Here, then, is the complete boat, ready to sail. Most of today's popular daysailers have a fairly close resemblance to this open-cockpit sloop (a boat with one mast and two basic sails). Some boats are most complex in their rig, and some are markedly simpler. On the next page are a few other types of boats you may see on American waters.

Sailboard
Essentially a surfboard with a mast and sail, this is about as simple a boat as one can find. Its type of sail is called lateen and was invented by Arab sailors in the Mediterranean. While very fast and much fun to sail, boardboats like this one require very quick reactions and capsize frequently. They can be easily righted, however, often in a matter of seconds.

Fig. 9-11   Sailboard

Fig. 9-12   Classic Catboat

Catboat

The native American catboat originated as a working fishing boat well over a hundred years ago. Its single sail is called a gaff rig, because of the extra spar--the gaff--which extends the upper edge of the sail. It is an easy boat to sail in gentle winds but can be demanding in breezes over 10 to 15 miles per hour.

Sloop

The most popular sail arrangement is the sloop, an arrangement of one mast and two sails, a main and a jib, which can be in many different sizes. In certain wind conditions, a third sail, a spinnaker, may be used.

Fig. 9–14 Ketch

Wind

Whatever the boat's shape or rig, it uses the same fuel—wind. Defined generally as air in motion, wind for the sailor is two different things, true wind and apparent wind.

Fig. 9–13 A Modern High Performance Sloop

Two or more Masts

When individual sails get too big to handle, the obvious thing to do is divide them up into more sails, as on this ketch, a popular type of cruising boat. Other two-master boats include the yawl and schooner.

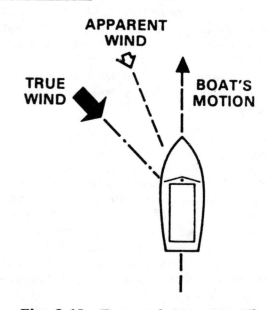

Fig. 9–15 True and Apparent Wind

True wind is what you feel when you stand in one spot on shore. True wind is the wind which is indicated by weather vanes or flags on fixed objects.

Apparent wind, which is what these indicators measure in a moving vehicle, is a combination of true wind and apparent wind, which is wind created by motion.

On a windless day, you set out from shore in a motorboat moving at 10 miles per hour. If you put your head up over the windshield, you'll feel a 10-mile-per-hour wind blowing directly in your face—but if you throttle back, the wind drops. This is a false wind, caused by the boat's moving through the air—not air moving past an unmoving boat. It is the apparent wind.

Later in the day, a north wind of 5 miles per hour springs up, and you head your motorboat, at 10 MPH, directly into it. Put your head over the windshield and you'll feel an apparent wind of 15 MPH: the true wind of 5, plus false wind of 10. Now turn and run in the opposite direction: the apparent wind drops off to 5 MPH, false wind of 10, minus true wind of 5.

If you are moving at an angle to the wind and not directly into it or away from it, the apparent direction of the wind as well as the apparent force of the wind will change. Both the force and the direction of the apparent wind are the vector sum of the true wind and the wind created by motion. Vector sums are beyond the scope of this course.

Thus, the wind you experience on a moving boat may be very different from the wind you would feel ashore. The boat's sails, too, feel the apparent wind, and you must adjust them to that apparent wind, and not to the true wind. Therefore, you cannot trim your sails according to true wind indicators, such as flags on buildings or plumes of smoke. Many sailors find it extremely useful to tie bits of yarn in the rigging or to install wind vanes at the masthead to

indicate the apparent wind where they are, so that they can trim their sails accordingly.

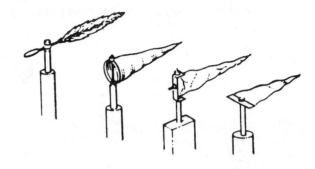

Fig. 9-16   Types of Masthead Wind Vanes

Running

It's easy to understand how a boat can sail with the wind astern. With the boom fully extended to one side or the other, the sail simply obstructs the wind; the boat is pushed forward. Because of wind eddies off the mainsail, the jib often flutters helplessly when a boat is running. If the jib will stand out on the opposite side to the main (sailing wing-and-wing, it's called), you may be able to add a bit of speed. This kind of sailing is called running, or running free.

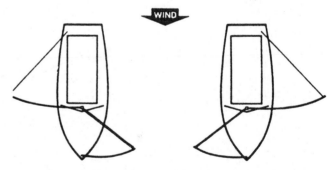

**Fig. 9-17   Running:
Wind From Dead Astern**

Beating

Ancient sailing vessels nearly always sailed more or less directly before the wind, yet modern sailboats can head to within about 45° of the direction from which the true wind is blowing. Because of the effect of apparent wind, it often feels as if your boat were sailing almost directly into the wind.

How is this possible? Basically, what happens is that the sail which acted like a wall when the boat was running now behaves like an airplane's wing. Looked at from above, a sail's shape is not unlike a side view of an airplane wing.

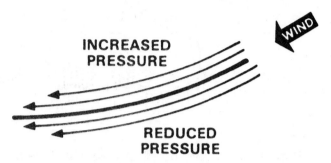

Fig. 9-18   Air Pressure On a Sail When Beating

The air passing over the convex wing or sail creates a low pressure area (see the discussion of propeller action in Chapter 2), and the higher pressure on the opposite side pushes the wing or sail along.

The lifting force operates most strongly in the forward third of the sail's area, and the lift itself is at right angles to the sail at any given point. Therefore, only part of the lifting impetus presses the boat forward, while much of the force urges the boat sideways. Because the underwater shape of a sailboat hull is designed to take maximum advantage of forward pressure, while at the same time resisting sideways pressures, the boat moves forward—into the wind. This kind of sailing is called beating, or sailing close-hauled (because the boom is hauled as close in to the boat's centerline as possible).

Any time a boat is not beating or running, it is said to be reaching. There are three kinds of reaches—a close reach, when the apparent wind is coming from forward of amidships; a beam reach, when the apparent wind is at right angles to the boat; and a broad reach, when the wind is coming from aft of amidships. In most reaching, the forces operating on the sail are a combination of push and

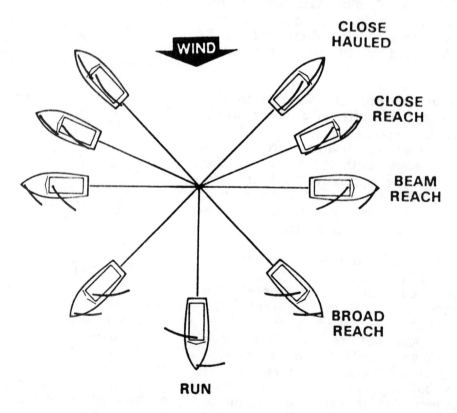

Fig. 9-19   Sail and Boat Attitudes Relative to Wind When Close Hauled and Reaching

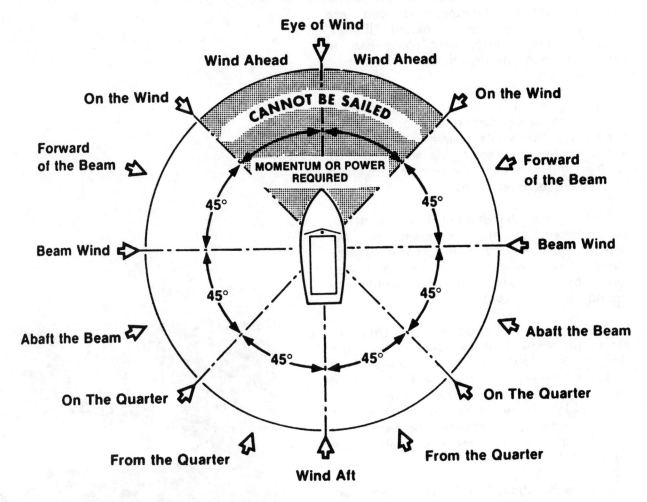

Fig. 9-20 Possible Headings Relative to Wind Direction

The Points of Sailing

Fig. 9-20 is a diagram showing all the possible headings for a modern sailboat reacting to winds from different directions. Note the shaded area, an arc which cannot be sailed. This unusable portion of the available headings extends approximately 45° on either side of the eye of the wind—the direction from which the wind is blowing.

These are true wind directions, of course. Close-hauled, a skipper will find

lift, and on a beam reach, the boat often gets the most possible help from each force—which is why beam reaching is often the fastest kind of sailing.

his wind vane seems to indicate that he is sailing to within 10° or 15° of the wind's eye, but that's only the effect of apparent wind aboard the boat.

Winds blowing from the right side of the diagram are coming over the boat's starboard side. When the wind blows from starboard, a boat is said to be sailing on the starboard tack. When the wind blows over a boat's port side—whether forward of, or abaft, the beam—the boat is on port tack.

Sooner or later it will be necessary to change from one tack to another. There are two ways of doing this, depending on whether you are sailing close-hauled or running. If you are sailing close-hauled, the maneuver of changing to the other tack is called "tacking." If you are running, the maneuver is called "jibing." Bear in mind, though, that jibing can be dangerous. See the description below.

Tacking, or Coming About

Tacking is the safest and most common way of changing direction and is always used when the boat's course is toward the wind. Successful tacking is a matter of timing, and practice is necessary to make it a clean, efficient move.

Tacking can be divided into six steps, each taken at the command of the skipper. For safety and general understandability, the commands for each step have become standard and should be learned by every sailor.

1. "Stand by to come about." This call alerts the crew well in advance that the skipper is about to change course and tack. Normally, the crew will be seated on the windward ("weather," toward the wind) side of the boat for balance. At this command, everyone prepares to move, and one crew member readies the jib sheet for release.

2. "Ready about." This is a cue that indicates the tacking maneuver is eminent.

3. "Hard alee." At this call, the skipper pushes the tiller "down" (to leeward, "alee," away from the wind), causing the rudder to turn the bow of the boat INTO the wind. (If the boat is equipped with a steering wheel, the wheel is turned in the corresponding direction.) The crew, keeping low to keep their balance and to avoid the boom, begins to move to the other side of the boat while one of their number releases the jib sheet and allows it to run free.

4. Through the wind: The bow of the boat passes through the eye of the wind. If the boat maintains enough momentum, it will swing all the way across so that the wind strikes the sail from the opposite side. The jib may be held on the

Fig. 9-21   Tacking: "Ready About."

Fig. 9-22   Tacking: "Hard Alee."

"wrong" side ("backed" or "backwinded") at this point to help the boat through the wind.

Fig. 9-23 Tacking: Through the Wind

5. Boom across: The mainsail boom swings to the opposite side of the boat as the mainsail refills with wind. The crew takes in the leeward (downwind) jib sheet (which was, until the tack, the windward jib sheet) until the sail stops fluttering (luffing). The mainsheet was not released; so it allows the boom to swing over to leeward to a position which is a mirror image of where it was before the tack, and the mainsail refills with wind.

Fig. 9-24 Tacking: Boom Across

6. Settled down on the new tack, the crew gathers up and coils loose running rigging (primarily the jib sheet) and assumes balancing positions in the (now) windward (weather) side of the boat as they once again pick up speed.

Fig. 9-25 Tacking: On the New Tack

Tacking Along a Course

It often happens that a sailboat must travel some distance to windward, in a direction which makes a direct heading to the destination impossible. In a situation like this, the sailboat skipper zig-zags in a series of tacks toward his mark, as shown in Fig. 9-26.

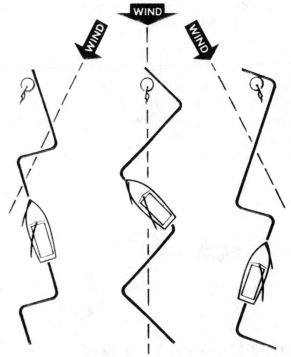

Fig. 9-26 Tacking to a Windward Objective

When the mark isn't directly upwind, yet cannot be reached on a single heading, the course will not be composed of equal port and starboard tacks: one or the other tack, as illustrated, will be much more advantageous.

In calculating when to tack, the skipper should take into account the leeway (or sideways slippage) of his boat. All boats make leeway when sailing close hauled, and the amount of leeway depends largely on a boat's design. Generally speaking, it's a mistake to try to sail too close to the wind: this causes the boat to stall for lack of lift, and to lose speed gradually. Keep the sails full and keep the boat moving at all times, and if a wave slows you up, head away from the wind to a close reach until you regain speed.

Jibing

Timing is also the key to changing tacks when heading downwind, which is called jibing. Note, however, the one important difference between the two maneuvers: whereas the attached edge of the sail passes through the wind's eye when tacking, the free edge does the swinging when you jibe. The effect can be similar to what happens when the wind gets behind an open door and slams it closed. Hence, jibing is a maneuver to be performed with great caution!

1. "Stand by to jibe." calls the skipper. Uncleat the mainsheet and begin to take it in quickly, coiling it so that it will be ready to run free when needed. Don't worry about the jib. Get ready to shift crew weight.

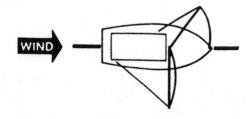

Fig. 9-27   "Stand By to Jibe."

2. "Ready." again a final cue, warning the crew that the maneuver is coming soon.

3. "Jibe-ho." and the skipper puts the tiller over—not too hard—toward the wind (or away from the boom: it's the same thing). Crew stands by to let the mainsheet run.

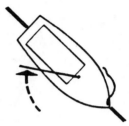

Fig. 9-28   "Jibe-ho."

4. Boom across—but it will swing fast, picking up speed as it comes. The crewman's role is vital: Do <u>not</u> snub the mainsheet up short, so that the boom fetches up with a jerk. Rather, let the sheet out in a controlled run (wearing gloves is a good idea the first few times). When the boom is out at right angles to the boat, snub its sheet.

Fig. 9-29   Boom Across

5. Off on the new tack. Now you can try to get the jib to set wing-and-wing on the opposite side, if you want.

Fig. 9-30   On New Tack

Accidental Jibe

We saw earlier that a jibe is, by its nature, a less controlled maneuver than coming about. In high winds, or when the skipper is careless, a jibe is dangerous:

Fig. 9-31 Possible Result of an Uncontrolled Jibe

1. If the mainsheet is snubbed too abruptly, the boat may be jerked over and swamp or capsize.

2. If the sheet is not snubbed, the swinging boom may hit the leeward shroud, damaging the boom or shroud, or even dismasting the boat.

3. If the sheet is not controlled as the boom swings, the boom may arc upward and snag the backstay, breaking it or capsizing the boat.

Tacking Downwind

When winds are gusty, the prudent skipper whose course lies downwind will frequently change direction by tacking instead of jibing, and will sail a series of broad reaches, instead of heading directly downwind on a course where a small wind shift may invite an accidental jibe.

To tack downwind, the boat must first be brought round to a close reach, then swung through the wind's eye. Trying to come about from a broad reach will seldom work, as the boat will lose its turning momentum as the wind ceases to fill the extended sail.

Rigging Your Boat

Many small boat skippers keep their craft at a pier or mooring all season, but an increasing number rig and launch their boats each time they go sailing. Rigging a small boat is no great problem, and every sailor should know how to set up and tune his own rigging.

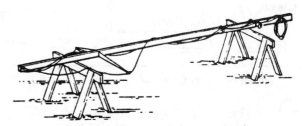

Fig. 9-32 Set Mast on Supports to Check Rigging

First lay the mast on supports--a pair of carpenter's horses are ideal--and make sure the stays, shrouds, and halyards are all properly attached: do not lose track of which is the forward side of the mast. When everything's ready, bundle the standing rigging and halyards loosely and lash them to the mast with a couple of turns of twine or shock cord. Don't put these lashings on any higher than you'll be able to reach when the mast is raised, however.

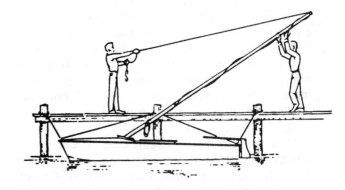

Fig. 9-33 Stepping the Mast

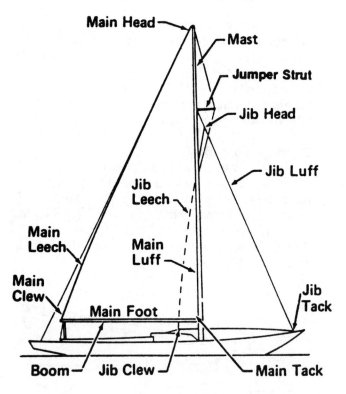

Fig. 9-34 Nomenclature of a Sloop Rigged Daysailer

Labels: Main Head, Mast, Jumper Strut, Jib Head, Jib Luff, Jib Leech, Main Leech, Main Luff, Main Clew, Jib Tack, Main Foot, Boom, Jib Clew, Main Tack

Now have one crew member guide the mast into its step—facing the right way—while the other walks the mast forward: watch where you're putting your feet. If the mast is large, it may be necessary to have one crew member take the jib halyard to help pull the mast upright (but first be sure the other end of the halyard is made fast!).

Before stepping the mast it is EX-TREMELY IMPORTANT to take a good look around for overhead wires or other obstructions. Many parking lots and launching ramps have lighting or other cables and wires overhead which may catch a mast and cause damage or cause it to become unbalanced and fall. An even more serious hazard is electrocution, as a metal mast, stay or shroud contacts wires carrying electric current.

You should be certain that there is no overhead obstruction of any kind near enough that the mast could possibly reach it, no matter what direction it is moved. Furthermore, if the mast is being stepped

while the boat is on the trailer, make sure there is a clear overhead path between the place where the mast is being stepped and the actual launching ramp.

When the mast is upright and firmly stepped, attach the stays and shrouds to the proper turnbuckles or directly (in smaller boats) to the chainplates. Now wind the turnbuckles or shroud attachments with waterproof tape, to prevent the hardware from ripping the sails.

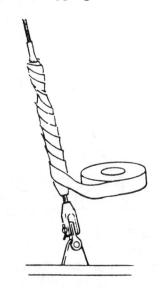

Fig. 9-35 Taping a Turnbuckle

Now attach the boom by its universal joint (the gooseneck). Insert the pintles of the rudder into the gudgeons on the transom. Lower the centerboard or daggerboard (assuming the boat's in the water). Make fast the mainsheet to its deck fitting and to the boom.

You're ready to put on the sails. Head the boat as nearly into the wind as you can. (If you're at anchor, the boat will probably head into the wind by itself.) Bend on the mainsail first: take it from the sailbag, making sure you know which corner you have in your hand—it should be the clew. Insert this into the groove along the upper edge of the boom, feeding the foot of the sail into the groove until the clew is as far out along the boom as it will go. Now attach the tack of the sail to the tack fitting. There's a fitting at the outer end of the boom—the outhaul—designed to set up tension on the foot of the sail, and this should be pulled reasonably tight.

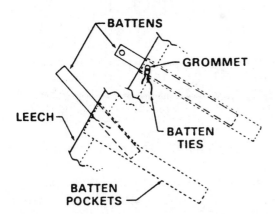

Fig. 9-36 Two Types of Batten Pockets

Your sail may have a track on boom and mast, in which case the corresponding foot and luff of the sail will be fitted with slides that ride the track. If this is the case, you can test the tension of the outhaul by tweaking the foot of the sail: it should be taut enough, when set up, to vibrate slightly.

Insert the battens in the batten pockets, as shown in Fig. 9-36. Most mainsails have two or three different sizes of battens, with matching pockets. Make sure the thin end of the batten goes in the pocket first.

Make fast the halyard to the head of the sail. A bowline is a good knot to use. After checking to be sure the halyard isn't fouled on any of the rigging, and that the mainsheet is uncleated, so that the boom can swing free, raise the sail, feeding its luff into the mast groove. The sail should be hoisted until there are parallel creases visible along the luff.

Now cleat and coil the halyard neatly as shown in Fig. 9-37. Exactly how you do it isn't that important, so long as the halyard is stowed so that it cannot escape and, at the same time can be released quickly.

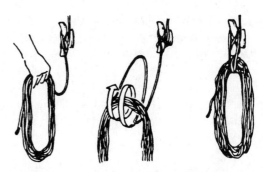

Fig. 9-37 Coiling the Halyard

To raise the jib, attach its tack to the tack fitting which is usually a part of the forestay chainplate. Next, clip the snaps along the luff to the forestay. Make sure all the snaps are facing in the same direction: if they're not, you have a twist in the luff. Make fast the sheets to the clew and the halyard to the head of the jib, again using a bowline knot if special hardware snaps are not provided.

Raise the jib until the sail's luff is as taut as you can get it (but not so taut that the forestay begins to sag). Cleat and coil that halyard. As a point of interest, mainsail halyards are generally led to the starboard side of the mast, jib halyards to port. It's not a vital thing, but if you always lead the halyards the same way, you won't have to worry about which is which.

Sail Trim

Your mast should be straight on all points of sailing—if it isn't, correct the adjustment of turnbuckles until it is. Proper sail trim does <u>not</u> require that the boat be on its ear, foaming along. Most boats, remember, sail best on their bottoms. When coming to a new heading, let out or take in the sheets until the sails stop luffing—no more. If the wind changes direction, but your heading remains the same, retrim the sheets accordingly.

Final Check

When you're learning to sail, its a good idea to make a final pre-voyage check before leaving the pier or anchorage.

1. Weather: Does the sky look as good as the forecast? If not, recheck the forecast or stay home.

2. Equipment: Is everything aboard? Accessible? Stowed so that it won't fall or fly overboard?

3. Float Plan: All boatmen should leave the following information with a reliable person ashore—(1) Where you're going; (2) When you expect to return; (3) Who's aboard; (4) What the boat looks like, in detail. When you get back, remember to cancel your float plan.

Setting Out

Leaving a pier, beach or mooring is the first test of your sailing skill. Before you cut loose from shore, plan ahead: know what to expect, and what you're going to do next. Don't act until you have a good idea what nearby skippers, swimmers and fishermen are up to. And bear in mind that a boat has no brakes: the only way to stop a sailboat (short of running into something solid) is to head into the wind.

1. Start headed into the wind, with centerboard fully lowered. While you're still learning, it's not a bad idea to paddle to some quiet, deserted spot in the harbor and drop an anchor with a float, to serve as a practice mooring.

2. When all is clear around you, have your crew member cast off the line to the mooring buoy or float. As the boat drops back, the crew member backs the jib, grasping its clew and holding it out to one side of the boat or the other to catch the wind. At the same time, you put the tiller over on the opposite side the jib is extended. The boat will begin to turn in the opposite direction, as in the illustration.

Fig. 9-38 Backing the Jib

3. As soon as the boat is approximately at right angles to the wind, the crew member lets go of the jib clew and pulls the lee side jib sheet taut, while the skipper takes in the mainsheet. The sails should be taken in just enough to stop luffing.

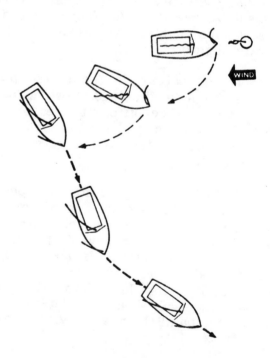

Fig. 9-39 Leaving the Mooring

Anchoring

Anchoring is discussed in detail in Chapter 2. There are some aspects to anchoring a sailboat, however, which deserve special attention.

When anchoring a sailboat, follow these simple steps:

1. Drop and stow the jib as you approach your chosen anchorage. You need working space on the deck, and a sail is slippery and easily damaged if you leave it in place while you attempt to set the anchor.

2. Head into the wind under the main alone and allow the boat to come "in irons." As forward momentum is lost, lower the anchor over the bow and pay out the rode. Make sure the anchor rode clears the rigging, lifelines, etc., and that there is a strong fitting available to secure it to.

3. As the boat drifts backwards, feed out additional rode until you have adequate scope of line out (see Chapter 2). Set the anchor by snubbing the rode on the deck cleat. Check the "feel" of the anchor rode to see if the anchor is holding or skipping over the bottom. If it is not holding, increase the scope until you feel it "bite."

4. Check your position by taking bearings on landmarks, and check from time to time to make sure you are not drifting.

To retrieve your anchor, much the same process is followed in reverse. If the boat is small, it may be possible to pull up on the anchor rode hand over hand. With most boats, however, this is apt to set the anchor more firmly and can result in rope burns or even in someone's slipping overboard.

The boat must be moved forward over the anchor, either under sail or power. If you have auxiliary power, this is probably the time to use it.

Move slowly up over the anchor while one crew member takes in the anchor rode. When the rode tends to be straight up and down, it should be easy to pull the anchor up from the bottom. If the anchor is set very hard, sailing on over it with the line cleated off to a strong fitting should break it loose.

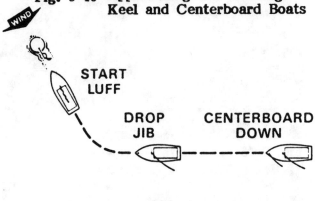

Fig. 9-40 Approaching the Mooring: Keel and Centerboard Boats

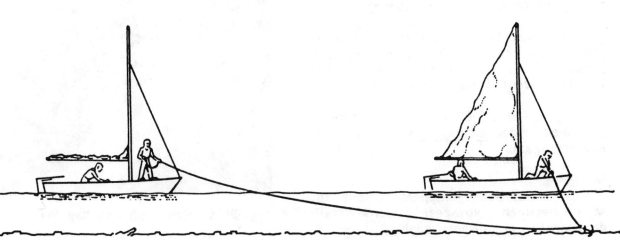

Fig. 9-41 Anchoring and Lowering Sail

Clean off the anchor before bringing it aboard, and stow the anchor and rode where it will not be in the way or interfere with crew, sails or rigging.

Bend on the jib, raise and trim it, and resume your sailing.

Landing

Whenever you come in for a landing, it seems the whole world is watching. The important thing is to avoid getting flustered: even the best sailors have been novices in their time, and they'll understand.

1. As you approach, note how the other boats are riding. Lower your centerboard all the way. The idea is to time your turn into the wind, as shown in the illustrations, so that you arrive at dock or mooring with little or no momentum.

2. Best final approach is usually close-hauled, if the location of other boats allows. Remember to allow for leeway!

3. At one or two boat lengths downwind of the pier or buoy, head up sharply into the wind. If you've calculated right, your boat will coast to a halt, sails luffing, right at the buoy—but have a crew member ready to grab it. If you're approaching a dock, the crew can fend off. Be careful to avoid catching body parts between the boat and pier, and beware of being thrown overboard.

Remember: In an emergency, wood or fiber glass can be repaired or replaced; limbs cannot. Do not risk serious injury just to prevent damage to a boat.

If you miss, follow the procedures described under setting out, swing round and try again.

Unrigging

Most small boats' skippers remove the sails between voyages: Dacron sails deteriorate in direct sunlight, and in many harbors, airborne dirt may foul sails left furled on a boom for a few days.

Before bagging your sails, remove the battens and lay each sail out—if possible—on a clean surface, such as a parking lot, driveway or lawn. Check for tears or worn spots. Now fold the sail as shown until it's a long, narrow strip, and then roll it up gently. Don't fold it or roll it hard—try to avoid creases.

Fig. 9-42   Fold Sail . . .

Fig. 9-43   . . . into Narrow Strip

Fig. 9-44   Now Roll and Bag Sail

If you do furl the mainsail on the boom, here's how:

1. Drop the sail and gather it on one side of the boom in one large fold of sail. (See Fig. 9-45.)

2. Roll it toward the boom, gathering the sail as you go. It's a good idea to remove the battens, as they are likely to take a permanent warp. (See Fig. 9-46.)

3. Lash the sail with elastic sail ties, just tight enough to hold it in place. The roll should have its open side facing down, so that rain and spray will run off the sail and not be caught inside. If you have a sail cover, put it on over the furled sail. (See Fig. 9-47.)

Now remove your tiller and rudder, raise the centerboard all the way, and clean out the boat. Be sure, if you sail in salt or heavily polluted water, to wipe off all varnished wood and bright metal with a clean cloth.

Fig. 9-45   Gather Sail on One Side of Boom

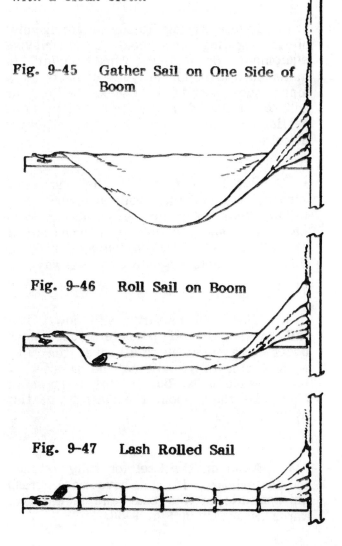

Fig. 9-46   Roll Sail on Boom

Fig. 9-47   Lash Rolled Sail

In Heavy Weather

Sooner or later, every sailor can expect to encounter weather severe enough to make sailing difficult or even dangerous. For the beginner, a careful attention to weather forecasts and to the appearance of sea and sky should postpone an encounter with heavy weather until you and your boat are enough of a team to handle it.

If you do get caught out in a sudden squall, however, chances are you'll get through it with no great trouble, if you keep your head and follow the principles of good seamanship.

Some days, especially muggy, hazy summer afternoons, breed dangerous squalls that can creep up on you before you're aware of what's happening. If you're sailing along and suddenly find the wind increasing dramatically, or see that a thunderstorm is going to strike before you can reach harbor, the first thing to do, preferably before the gusts get too strong, is drop and furl all sail. To do this, head up into the wind, let the sheets fly, and lower the sails as quickly as you can, gathering them and furling them as you do. Lash sails to boom or deck hardware, to prevent them from billowing and tearing.

Once the sails are under control, put out your anchor. Even if you haven't enough line to anchor securely, the weight of line and anchor will hold your boat's bow up into the wind—the safest attitude for any boat with difficult weather.

Have your crew put on life jackets—and set a good example yourself. It's much easier to put on any lifesaving device in the boat than in the water. Tie down all loose gear and, if significant amounts of rain or spray get in the boat, don't wait to bail.

One good thing about sudden squalls is that they're usually over fairly quickly. In 15 minutes or so, the wind should moderate enough for you to sail home under reduced sail.

The kind of sail you set in strong winds will depend on how your boat is rigged, what sails you carry, and in what direction you want to go. Generally speaking, most small sailboats will sail reasonably well under mainsail alone, on any heading from a broad reach up to nearly close-hauled. In a gusty wind, it's especially important to keep the boat moving; so don't try to sail as close to the wind as you normally would. Also, if you're broad-reaching, be awake for sudden wind shifts: this is not the time for an unexpected jibe.

If your course is downwind, your boat may handle better under jib alone. Be sure the main is tightly furled and the boom secured. And keep the jib from unnecessary flapping, which can rip the stitching along seams.

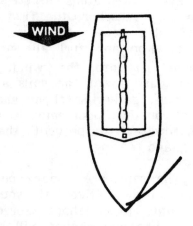

Fig. 9-48 Sailing Under Jib Alone

Your boat may be equipped with reefing gear, in which case you can reduce the area of the mainsail, while still retaining some of it for a balanced sail plan. On most small boats today, reefing is accomplished by easing off the main halyard while simultaneously rotating the boom with a built-in or attachable crank, to roll the sail around it like a window shade. If your boat has reefing gear, practice using it in harbor before you try it under way.

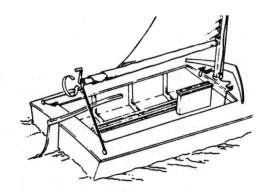

Fig. 9-49 Rolling in a Reef

Emergency

It may happen that, despite your best efforts, the boat capsizes, or turns over on its side. With most modern daysailers, this is an irritation, but hardly a disaster. Know how to right your boat and the worst you'll suffer is a wetting.

1. Before trying to do anything else about righting the boat or retrieving equipment, do a quick "head count" to make sure that all of your crew is safe. Make sure nobody is trapped under the sail or entangled in the rigging, and avoid getting entangled during your recovery efforts.

2. Put on PFDs (if they are not already on), and plan your recovery. It is usually best to begin by gathering loose equipment and stuffing it into a sailbag or other container to keep it from drifting off and/or getting in the way.

3. Cast off halyards and lower the sail to the deck if possible. (Some small boats have sails which fit over the mast with a sleeve. It will not be possible to lower these sails, but it may be possible to gather them about the mast by casting off the outhaul.)

4. Stand on the keel (or fully extended centerboard, if you have one), grasp the gunwale of the boat and lean backwards as shown in Fig. 9-50.

Fig. 9-50   Righting Capsized Boat

5. Chances are the boat will come upright by herself. Full of water, she will be very unstable. Swim alongside and bail until the water is six inches or so lower than the boat's sides.

6. Now a light-weight crew member can climb in over the stern and finish bailing, after which sails can be raised again. With practice, especially in easily capsized board boats, you'll learn how to right the boat without lowering sail.

Distress

Sometimes a mast or boom is damaged to the point where the boat cannot easily be sailed. If this happens to you, or if your sail develops a sudden tear, it may be best to call for help, rather than pushing onward to incur a big repair bill. Distress signals can be carried on the smallest boat: they should be stowed in a watertight box or bag, out of the reach of small children, in a place where a capsize won't cause them to fall from the boat. Here are common ways to ask for help—never be ashamed to do so if you feel the situation is getting out of control:

1. Flare or smoke signal: Hand-held orange smoke signals can be seen a long way. Be sure to follow instructions on the device, and hold the burning signal away from yourself and the boat.

2. A distress flag—usually a bright International Orange square of plastic—can be hoisted in the rigging.

3. A horn or whistle, repeatedly sounded in patterns of five blasts, is a recognized distress signal.

4. With no signals at all, simply raising your arms over your head and lowering them level with your shoulders, over and over, is a standard distress signal.

When making any distress signal, be sure you do it vigorously. You may know you're in need of help, but the other fellow may think you're just waving or tooting to be friendly.

Conclusion

There's nothing difficult or mysterious about sailing, once you have the hang of it, but don't think that you'll ever know it all. That's one of the fascinations of the sport: there's always something new to learn, some way to improve your sailing skills.

Now that you've completed this introduction to sailing, there are two complementary things to do next. First, practice what you've learned: use it until you can come about, jibe, enter and leave tight corners with real confidence. As noted earlier, a good way to learn more quickly is to crew for an experienced sailor.

Second, take another sailing course. One you may want to consider is the Coast Guard Auxiliary's own Sailing and Seamanship, a fourteen-lesson course that explains in depth what you've learned here in outline, and which will teach you more about fine points of sailing than we've had room to touch on in this short space.

Chapter 10

Trailering

The average small sailing cruiser meanders along at about four knots. Power boats average a little faster. Ten hours of cruising, given decent conditions, and you're only a few miles from where you started. Or consider the price of marina accommodation for a small boat – even assuming the berths are available. By fitting your boat with a trailer, you can start your boating vacation 500 miles from your usual cruising grounds, visit places you would normally never see, and avoid the costs and hazards of marinas. At season's end you can store your boat at home where you can work on her through the winter months as the weather allows.

Trailer boating has become increasingly popular in recent years. Of the approximately 13 million recreational boats in the United States, over 95% are trailerable.

The Trailerable Boat

The first requirement is a suitable boat. One of the few absolute limiting factors of such a boat is its width. For trailering without a special permit, the maximum width of the boat and trailer combination is eight feet on some state roads or 8 feet 6 inches on Interstate and other Federal-aid highways with 12-foot lanes. Most manufacturers and designers make a special point to make sure that the beam falls within the trailerable limit, if the design permits. Although boats over 30 feet have been built with an eight-foot beam, the maximum length of most trailerable sailboats is under 25 feet. Boats with unusual hull shapes, and

Fig. 10-1   Trailerable   Keel–Centerboard Hull

especially sailboats, can pose special problems.

It's obvious that hull shape is also a major factor. The ideal hull from a trailering point of view is flat-bottomed or gently rounded, with no protrusions. This kind of hull is virtually required if you are going to launch at a municipal ramp or off a beach. If in doubt, get in touch with the dealer who handles your boat, and if he doesn't know, have him ask the manufacturer. Chances are that the designer had a standard brand of trailer in mind when designing the boat. Whatever the hull shape, it is essential that it be supported evenly by the trailer.

The Trailer

Width and length aside, highway requirements for a trailer to be towed at high speeds are fairly serious. These requirements fall into two general categories - what is legally necessary, and what is derived from common sense. Legal requirements are still changing in many areas, as more and more states turn their attention to the dangers inherent in trailering. Consult your state police and your motor vehicle bureau for up-to-the-minute information.

Trailers are divided into classes based on the total weight of the trailer and its load at a standard speed. A decrease in speed will allow a slight increase in weight.

CLASS 1.   Gross weight of trailer including load not to exceed 2000 pounds.
CLASS 2.   Gross weight of trailer including load of over 2000 pounds through 3500 pounds.
CLASS 3.   Gross weight of trailer including load of over 3500 pounds through 5000 pounds.
CLASS 4.   Gross weight of trailer including load of over 5000 pounds.

Federal Law requires that all trailers have certain important capacity information displayed. The Gross Vehicle Weight Rating (GVWR) for the trailer must be displayed, which includes the trailer and all weight it is expected to carry. If the rating of the trailer is within 15% of the total weight of your boat, gear and trail-

er, it is recommended that you select the next larger capacity trailer. The Gross Axle Weight Rating (GAWR) Capacity information will show the size of tires needed to carry the load for which the trailer is rated. On multi-axle trailers, the combined Gross Axle Weight Rating (GAWR) of all axles must be equal to or greater than the Gross Vehicle Weight Rating (GVWR) for the trailer.

Your trailer will probably require license plates and lights. If possible, get a rear light and license-plate set that's demountable, so that you can remove them before backing the trailer into the water. Lights like this normally clamp to the boat's transom. No lighting system made can resist repeated immersion, despite what a manufacturer may claim. You will also need turn-indicator lights and, if your rig nears the eight-foot maximum, side lights as well.

Pay special attention to the electrical plug and socket arrangement connecting the car's lighting system to the trailer. The wiring should be under no stress, should be as weatherproof as possible, and should not sag or loop so that it can get caught in machinery or drag along the ground. Stranded wire is recommended to reduce vibration damage. A good ground is essential, and a separate ground cable between the trailer and the tow vehicle may be necessary. The addition of lights and reflectors to the rear of the boat or trailer, beyond that required by law, will significantly increase safety at night.

Brake requirements vary greatly from state to state, but the American Boat &

☐ SAFE LOADING CAPACITY

☐ MOTOR UP

☐ REAR VIEW MIRRORS

☐ LIGHTING EQUIPMENT

WEIGHT DISTRIBUTED EVENLY

☐ SAFETY CHAINS

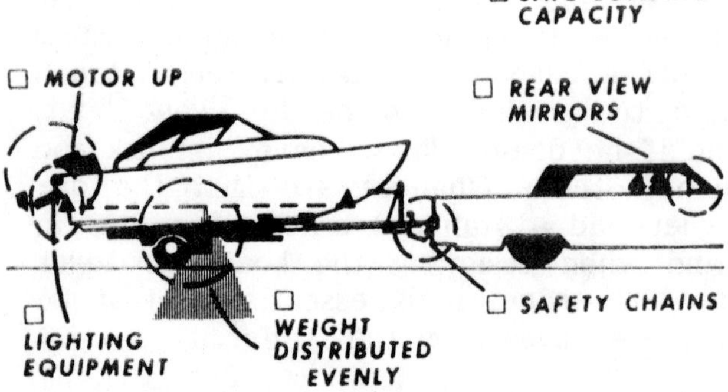

Fig. 10-2   Consider All Of the Pieces: Boat, Trailer, and Towing Vehicle

Fig. 10-3   Typical Electrical Connector

Yacht Council recommends that trailer manufacturers offer brakes of some sort for all wheels of trailers designed for a gross weight of 1,500 lbs. or more. Legal requirements can be met by any one of the three common brake systems—electrical, hydraulic or surge. The first two are integrated into the tow vehicle's own brake system; the surge brake is activated by the trailer's own momentum. Your trailer's brakes should operate automatically when the towing car's service brakes are applied, and should continue to operate even if the trailer separates from the tow car.

The Hitch

Choosing the proper class of hitch for the weight of the trailer being towed is very important. There are two basic types of hitch, the weight-carrying hitch and the weight-distribution (or load-equalizer) hitch.

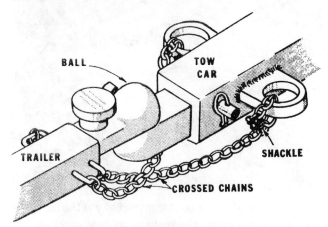

Fig. 10-4 Trailer Hitch

The class of hitch required depends on the gross trailer weight and its tongue weight. The dealer that supplied the towing vehicle can normally provide guidance in purchasing a suitable hitch.

Weight-Carrying Hitches

The simplest and most inexpensive weight hitch is the so-called "bumper hitch," which is mounted on the rear bumper of the car. While it may be adequate for very light trailers, it is not recommended, and is banned in several states. (The "step-bumper" hitch mounted on many light trucks is <u>not</u> considered a bumper hitch and may be acceptable.)

Weight-carrying hitches come in various sizes and configurations depending upon the gross trailer weight, the tongue weight and the tow vehicle characteristics. As the name implies, the weight-carrying hitch holds the trailer's entire tongue weight.

Fig. 10-5 Front Hitch

Weight-Distribution Hitch

The rear of a tow vehicle is generally loaded with luggage, gear, and, sometimes a back seat full of kids. When you add the tongue weight of a loaded trailer, you can place heavy strain on the rear tires, shocks and springs of the tow vehicle. There may be so much weight on the rear of the car that some of the weight on the front wheels is removed, making it difficult to control the car. A weight-distribution hitch redistributes much of this weight to all four wheels of the tow vehicle as well as the wheels of the trailer, resulting in better handling, safer operation and less wear on the tow vehicle. Some weight-distribution hitches are also equipped with anti-sway bars, which help control trailer sway and improve control.

Coupler and Ball

The coupler is the mechanism which

attaches the trailer to the hitch. It is generally one of two basic types, the latch or the screw type.

The coupler must be of a size which matches the ball. The size of the ball is determined by the Gross Vehicle Weight Rating (GVWR). All couplers manufactured after 1973 have the Gross Vehicle Weight Rating stamped on them.

Fig. 10-6 Tongue in Position to Engage Ball

Fig. 10-7 Locking Ball in Cup

Among your trailer-gear spares, you should carry an extra ball, in case wear or turning stresses force yours out of roundness. Like all trailer bolt fittings, the ball should be secured by a lock nut.

Safety Chains

The final legal requirement in most states is safety chains. These consist simply of a pair of chains running from the tongue of the trailer to the towing hitch. The chains are crossed under the hitch in such a way that if the ball and coupler should fail, the trailer tongue won't hit the ground, dig in and cause the trailer to somersault. The chains should be just long enough to permit free turning and should be fastened securely to the vehicle. If S-hooks are used, they should be hooked with the S facing back toward the trailer to prevent their jumping free. Although S-hooks are acceptable, it is a safer practice to use a shackle and safety wire in place of the S-hook.

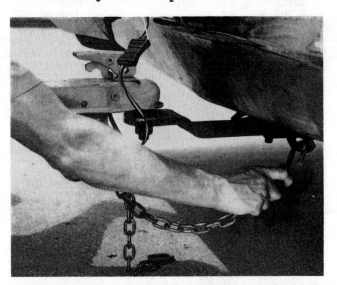

Fig. 10-8 Attaching Safety Chain

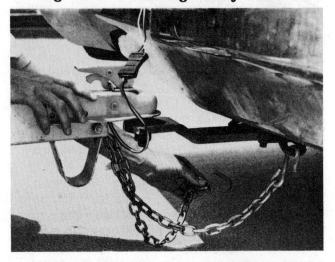

10-9 Crossing Second Chain Under First

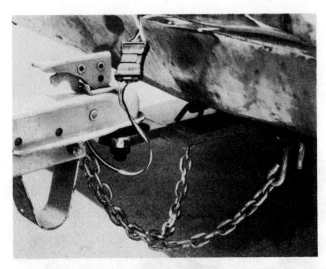

10-10 Hookup Complete

The chains themselves should be of welded steel, with a working test-load equivalent to the trailer's recommended gross weight, which is marked on the trailer itself. Although a single length of safety chain, looping through the eyes on the trailer tongue, may be used, individually attached chains provide an extra safety factor. The chains should never be made fast to a fitting common with the ball, but to some separate solid attachment point.

Fig. 10-11   Outboard Chained to Transom
and Drain Plug in Place

Support Points

After safety considerations, the most important thing about a trailer is its sup-

port of your boat's hull. Even sturdy fiberglass boats can be badly wrenched out of shape if they're not braced at critical points. The problem is that no roller-supporting system can support a hull on all points as evenly as water. All hull support systems are a compromise, and there are a few key things to watch out for.

For most hulls, vital support points are the forefoot, the keel, the turn of the bilge (especially where interior weights are concentrated) and the transom. Any other spot where a specially heavy downward force is exerted on the hull should also be braced from below when the hull is fully seated on the trailer. In the general category of concentrated weights you can include retractable keels or weighted centerboards on sailboats, water and fuel tanks, batteries, and engines. If your boat has an inboard engine, this is an absolutely overriding weight concentration that must be carefully braced beneath the engine bed stringers.

On most commercial trailers, the rollers and bolsters are adjustable, both up and down and fore an aft, and the winch column and wheel assemblies can also be moved along the frame. Given a trailer of adequate length and width, therefore, it should be possible to adjust the various elements of the frame and the supports to match the boat with some precision. Remember to be careful when adjusting any element that has a matching component on the boat's other side. An inch or so of fore-and-aft difference between the rollers can make a serious riding problem for the whole rig.

Fig. 10-12   Roller Supporting System

Tires

A trailer's tires and wheels undergo far more strain than do those on your car. Not only are a trailer's wheels often smaller to begin with, turning at higher speeds, but they are also subject to immersion, often in corrosive salt water. Maximum tire-load capacity and pressure are marked on the tire itself. These pressures are considerably higher than those of the tires on your family car. You should carry a suitable tire-pressure gauge and check your trailer's tires frequently. If you err, it should be on the side of more air in the tires, not less. Low air pressure in small, high-speed tires causes them to heat up faster and fail sooner.

The Winch

Under way on the open road, a trailered boat is subject to a type of motion that it will never encounter on the water. Every unattached piece of gear in the trailered boat should be firmly secured, and the boat itself should be firmly lashed in place.

The primary point of attachment is forward, at the trailer winch. If you plan to launch and recover off the trailer with some frequency, this winch is an especially important piece of equipment. It is usually an extra-cost option, so you have some choice as to type.

Your winch should have an anti-reverse gear so that the boat cannot slide backwards, and unless the boat is very light, the standard rope on the winch drum should be replaced with stainless steel wire. For larger boats, geared winches and electrical winches running off the towing vehicle's battery are available. The winch drum should be mounted, if possible, approximately on a line with the towing eye on your boat's bow when the boat is fully cradled. If there is no towing eye, the angle of pull from the bow chocks should be slightly downward.

Do not expect the winch alone to hold the bow in place. An additional wire cable, preferably with a turnbuckle, should

Fig. 10-13 Winch Cable Hooked to Eye of Stem

connect the boat's stem to the winch pillar. There should also be a non-stretching strap across the after part of the boat. Webbing like that used for auto seat belts or sailboat hiking straps will do well enough, but pad the hull or wood trim directly under the strap with old carpeting to preserve gel coat and varnish. A pair of spring lines (these can be your boat's dock lines) should be run aft from the bow cleat to the trailer frame about even with the wheels.

Important extras, after a winch and brakes, include the following: spare trailer wheel, bearing grease and a complete set of wheel bearings, bulbs for the trailer's lights, a jack that suits the trailer's frame and can lift the trailer and boat, a set of long-handled wrenches for tightening the various body bolts regularly, outside mirrors for the towing vehicle, flares, trouble flag and trouble light.

The Tow Vehicle

The average passenger car is designed to carry only people. You will need to beef it up if you want to tow anything but the lightest of trailers. The advent of front-wheel drive makes the load distribu-

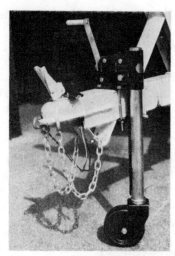

**Fig. 10-14 Trailer Tongue Jack
and Dolly Wheel**

tion between the front and rear axles even more important than it was on the older, heavier cars. Both steering and traction now depend on sufficient weight on the front axle. The owner's manual of a typical front-wheel drive car with a gross vehicle weight of 2800 pounds indicates that the permissible trailer gross weight without brakes is only 885 pounds. The same car can tow a 2200 GVW trailer with brakes, but only on hills with less than a 12% gradient if the car has a manual transmission, or less than 16% with an automatic transmission. Trailer-tongue loading is limited in all cases, often to as little as 110 pounds.

Except for specially equipped utility vehicles, you should not tow a trailer heavier than your car. Many manufacturers sell towing packages including items such as a non-slip differential, heavy-duty cooling system, heavy-duty flashers, oversize battery and alternator, heavy-duty suspension, special wiring, special rear-axle ratio, and larger tires and wheels. Such packages are suitable when included in an order for a new car but are not a viable addition to the car you already own.

The essentials for a towing vehicle include:

Adequate Power - The tow vehicle must have enough power to merge safely with highway traffic when towing maximum load. It must also be able to climb commonly encountered hills without losing speed; therefore, get the largest engine available.

Cooling - For cooling, the engine may need a heavy-duty, high-capacity radiator with more core tubes to speed heat release, possibly a special fan shroud, and a coolant-recovery unit. A thermostat-operated spray-coolant unit to spray cool water on the radiator core tubes when the temperature of the coolant goes too high is also available.

Transmission - Towing a trailer places an extra load on the transmission. This may generate enough heat to thin out the transmission fluid and damage the transmission. To prevent this, it may be necessary to install a small radiator to cool the transmission fluid. The driver of a towing vehicle must always be on the alert for transmission leaks, slippage or rough shifting, all of which are indicative of transmission problems.

Brakes - Cars ordered with a towing option have oversized drums and/or special heavy-duty brake linings. Standard auto brakes are undersized for towing all but very light trailers. Brakes should have premium linings, especially on the rear, as the tongue weight keeps wheels in tighter contact with the pavement.

Suspension System - 100 pounds of tongue weight 4 feet behind the rear axle have the same effect as 400 pounds added to the trunk of the car. To avoid excessive sagging and "bottoming out," the suspension should be beefed up with heavy-duty springs, air shocks, or air bags. Heavy-duty shock absorbers are necessary to control the added weight. This will allow the vehicle to ride in a nearly normal attitude and improve visibility and handling.

Proper Loading
Balancing the load on your trailer is really the key to successful towing. What it amounts to is adjusting the boat's gross weight - the boat and its contents - so that the load on the trailer tongue is somewhere between five and seven percent of the total gross weight of the

tow: boat + contents + trailer. For the average small passenger car, the weight at the tongue shouldn't be much more than 100 lb. Working backward, that indicates a gross weight of 2,000 lb. as the maximum an ordinary sedan should be asked to pull. If you're in doubt about the towing capabilities of your car, check with the dealer.

To measure tongue weight, load the boat (which is on the trailer) with the gear she would normally carry on the road. Then stack two or three cinder blocks under a set of bathroom scales and ease the trailer's tongue down on this platform. If the weight involved is over about 75 lb., consider fixing an accessory jack and caster to the tongue. The jack-and-caster assembly was developed to facilitate the mating of heavy trailers to the trailer hitch. It allows raising and lowering the trailer tongue and facilitates moving the trailer for parking and other purposes. Raising the trailer tongue will also tilt the boat to allow for drainage when the boat is stored. (See Fig. 10-14)

If the weight at the trailer tongue is much more than the recommended maximum, the tow car will have too much load behind and be hard to handle at speed. If the tongue weight is too little, the trailer is likely to fishtail. What you want, then, is the happy medium. If you're pulling a load over about 4,000 pounds, by the way, you'll want a tandem, or four-wheel, trailer as well as a special towing vehicle.

You can determine the gross vehicle (trailer) weight by loading the trailer with everything that normally would be on it during transportation and taking the rig to the nearest scales with a platform (highway weighing station, building supply company, trucking company, junk yard, etc.). Weigh the trailer by itself, unhitched and supported on the jack. This will give the gross trailer weight. It is important that the gross trailer weight (Gross Vehicle Weight) does not exceed the Gross Vehicle Weight Rating as shown on the capacity label. Keep the trailer in

a level attitude by adjusting the jack-caster assembly.

Even before loading a new trailer for the first time, it might be wise to consider what might happen if you get a flat tire after the trailer is loaded. Check the wheel nuts for tightness. Factories tend to install wheelnuts with air wrenches; the nuts may be too tight for you to loosen with a tire iron. You might also let the air out of a tire to make sure your jack will fit under the axle when you really need to use it.

Pre-Departure Checks

Before setting out, you should check the items loaded in the boat to be sure they are properly secured in place. Make certain that no one has tossed in last-minute items that can significantly alter the trailer's balance. Check also that the trailer's bolts are all tightened up. They can work loose slowly and insidiously. Check boat tie-downs, trailer lights and brakes. Spare a moment to make certain that the car-to-trailer umbilicals will stay secured when under way.

If you trailer a sailboat, the mast and boom should be firmly lashed down, preferably in a padded rack. Some trailerable-boat manufacturers supply just such a fitting, but you can usually rig one yourself. The standing and running rigging should be bundled together and tied to

Fig. 10-15   Mast Padded at the Rack and Transom

the spar at intervals so that it can't work loose. If you travel rough roads or long distances, consider a covering for at least the winch cluster at the base of the spar and the sheave arrangement at the masthead, just to keep out highway dirt. If the mast protrudes aft, it should have a red flag lashed to its end.

The rudder of a sailboat should be removed before trailering, if it's removable. A bracket-mounted outboard can stay on the boat as long as the transom is supported directly beneath the motor. Protect the motor (or lower unit, if an I/O) from excessive and uncontrolled swinging or bouncing. Avoid supports which concentrate stress in fragile castings, or which rely on hydraulic cylinders, which may suffer damaged seals.

If your sailboat has a swing-keel or a weighted centerboard, it should be lowered until it rests on a frame cross-member. This will save much wear on the centerboard pennant (the wire rope used to raise the centerboard) and a certain amount of stress on the hull, as well.

Underway, remember that you've got a long, heavy, awkward tail behind you. This sounds very obvious, until you see someone pulling a trailer cut in ahead of you, oblivious to the fact that his vehicle is 20 or 25 feet longer than normal.

Start your towing car slowly, in low gear, and take it up through the speeds gently and smoothly. Think twice about passing other cars, but if you decide to pass, pick a spot and go - don't hesitate. When rounding corners, swing wide, after having checked traffic just behind and alongside you. Give plenty of warning with your turn signal.

Remain sensitive to any unusual sounds or handling factors, and if you notice anything at all out of the ordinary, pull over at once and check. In fact, you should get off the road and check out the entire rig every hour or so - look for high temperatures in the wheel bearings, loosening tie-downs, slacked-off bolts,

brake and turn lights, tire pressure and car-engine temperature.

Heavy-duty flashers can slow down the blinking of your turn signal to a "normal" rate, but they have the disadvantage of not revealing a burned-out bulb by failing to flash. If you have them, you should turn on your parking lights and hazard flashers every time you stop and walk around to make sure that all the bulbs are working. This problem exists even if you are not towing your trailer as long as the heavy-duty flasher is installed.

Launching

Before you attempt a real launching, put in a couple of hours some Sunday in an empty parking lot learning how to line up and back the trailer effectively. Have someone help you by acting as a guide, and develop a set of simple hand signals. Backing a trailer is much easier than docking, but it does take practice. If you have an exceptionally heavy or unwieldy rig, consider buying a front bumper hitch. With this accessory, you can make the launch while moving the towing vehicle forward, and close-quarters maneuvering will be simpler.

When launching, try to avoid getting the trailer hubs in the water. If you can't avoid immersing them, at least let them cool off first, or the heat will simply suck the bearing full of water.

One way to pass the time while waiting for the trailer wheels to cool down from highway temperatures is by preparing the boat. If you have a sailboat, one thing you must do is step the mast. Before you try this, check to be sure that there are no low power lines or other overhead obstructions between you and the launching ramp. Many municipal ramps were laid out for outboard skiffs, not masted vessels. Be certain that no matter how the mast could fall, there are no overhead obstructions that it could hit, especially wire.

Sailboat Trailering - Raising the Mast

Many sailboats have some form of

Fig. 10-16   Mast Step on Hinge

tabernacle for raising the mast. This is essentially a mast stepped on a hinge, and most of them are so arranged that the mast swings up from astern. Smaller boats, of course, don't require this kind of fancy gear, and the mast goes into the normal step guided by a crewmember, as described earlier in this book.

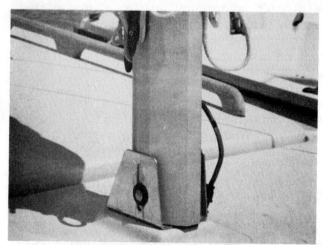

Fig. 10-17   Mast Tabernacle

Before beginning to raise the mast, check overhead for wires and obstructions. Check too, that there is a clear overhead path from the set-up area to the actual launching area and beyond.

Masts that pivot up and forward are simple to raise but require a fair amount of muscle power from the crew. With the mast in its hinged tabernacle, attach the upper shrouds and the backstay and tie a

pulling line - a good, thick one, comfortable to the hand - to the forestay just above the turnbuckle. As one person stands in the cockpit and raises the spar, the other crewmember at the bow, who should be the stronger of the two, pulls on the forestay extension.

If the boat is very small and light, the person raising the spar should stay out of the boat while doing it, since the unsupported hull might be damaged by the weight of the person inside. As the mast approaches the point where the person aft can exert no more lift, it may be necessary to tie off the forestay extension until the cockpit hand can get around forward to help pull. Until you're used to the stresses involved, don't take anything for granted: even a light mast can exert an enormous pull at certain acute angles.

The mast may, in some cases, swing up and aft from the bow. The spar thus lies flat over the foredeck after being made fast in its tabernacle. In this case, first make fast the upper shrouds and the forestay. Then attach the boom to its gooseneck at right angles to the mast, holding it in place with the topping lift and temporary guys to the deck at either side.   To raise the mast, you simply employ the four- or five-part mechanical advantage of the mainsheet tackle system, amplified if necessary by the genoa sheet winch.

Launching and Recovery

Before launching (or recovery) make sure that there is nothing protruding down from the boat to snag on the trailer frame. The outboard should be raised and locked, and the sailboat's centerboard or swing keel should be pulled all the way into its well and the pennant lashed. Don't forget to release the tiedowns and disconnect or remove the trailer's stop and directional lights, and make one last check to see to it that all drain plugs, etc., are in place.

Make sure you NEVER, NEVER cast off all the lines from the boat before launching. Someone on shore must have a

Fig. 10-18 Backing Down the Launch Ramp

line that is made fast to the boat. The line makes it easy to shove the boat off the trailer and then pull the boat to a dock or boarding platform or back to the trailer at a wide, busy launching ramp.

Back the trailer slowly down the ramp until the boat's stern is afloat, then ease it off the trailer. A person ashore should hold a bow line while this is being done. If you can remain in the car, it is a good idea not to turn the engine off so that the car won't roll back into the water when you try to start it again. Put an automatic transmission in "park" and keep a foot on the brake. If you are driving a manual shift vehicle, put the gearshift in first gear and keep your feet on both the clutch and the brake. Remember that the trailer's brakes do not operate from your parking brake lever, and that surge brakes do not work in reverse in any event.

If you must get out of your car to assist in the launching, it is not a good idea to leave your engine running. An

Fig. 10-20 Launched

automatic transmission can slip out of park into reverse with obvious results. If you leave your manual shift in neutral, you are depending entirely on your parking brake. How many times have you backed down your driveway and then shifted into a forward gear before you discovered you had forgotten to release your parking brake? The safest course of action is to set your automatic transmission in park, let up on the footbrake to make sure the transmission is locked,

Fig. 10-19 Releasing the Stem Hook

Fig. 10-21 Beginning Recovery Process

10-11

Fig. 10-22 Boat Recovered and on Trailer

then put on the parking brake and shut off the engine. A standard transmission should be left in first gear with the parking brake set and the engine off.

Today, many trailers have special bearings that resist moisture if they are not hot when they are immersed in water. If your trailer does not have immersible bearings and the wheels get wetted down, repack the bearings with grease. It doesn't take long and is easier than changing a burnt-out bearing on the road home.

Trailer Storage

When the boat is on her trailer for any length of time, get the weight off the trailer suspension and wheels. Jack up the trailer frame and support it with cinder blocks, shimmed up if necessary with pieces of planking. Once the frame is fully jacked up, check underneath to be sure the boat is still evenly supported – the frame can be easily and imperceptibly wrenched out of shape during the jacking process.

Boat Covers

Your boat cover should be tailored to your specific boat to stay in place under a variety of conditions. A top drawstring allows for pulling the cover high enough to shed water. Remember that puddling of water must be prevented since rain weighs about 8.3 pounds per gallon. The weight of collected water stretches the cover, allowing the puddle to grow larger until the cover rips or the bottom edge comes up, allowing the water to funnel into the boat. The bottom drawstring and tiedowns, which go under the boat, are handy to prevent the cover from whipping while trailering. Sandbags or other weights sewn into pockets along the bottom drawstring will help keep the cover in place. A tire cover for storage extends tire life by eliminating harmful sun rays.

Chapter 11

Weather

Introduction

Boating people are, as a group, directly concerned with weather. Boaters have a special need to know about sea and wind conditions. Although many sailors tend to regard wind as synonymous with weather, the first is but one aspect of the second. Weather also includes temperature, pressure and moisture, all of which affect the condition of the atmosphere. This chapter will deal with the essentials of weather on two levels, systemic and local. The weather system information here won't make you a meteorologist. But it should help, with practice, in making you aware of what weather to expect before you set out. Weather can turn nasty during an afternoon's outing. Knowing what to expect from local weather signs can reduce your chance of being caught unprepared.

What Makes Weather Work

All weather is ultimately brought about by heat from the sun within the shallow envelope of gas we call the atmosphere. And all weather change is brought about by rising or falling temperature.

In very simplified terms, the large-scale movement of air around the earth is caused by the air becoming heated from contact with the ground or ocean near the Equator. The heated air rises and spreads around the globe while colder air from the north and south replaces it. If the world didn't rotate, air circulation around it would be much simpler. Because of the earth's rotation, the basic wind patterns are as shown, with prevailing winds that are generally quite reliable. In the continental United States, most of which is located between Latitudes 30° and 60° North, the prevailing winds are

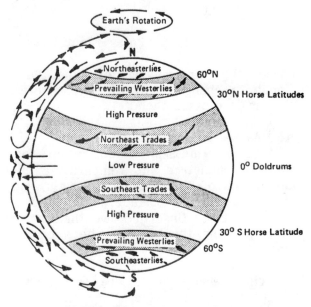

Fig. 11-1 Global Atmospheric Circulation

from the west—a fact that influences not only boating habits, but also marina and harbor layouts.

Although the majority of winds across our country blow from a generally westerly direction, there are many days when this isn't the case. Seasonal changes, differences in heat distribution over water and land, geographic features, uneven local heating—all contribute to making weather variable. In the United States, the position of the **Polar Front**, the boundary between the polar easterlies and our prevailing westerlies, normally lies around 60° North. But when the cold polar air moves south, violent weather is sometimes the result.

Another major influence on weather change is the Rocky Mountains, which

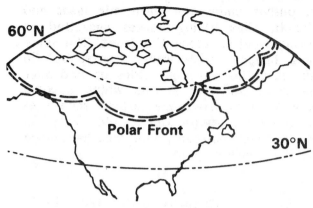

Fig. 11-2   Polar Front

cause the air moving off the Pacific Ocean to change many of its characteristics as it crosses them.

Air Masses and Fronts

Huge air masses, which retain for a time the moisture and temperature characteristics of their place of origin, move over the earth's surface, and determine our weather. Unsettled weather regions develop along the boundary between these masses.

High pressure areas are formed when air (for any of several reasons) cools, becomes more compressed, and consequently sinks. In the northern hemisphere the circulation of air is clockwise around a high and the wind directions are both

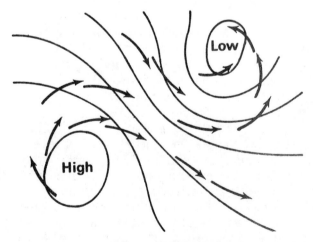

Fig. 11-3   **Air Circulation—Clockwise Around Highs, Counterclockwise Around Lows in the Northern Hemisphere**

clockwise and outward from the high's center, as shown in Fig. 11-3. High pressure areas may cover immense stretches of the earth's surface--half the United States, under certain conditions--but they are usually a few hundred miles in diameter. Highs originating in the polar area move south and east. Cool, dry air and fair weather is generally characteristic of a high, as are light winds and steady temperatures.

Low pressure areas, in most respects, are the opposite of highs. A low's center is constantly being filled with air moving into it in a generally counterclockwise direction (in the Northern Hemisphere). Winds are strong, but lows, like highs, generally move from west to east across our continent.

There are, however, semi-permanent high and low pressure areas. Off the West Coast of the United States is the **Pacific High**, somewhat larger in summer than in winter. The **Azores High**, over the Atlantic, shows the same seasonal changes in size. In winter, a low frequently exists in the Aleutians, while in summer there is a low that extends from northeast Africa all the way to Indochina. The semi-permanent highs form largely over water, when the sea is cooler than the land.

Localized low pressure areas may also form under a thundercloud formation, where air is rising with great speed, or over very hot areas into which the cooler air flows as the heated air is elevated.

It can be useful to know where a low pressure area is in relation to you, since lows are usually the source of bad boating weather. In the northern hemisphere, stand with your back to the present surface wind, then turn 45° or so to the right. This aligns you with the existing wind aloft, which blows in a somewhat different direction than the breeze at ground level. Under normal circumstances, where the true wind is not affected by highly localized conditions, the high pressure center is now to your right, the low center to your left. The pressure area to

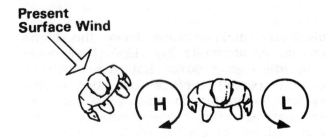

Present Surface Wind

Fig. 11-4   Buys-Ballot's Law for Determining Low Pressure Area

the west of you is, generally speaking, the one that will reach you, while weather to the east has already passed.

Besides highs and lows, it is useful to consider the great air masses, bodies of air in which conditions of temperature and moisture are the same or similar from one side to the other. Air masses take their names from their characteristics, and the masses which cross our country can be very different.

Although air masses change somewhat according to the surfaces they cross, they remain essentially the same. In the United States, there are two origins of such masses, called **Tropical** and **Polar**. Obviously the former comes from southern latitudes, while the latter originates in the north. But each may be further defined as **continental**—having formed over land—or **maritime**, having formed over the sea.

The air masses that affect us are:

Continental Polar (cP)—cold and dry

Maritime Polar (mP)—cold or warm, but moist

Maritime Tropical (mT)—warm and moist

<u>Fronts</u> form when air masses of different characteristics collide--the front being the boundary between two such masses. The front takes its name from the type of air which is arriving. That is, when an eastward-moving mass of cold air catches up with warm air, also moving east, but

not so quickly, a <u>cold front</u> is formed. Cold air, being more compact and heavier, pushes under the warm air mass and lifts it. This lifting causes unsettled or stormy weather along the front. The same thing happens with warm fronts, but in this case the warm air rides up and over the cold, and the storms which accompany a warm front are not so severe as those characteristic of a cold front. In either case, however, the weather along the front is not good.

Cold Fronts

Cold fronts move at speeds from 10 to 50 knots, depending on the time of year—they are two or three times as fast in winter as in summer. If a cold front is moving fast, it may be preceded by a **squall line**, a roll of black, towering clouds that may reach heights of 40,000 feet, with violent storms and even tornadoes. Wind shifts along the front will be sudden and velocities will increase dramatically. Behind the squall line are heavy rains, followed by clearing.

About 150 miles ahead of the usual cold front are high sheets of Altocumulus cloud, followed by lowering, thickening Nimbostratus, a low cloud with rain and wind. The barometer falls, sometimes very fast, and the wind becomes gusty. As the actual front passes overhead, the winds increase and the barometer contin-

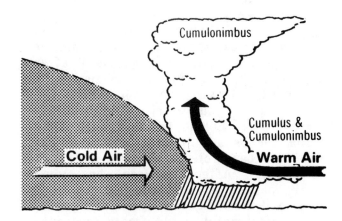

Fig. 11-5   Collision of Cold and Warm Fronts Results in Bad Weather for the Boater

ues to drop, then as the barometer hits bottom, the wind direction shifts abruptly clockwise, continuing gusty, and the barometer begins to rise quickly as the temperature falls.

A cold front is normally followed by some heavy rain, then clearing and gusty winds from west or northwest. At least a couple of days of clear, cool weather, often with excellent sailing winds, are in prospect.

Warm Fronts

The warm front is a different creature. Its cloud warnings—high, thin Cirrus—extend as much as 1,000 miles ahead, clouds representing warm air that has climbed up and over the retreating cold

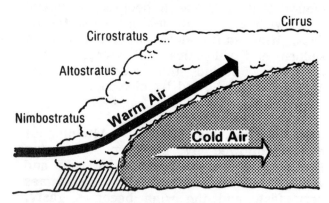

Fig. 11-6 Warm Front Storm

air mass. As the front slowly advances, clouds thicken and lower. The barometer starts a steady fall and the winds pick up. High-level **Cirrostratus** clouds become mid-level **Altostratus** clouds and rain or snow begins to fall, continuing until after the front passes. As this occurs, the winds shift clockwise and decrease. The temperature begins to rise and visibility is often poor. Behind the front are some **Stratus** clouds and perhaps a little more rain. The barometer may rise and then fall slightly. After the front has completely passed, the skies will clear and winds will normally be from the southwest. Unfortunately, cold fronts frequently follow hard on the heels of warm fronts, so the duration of good weather may be short.

It's very useful to know these normal sequences of weather as fronts pass through. Although the time it takes for an individual front to pass through an area will vary, it's possible to predict the actual weather sequence with considerable accuracy. Weather fronts are accompanied by specific cloud formations which are developed by the front itself, as you saw in Figures 11-5 and 11-6. If you learn to recognize these cloud formations you can relate the approaching weather pattern with the clouds you can see overhead.

Clouds

As indicated earlier, weather changes are caused by changing temperatures. When air cools below its saturation point, the water vapor in the air condenses and forms clouds. The two basic cloud types are called **Cumulus**, which are fluffy,

Fig. 11-7   Scattered Cumulus Clouds— Good Weather

piled up clouds (Fig. 11-7), and **Stratus**, which are flat and frequently layered (Fig. 11-8).

Specific cloud names include a description of the altitude where the clouds form. Three types of high clouds exist. **Cirrus** are thin, wispy high clouds that sometimes stretch right up to the lower

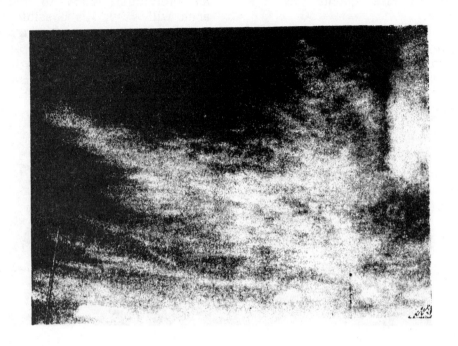

Fig. 11-8   Stratus Clouds— Overcast
Sky

Fig. 11-9   Cirrostratus Clouds—Cause
Sun and Moon Halo—Maybe
Rain

Fig. 11-10   Altostratus Clouds—
               Overcast Sky or Rain

Fig. 11-11   Altocumulus Clouds

level of the stratosphere. They are composed entirely of ice crystals and are often called "mares tails." The second type of high cloud is called **cirrocumulus.** It often appears as faint ripples like those on windblown sand, sometimes called a mackerel sky. The **cirrostratus** (Fig. 11-9) is the lowest of the high clouds, although it may be as much as four or five miles up. It is veil-like, causing the sky to look milky and causing those rings or halos around the sun or moon that are said to forecast approaching rain.

The middle clouds, averaging 10,000 feet in altitude, contain the prefix "alto." **Altostratus** have a fibrous, frosted appearance (Fig. 11-10); **altocumulus** resemble them except they are puffier (Fig. 11-11).

Of the three types of low clouds, ranging from ground level to 6,500 feet, the **nimbostratus** is the typical rain cloud

Fig. 11-12   Nimbostratus Clouds—Rain or Snow

(Fig. 11-12). At a low altitude, it is a dark grey color and nearly uniform. Low **stratus** cloud, on the other hand, consists of an even, continuous layer all the way

through. It sometimes looks like a high bank of fog and causes only drizzle. The atmosphere below a sheet of stratus is often very clear and distant objects look to be quite close. **Stratocumulus** appears as a layer or patches of globular cloud masses, regularly arranged. The smallest are quite large, and are mostly soft and grey, with some darker parts (Fig. 11-13). While they may indicate rain is on the way, they are not rain clouds.

Fig. 11-13   Stratocumulus Clouds—Rain Warning

There are also two types of clouds that form vertically, including the **cumulus.** These cauliflower-like puffs mean fair weather and can form at any altitude (Fig. 11-7). The second is the **cumulonimbus,** the common thunderhead which can grow to 50,000 feet and develop an anvil top where the cloud reaches the high altitude "jet-stream" winds (Fig. 11-14).

Fig. 11-14 Cumulonimbus Clouds—Note Anvil Shaped Cirroform Cap

Weather Clues from the Clouds

Clouds not only tell you where you are in relation to an approaching front, but also indicate something about the weather in general. When you see clouds moving leisurely across the sky, you can anticipate continued fair weather. You can look for wind and rain when they scud rapidly overhead. When small clouds decrease or melt away towards sunset, fair weather can be expected, but increasing clouds indicate unsettled weather ahead. Near the end of a long spell of good weather, clouds sometimes begin to form high in the sky. This is said to indicate that the change in weather will be gradual with the bad weather as much as two days away. It can also mean that the bad weather will be around for awhile. When the higher clouds are moving in a different direction than the lower prevailing wind, or the lower clouds, it means that a general change of wind direction to the direction of the higher clouds is coming.

Even the color of the sky can be revealing since moisture in the atmosphere can act like a prism to break up the sunlight. On a good day when little moisture is present, the blue rays are not scattered.

As the moisture increases, the blue rays are turned aside and the long-wave reds and yellows dominate. Yellow is often the forerunner of heavy rain and wind within the next day and a half.

A red glow over the western sky at sunset, or in long narrow streaks of high cloud showing across the setting sun, means fine weather tomorrow. But red reflecting over lowering masses of ragged clouds at sunset indicates stormy weather ahead. Red is also a bad sign in the eastern sky at dawn because it indicates the approach of clouds. The red is caused by high thin clouds that are often otherwise invisible.

Green appearing sky in the clearing areas between showers indicates the upper atmosphere is very moist and intermittent showers will continue, interspersed with sunshine. A soft light blue sky means settled weather, but very dark blue sky that sharply outlines the clouds means a storm is coming.

Thunderstorms

The localized thundersquall is probably the one kind of weather most feared by experienced boaters. It need not be associated with major weather systems, as it can arise in a very short time, or it may lurk concealed in a hazy sky, and it can produce winds of shattering force. Add to that the fearful and often dangerous effect of lightning, and you have a natural demonstration that should inspire respect in any seafarer.

Causes of thunderstorms vary, but they are all characterized by a violent uplifting of air, sometimes to heights of 75,000 feet. There are usually three stages in the life cycle of an average thunderstorm. The early, or cumulus, stage occurs when a **cumulus cloud**—the detached,

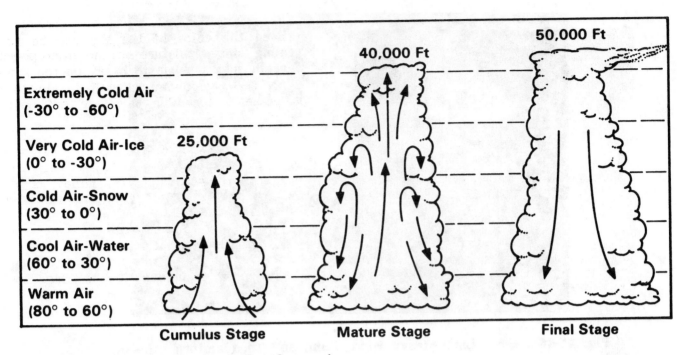

Fig. 11-15 Thunderstorm Development

puffy cloud of summer fair weather—develops vertically from 15,000 to 25,000 feet. This means that the rising air currents within it may be cooled as much as 80° while ascending, to well below freezing at the cloud's top. The air in the cloud is still warmer than the air outside.

In the second stage, when the cloud reaches a height of approximately 40,000 feet, its full vertical development, precipitation occurs and falling rain or hail cools the air inside, creating downdrafts and heavy rains. In the terminal third stage, the entire cloud becomes sinking air. With no ascending air to be cooled, rain stops. At this point, the cloud at the top of the thunderhead has been blown into the familiar anvil shape—the sign of an aging storm.

On most summer days, the cumulus clouds of afternoon have at least some potential for becoming thunderheads. As long as you keep an eye on them, you can usually make for safety long before there's any danger. On the other hand, when visibility is limited by haze, as it sometimes is during ideal thunderstorm conditions, the formation of the towering,

sharp-edged cloud—called **cumulonimbus**—typical of thunderstorms, may be veiled by haze.

On such hot, muggy, hazy afternoons, you should be alert for static on AM (not FM) radios, the sound of distant thunder, or the flicker of lightning. You should stay close to port, as the wind may die shortly before the storm itself begins. Anytime there is a threat of bad weather all hands should don their PFDs.

Once you can see the cumulonimbus cloud, you can estimate your distance from the thunderstorm. Since thunder and lightning occur simultaneously at the point of the lightning discharge, you see the lightning flash before you hear the thunder unless it is directly overhead. The sound takes approximately five seconds to travel one statute mile. Therefore if you slowly count one thousand, two thousand, ..., every five counts indicates the lightning is one mile away. You must take care that you relate the sound to its appropriate flash, a difficult task if the lightning is nearly continuous.

Fig. 11-16 Squall Line—Heavy Wind, Rain, and Thunderstorm Ahead

Squall Lines

Squall lines may precede fast-moving cold fronts. They are an unbroken line of black, ominous clouds, towering 40,000 feet or more into the sky, including thunderstorms of almost incredible violence and occasional tornadoes. Such squall lines are extremely turbulent, sometimes more so than a typical hurricane. From the water, a squall line looks like a wall of rolling, boiling black fog. Winds shift and sharpen suddenly with the approach of the squall line, and downward-pouring rain may carry the cloud clear to the water in sharp, vertical bands. Torrential rains fall behind the leading edge of the squall line.

Squall lines occur when winds above a cold front, moving in the same direction as the front's advance, prevent the lifting of a warm air mass. This is why little bad weather occurs right at the surface front. But miles ahead of the front the strong winds force up the warm air with almost explosive violence, producing the squall line.

Tornadoes

When numerous thunderstorms occur along a single cold front, they are often organized into a long, narrow band. The front of this band is usually marked by a squall line. The cold downdrafts from the thunderstorms meet the warm air along these squall lines, causing the wind direction to change suddenly in strong gusts. The temperature also drops suddenly. Such conditions often spawn tornadoes. The tornadoes formed at squall lines often occur in families and move with the prevailing wind in the warm sector ahead of the cold front. This is usually a southwest wind which moves the tornadoes in a northeast direction.

A **tornado** is a whirlpool of air of relatively small diameter which extends downward from a cumulonimbus cloud. It has a funnel-like appearance, the average diameter of the visible funnel is about 750 feet. The destructive effects of the whirling winds associated with the funnel may extend as much as one-half mile on each side of the center. Wind speed near the tornado's center has been estimated in excess of 200 knots. Tornadoes occur in boating areas along the Atlantic and Gulf of Mexico coasts and in all inland boating areas east of the Rocky Mountains.

Microbursts

In 1976 the U. S. Government first identified the microburst phenomenon as a possible hazard to landing aircraft and to pleasure boats. The downdrafts from a single thunderstorm act in the same manner as the downdrafts in front of a squall line, meeting the warm air and causing the wind direction to change suddenly in the form of strong gusts. These gusts usually flow radially from the point where the downdraft hits the surface and are strongest in the direction in which the thundercloud is moving. Such microburst winds have been estimated to exceed 100 knots.

Microbursts may occur even when no rain is apparent below the thunder-cloud since within the cloud there may be rainfall which evaporates before it reaches the surface. This phenomenon is known as a dry microburst. The gusts of wind associated with microbursts are called "windshear." Because there is no visible indication of windshear, it is very difficult to forecast. Microbursts can occur several miles away from an associated squall line, so you should be alert to the possibility of strong gusts from a different direction than the prevailing wind whenever you are sailing near a thunderstorm area, whether it is raining or not.

Waterspouts

A **waterspout** is the marine equivalent of a tornado. It forms under the same conditions and may have a diameter of from 20 to 200 feet. Waterspouts begin as a funnel-shaped protuberance at the base of a cumulonimbus cloud and grow downward toward the sea. A cloud of spray forms below the funnel where the water surface is agitated. The funnel-like cloud descends until it merges with the spray, then the water spout appears as a tube reaching from the sea to the cloud. Although waterspouts are less violent than tornadoes, they are still a real danger to pleasure boats. They are more common to the tropics than to the middle latitudes and may last from ten minutes to a half an hour before the tube breaks and the "spout" at the water surface subsides.

Hurricanes

A hurricane is not related to warm or cold fronts. It is a storm that originates in the tropics and is characterized by its counterclockwise circulation. A hurricane begins as a **tropical depression**. Once its winds reach 33 knots, it becomes a **tropical storm**. It is classified as a **hurricane** when it reaches sustained speeds of 64 knots. Hurricanes are a form of a **Tropical Cyclone** as are the **Typhoons** which occur in the western Pacific Ocean. Typhoons are often larger and more intense than hurricanes because of the greater expanse of the Pacific Ocean.

A well developed hurricane may average 400 miles in diameter. Its center or eye is a low pressure area (which accounts for the hurricane's counterclockwise circulation) and may be 15 to 25 miles in diameter. While hurricane winds, by definition, are more than 64 knots, the winds in the eye seldom reach 15 knots, although seas within the eye are heavy and confused.

The Atlantic Ocean hurricane season is June through November, August through October is the season of greatest hurricane frequency. Hurricanes usually mature near the West Indies and move westward toward the Gulf of Mexico. They often follow a route around the semi-permanent Azores-Bermuda high-pressure area and track northward. However, their exact route over the water can be erratic and unpredictable.

Hurricanes move at around 15 knots while they are traveling westward in the low latitudes. After they have finished their turn to a northerly direction, they usually pick up speed, traveling at 25 knots or better, sometimes as fast as 50 or 60 knots if they remain over open water. They lose their intensity as they move over the cooler waters in the middle and upper latitudes or when they move over land.

Since the government has an imperfect record of forecasting the movement of specific hurricanes, you should not try to outguess either the hurricane or the fore-casters, and should stay ashore if a hurricane threatens. While you should take every precaution to secure your boat properly before a hurricane arrives, you should not try to "ride out" a hurricane on your boat. No boat is worth the loss of a life in order to protect it.

Fog

One weather feature that is of particular concern to boaters is fog. **Fog** is formed when air at the surface is cooled to the point (dew point) where its moisture condenses into very small droplets. This is similar to the way a cloud forms. Fog is really a cloud that is on, or near the ground.

To understand more about fog, let's review some facts we discussed earlier. Cool air cannot hold as much moisture as warm. Thus, if air that is already moist is made cooler, fog will form. This occurs in several ways.

On land, if the air is very humid at sunset, the land, and the air close to it, will cool off and fog may form. This is known as **radiation** fog. When the sun rises the following morning, it will warm the air a few degrees. The condensed moisture will disappear and the fog will dissipate ("burn off").

The fog most common to boaters is caused by moist air moving over a cool surface. An example of this is warm moist air from land blowing over cold coastal waters. This is called **advection** fog because the temperature change is brought on by air moving to a cooler location. It is a particular hazard to boaters because it commonly occurs on coastal waters especially in cold seasons, and it moves in a "bank" that can over-take and surprise the unwary boater. The fog will usually be concentrated close to the water's surface and may be absent at a height of 50 feet. This is because the water is the cooling agent.

Fog is likely wherever an area of cold water exists; as for example, on the Pa-cific coast, where upwelling brings cold water to the surface. For this same reason, fog can form on rivers where cold water flows through areas with very moist air. The cold river will cool air near the surface causing fog. Sometimes this situation occurs below dams because the water becomes cold in the deep pool behind the dam.

Fortunately, weathermen, by carefully predicting temperature change and measuring dew point (the temperature at which moisture condenses), can predict fog with high reliability. Marine weather forecasts include information about any anticipated fog. Inasmuch as the normal weather forecasts often don't give this information, wise boaters always get the marine forecast before departing.

Sources of Weather Information

The best source of weather information is the one that is easiest for you to get and most up to date. You will, of course, want to have the very best information you can get, but you must also recognize that conditions can be very localized, and can change very quickly. You should de-velop the ability to analyze developing weather conditions and be prepared to change your plans as conditions dictate.

In some areas, principally large metro-politan areas, recorded telephone marine weather forecasts are available. Call while you are planning your trip, then again just before you leave, to get the latest update.

VHF-FM weather broadcasts are proba-bly the best overall source of weather information for the boater. These broad-casts, transmitted continuously from Na-tional Weather Service stations, repeat every few minutes, and include detailed reports of conditions and forecasts for the coverage area. They are updated fre-quently, and may be interrupted with live updates as developing situations require.

VHF weather broadcasts draw on Na-tional Weather Service computers, reports from Coast Guard and other units in the area, and represent the best information available. Reception on suitable radios is excellent over very wide areas, since the transmitting antennas are generally located on very advantageous sites.

Most VHF-FM radiotelephones are equipped for two or more weather channels (receive only - you cannot transmit), identified as "WX-1," "WX-2," etc. (See Chapter 12, Radiotelephone.)

Scheduled weather forecasts on commercial radio and television stations are also available to you. Some of these come directly from the National Weather Service, and others augment NWS forecasts with more specific forecasts developed by consultant meteorologists.

You should understand, however, that many forecasts on commercial broadcast stations are intended for a different audience, and may lack the details, or the areas of coverage, that you as a boater may need.

Newspapers generally include weather forecast information, and may also show weather maps from which you may be able to gain a general idea of the weather patterns that are approaching your area. Use these data with caution, however, since they may be from 12 to 24 hours old by the time you see them. Outdated information can be worse than no information at all, and conditions can change very seriously over a 24-hour period.

Yachtsmen who routinely make long passages know the importance of good, up-to-date weather information, and sometimes go to great lengths to obtain it. Coded weather data are broadcast by short-wave radio, but they require a good deal of sophistication to decode, plot and develop into a forecast for your region. Facsimile weather maps and forecast information are also available from short-wave broadcasts. Special and very expensive equipment is necessary to convert these radio signals into weather maps, but

if you are caught in mid-ocean by a developing tropical storm, the cost may be negligible compared to the cost of a catastrophe.

Pennants and Lights

Visual warning displays may be shown by yacht clubs, marinas, and some Coast Guard facilities when conditions warrant. The most common of these is the "small craft advisory." It forecasts possible hazards to small craft, such as winds over 30 knots or scattered afternoon thunderstorms. These warnings should not be disregarded, no matter how good conditions appear to be at the time. Remember, too, that "small craft" includes some rather large boats — up to 65' in length.

Gale and storm warnings also may be shown, and indicate that even more severe weather conditions are anticipated. And, of course, the hurricane warning signals warn of the development of very serious weather, indeed.

In order for you to relate these various wind velocities to visual aids, the Beaufort Wind Scale is shown in Fig. 11-18.

Before you start out on a boating trip, whether it be an extended cruise or merely an afternoon outing on a local lake, check the weather patterns. If you anticipate a lengthy trip, you might begin watching some days in advance of the trip so you can have a feeling for the kinds of trends that develop over time.

Even more important than gathering forecast information, keep your "weather eye" peeled for the approach of conditions that suggest a storm. Dark, threatening clouds, with or without lightning, should be avoided.

Storms that are too distant to be seen or heard can sometimes be detected by listening to static, caused by lightning activity, on AM broadcast radios.

Take special note of any changes in wind direction or strength that is not expected, and watch for changes in the character or direction of waves. If you have any doubts about the weather, look for a protected anchorage. In any case, you should always have an alternative port in mind should weather conditions change suddenly and catch you unprepared.

Local Weather

All weather lore and forecasts aside, local weather conditions may be unique, and your ability to handle them may depend more on your knowledge--and the knowledge and experience of others--of these local conditions. This is especially true of conditions in the vicinity of mountains, islands, or even large cities. Forecast winds from a particular direction may be deflected and appear to come from a very different direction if structures and land masses intervene. Many sailors have been capsized, for instance, when they failed to note a "notch" in the shore line, or a bay entrance. The wind or waves funneled through that opening could easily upset sail trim, and could even knock the boat on her beam ends.

SMALL CRAFT

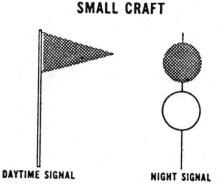

DAYTIME SIGNAL   NIGHT SIGNAL

One RED pennant displayed by day and a RED light over a WHITE light at night to indicate winds as high as 33 knots (38 m.p.h.) and/or sea conditions considered dangerous to small craft operations are forecast for the area.

STORM

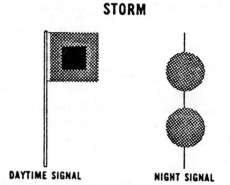

DAYTIME SIGNAL   NIGHT SIGNAL

A single square RED flag with a BLACK center displayed during daytime and two RED lights at night to indicate that winds 48 knots (55 m.p.h.) and above are forecast for the area. If the winds are associated with a tropical cyclone (hurricane), the "Storm Warning" display indicates winds 48 to 63 knots (55 to 73 m.p.h.) are forecast.

HURRICANE

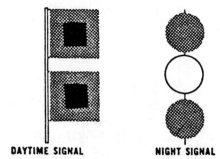

DAYTIME SIGNAL   NIGHT SIGNAL

Displayed only in connection with a tropical cyclone (hurricane). Two square RED flags with BLACK centers displayed by day and a WHITE light between two RED lights at night to indicate that winds 64 knots (74 m.p.h.) and above are forecast for the area.

GALE

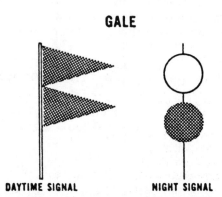

DAYTIME SIGNAL   NIGHT SIGNAL

Two RED pennants displayed by day and a WHITE light above a RED light at night to indicate winds within the range 34 to 47 knots (39 to 54 m.p.h.) are forecast for the area.

Fig. 11-17 Warning Signal Displays

BEAUFORT WIND SCALE

Beaufort number	Seaman's description of wind	Velocity m. p. h.	Estimating velocities on land	Estimating velocities on sea	Probable mean height of waves in feet	Description of Sea
0	Calm	Less than 1 ...	Smoke rises vertically.	Sea like a mirror	....	Calm (glassy)
1	Light air	1-3	Smoke drifts; wind vanes unmoved.	Ripples with the appearance of scales are formed but without foam crests.	½	Rippled
2	Light breeze	4-7	Wind felt on face; leaves rustle; ordinary vane moved by wind.	Small wavelets, still short but more pronounced; crests have a glassy appearance and do not break.	1	Smooth
3	Gentle breeze ...	8-12	Leaves and twigs in constant motion; wind extends light flag.	Large wavelets. Crests begin to break. Foam of glassy appearance. Perhaps scattered white caps.	2½	
4	Mod. breeze	13-18	Raises dust and loose paper; small branches are moved.	Small waves, becoming longer, fairly frequent white caps.	5	Slight
5	Fresh breeze	19-24	Small trees in leaf begin to sway; crested wavelets form on inland water.	Moderate waves, taking a more pronounced long form; many white caps are formed. (Chance of some spray.)	10	Moderate
6	Strong breeze ..	25-31	Large branches in motion; whistling heard in telegraph wires; umbrellas used with difficulty.	Large waves begin to form; the white foam crests are more extensive everywhere. (Probably some spray.)	15	Rough
7	Moderate gale .	32-38	Whole trees in motion; inconvenience felt in walking against wind.	Sea heaps up and white foam from breaking waves begins to be blown in streaks.	20	Very rough
8	Fresh gale	39-46	Breaks twigs off trees; generally impedes progress.	Moderately high waves of greater length; edges of crests break into spindrift. The foam is blown in well-marked streaks along the direction of the wind.	25	High
9	Strong gale	47-54	Slight structural damage occurs.	High waves. Dense streaks of foam along the direction of the wind. Sea begins to roll. Spray may affect visibility.	30	
10	Whole gale	55-63	Trees uprooted; considerable structural damage occurs.	Very high waves with long, overhanging crests. The surface of the sea takes a white appearance.	35	Very high
11	Storm	64-73		The sea is completely covered with long white patches of foam lying along the direction of the wind. Everywhere edges of the wave crests are blown into froth. Visibility affected.	40	
12	Hurricane	74-82		The air is filled with foam and spray. Sea completely white with driving spray; visibility very seriously affected.	45 or more ..	Phenomenal

Fig. 11-18 Beaufort Wind Scale

Weather Instruments

There are several devices used to describe the weather by measuring physical properties of the atmosphere. Unless you are planning to formulate your own forecast, having a lot of weather instruments will not be of much benefit to you. However, you may wish to purchase an inexpensive barometer. Barometers will give a rough indication of approaching fronts and low pressure systems. Leave the reading and interpreting of the highly technical instruments to the professionals.

The following definitions are intended for your general information only. An **Anemometer**, measures wind speed. A **Barometer** measures atmospheric pressure in either inches of mercury or millibars. A **Thermometer** measures degree of temperature. A **Hygrometer** measures relative humidity. A **Psychrometer** measures wet and dry bulb air temperatures.

Further explanation here might be helpful. **Relative humidity** is the ratio of water vapor in the air to the amount the air could hold at that temperature. The **dew point** is the temperature below which moisture will condense out of the air to form droplets as fog or cloud. A psychrometer is a set of two thermometers with the bulb of one enclosed in a wet gauze. The "wet bulb" thermometer will read lower because of the cooling effect of evaporation. The amount of evaporation depends on the relative humidity of the air. If the air is humid, there will be little evaporation and the "wet bulb" thermometer will not read very much lower than the "dry bulb" thermometer. In other words, the difference between the two thermometer readings varies with the relative humidity.

Forecasting with a Barometer

Let's review the weather sequence associated with a passing cold front again, this time noting the changes in barometric pressure and wind direction which occur as the front moves through. When a **strong cold front** approaches, we first notice a sharpening of wind from the south or southwest and altocumulus clouds appear on the west or northwest horizon. The barometer begins to fall.

As the front approaches, the clouds lower and cumulonimbus clouds begin to appear overhead. Once it begins to rain, the rain increases in intensity very rapidly. The wind may increase and the barometer may fall still further. As the front passes overhead, the wind shifts (veers) rapidly to the west or north and begins to blow in strong gusts. Squall-like rains continue and the barometer reaches its lowest reading. Once the front passes, the weather improves rapidly, the barometer rises rapidly, and the temperature drops as the winds steady out of the west or northwest.

Each phase in the passing of a cold or warm front is tied to a wind direction and barometric reading. As with any type of weather instrument, a single observation is of little use. A sequence of measurements will reveal a trend—most of the time. As a general rule, the more rapid the drop in the barometer reading, the closer and more severe an approaching storm will be. Fig. 11-19 correlates wind direction and barometric tendency. With it and little else you can sometimes forecast local weather with tolerable accuracy.

Other weather indicators are more subjective, but can frequently aid you in predicting local weather patterns. Here are some that have proven quite accurate over many years, in some cases many centuries:

Indicators of Deteriorating Weather
- Clouds lowering and thickening
- Clouds increasing in number, moving fast across the sky
- Veils or sheets of gray cloud increasing on the western horizon
- Clouds moving in different directions at different heights
- Clouds moving from east or northeast toward the south
- Barometer falling steadily or rapidly
- Static on AM radio
- Strong wind in the morning

- Wind shifts from north to east and possibly through east to south (veering wind)
- Temperatures far above or below

Indicators of Strong Wind
- Light scud clouds alone in a clear sky
- Sharp, clearly-defined edges to clouds
- Yellow sunset

Wind Direction	Sea-Level Pressure	Forecast	Wind Direction	Sea-Level Pressure	Forecast
SW to NW	30.10 to 30.20 and steady	Fair, with little temperature change, for 1 to 2 days.	E to NE	30.10 or higher; falling slowly	In summer, with light winds, rain may not fall for 2 to 3 days. In winter, rain within 24 hours.
SW to NW	30.10 to 30.20 rising rapidly	Fair, followed within 2 days by rain.	E to NE	30.10 or higher; falling rapidly	In summer, rain probably within 12 to 24 hours. In winter, rain or snow within 12 hours and increasing winds.
SW to NW	30.20 or higher and steady	Continued fair with little temperature change.			
SW to NW	30.20 or higher; falling slowly	Fair for 2 days with slowly rising temperature.	S to SW	30.00 or below; rising slowly	Clearing within a few hours. Then fair for several days.
S to SE	30.10 to 30.20; falling slowly	Rain within 24 hours.	S to E	29.80 or below; falling rapidly	Severe storm within a few hours. Then clearing within 24 hours-followed by colder in winter.
S to SE	30.10 to 30.20; falling rapidly	Increasing winds and rain within 12 to 24 hours.			
SE to NE	30.10 to 30.20; falling slowly	Increasing winds and rain within 12 to 18 hours.	E to N	29.80 or below; falling rapidly	Severe storm (typical nor'easter) in a few hours. Heavy rains or snowstorm. Followed by a cold wave in winter.
SE to NE	30.10 to 30.20; falling rapidly	Increasing winds and rain within 12 hours.			
SE to NE	30.00 or below; falling slowly	Rain will continue 1 to 3 days, perhaps even longer.	Hauling to W	29.80 or below; rising rapidly	End of the storm. Followed by clearing and colder.
SE to NE	30.00 or below; falling rapidly	Rain with high winds in a few hours. Clearing within 36 hours-becoming colder in winter.	NOTE: **Falling** or **rising rapidly** means a pressure change of .24 inches or greater within three hours. **Falling** or **rising slowly** means a change of approximately .09 inches or less in a three-hour period.		

Fig. 11-19 **Wind/Barometer Table (Eastern United States)**

Indicators of Impending Precipitation
- Distant objects seem to stand above the horizon
- Sounds are very clear and heard for great distances
- Transparent, veil-like clouds thickening and lowering
- Halo around sun or moon
- Increasing south wind, with clouds moving from the west
- Wind (especially north wind) shifts to west and then to south (backing wind)
- Steadily falling barometer
- Pale sunset
- Red sky at dawn
- No dew after a hot day.

Indicators of Clearing Weather
- Cloud bases rise
- Wind shifts to west, especially from east through south
- Barometer rises quickly
- Gray early morning
- Morning fog or dew.

Indicators of Continuing Fair Weather
- Early morning fog that clears
- Gentle wind from west or northwest
- Barometer steady or rising slightly
- Red sunset
- Bright moon and light breeze
- Heavy dew or frost
- Clear blue morning sky
- Dull hearing, short range of sound.

Chapter 12

Radiotelephone

The marine radiotelephone system exists to (1) provide monitored distress and safety frequencies, (2) allow exchange of information pertaining to navigation, movement or management of vessels, (3) allow communication between private vessels and local and Federal agencies, (4) provide communications for stations and vessels engaged in commerce, (5) allow common-carrier (telephone) service to vessels afloat, and (6) provide for the communications needs of recreational boaters.

Recreational boats are not required by law to be equipped with radiotelephone equipment, as certain types of commercial vessels are, but many people find a marine radiotelephone to be an enormous convenience. And there is no doubt that it can be an important safety factor in emergencies.

Boats carrying more than six passengers for hire, as well as many other commercial craft, are required to carry radio equipment. If you operate any type of commercial vessel, consult your nearest FCC office to determine the requirements which may apply to you and your boat.

To provide these services, special frequency bands have been set aside in the high frequency (HF) and very high frequency (VHF) portions of the radio spectrum. Most marine radiotelephone service is provided in the VHF band, where the assigned frequencies are identified as "channels." Certain other services (such as very long-distance communications, for instance) can only be provided in the HF band, due to technical limitations.

The VHF system is essentially a line-of-sight system, limited in range to only a little beyond the horizon. This is sufficient for the vast majority of important marine communications, especially since important land stations have very high antennas, and therefore have very wide horizons.

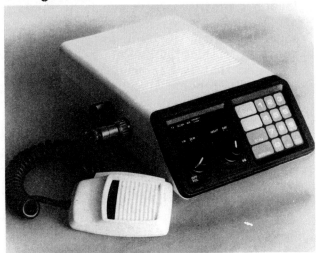

Fig. 12-1 Radiotelephone Set.

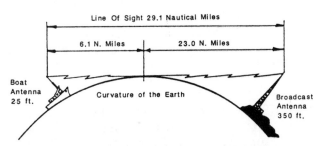

Fig. 12-2 Line of Sight Distances for Radio

The long-range characteristics of the HF system are an advantage for vessels that typically cross oceans or cruise several hundred miles offshore.

Marine radiotelephones require a license from the FCC.

The station license is obtained by submitting forms obtained from the FCC. Many manufacturers include copies of the necessary forms in the package with a new marine radiotelephone.

Typically, it takes several weeks for a license application to be processed and a license issued. The FCC has made provisions for a temporary station license for use while the actual license application is pending.

With the station license comes a call sign. The call sign, which is a combination of letters and numbers, identifies your station uniquely, and must be given at prescribed times during a series of transmissions. (See Operating Procedures, below.)

The station license covers all transmitting radio equipment aboard used in the marine radio service. That is, it covers VHF and HF radiotelephones, radar, or an Emergency Position Indicating Radio Beacon (EPIRB), if the license so states. It does not cover receiving equipment, such as receivers for broadcast stations, radio direction-finding receivers, LORAN navigation receivers, etc., which do not need to be licensed. It also does not cover amateur (ham) radio transmitters or Citizens' Band (CB) transmitters, which are covered by a different set of licensing regulations, or mobile (cellular) telephones, which are licensed under the common carrier providing the connecting service.

If you have an existing license and you add one of these covered pieces of equipment, the FCC must be notified and the license must be modified to cover the new equipment.

Modern radiotelephone equipment is reliable, generally reasonable in cost, available with a broad array of features, and simple to use.

All marine radiotelephone transmitters are "type accepted" by the FCC. That is, the design of the equipment is such that it meets certain minimum technical standards, and cannot be operated on frequencies outside the marine channels. The owner/operator of the equipment is not permitted to make any internal adjustments to the set that could alter its transmitting characteristics, and repairs must generally be carried out by licensed technicians specially qualified to work on marine radio equipment.

Installation can be performed by the owner, however, but you should be aware that improper power and antenna connections can seriously impede performance, and can result in damage to the equipment.

The units used in recreational craft are typically combined transmitter and receiver units, called "transceivers." The controls are simple: a channel selector knob, a volume control (which usually is also the on-off switch), a "squelch control," and a high power-low power switch.

The volume control controls the loudness of the received signal; it has no effect on the transmitted signal. The squelch control is used to eliminate the constant rushing noise which is produced by radio that is not receiving a signal. It essentially renders the radio quiet until a signal is received. Unfortunately, it is possible to set this control so high that even a strong signal will not "break squelch." This has the effect of turning the receiver off, and no signals can be heard. The squelch control should be set so that the no-signal noise just disappears, and no higher, lest important calls be missed.

The high power-low power switch is provided so that you can raise the power of your transmitter for longer range communications. It is normally kept on the low setting since many times it is necessary to communicate with a station just a short distance away, and even within sight of you, as when getting instructions from a lock master or a bridge tender, for instance. The low power setting allows you to do that without interfering with other communications a longer distance away. The high power setting is used only when necessary.

Since the radiotelephone is a "transceiver," it cannot both transmit and receive at the same time, but must be switched between transmitting and receiving. This is usually done with a switch or pushbutton on the microphone, the "push-to-talk" button.

Adjustments of Transmitting Equipment

You are responsible for the proper technical operation of your equipment. All transmitter measurements, adjustments, or repairs that may affect the proper operation of the transmitter must be made by or under the immediate supervision and responsibility of a person holding a valid First- or Second-Class Radiotelegraph or Radiotelephone Operator License. A special license endorsement is required to service a radar set.

Selecting a VHF Radiotelephone

Before purchasing a VHF-FM radiotelephone, you should consider your requirements carefully and select a unit that will meet these needs. You should remember that VHF communications are essentially "line of sight." The average ship-to-ship range is about 10 to 15 miles, while the normally expected ship-to-shore range is 20 to 30 miles, since the shore station typically has a much higher antenna. These figures vary depending upon transmitter power, antenna height, and terrain.

The FCC limits the transmitter power for VHF-FM to 25 watts for vessels and also requires the capability to reduce transmitter power to not more than one watt for short range communication.

No matter how powerful your transmitter is, if you can't hear the other station—you can't communicate. The receiver performance of your radiotelephone is therefore an important aspect of your communication capability.

Antennas

The quality of the antenna and of its installation can be the largest single factor determining how well a marine radiotelephone installation works. Two design factors are vital, height and gain.

Since the VHF system is essentially a line-of-sight transmission system, it is obvious that the higher the antenna, the further it can "hear," and the further you can communicate. Sailboats with antennas mounted at the top of the mast have an advantage over small powerboats in this area, an advantage which may even outweigh the advantage that most power boats have in readily available electrical power. Some power boaters compensate by mounting the antenna at the highest point on the boat or by using extension masts made just for that purpose, but there is a limit to how many extensions one can support.

The other factor is "gain." Generally, the station to be communicated with is located somewhere toward the horizon. Energy that is radiated upward into space or downward into the water is effectively wasted energy. Some antenna designs redirect some of this wasted energy so that it is radiated outward toward the horizon, effectively boosting the output of the transmitter.

But, as with all good things, there is a limit to this, too. If a very high gain antenna is used (greater than 9dB, typically) and the boat heels or rocks, much of the signal is directed into the water or out into space. In this situation a lower gain antenna would be more effective.

Operating Procedures

Maintain a Watch

Whenever your radio is turned on, keep

the receiver tuned to the appropriate distress and calling frequency, 156.8 MHz. This listening watch must be maintained at all times the station is in operation and you are not actually communicating.

You should expect to do far more listening on the radiotelephone than talking. Not only is the marine radiotelephone an extremely busy "party line," with a great many users, but it is also a vitally important link for emergency communications that must not be interfered with. A general rule to follow is to listen carefully before transmitting, preferably with the squelch turned all the way off so that very weak signals can be heard. There may be an emergency condition in effect, and you must avoid interfering.

VHF Channel 16 and SSB 2182 kHz have been designated as BOTH the emergency channel and the calling channel. All calls originate on Channel 16, but ONLY call originations or emergency traffic are permitted on that channel. This ensures that virtually every vessel with a radiotelephone that is not in use on another channel will be available to hear an emergency call, since all monitor channel 16 for incoming messages.

Operating Procedures

The operation of marine radiotelephones is governed by regulations of the Federal Communications Commission (FCC). These regulations are set forth in detail in Volume IV, Part 83, of the FCC Rules and Regulations available from the Superintendent of Documents, U. S. Government Printing Office, Washington, D. C. 20402.

The FCC has been a leader in government agencies in presenting regulations to the public in a readable form, avoiding much of the legal language that makes so many regulations difficult to understand.

There are very specific procedures (detailed below) for placing calls to other

vessels and for answering calls to your vessel. These procedures are intended, (1) to ensure clear communications with a minimum risk of confusion of intent, and (2) to tie up the limited available radio channels as little as possible.

Choose the Correct Channel or Frequency

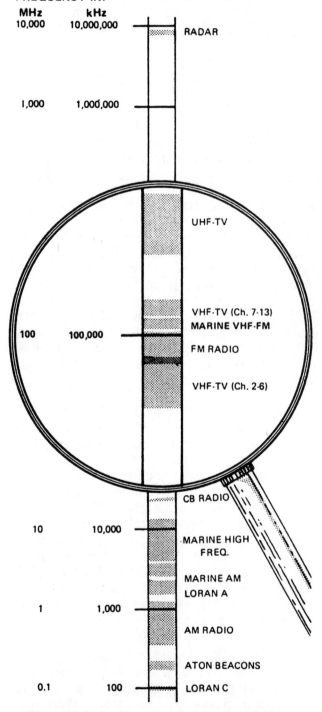

Fig. 12-3 Radio Frequency Spectrum

TABLE 12-I

Channel Numbers	Type of Communication	Suggested Channel Selection for Recreational Vessels	
		6 Ch.	12 Ch.
16	DISTRESS, SAFETY & CALLING Intership & ship to coast	*	*
6	INTERSHIP SAFETY Intership. NOT to be used for non-safety intership communications	*	*
22	Communications with U. S. Coast Guard ship, coast, or aircraft stations.	1	1
65, 66, 12, 73, 14, 74, 20	PORT OPERATIONS Intership & ship to coast		1
13	NAVIGATIONAL		1
68, 9	NON-COMMERCIAL Intership & ship to coast	1	2
69, 71, 78	NON-COMMERCIAL Ship to coast		1
72	NON-COMMERCIAL Intership		2
24, 84, 25, 85, 26, 86, 27, 87, 28	PUBLIC CORRESPONDENCE Ship to public coast	2	2
162.40 & 162.475 MHz 162.55 MHz	NOAA WEATHER SERVICE Ship receive only Ship receive only	** **	** **

* These stations are required to be installed in every ship station equipped with a VHF radio.

**The weather receive channels are half-channels (receive only) one or both of which are recommended to be installed in each ship station. Many manufacturers include one or both of these channels in their sets in addition to the normal six or twelve channel capacity.

TABLE II

CHANNEL USAGE

Channel Number	Ship Transmit	Ship Receive	Intended Use
6	156.300	156.300	INTERSHIP SAFETY. Required for all VHF-FM equipped vessels for intership safety purposes and search and rescue (SAR) communications with ships and aircraft of the U. S. Coast Guard. Must not be used for non-safety communications.
9	156.450	156.450	COMMERCIAL AND NON-COMMERCIAL (INTERSHIP AND SHIP-TO-COAST). Some examples of use are communications with commercial marinas and public docks to obtain supplies to schedule repairs and contacting commercial vessels about matters of common concern.
12	156.600	156.600	PORT OPERATIONS (INTERSHIP AND SHIP-TO-COAST). Available to all vessels. This is a traffic advisory channel for use by agencies directing the movement of vessels in or near ports, locks, or waterways. Messages are restricted to the operational handling, movement and safety to ships and, in emergency, to the safety of persons. It should be noted, however, in the Ports of New York and New Orleans channels 11, 12 and 14 are to be used exclusively for the Vessel Traffic System being developed by the United States Coast Guard.
13	156.650	156.650	NAVIGATIONAL — (SHIP'S) BRIDGE TO (SHIP'S) BRIDGE. This channel is available to all vessels and is required on large passenger and commercial vessels (including many tugs). Use is limited to navigational communications such as in meeting and passing situations. Abbreviated short

operating procedures and 1 watt maximum power (except in certain special instances) are used on this channel for both calling and working. For recreational vessels, this channel should be used for *listening* to determine the intentions of large vessels. This is also the primary channel used at locks and bridges operated by the U. S. Army Corps of Engineers.

14	156.700	156.700	PORT OPERATIONS (INTERSHIP AND SHIP-TO-COAST). Same as channel 12.
15	156.750	156.750	ENVIRONMENTAL (RECEIVE ONLY). A receive only channel used to broadcast environmental information to ships such as weather, sea conditions, time signals for navigation, notices to mariners, etc. Most of this information is also broadcast on the weather (WX) channels.
16	156.800	156.800	DISTRESS, SAFETY AND CALLING (INTERSHIP AND SHIP-TO-COAST). Required channel for all VHF-FM equipped vessels. Must be monitored at all times station is in operation (except when actually communicating on another channel). This channel is monitored also by the Coast Guard, public coast stations and many limited coast stations. Calls to other vessels are normally initiated on this channel. Then, except in an emergency, you must switch to a working channel. For additional information see the sections on operating procedures.
17	156.850	156.850	STATE CONTROL. Available to all vessels to communicate with ships and coast stations operated by state or local governments. Messages are restricted to regulation and control, or rendering assistance. Use of low power (1 watt) setting is required by international treaty.
20	157.000	161.600	PORT OPERATIONS (SHIP-TO-COAST). Available to all vessels. This is a traffic advisory channel for use by agencies directing the movement of vessels in or near ports, locks, or waterways. Messages are restricted to the operational handling, movement and safety of ships and, in emergency, to the safety of persons.
21A	157.050	157.050	U. S. GOVERNMENT ONLY.
22A	157.100	157.100	COAST GUARD LIAISON. This channel is used for communications with U. S. Coast Guard ship, coast and aircraft stations after first establishing communications on channel 16. *It is strongly recommended that every VHF radiotelephone include this channel.*
23A	157.150	157.150	U. S. GOVERNMENT ONLY
24	157.200	161.800	PUBLIC CORRESPONDENCE (SHIP-TO-COAST). Available to all vessels to communicate with public coast stations operated by telephone companies. Channels 26 and 28 are the primary public correspondence channels and therefore become the first choice for the cruising vessel having limited channel capacity.
25	157.250	161.850	PUBLIC CORRESPONDENCE (SHIP-TO-COAST). Same as channel 24.
26	157.300	161.900	PUBLIC CORRESPONDENCE (SHIP-TO-COAST). Same as channel 24.
27	157.350	161.950	PUBLIC CORRESPONDENCE (SHIP-TO-COAST). Same as channel 24.

28	157.400	162.000	PUBLIC CORRESPONDENCE (SHIP-TO-COAST). Same as channel 24.
65A	156.275	156.275	PORT OPERATIONS (INTERSHIP AND SHIP-TO-COAST). Same as channel 12.
66A	156.325	156.325	PORT OPERATIONS (INTERSHIP AND SHIP-TO-COAST). Same as channel 12.
68	156.425	156.425	NON-COMMERCIAL (INTERSHIP AND SHIP-TO-COAST). A working channel for non-commercial vessels. May be used for obtaining supplies, scheduling repairs, berthing and accommodations, etc. from yacht clubs or marinas, and intership operational communications such as piloting or arranging for rendezvous with other vessels. It should be noted that channel 68 (and channel 70 for intership only) is the most popular non-commercial channel and therefore is the first choice for vessels having limited channel capacity.
69	156.475	156.475	NON-COMMERCIAL WORKING. For pleasure boats ship-to-ship and ship-to-shore communications only.
72	156.625	156.625	NON-COMMERCIAL (INTERSHIP). Same as channel 68 except limited to intership communications.
73	156.675	156.675	PORT OPERATIONS (INTERSHIP AND SHIP-TO-COAST). Same as channel 20.
74	156.725	156.725	PORT OPERATIONS (INTERSHIP AND SHIP-TO-COAST). Same as channel 20.
78A	156.925	156.925	NON-COMMERCIAL WORKING. For pleasure boats ship-to-ship and ship-to-shore communications only. (Not available for pleasure boat use in Canada.)
81A	157.075	157.075	U. S. GOVERNMENT ONLY.
82A	157.125	157.125	U. S. GOVERNMENT ONLY.
83A	157.175	157.175	U. S. GOVERNMENT ONLY.
84	157.225	161.825	PUBLIC CORRESPONDENCE (SHIP-TO-COAST). Same as channel 24.
85	157.275	161.875	PUBLIC CORRESPONDENCE (SHIP-TO-COAST). Same as channel 24.
86	157.325	161.925	PUBLIC CORRESPONDENCE (SHIP-TO-COAST). Same as channel 24.
87	157.375	161.975	PUBLIC CORRESPONDENCE (SHIP-TO-COAST). Same as channel 24.
WX1	—	162.550	WEATHER (RECEIVE ONLY). To receive weather broadcasts of the Department of Commerce, National Oceanic and Atmospheric Administration (NOAA).
WX2	—	162.400	WEATHER (RECEIVE ONLY). Same as WX1.
WX3	—	162.475	WEATHER (RECEIVE ONLY). Same as WX1.

NOTE: The addition of the letter "A" to the channel number indicates that the ship receive channel used in the United States is different from the one used by vessels and coast stations of other countries. Vessels equipped for U. S. operations only, will experience difficulty communicating with foreign ships and coast stations on these channels.

TABLE 12-II

Each of the marine frequencies and channels is authorized for a specific type of communication. It is therefore required that you choose the correct channel for the type of communications you wish to engage in. For example, certain channels are set aside exclusively for intership (ship-to-ship) use and may not be used for ship-to-coast communications. Channels are further classified according to the subject matter or content of the communications. For example, commercial communications are limited to matters pertaining to the commercial enterprise the vessel is engaged in.

The authorized use of each of the VHF channels is given in Table 12-II. For recreational boats, most of the communications will be limited to what is known as Non-commercial (Operational in the MF band) communications and Public Correspondence.

Public Correspondence

By using the channels set aside for Public Correspondence and establishing communications through the facilities of the public coast stations, you are able to make and receive calls from any telephone on shore. There is no restriction on the content of your communication and you do not have to limit your messages strictly to ship's business. Except for distress calls, public coast stations will charge for this service.

One other comment about using public correspondence channels--other people are listening! You have a private channel through the telephone lines, but the radio link between the vessel and the shore station is very public!

Calling Intership

Turn your radiotelephone on and listen on the appropriate distress and calling frequency, Channel 16 or 2182 kHz, to make sure it is not being used. If it is clear, put your transmitter on the air. This is usually done by depressing the "push to talk" button on the microphone.

You must release the microphone button when you are through transmitting. You cannot receive transmissions directed at you until you release the microphone button and switch your radio to "receive." It is also good practice to pause just a fraction of a second after you press the button before you begin to speak. This allows time for the receiving radio on the other end of your communication link to "break squelch," it allows the listener a fraction of a second to get ready to listen, and it also helps you to avoid the common error of rushing things and starting to talk before the button is pushed. Both of these factors tend to clip off the beginning of the message and make communication difficult.

Speak directly into the microphone in a normal tone of voice. Check the manufacturer's recommendation for distance to be used. Speak clearly and distinctly. Call the vessel with which you wish to communicate by using its name; then identify your vessel with its name and FCC assigned call sign. Do not add unnecessary words and phrases such as "Come in, Bob" or "Do you read me?" Limit the use of phonetics to poor transmission conditions.

This preliminary call must not exceed 30 seconds. If contact is not made, wait at least 2 minutes before repeating the call. After this time interval, make the call in the same manner. This procedure may be repeated no more than three times. If contact is not made during this period, you must wait at least 15 minutes before making your next attempt. Again, avoid unnecessary transmission, such as, "negative contact." It is unnecessary and very unprofessional.

Once you establish contact on the calling channel, you must switch to a "working channel" to carry out the rest of your business.

As a recreational boater, you have access to only a few of the many channels that your radio may have. There are 73 channels of which 55 may be used in the United States.

These remaining channels include twelve that are designated for commercial operator use only, for communication between commercial vessels and their operational headquarters, etc.

There are also several channels set aside for government use. For instance, Channel 21A is a "U. S. Government Use Only" channel, designated for the U. S. Coast Guard. There are also several channels that are designated "Public Correspondence" channels, where common carrier operators provide ship-to-shore telephone service.

All radios are equipped with Channel 16, the internationally recognized emergency and calling channel. They also are equipped with Channel 06. Thus, wherever in the world you may go where VHF radiotelephones are used, there will be at least two channels you will have in common with anyone else you may meet.

Monitor the "working" frequency you wish to use, briefly, before initiating the call on Channel 16 or 2182 kHz. This will help prevent you from interrupting other users of the channel.

All communications should be kept as brief as possible and at the end of the communication each vessel is required to give its call sign, after which, both vessels switch back to the distress and calling channel and reestablish the watch.

Operating Procedures
There are accepted and established procedures for establishing and maintaining effective communications, and it is your responsibility to learn them and use them.

These procedures are based on extensive practical experience, and are carefully thought out to give effective communication with the minimum usage of radio spectrum and time.

A key to efficient use of the radiotelephone is the use of PROCEDURE WORDS, or "prowords." They are a form of shorthand, and as long as everybody understands and uses them correctly, a great deal of time can be saved. There is a fixed amount of radio spectrum and time available; the more people who can use it, the better. The basic prowords are shown in Table 12-III.

TABLE 12-III   Procedure Words (PROWORDS) and Phonetic Alphabet.

PROCEDURE WORD	MEANING
OUT	This is the end of my transmission to you and no answer is required or expected.
OVER	This is the end of my transmission to you and a response is necessary. Go ahead and transmit. (Note: Observe the considerable difference between "Over," used during a message exchange, and "Out," employed at the end of an exchange. "Over" should be omitted when the context of a transmission makes it clear that it is unnecessary.)
ROGER	I have received your last transmission satisfactorily.
WILCO	Your last message has been received, understood, and will be complied with.
THIS IS	This transmission is from the station whose name or call sign immediately follows. (Note: Normally used at the beginning of a transmission: "BLUE DUCK — THIS IS — GIMLET — WHISKEY ZULU ECHO 3488." Sometimes omitted in transmissions between experienced operators familiar with each other's boat names.)
FIGURES	Figures or numbers follow. (Used when numbers occur in the middle of a message: "Vessel length is figures two three feet.")
SPEAK SLOWER	Your transmission is at too fast a speed, speak more slowly.
SAY AGAIN	Repeat.
WORDS TWICE	Communication is difficult — give every phrase twice.
I SPELL	I shall spell the next word phonetically. (Note: Often used where a proper name or unusual word is important to a message; "Boat name is *Martha*. I spell — Mike; Alfa; Romeo; Tango; Hotel; Alfa." See phonetic alphabet.)
MESSAGE FOLLOWS	A message that requires recording is about to follow.
BREAK	I separate the text from other portions of the message; or one message from one immediately following.
WAIT	I must pause for a few seconds; stand by for further transmission. (Note: This is normally used when a message must be interrupted by the *sender*. If, for instance, one station is asked for information not instantly available, its operator might send "WAIT" while looking up the required data. In addition, WAIT may also be used to suspend the transmission of an on-the-air test. If a station announces its intention of making such a test, another station using the channel may transmit the word "WAIT;" the test shall then be suspended.
AFFIRMATIVE	You are correct, or what you have transmitted is correct.
NEGATIVE	No.
SILENCE (said three times)	Cease all transmissions immediately. Silence will be maintained until lifted. (Note: Used to clear routine business from a channel when an emergency is in progress. In this meaning *Silence* is correctly pronounced SEE LONSS.)

SILENCE FINI	Silence is lifted.

(Note: Signifies the end of the emergency and the resumption of normal traffic. Correctly pronounced SEE LONSS FEE NEE.)

5	FIVE	FI FE
6	SIX	SIX
7	SEVEN	SEVEN
8	EIGHT	ATE
9	NINE	NINER

PHONETIC ALPHABET

Letter	Phonetic Equivalent	Pronunciation
A	ALFA	*AL* FAH
B	BRAVO	*BRAH* VOH
C	CHARLIE	*CHAR* LEE
D	DELTA	*DELL* TAH
E	ECHO	*ECK* OH
F	FOXTROT	*FOKS* TROT
G	GOLF	GOLF
H	HOTEL	HO *TELL*
I	INDIA	*IN* DEE AH
J	JULIETT	JEW LEE *ETT*
K	KILO	*KEY* LOH
L	LIMA	*LEE* MAH
M	MIKE	MIKE
N	NOVEMBER	NO *VEM* BER
O	OSCAR	*OSS* CAH
P	PAPA	PAH *PAH*
Q	QUEBEC	KEH *BECK*
R	ROMEO	*ROW* ME OH
S	SIERRA	SEE *AIR* RAH
T	TANGO	*TANG* GO
U	UNIFORM	*YOU* NEE FORM
V	VICTOR	*VIK* TAH
W	WHISKEY	*WISS* KEY
X	XRAY	*ECKS* RAY
Y	YANKEE	*YANG* KEY
Z	ZULU	*ZOO* LOO
0	ZERO	ZERO
1	ONE	WUN
2	TWO	TOO
3	THREE	THUH REE
4	FOUR	FO WER

You should not be sensitive about using these prowords. Nobody will think you are imitating the dialog on the late movie if you say "Wilco," as long as you use it appropriately.

On the other hand, there are other words and phrases that have come into common usage that have the "flavor" of prowords, but which accomplish nothing. A recent example heard on Channel 16: Several calls to a particular boat went unanswered, whereupon the caller said, "Negative contact. This is XXXXXX, out."

We will ignore for the moment the fact that "negative contact" is meaningless. What is important is that it was obvious to anybody listening that the attempt to establish contact was fruitless, since there was no reply. The time taken to announce that obvious fact to the world was enough that someone else, more efficient, could have placed a call. Worse, the unnecessary announcement could have masked an emergency call.

Calling Ship to Coast

The procedures for calling coast stations are similar to those used in making intership calls with the exception that you normally initiate the call on the assigned frequency of the coast station.

Routine Radio Check

Radio checks may be made by calling a specific station. (General calls even for radio checks, are not permitted except for special situations.) Begin by initiating a call on Channel 16, but shift to a working channel as quickly as possible.

Listen to make sure that the Distress and Calling frequency is not busy. If it is free, put your transmitter on the air and call a specific station or vessel and include the phrase "request a radio check" in your initial call. For example, "MARY JANE - THIS IS BLUE DUCK - WHISKEY ALFA 1234 - REQUEST RADIO CHECK CHANNEL _____ (names working channel) - OVER." After the reply by Mary Jane, Blue Duck would then say "HOW DO YOU HEAR ME? - OVER."

The proper response by Mary Jane, depending on the respective conditions, would be:
  "I HEAR YOU LOUD AND CLEAR," or
  "I HEAR YOU WEAK BUT CLEAR," or
  "YOU ARE LOUD BUT DISTORTED," etc.
Do not respond to a request for a radio check with such phrases as:
  "I HEAR YOU FIVE BY FIVE," or
  "I READ YOU LOUD AND CLEAR."
Figures are not a clear response as to the character of the transmission and the word "read" implies a radio check by a meter.

It is illegal to call a Coast Guard station on 156.8 MHz or 2182 kHz for a radio check. This prohibition does not apply to tests conducted during investigations by FCC representatives or when qualified radio technicians are installing equipment or correcting deficiencies in the station radiotelephone equipment.

Radiotelephone Station Log
A radio log when used should have each page (1) be numbered; (2) bear the name of the vessel and call sign; and (3) be signed by the operator. Entries should show the time each watch begins and ends. All distress and alarm signals should be recorded as completely as possible. This applies to all related communications transmitted or intercepted, and to all urgency and safety signals and communications transmitted. A record of all installations, services, or maintenance work performed that may affect the proper operation of the station should also be entered by the licensed operator doing the work, including his address and the class, serial number, and expiration date of his license.

The 24-hour system is used in a radio log for recording time; that is, 8:45 a.m. is written as 0845 and 1:00 p.m. as 1300. Local time is normally used, but Eastern Standard Time (EST) or Universal Coordinated time (UTC) must be used throughout the Great Lakes. Vessels on international voyages use UTC exclusively. Whichever time is used, the appropriate abbreviation for the time zone must be entered at the head of the time column.

Radio logs must be retained for at least a year, and for 3 years if they contain entries concerning distress, and for longer periods if they concern communications being investigated by the FCC or against which claims or complaints have been filed.

Station logs must be made available for inspection at the request of an FCC representative.

Secrecy of Communications
The Communications Act prohibits divulging interstate or foreign communications transmitted, received, or intercepted by wire or radio to anyone other than the addressee or his agent or attorney, or to persons necessarily involved in the handling of the communications, unless the sender authorizes the divulgence of the contents of the communication. Persons intercepting such communications or becoming acquainted with them are also prohibited from divulging the contents or using the contents for the benefit of themselves or others.

Obviously, this requirement of secrecy does not apply to radio communications relating to ships in distress, nor to radio communications transmitted by amateurs or broadcasts by others for use of the general public. It does apply, however, to all other communications. These statutory secrecy provisions cover messages addressed to a specific ship station or coast station or to a person via such station.

Obscenity, Indecency and Profanity
When two or more ship stations are communicating with each other, they are

talking over an extensive party line. Users should always bear this fact in mind and assume that many persons are listening. All users therefore have a compelling moral obligation to avoid offensive remarks. They also have a strict legal obligation inasmuch as it is a criminal offense for any person to transmit communications containing obscene, indecent, or profane words, language, or meaning. Whoever utters any obscene, indecent or profane language by radio may be fined up to $10,000 or imprisoned up to 2 years, or both.

Crew Training

As with all other aspects of boat operation, more than one person on board should be familiar with the operation of the radiotelephone. You should be sure to check out all members of your "regular" crew on radiotelephone operation, and include a brief introduction to the basic operation of the radiotelephone as part of your familiarization tour for guests on board your boat. Finally, you should complete the form in Table 12-IV and post it in a conspicuous location near the radiotelephone so that in an emergency anyone on board will be able to summon assistance.

Some of these precautions may seem unnecessarily simple-minded, but under stress even experienced people sometimes fail to do seemingly simple tasks. An emergency broadcast that fails to summon help because the rattled operator does not turn on the power, or calls on the wrong channel, or the return call that is missed because the squelch is set too high or the operator fails to release the microphone button, is tragic.

Remember: The RMS TITANIC sank, with the loss of over 1,700 lives, while another ship sat just a few miles away, unaware of the situation. TITANIC sent out radio distress calls that were heard hundreds of miles away in New York, but

---

MARINE DISTRESS COMMUNICATIONS FORM

Instructions: Complete this form now (except for items 6 through 9) and post near your radiotelephone for use if you are in DISTRESS.

****

SPEAK: SLOWLY — CLEARLY — CALMLY

1. Make sure your radiotelephone is on.
2. Select either VHF Channel 16 (156.8 MHz) or 2182 kHz.
3. Press microphone button and say: "MAYDAY—MAYDAY—MAYDAY."
4. Say: "THIS IS _____
   _____ Your Call Sign/Boat Name repeated three times
5. Say: "MAYDAY _____."
   _____ Your Boat Name
6. TELL WHERE YOU ARE (What navigational aids or landmarks are near?).
7. STATE THE NATURE OF YOUR DISTRESS.
8. GIVE NUMBER OF PERSONS ABOARD AND CONDITIONS OF ANY INJURED.
9. ESTIMATE PRESENT SEAWORTHINESS OF YOUR BOAT.
10. BRIEFLY DESCRIBE YOUR BOAT: _____ FEET; _____ ; _____ HULL;
    _____ Length   Type   Color
    _____ TRIM; _____ MASTS; _____
    Color   Number   Anything else you think will help rescuers find you.
11. Say: "I WILL BE LISTENING ON CHANNEL 16/2182."
    Cross out one which does not apply
12. End Message by saying: "THIS IS _____ o . OVER"
    Your Boat Name and Call Sign
13. Release microphone button and listen: Someone should answer.
    IF THEY DO NOT, REPEAT CALL, BEGINNING AT ITEM NO. 3 ABOVE.
    If there is still no answer, switch to another channel and begin again.

TABLE 12-IV

the vessel nearest and best able to render assistance did not hear them because her radio was turned off!

Operating Procedures (Distress, Urgency and Safety)

General

If you are in distress, you may use any means at your disposal to attract attention and obtain assistance. You are by no means limited to the use of your marine radiotelephone. Often, visual signals, including flags, flares, lights, smoke, etc., or audible signals such as your boat's horn or siren, or a whistle, or megaphone will get the attention and help you need.

For boats equipped with a marine radiotelephone, help is just a radio signal away. Two marine radiotelephone channels have been set aside for use in emergencies. Channel 16 (156.8 MHz), the VHF-FM Distress, Safety and Calling frequency is the primary emergency channel in the VHF marine band. For those who have medium frequency (MF) radiotelephone also, 2182 kHz is the emergency frequency for use in that band. You are not limited to the use of these channels; you may use any other frequency channel available to you. The working frequency of the local marine operator (public telephone coast station) is a good example of a channel that is monitored.

There are other types of marine stations located ashore that are listening to Channel 16 and 2182 kHz along with the marine radio equipped vessels operating in the area. Because of this coverage, almost any kind of a call for assistance on Channel 16 (0r 2182 kHz) will probably get a response. There are times, however, when the situation demands immediate attention; when you just can't tolerate delay. These are the times when you need to know how to use (or respond to) the Distress and Urgency signals and how to respond to the Safety signal.

Spoken Emergency Signals

There are three spoken emergency signals:

1. Distress Signal: MAYDAY
The distress signal MAYDAY is used to indicate that a mobile station is threatened by grave and imminent danger and requests immediate assistance. MAYDAY has priority over all other communications.

2. Urgency Signal: PAN PAN (Properly pronounced PAHN PAHN)
Used when the safety of the vessel or person is in jeopardy. "Man overboard" messages are sent with the Urgency signal. PAN PAN has priority over all other communications with the exception of distress traffic.

3. Safety Signal: SECURITY (Pronounced SAY-CURITAY)
Used for messages concerning the safety of navigation or giving important meteorological warnings.

Any message headed by one of the emergency signals (MAYDAY, PAN PAN, or SECURITY) must be given precedence over routine communications. This means listen. Don't transmit. Be prepared to help if you can. The decision of which of these emergency signals to use is the responsibility of the person in charge of the vessel.

Radiotelephone Alarm Signal

This signal consists of two audio frequency tones transmitted alternately. This signal is similar in sound to a two-tone siren used by some ambulances and lasts 30 seconds to 1 minute. The purpose of the signal is to attract attention of the person on watch or to actuate automatic devices giving the alarm. The radiotelephone alarm signal shall be used only with the distress signal except in two situations dealing with the Urgency Signal.

Sending Distress Call and Message

First send the Radiotelephone Alarm Signal, if available.

1. Distress signal MAYDAY (spoken three times).

Fig. 12-4   Coast Guard Communication
Station

2. The words THIS IS (spoken once).
3. Name of vessel in distress (spoken three times) and call sign (spoken once).

The Distress Message immediately follows the Distress Call and consists of:

4. Distress signal MAYDAY (spoken once).
5. Name of vessel (spoken once).
6. Position of vessel in distress by latitude and longitude or by bearing (true or magnetic, state which) and distance to a well-known landmark such as a navigational aid or small island, or in any terms which will assist a responding station in locating the vessel in distress.
7. Nature of distress (sinking, fire, etc.).
8. Kind of assistance desired.
9. Any other information which might facilitate rescue, such as:
   - length or tonnage of vessel,
   - number of persons on board and number needing medical attention,
   - color of hull, decks, cabin, masts, etc.
10. The word OVER.

Acknowledgement of Distress Message
If you hear a Distress Message from a vessel and it is not answered, then YOU must answer. If you are reasonably sure that the distressed vessel is not in your vicinity, you should wait a short time for others to acknowledge. In any event, you must log all pertinent details of the Distress Call and Message.

Offer of Assistance
After you acknowledge receipt of the distress message, allow a short interval of time for other stations to acknowledge receipt, if there are any in a position to assist. When you are sure of not interfering with other distress-related communications, contact the vessel in distress and advise them what assistance you can render. Make every effort to notify the Coast Guard. The offer-of-assistance message shall be sent only with permission of the person in charge of your

vessel.

Urgency Call and Message Procedures

The emergency signal PAN PAN (pronounced PAHN PAHN), spoken three times as PAN PAN, PAN PAN, PAN PAN, begins the Urgency Call. The Urgency Call and Message is transmitted on Channel 16 (or on 2182 kHz) in the same way as the Distress Call and Distress Message. The Urgency signal PAN PAN indicates that the calling person has a message concerning the safety of the vessel, or a person in jeopardy. The Urgency signal is authorized for situations like the following:
- Transmission of an urgent storm warning by an authorized shore station.
- Loss of person overboard but only when the assistance of other vessels is required.
- No steering or power in shipping lane.

Sending Urgency Call and Message

The Urgency Call and Message usually includes the following:
1. The Urgency signal PAN PAN (spoken three times).
2. Addressee ALL STATIONS (or a particular station).
3. The words THIS IS.
4. Name of calling vessel (spoken three times) and call sign (spoken once).
5. The Urgency Message (state the urgent problem).
6. Position of vessel and any other information that will assist responding vessels. Include description of your vessel, etc.
7. The words THIS IS.
8. Name of calling vessel and radio call sign (spoken once).
9. The word OVER.

Safety Call and Message Procedures

The Safety Call, headed with the word SECURITY (Say-curitay, spoken three times), is transmitted on the Distress and Calling frequency (Channel 16 or 2182 kHz), together with a request to shift to a working frequency where the Safety Message will be given. The Safety Message may be given on any available working frequency.

United States Coast Guard stations routinely use the Safety Call SECURITY to alert boating operators that they are preparing to broadcast a message concerning safety of navigation. The call also precedes an important meteorological warning. The Safety Message itself usually is broadcast on Coast Guard VHF/FM Channel 22 (157.1 MHz) and AM 2670 kHz. Although recreational boating operators may use the Safety Signal and Message, in many cases they would get better results by giving the information to the Coast Guard without making a formal Safety Call. The Coast Guard usually has better broadcast coverage from its shore stations and will rebroadcast the information if it is appropriate.

Public Coast Stations

General

By utilizing the services of Public Coast Stations, ships may make and receive telephone calls to and from any telephone with access to the nationwide telephone network, including telephones overseas and on other ships and aircraft. In effect, these coast stations extend the talking range of ship telephones almost without limit.

Description of Public Coast Stations

Three categories of Public Coast Stations operate in different frequency bands to provide for telephone service over a wide range of situations. The following brief descriptions of these services are of interest in selecting a service appropriate for your requirements. This information is followed by some suggestions for operating ship stations on public correspondence channels.

VHF-FM Marine Operator Service

VHF-FM service offers reliable operation with good transmission quality over relatively short distances up to 20-50 miles, using channels in the 157-162 MHz range. Channels 24, 25, 26, 27, 28, 84, 85, 86 and 87 are available for assignment to public coast stations in the United States. Channels 26 and 28 are used in more areas than any others. To obtain information on VHF-FM ship-to-shore telephone coverage in your area, call your local Marine Operator, according to instructions in your telephone directory.

In addition, in some localities not yet served by VHF-FM coast stations, ships are permitted to make telephone calls through local VHF-FM base stations operating in the land mobile radio telephone service. In these instances, a different license authorization as well as different transmitting equipment is required.

Medium Frequency Service

The Medium Frequency Service operates over considerably greater distance ranges than VHF-FM, but ranges vary widely with time of day and a variety of other circumstances. Distances in excess of 1,000 miles are possible at certain times, but may be limited to less than 100 miles at other times.

Medium Frequency Coast Stations operate on frequencies in the 2 MHz band along the sea coasts and Gulf of Mexico. Stations serving the Great Lakes and the Mississippi River valley also operate on frequencies in the high-frequency bands.

High Frequency

A High Seas Service using high frequencies provides long-range radiotelephone communications with suitably equipped vessels throughout the world. Service is provided via four coast stations within the United States coastal areas plus one station in the state of Hawaii. These stations operate on various radio channels in the 4 through 23 MHz HF bands and are equipped for single sideband operation.

Registration With Your Public Coast Station

It is important for the vessel owner who plans on using the public radiotelephone service to register with the telephone company in the location where you wish to be billed.

This registration provides all coast stations with the name and address to be used in billing for ship-originated calls. Public coast stations are supported by charges made in accordance with tariffs filed with regulatory authorities. If a ship is not registered, billing information must be passed to the coast station operator each time a call is made, with consequent expenditure of time and effort. Registration may also serve to establish the procedures under which a coast station will call the ship in completing land-originated calls. Should you encounter any problems, contact your local telephone company business office and request assistance in registering your vessel.

Making Ship-To-Shore Calls

Use the VHF-FM Service (up to 20 to 50 miles) in preference to the Medium Frequency or High Frequency Services, if within range.

1. Select the public correspondence channel assigned to the desired shore station. Do not call on Channel 16 or on 2182 kHz except in an emergency.

2. Listen to determine if the working channel of the desired coast station is busy. A busy condition is evidenced by hearing speech, signaling tones, or a busy signal.

3. If the channel is busy, wait until it clears or switch to an alternate channel if available.

4. If the channel is not busy, press the push-to-talk button and say: (Name of the coast station) - THIS IS - (your call sign once). Do not call for more than a few seconds.

5. Listen for a reply. If none is received, repeat call after an interval of two minutes.

When the coast station operator answers, say:

THIS IS - Name of vessel, call sign, and ship's telephone or billing number (if assigned), CALLING (city, telephone number desired).

If your vessel is not registered or if the coast station operator does not have the listing, the operator will ask for additional information for billing purposes. At completion of call say:

Name of vessel - Call sign - OUT.

Receiving Shore-to-Ship Calls

Obviously, to receive public coast station calls, a receiver must be in operation on the proper channel. When calling on VHF-FM frequencies, coast stations will call on Channel 16 unless you have selective signaling, in which case the shore station will dial your number on a working channel. When calling on SSB medium frequencies, the preferred channel is the working channel of the coast station. Commercial coast stations operating on channels in the 2 MHz band routinely call on a working channel, but will call on 2182 kHz when requested to do so by the calling party. If you are expecting calls on medium frequencies and are not planning to monitor the working channel, you should tell prospective calling parties to so advise the Marine Operator. Note: A guard must be maintained on the distress, safety and calling channel; therefore a second channel receiver capability is essential if a guard is to be maintained on a coast station working channel.

Selective signaling, of course, requires a second receiver, since monitoring of the working channel would be essential. It is illegal to send dial pulses over Channel 16 or 2182 kHz.

Making Ship-to-Ship Calls Through a Coast Station

Although contacts between ships are normally made directly, ship-to-ship calls can be made by going through your coast station, using the same procedure as you do for the ship-to-shore calls.

How to Place a Shore-to-Ship Call

The basic procedure that the telephone subscriber should follow in placing a telephone call to a ship station from his home or office is found in the first few pages of most telephone directories. These instructions generally consist of dialing "O" (Zero) for the Operator, and asking for the "Marine Operator."

It is further necessary to know the name of the vessel being called (not the owner's name) and the approximate location so that the marine operator may judge which coast station to place the call through.

More specific information about the vessel is often useful. For instance, the channel generally monitored for receiving calls, a selective signaling number (if applicable), and the coast station through which calls can generally be received.

Remember that the ship station generally operates using push-to-talk techniques, so that it is impossible for you to break in while the ship station is transmitting.

Limited Coast Stations

The term **limited coast stations** includes coast stations that there to serve the operational and business needs of vessels, but are not open to public correspondence. Many, such as those operated by a harbor master coordinating the movement of vessels within a confined area, or a station at a highway bridge, serve a safety function as well. Shore stations operated by the United States Coast Guard provide a safety communications service rather than business or operational. They are classified as Government stations rather than as limited coast stations although they also are not open to public correspondence.

While limited coast stations are not new to the Marine Service, most small vessel operators are finding this service available for the first time on VHF-FM. Thus, tug companies may have a limited coast station for the purpose of dispatching their own tugs. A fleet of fishing vessels may be directed from a limited coast station operated by a fish cannery.

Yacht clubs having docking facilities, marina operators, ship chandlers, boatels, harbor masters, dock-side restaurants, marine police, and marine radio service shops are among those who maintain and operate limited coast stations as a part of their regular operations. No charge is made for the communications service, which is incidental to their business.

How to Use the Services of Limited Coast Stations

Vessels should call limited coast stations on the limited coast station's working channel. All limited coast stations have Channel 16 plus one or more working channels. Limited coast stations, on the other hand, will call boats on Channel 16; therefore you do not need to monitor his working channel even if you are expecting a call.

As a general rule, limited coast stations operate only during their normal working hours. The calling procedure to use is the same as you would use to call another vessel except that you should initiate the call on the coast station's working channel. Be sure to give them plenty of time to answer your call as operating the radio is secondary to the operator's normal tasks. Many of these stations monitor Channel 16 as well as their working channels. If you don't know their assigned working channel, or if they don't appear to be watching their working channel, call on Channel 16.

Other Radio Services

CB

Citizens' Band (CB) radio is inexpensive and popular with both fixed land and land mobile stations, and in many inland areas CB radios are very common on boats, as well. In inland areas where marine radiotelephone services are not available, some boaters have only CB radio.

CB radio may be very useful for local communications, such as between boats traveling together on a river cruise, etc. As such, it can actually relieve some usage pressure on the marine VHF system.

On the other hand, there is no established standard channel which is generally monitored for marine use, and actively monitored channels vary from region to region. There are active volunteer groups which monitor CB channel 9 (the highway emergency calling channel), but in most cases the likelihood that you will be able to reach competent help in an emergency is slight. Add to this the fact that the effective range of CB radio under most conditions is limited (typically 4-5 miles) and it becomes clear that dependence on CB for emergency communications is risky.

The Coast Guard does monitor CB channel 9, but only on a "not to interfere" basis. What this means is that the CB is a secondary concern, after the VHF system. If the VHF radio requires attention, the CB will not be monitored.

In summary, then, the CB radio may be a useful addition to your boat's radio equipment, but it should not be looked on as a primary means of emergency communications except in extreme situations.

Amateur Radio

Some boaters who plan extended long-distance cruises offshore equip their boats with amateur ("ham") radio gear. If they are already amateur radio operators and wish to combine their hobbies, or if they want to maintain contact with their ham friends at home and elsewhere, this is fine. However, if the intent is to substitute amateur radio for marine radiotelephone, it is a serious mistake.

Amateur radio and HF-SSB marine radiotelephones are superficially similar. Amateur equipment is available that operates at frequencies NEAR the marine HF frequencies. Much amateur equipment uses SSB transmissions, and similar levels of power are available. An additional inducement is that amateur equipment is available for a fraction of the cost of a typical marine HF radiotelephone.

The problems, however, are many. While there are many boaters who are also hams, there are no internationally-recognized frequencies where assistance is consistently available, and there is no watch maintained for emergency calls, let alone for routine calls.

As with CB radio, the likelihood that a boater in distress will be able to reach someone in a position to help is slim. The people who might happen to be listening to hear your call at that time and at that frequency is a random sample of all hams in the world. The very long-range nature of ham communications which makes it so seductive as an alternative could also mean that your call for distress could be heard by someone halfway around the world from you!

Then there is the issue of equipment reliability. Marine radiotelephone equipment is quite a bit more expensive than amateur equipment, and that extra expense is reflected largely in quality of construction and added reliability. Just as slim as the chance that you will be able to contact somebody nearby is the chance that the equipment will still be working during an emergency, just when you need it most.

Approved marine radiotelephone equipment is designed to be nearly fool-proof, and very easy to operate. Amateur radio gear is considerably more difficult to operate, and relatively easy to make operate improperly. If you already have an electronics hobby, this is no major concern. But if you are a boater who wants reliable communications, you may not want to have to deal with a sensitive and delicate piece of equipment.

Finally, there is the matter of licensing. Amateur radio requires a special license, which in turn requires an examination. Various technical and legal matters are covered in the examination, and you will be tested on your ability to send and receive International Morse code. Once again, this is beyond the interests of most boaters who just want to talk to the folks back home from time to time.

In summary, amateur radio is an excellent hobby, and combines well with boating, once certain technical problems are resolved. It may even serve on occasion to supplement regular marine radiotelephone communications, or in rare instances may even serve in an emergency when the marine radiotelephone has failed. However, it has no place as a complete substitute or replacement for proper marine radiotelephone, properly installed and operated.

Chapter 13

Inland Waterways, Locks And Dams

River Boating

Some of the finest boating this country offers can be found on the inland waterways of interconnected rivers and lakes. Throughout the United States there are nearly 30,000 miles of inland waterways. The Mississippi River system alone covers more than 12,000 miles. Rivers as a rule seldom offer large open expanses, but they do require unique piloting skills.

Changing conditions on the rivers put a premium on local knowledge and raise river navigation to an art. Piloting the riverways is both exciting and interesting. Although the rivers hold no dark secrets, they do have peculiarities that offer new challenges to the coastal and lake boater.

Fig. 13-1 Dam with Double Locks.

While the coastal boater keeps close watch on the tides and water depth, the river boater watches overhead clearance, buoys, channels, dikes, wing dams, and low water dams in back channels. Except for flooding conditions that occur following a heavy rain, the only fluctuation in river level is seasonal. In some of the navigable streams, sudden rains may raise the level several feet in a very few hours.

Maintained Channels

Federal waterways are maintained by the U. S. Army Corps of Engineers. They attempt to maintain a minimum channel depth and width through dredging and other maintenance activities. Minimum channel depths vary depending on the river and (to some extent) the season of the year. But like Mean Low Water in tidal waters, this is a target (reference) level, and under special conditions the water may actually be more shallow than indicated. Commercial interests plan on these minimum depths, and load their barges and plan schedules accordingly.

If changes occur in the river channel that will affect the channel depth, announcements are published in the LOCAL NOTICE TO MARINERS. Minute-to-minute updates are also available for critical situations through broadcast messages on the VHF-FM radiotelephone system from the Coast Guard. (See Chapter 12.)

Currents

Currents can be of great concern to the river boater. Vessels moving upstream, against the current, may make very little advance over the ground, while making considerable speed through the water and using up a substantial quantity of fuel. Some slower houseboats and sailboats may not be able to make headway upstream at all.

Movement downstream is aided by a current, and speed and fuel economy are boosted by the amount of the current flow. But this is not an unmixed blessing, as a vessel that is being carried downstream by a substantial current is to a large extent at the mercy of that current, and lacks an element of control. (It is for this reason that the Inland Navigation Rules make vessels headed downstream the "stand-on vessel," and place the burden of avoidance on those headed up, who have more control, even if they are making less headway.) [See Chapter 4.]

Currents in the river can also be complex, as they respond to changes in the channel direction and bottom configuration. Currents at various depths, too, may run contrary to one another. Deep-draft vessels may be affected by deep currents, while shallow-draft vessels may be in a current running in the opposite direction. (Needless to say, this can create some interesting situations for two vessels maneuvering alongside one another.)

Knowledgeable river boaters learn to read these currents and to take advantage of them. Vessels headed upstream may move to the inside of a bend, where currents are lessened, or may actually reverse and head upstream. This can result in significant fuel savings, which is important for recreational and commercial users alike. (Of course, the inside of the bend is usually the shallowest part of the river, so this maneuver must be used with caution.)

The rivers and the river boatmen who plied them were a vital part of commerce in the 18th and 19th Centuries, and played an important role in opening up the western territories. But much depended on the individual skill and knowledge of the river pilots, whose local knowledge was all that stood between reliable transportation and a series of groundings, wrecks and sinkings.

Those rivers that were navigable suffered from water levels that changed rapidly and often unpredictably, and wandering channels and sandbars that could open up or close the river over night.

Early efforts to control some of the rivers, to maintain a clear channel and control the random meandering of sandbars, involved the construction of "wing dams." These structures diverted the current to the center of the channel. This kept the channel scoured out and reduced shoaling. Wing dams could not control the river level, however, and spring floods were inevitably followed by late summer dry weather and shallow water.

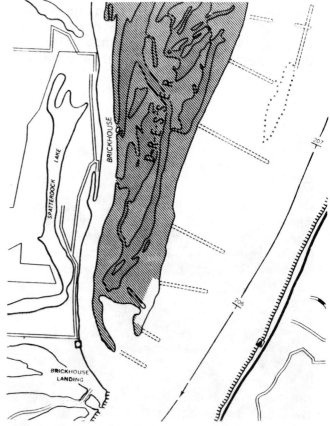

Fig. 13-2 Wing Dams On a River Chart.

Later, full dams were built that changed the rivers from a continuous flow of water from higher to lower elevation into a stepwise series of "pools." Excess water could be retained upstream of the dams and released into the lower pool as needed to maintain water depth and control shoaling.

These dams not only aided in controlling the channel, but also helped regulate the flow of water, so that the water accumulated during the spring floods can be held back and released later in the summer when the rains upstream are less plentiful.

The construction of the full dams, however, while it brought many benefits, created two new problems. The first is how to get vessels through the barriers created by the dams; the second is the wing dams, which were left in place but which are now generally under the surface and invisible.

The problem of navigation through the dams was solved by the construction of LOCKS. (See below.) The wing dams remain as a potentially serious navigation hazard for the unwary. They are clearly marked on navigational charts of the river, however, and many are further marked with warning buoys. As a result, they constitute no real problem if you are aware of them and stay in the channel or move outside the channel with care.

Commercial Traffic (Barges & Tows)

One of the fascinating aspects of the inland waterways is the commercial traffic you encounter there. In some areas this traffic consists of ships, often from foreign ports. But in most cases the vessels are integrated collections of barges and towboats. Most generally the barges are lashed alongside the towboat or pushed ahead. All of the units are connected to one another in such a way that the whole collection can be maneuvered as one vessel, yet individual barges can be broken out and left at various intermediate locations for unloading

while the rest of the tow goes on about its business.

Fig. 13-3 View from Towboat Pilothouse.

Large tows may also be equipped with a "bowboat," sometimes specially built for the job, to assist in controlling the combination.

Tows can be 1000 feet or more in length, and comprise some of the largest vessels to be seen anywhere. They require a great deal of maneuvering room, and special attention is necessary for small boats operating in their vicinity.

These extremely large vessels may require a mile or more to stop in an emergency, and they often cannot maneuver laterally to avoid difficulty, either.

Second, since the helmsman is usually located at the after part of the tow, he has limited visibility forward. That is to say, there is a large area immediately in front of the tow that is blocked to his view. Many towboats have very high pilothouses, and other towboats that must be lower to operate under bridges, etc., have pilothouses mounted on hydraulic rams to allow them a higher vantage point whenever possible. These measures only lessen the problem, however. They do not eliminate it.

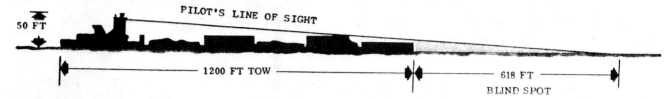

Fig. 13-4 Towboat Danger Area (Blind Spot)

The visibility problem is made even worse when the tow includes empty barges. Empties are almost always carried at the head (front) of the tow. Otherwise the whole tow becomes almost unmaneuverable. But empties ride high in the water, and block even more of the forward view.

When you are operating in the vicinity of a tow, then, be especially sensitive to the helmsman's field of view, and avoid running into his blind zone. It is tempting to move back to the center of the channel quickly after you pass a tow. But this almost invariably means that you move into the blind zone. If you were to suffer an engine failure, or strike a submerged object and become disabled at that point, the towboat operator might never know you were there, even after he had run over you. Even if he had a lookout posted on the bow, as many do in congested waters, he might not be able to stop in time to avoid hitting a stalled boat.

The third issue has to do with maneuverability outside the channel. Most towboats and barges are loaded to the maximum depth the channel will accommodate. They may have only a few inches clearance on the bottom. As a result, they do not have the ability to operate outside the buoyed channel. Most recreational boats, on the other hand, have more flexibility in this regard. It is only common courtesy and common good judgment to avoid forcing the issue.

It may be possible to feel the effects of an approaching tow in the water a considerable distance ahead and behind, as water is alternately pulled toward the tow, then pushed away behind it. Large, powerful screws acting in a narrow channel close to the bottom can create pressure waves that can be felt through the hull of a small boat and can give advance warning of the approach of a tow.

In addition to the wave action produced by the towboat's screws, the disturbance produced by its passage may cause submerged objects lying on the bottom to be stirred up to depths where they may be a hazard to small craft following behind. Waterlogged trees, sunken steel drums, even sunken barges, may be encountered this way. For this reason alone it is wise to avoid running in the wake of any deep-draft vessel on the river (including large pleasure boats).

Dams [View of Dam upper level]

Fig. 13-5 TAINTER GATE DAM

Dams are not simply solid walls built across the river. They may actually be very complex structures, and may incorporate hydroelectric generating plants and other structures that present a very confusing picture when viewed from water level.

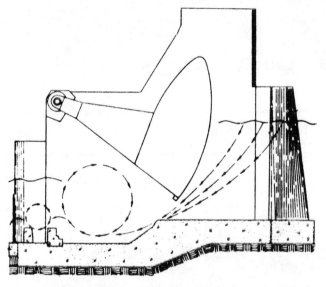

Fig. 13-6 Tainter Gate

Dams must make provision for allowing water to flow to the downstream pool, and for controlling that flow. To do this they have various types of "gate." So-called "tainter" gates allow water to flow downstream from the bottom of the dam. This allows accumulated sediment to be flushed downstream so it doesn't collect

Fig. 13-7 Dam and Lock

at the base of the dam. However, it also means that you cannot tell by looking if the dam gates are open or not. Open gates mean turbulent water, and this in turn means a potentially dangerous situation for small boats.

Another type of dam uses "wicket" gates, which can be lowered to lie along the bottom and which allow water to flow over the top of the wickets. The principle advantage of wicket dams is that in times of high water the wickets can be lowered completely and river traffic can pass over the dam without hinderance and without having to pass through the locks.

From the small boater's point of view, wicket dams present a potential hazard, since a small boat can be swept over a partially open wicket. A small boat caught up against the wall of a tainter dam, on the other hand, will be held there and can be rescued if it does not capsize and if the occupants stay with the boat.

Locks

Locks are a means of passing vessels through the dam and, at the same time, raising or lowering them to the level of the next pool. A lock is a large chamber, typically 800-1200 feet long and 100-120 feet wide, and equipped with gates at each end.

A vessel headed upstream enters the lock chamber through the downstream gates, which are closed behind. Valves are then opened which permit water to enter the chamber from the upstream pool. No pumps are used; gravity powers the lock.

As the water level rises in the chamber the vessel rises with it. When the water level in the lock comes even with the level in the upstream pool the flow of water slows, then stops. The upstream gates are then opened, and the vessel moves out of the chamber and continues on its way.

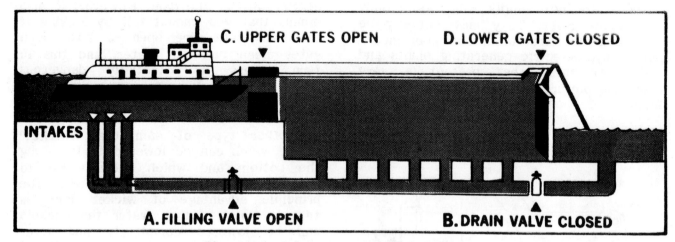

Fig. 13-8   Lock Open to Upper Pool.

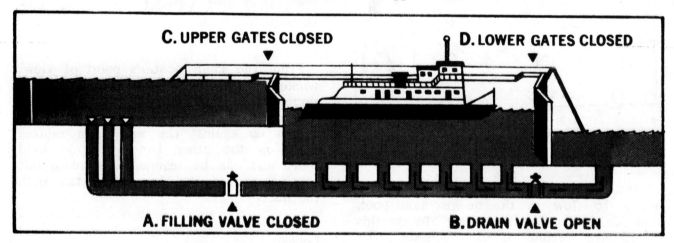

Fig. 13-9   Water Level Lowering.

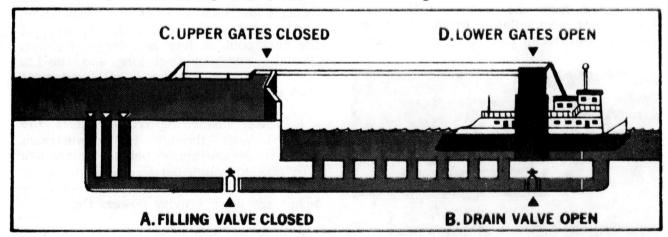

Fig. 13-10   Lock Open to Lower Pool.

A downbound vessel enters through the upstream gates, which are then closed. Valves are opened which allow the water in the lock chamber to flow into the downstream pool. When the level of water in the chamber is the same as the downstream pool, the lower gates are opened and the vessel moves out.

The building, maintenance and operation of river locks are the responsibility of the U. S. Army Corps of Engineers. Each lock is under the control of a lockmaster, who is entirely responsible for lock operations. A lockmaster will accommodate your needs if possible, but he may have other, more pressing priorities that may result in some minor inconvenience for you. Understanding all the way around will make the whole process of passing through locks much more pleasant.

Federal law establishes clear priorities for the use of locks. First priority goes to U. S. naval and military vessels, followed by mail-carrying vessels, vessels carrying passengers for hire, fishing vessels, and vessels carrying freight. Finally, at the lowest priority, is recreational boats.

This is not as bad as it may sound. As a matter of fact, naval and military vessels and mail packets are seldom seen on the waterways, and passenger-carrying vessels are not common, either. In most cases, the "competition" for lockage is commercial barge traffic.

On occasion it is possible to pass through locks in company with commercial vessels. This depends on the space available in the lock chamber, the nature of the cargo being carried, and the wishes of the towboat operator, whose first responsibility is for the safety of his vessel.

Regardless of space availability, no other vessels will be locked through with a hazardous cargo (e.g., gasoline, sulphuric acid, etc.). Such cargos are marked by the international code flag "BRAVO," a red swallow-tailed pennant, usually constructed of sheet metal so it is always visible. You should avoid such "red-flagged" barges, and give them extra consideration. While river transport of such cargos in bulk is well-proven and exceptionally safe, any accident that DOES occur has the potential of being a major disaster.

All things considered, then, you should plan on a certain amount of delay at locks. If commercial traffic is heavy and several tows are waiting at a lock, the delay may be several hours. As a practical matter, no lockmaster wants to have several dozen pleasure boats loitering in the approaches to his lock, and will make every effort to move small boat traffic through quickly.

Sometimes a barge string is too large to fit into the lock chamber. In these cases, the barge string will be broken into two or more parts and locked through in halves. It may be possible to lock pleasure boats in the opposite direction as the chamber is being filled or drained in preparation for the second half, since there is not space enough to move another tow in for that cycle. Time is of the essence, and pleasure boaters should be prepared to move quickly to take advantage of opportunities like these. Quarters will also be very tight, and you may be moving very close to the tow and/or the lock gates, so extra caution is called for.

Lockmasters may be reached by VHF-FM radiotelephone (see Chapter 12), and this can be very useful for all involved. If the lockmasters know what is headed their way they can plan their moves and make more efficient use of the facilities. If you know what is currently going on, you can adjust your speed or plans accordingly. You may be able to speed up and get into a group locking through, or you may simply plan to anchor or beach your boat for a lunch break if there is a large restricted ("red-flagged") tow being locked through.

If they are locking through a tow, or a number of recreational craft, the lockmasters may not be able to respond immediately to every radio call. If you make it a practice to listen to ongoing radio traffic you can keep track of what is happening, and may not have to make a call to the lockmaster.

Signals are provided near the entrance of the lock chamber with which the lockmaster regulates traffic. These signals typically resemble traffic lights, and indicate much the same sort of information. Horn signals are also used.

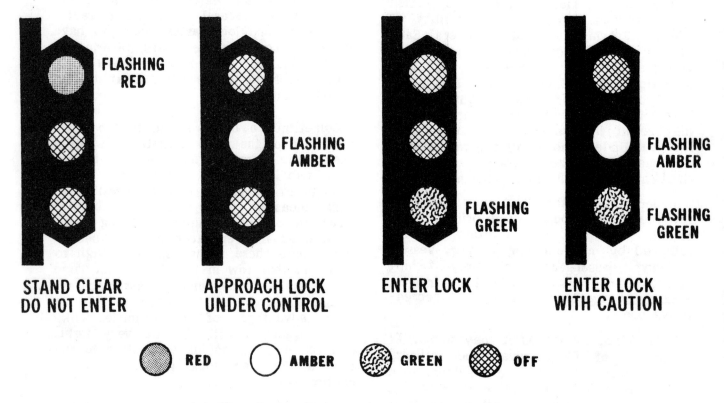

FLASHING RED

FLASHING AMBER

FLASHING GREEN

FLASHING AMBER

FLASHING GREEN

STAND CLEAR DO NOT ENTER

APPROACH LOCK UNDER CONTROL

ENTER LOCK

ENTER LOCK WITH CAUTION

RED   AMBER   GREEN   OFF

Fig. 13-11   How Signals Are Also Used.

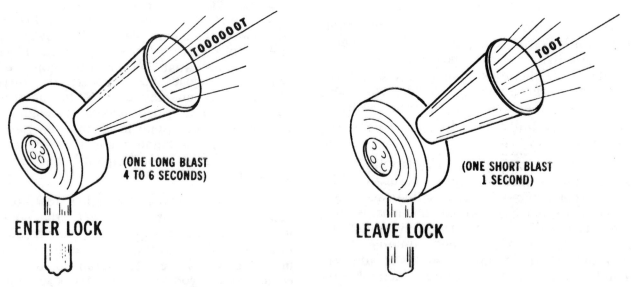

(ONE LONG BLAST 4 TO 6 SECONDS)

ENTER LOCK

(ONE SHORT BLAST 1 SECOND)

LEAVE LOCK

Fig. 13-12   Air Horn Signals.

A red light means "do not approach." A yellow light (often flashing) indicates that you should PREPARE to move into the lock, but do not move yet. The green light signals that the lock is ready to receive vessels. Note that the signal to enter MAY NOT APPLY TO YOU. If there are vessels waiting for lockage that have higher priority than you, the signal may apply to them.

As you approach the lock chamber, you should move at a strict no-wake speed. For most boats this means no more than a fast idle speed. There is a conflict between the urge to move into position quickly and the need to keep wakes down. Avoiding wakes should take priority. A lock chamber is a long, narrow chamber with flat concrete walls. With several boats moving in close proximity to one another, extra care is needed from everybody to avoid damaging boats or lock gate structures.

All crewmembers should wear PFD's during the entire locking operation. The lock chamber can be turbulent while the chamber is being filled, and crewmembers will be moving around tending lines, etc. It is very easy to fall overboard in these conditions, and this is nearly the worst possible conditions for a person overboard: several boats very close to one another, turbulent water, vertical walls.

A general precaution, you should also stop engines and extinguish all flames, including cigarettes. With several boats in close quarters in an enclosed chamber, a fire could be a disaster, indeed.

Locks may provide lines, or you may be expected to provide your own. You should have lines available that are AT LEAST as long as twice the depth of the lock. Small boats can be handled with one line, located midships; boats larger than 25-30' may require lines fore and aft.

Various types of locks have various means available for tying up. Small craft may use lines on bitts or bollards (large, rounded "knobs" mounted along the top of the lock wall) or on a railing. Other locks have ladders or series of recessed bollards set into the lock wall. It will be necessary to move your line from attachment point to attachment point as the boat is raised or lowered in these cases.

Perhaps the best of all arrangements is the system of floating bollards in some of the larger locks, such as those on the Tennessee River. These structures are

Fig. 13-13 Typical Lock Wall.

mounted on tracks set into the lock wall and float up and down as the water level changes. If you are fortunate enough to get one of these floating bollards, you will not have to feed out or take in line. You will, however, have to tend the lines and be prepared to take action in the unlikely event that the bollard should jam and not move up or down.

When many recreational boats are locked through, there may not be enough space available on the lock wall. You should, therefore, be prepared to raft up with other boats. The lockmaster will instruct you where to go on the wall, and may designate which boats should raft with you. You should be prepared with extra fenders and lines for this eventuality.

After the water in the lock chamber has reached its new level, do not move away from the wall until the lockmaster signals that you may. Again, move at a no-wake speed, paying close attention to other boats that will also be getting under way at the same time.

River Piloting
The charts that are used for river navigation differ somewhat from those used for coastal piloting. Since the extent

of the river is essentially one–dimensional, it is not practical to publish river charts in the same form as for broader expanses of water, such as coastal waters or the Great Lakes. Instead, river charts are published as spiral-bound books. Each page of the book represents a section of a few miles of the river, which is continued on an adjacent page. Because of this arrangement, river charts can conveniently be shown in a fairly large scale, and they can still be handled conveniently even on board fairly small boats.

Anyone who is familiar with coastal piloting charts and practices should feel comfortable with river charts in short order. There are some differences, however.

It is seldom necessary on the river to plot a compass course or maintain a dead reckoning plot. It is necessary, however, to stay in a relatively confined channel, and a number of special navigation aids are provided to assist you in doing this. These include traditional buoys and daymarks, plus a liberal number of ranges and a special type of daymark, called a "crossing daymark."

The banks of the river are identified as "right bank" or "left bank," as the river flows. Thus, the west bank of the Mississippi River, which flows south, is its right bank. The right margin of the channel is marked by green buoys and daymarks, while the left margin is marked with red buoys and daymarks. (See Chapter 5, Aids to Navigation.)

The river channel is the deepest portion of the river, a sort of river within the river. When a river basin is flooded, either naturally or because of the construction of control structures (dams) downstream, the deeper channel may be lost under a broad expanse of uniform-appearing water. Since the river can be very shallow outside the channel, it is important to know where the channel lies. This is especially true since the channel can meander considerably within the limits of its banks.

Standard daymarks (red triangles and green squares) as they are used on the river imply that the channel continues as it has. They are often referred to as "passing daymarks," since they are passed without any change of course other than that necessary to follow the curvature of the river itself.

A different sort of daymark, diamond-shaped, but still marked with red or green, depending on which side of the channel it marks, indicates that the channel swings to the opposite bank. This "crossing daymark" indicates that the next marker (buoy or daymark) to be seen will be on the opposite bank.

Fig. 13-14 Crossing Daymark.

Glossary of Nautical Terms

A

ABAFT - Toward the rear (stern) of the boat. Behind.

ABEAM - At right angles to the keel of the boat, but not on the boat.

ABOARD -- On or within the boat.

ABOVE DECK - On the deck (not over it -- see ALOFT).

ABREAST - Side by side; by the side of.

ADRIFT - Loose, not on moorings or towline.

AFT - Toward the stern of the boat.

AGROUND - Touching or fast to the bottom.

AHEAD - In a forward direction.

AIDS TO NAVIGATION - Artificial objects to supplement natural landmarks in indicating safe and unsafe waters.

ALEE - Away from the direction of the wind. Opposite of windward.

ALOFT - Above the deck of the boat.

AMIDSHIPS - In or toward the center of the boat.

ANCHORAGE - A place suitable for anchoring in relation to the wind, seas and bottom.

ASTERN - In back of the boat, opposite of ahead.

ATHWARTSHIPS - At right angles to the centerline of the boat; rowboat seats are generally athwartships.

B

BATTEN DOWN - Secure hatches and loose objects both within the hull and on deck.

BEAM - The greatest width of the boat.

BEAR - To "bear down" is to approach from windward, to "bear off" is to sail away to leeward.

BEARING - The direction of an object expressed either as a true bearing as shown on the chart, or as a bearing relative to the heading of the boat.

BELAY - To make a line fast. A command to stop.

BELOW - Beneath the deck.

BEND - To attach a sail to a spar. Also used as a term to describe a knot which fastens one line to another.

BIGHT - The part of the rope or line, between the end and the standing part, on which a knot is formed. A shallow bay.

BILGE - The interior of the hull below the floor boards.

BINNACLE - A stand holding the steering compass.

BITT - A heavy and firmly mounted piece of wood or metal used for securing lines.

BITTER END - The last part of a rope or chain. The inboard end of the anchor rode.

BLOCK - A wooden or metal case enclosing one or more pulleys and having a hook, eye, or strap by which it may be attached.

BOAT - A fairly indefinite term. A waterborne vehicle smaller than a ship. One definition is a small craft carried aboard a ship.

BOAT HOOK - A short shaft with a fitting at one end shaped to facilitate use in putting a line over a piling, recovering an object dropped overboard, or in pushing or fending off.

BOLLARD - A heavy post set into the edge of a wharf or pier to which the lines of a ship may be made fast.

BOOT TOP - A painted line that indicates the designed waterline.

BOW - The forward part of a boat.

BOW LINE - A docking line leading from the bow.

BOWLINE - A knot used to form a temporary loop in the end of a line.

BOWSPRIT - A spar extending forward from the bow.

BRIDGE - The location from which a vessel is steered and its speed controlled. "Control Station" is really a more appropriate term for small craft.

BROACH - The turning of a boat parallel to the waves, subjecting it to possible capsizing.

BROAD ON THE BEAM - At right angles to the beam. Abeam (not aboard the vessel).

BROAD ON THE BOW - A direction midway between abeam and dead ahead.

BROAD ON THE QUARTER - A direction midway between abeam and dead astern.

BULKHEAD - A vertical partition separating compartments.

BULWARK - The side of a vessel when carried above the level of the deck.

BUOY - An anchored float used for marking a position on the water or a hazard or a shoal and for mooring.

C

CABIN - A compartment for passengers or crew.

CAPSIZE - To turn over.

CAST OFF - To let go.

CATAMARAN - A twin-hulled boat, with hulls side by side.

CAULK - To stop up and make watertight by filling with a waterproof compound or material.

CHAFING GEAR - Tubing or cloth wrapping used to protect a line from chafing on a rough surface.

CHART - A map for use by navigators.

CHINE - The intersection of the bottom and sides of a flat or v-bottomed boat.

CHOCK - A fitting through which anchor or mooring lines are led. Usually U-shaped to reduce chafe.

CLEAT - A fitting to which lines are made fast. The classic cleat to which lines are belayed is approximately anvil-shaped.

CLOSE ABOARD - Not on but near to a vessel.

CLOVE HITCH - A knot for temporarily fastening a line to a spar or piling.

COAMING - A vertical piece around the edge of a cockpit, hatch, etc. to prevent water on deck from running below.

COCKPIT - An opening in the deck from which the boat is handled.

COIL - To lay a line down in circular turns.

COURSE - The direction in which a boat is steered.

CRADLE - A framework, generally of wood, to support a boat when it is out of the water.

CUDDY - A small shelter cabin in a boat.

CURRENT - The horizontal movement of water.

D

DAVITS - Mechanical arms extending over the side or stern of a vessel, or over a sea wall, to lift a smaller boat.

DEAD AHEAD - Directly ahead.

DEAD ASTERN - Directly aft.

DEAD RECKONING - A plot of courses steered and distances traveled through the water.

DECK - A permanent covering over a compartment, hull or any part thereof.

DINGHY - A small open boat. A dinghy is often used as a tender for a larger craft.

DISPLACEMENT - The weight of water displaced by a floating vessel, thus, a boat's weight.

DISPLACEMENT HULL - A type of hull that plows through the water, displacing a weight of water equal to its own weight, even when more power is added.

DOCK - A protected water area in which vessels are moored. The term is often used to denote a pier or a wharf.

DOLPHIN - A group of piles driven close together and bound with wire cables into a single structure.

DRAFT - The depth of water a boat draws.

DROGUE - Any device streamed astern to check a vessel's speed, or to keep its stern up to the waves in a following sea.

E

EASE - To slacken or relieve tension on a line.

EBB TIDE - A receding tide.

EVEN KEEL - When a boat is floating on its designed waterline it is said to be floating on an even keel.

EYE OF THE WIND - The direction from which the wind is blowing.

EYE SPLICE - A permanent loop spliced in the end of a line.

F

FAST - Said of an object that is secured to another.

FATHOM - Six feet.

FENDER - A cushion, placed between boats, or between a boat and a pier, to prevent damage.

FIGURE EIGHT KNOT - A knot in the form of a figure eight, placed in the end of a line to prevent the line from passing through a grommet or a block.

FISHERMAN'S BEND - A knot for making fast to a buoy or spar or to the ring of an anchor.

FLARE - The outward curve of a vessel's sides near the bow. A distress signal.

FLOOD TIDE - A rising tide.

FLUKE - The palm of an anchor.

FLYING BRIDGE - An added set of controls above the level of the normal control station for better visibility. Usually open but may have a collapsible top for shade.

FOLLOWING SEA - An overtaking sea that comes from astern.

FORE-AND-AFT - In a line parallel to the keel.

FOREPEAK - A compartment in the bow of a small boat.

FORWARD - Toward the bow of the boat.

FOULED - Any piece of equipment that is jammed or entangled, or dirtied.

FOUNDER - When a vessel fills with water and sinks.

FREEBOARD - The minimum vertical distance from the surface of the water to the gunwale.

G

GAFF - A spar to support the head of a gaff sail.

GALLEY - The kitchen area of a boat.

GANGWAY - The area of a ship's side where people board and disembark.

GANGPLANK - The temporary ramp or platform between the vessel and the wharf or pier.

GEAR - A general term for ropes, blocks, tackle and other equipment.

GRAB RAILS - Hand-hold fittings mounted on cabin tops and sides for personal safety when moving around the boat.

GROUND TACKLE - A collective term for the anchor and its associated gear.

GUNWALE - The upper edge of a boat's sides.

H

HATCH - An opening in a boat's deck fitted with a watertight cover.

HAWSER - A heavy rope or cable used for mooring or towing.

HEAD - A marine toilet. Also the upper corner of a triangular sail.

HEADING - The direction in which a vessel's bow points at any given time.

HEADWAY - The forward motion of a boat. Opposite of sternway.

HEAVE TO - To bring a vessel up in a position where it will maintain little or no headway, usually with the bow into the wind or nearly so.

HEEL - To tip to one side.

HELM - The wheel or tiller controlling the rudder.

HITCH - A knot used to secure a rope to another object or to another rope, or to form a loop or a noose in a rope.

HOLD - A compartment below deck in a large vessel, used solely for carrying cargo.

HULL - The main body of a vessel.

K

KEEL - The centerline of a boat running fore and aft; the backbone of a vessel.

KETCH - a two-masted sailboat with the smaller after mast stepped ahead of the rudder post.

KNOT - A measure of speed equal to one nautical mile (6076 feet) per hour.

KNOT - A fastening made by interweaving rope to form a stopper, to enclose or bind an object, to form a loop or a noose, to tie a small rope to an object, or to tie the ends of two small ropes together.

L

LAZARETTE - A storage space in a boat's stern area.

LEEWARD - The direction away from the wind. Opposite of windward.

LEEWAY - The sideways movement of the boat caused by either wind or current.

LINE - Rope and cordage used aboard a vessel.

LOG - A record of courses or operation. Also, a device to measure speed.

LONG SPLICE - A method of joining two ropes by splicing without increasing the diameter of the rope.

LUBBER'S LINE - A mark or permanent line on a compass indicating the direction forward parallel to the keel when properly installed.

M

MAST - A spar set upright to support rigging and sails.

MIZZEN - The after and smaller mast of a ketch or yawl; also a sail set on that mast.

MOORING - An arrangement for securing a boat to a mooring buoy or a pier.

N

NAUTICAL MILE - One minute of latitude; approximately 6076 feet — about 1/8 longer than the statute mile of 5280 feet.

NAVIGATION - The art and science of conducting a boat safely from one point to another.

O

OUTBOARD - Toward or beyond the boat's sides. A detachable engine mounted on a boat's stern.

OVERBOARD - Over the side or out of the boat.

P

PAINTER - A line attached to the bow of a boat for use in towing or making fast.

PAY OUT - To ease out a line, or let it run in a controlled manner.

PENNANT (sometimes PENDANT) - The line by which a boat is made fast to a mooring buoy.

PIER - A loading platform extending at an angle from the shore.

PILE - A wood, metal or concrete pole driven into the bottom. Craft may be made fast to a pile; it may be used to support a pier (see PILING) or a float.

PILING - Support, protection for wharves, piers etc.; constructed of piles (see PILE).

PILOTING - Navigation by use of visible references, the depth of the water, etc.

PITCHPOLING - A small boat being thrown end-over-end in very rough seas.

PLANING HULL - A type of hull shaped to glide easily across the water at high speed.

POINT - One of 32 points of the compass equal to 11 1/4 degrees.

PORT - The left side of a boat looking forward. A harbor.

Q

QUARTER - The sides of a boat aft of amidships.

QUARTERING SEA - Sea coming on a boat's quarter.

R

REEF - To reduce the sail area.

REEVE - To pass a line through a block or other opening.

RIGGING - The general term for all the lines of a vessel.

RODE - The anchor line and/or chain.

ROPE - In general, cordage as it is purchased at the store. When it comes aboard a vessel and is put to use it becomes line.

RUDDER - a vertical plate or board for steering a boat.

RUNNING LIGHTS - Lights required to be shown on boats underway between sundown and sunup.

S

SAMSON POST - A single bitt in the bow or stern of a boat, fastened to structural members.

SCOPE - The ratio of the length of an anchor line, from a vessel's bow to the anchor, to the depth of the water.

SCREW - A boat's propeller.

SEA ANCHOR - Any device used to reduce a boat's drift before the wind. Compare with DROGUE.

SEA ROOM - A safe distance from the shore or other hazards.

SEAWORTHY - A boat or a boat's gear able to meet the usual sea conditions.

SECURE - To make fast.

SEIZE - To bind two lines together with light line.

SET - Direction toward which the current is flowing.

SHACKLE - A "U" shaped connector with a pin or bolt across the open end.

SHEAVE - The grooved wheel or roller in a block (pulley).

SHEER - The fore-and-aft curvature of the deck as shown in side elevation.

SHEET - The line used to control the forward or athwartships movement of a sail.

SHEET BEND - A knot used to join two ropes. Functionally different from a square knot in that it can be used between lines of different diameters.

SHIP - A larger vessel usually thought of as being used for ocean travel. A vessel able to carry a "boat" on board.

SHORT SPLICE - A method of permanently joining the ends of two ropes.

SHROUD - The standing rigging that supports the mast at the sides of the boat.

SLACK - Not fastened; loose. Also, to loosen.

SLOOP - A single masted vessel with working sails (main and jib) set fore and aft.

SPAR - A general term for masts, yards, booms, etc.

SPLICE - To permanently join two ropes by tucking their strands alternately over and under each other.

SPRING LINE - A pivot line used in docking, undocking, or to prevent the boat from moving forward or astern while made fast to a dock.

SQUALL - A sudden, violent wind often accompanied by rain.

SQUARE KNOT - a knot used to join two lines of similar size. Also called a reef knot.

STANDING PART - That part of a line which is made fast. The main part of a line as distinguished from the bight and the end.

STANDING RIGGING - The permanent shrouds and stays that support the mast.

STARBOARD - The right side of a boat when looking forward.

STEM - The foremost upright timber of a vessel to which the keel and ends of the planks are attached.

STERN - The after part of the boat.

STERN LINE - A docking line leading from the stern.

STOCK - The cross bar of an anchor.

STOW - To put an item in its proper place.

SWAMP - To fill with water, but not settle to the bottom.

T

TACK - To come about; the lower forward corner of a sail; sailing with the wind on a given side of the boat, as starboard or port tack.

TACKLE - A combination of blocks and line to increase mechanical advantage.

THWART - A seat or brace running laterally across a boat.

THWARTSHIPS - At right angles to the centerline of the boat.

TIDE - The periodic rise and fall of water level in the oceans.

TILLER - A bar or handle for turning a boat's rudder or an outboard motor.

TOPSIDES - The sides of a vessel between the waterline and the deck; sometimes referring to onto or above the deck.

TRANSOM - The stern cross-section of a square sterned boat.

TRIM - Fore and aft balance of a boat.

TRUE WIND - The actual direction from which the wind is blowing.

U

UNDERWAY - Vessel in motion, i.e., when not moored, at anchor, or aground.

V

V BOTTOM - A hull with the bottom section in the shape of a "V".

W

WAKE - Moving waves, track or path that a boat leaves behind it, when moving across the waters.

WATERLINE - A line painted on a hull which shows the point to which a boat sinks when it is properly trimmed (see BOOT TOP).

WAY - Movement of a vessel through the water such as headway, sternway or leeway.

WHARF - A man-made structure bounding the edge of a dock and built along or at an angle to the shoreline, used for loading, unloading, or tying up vessels.

WHIPPING - The act of wrapping the end of a piece of rope with small line, tape or plastic to prevent it from fraying.

WINDWARD - Toward the direction from which the wind is coming.

Y

YAW - To swing off course, as when due to the impact of a following or quartering sea.

YAWL - A two-masted sailboat with the small mizzen mast stepped abaft the rudder post.

Hypothermia

Hypothermia is being cold. But it is being cold in a way that is far more serious than the discomfort you feel on a raw winter day. Hypothermia is life-threatening cold.

But hypothermia is not "freezing to death." It is not even frostbite. Hypothermia can kill at temperatures well above freezing, and can be a serious problem for some people even in comfortably mild temperatures.

Hypothermia is the reduction of the body's core temperature below the point where normal biological functions can occur. It represents a failure of the body's ability to generate sufficient heat to offset losses, either because heat loss is so rapid, or the resources for generating heat are not available, or the heat-generating mechanisms are impaired.

Hypothermia is a major killer of victims of aquatic mishaps, as well as people injured, ill, or unable to take shelter. It is commonly referred to in newspaper accounts as "exposure."

Hypothermia requires prompt and sophisticated medical treatment; it is not a "first aid" case. It is important to recognize the conditions that could lead to hypothermia early, take steps to avoid them, and seek prompt medical attention for people who are suffering from it. The successful management of hypothermia cases is not trivial, even for trained and well-equipped emergency medical centers.

Recognizing Hypothermia

It is unfortunate that one of the first things affected by hypothermia is the ability to recognize and understand the implications of what is happening. A person working alone must be aware of the conditions that can lead to hypothermia and take steps to avoid or minimize them, since he probably will not recognize the degradation of his abilities as hypothermia progresses, or overestimate his own ability to "tough it out." People in groups must assume the responsibility for monitoring each other and for taking steps to counter it, even in the face of protests that everything is "all right."

The human body has a remarkably efficient mechanism for maintaining its own internal environment. The chemical and biological processes that support life can operate only within a narrow range of temperatures, and the body uses food energy to help maintain its own temperature within that range. If the body heats up, excess heat is dumped to the surroundings. If the body cools down, automatic mechanisms work to conserve heat and to generate more.

Hypothermia is a failure of the regulatory mechanism that conserves and generates body heat.

As the body's temperature falls, the temperature drop is detected by a mechanism in the brain and several things begin to happen. The blood flow within the body is altered in subtle ways so that more of the body's heat is shunted away from the skin surface and toward the vital organs (brain, heart, lungs). Stored food energy is called upon and the metabolic "furnace" starts generating more heat. These adaptations to cold are generally not visible.

What is visible is the "gooseflesh" that is one indication of the routing of blood away from the skin, and the shivering that is part of the heat-producing activity.

If these actions are not able to keep up with heat losses, they become more intense. The reduction of blood flow to the extremities (hands, arms, legs) can be so severe that functioning of the small muscle groups required for fine movement is interfered with. This can happen within a very few minutes of immersion, and may not be a direct function of the chilling of the muscles of the hands and fingers themselves. Victims thrown suddenly into 65-70 degree water have reported that they were unable to cope with the straps and buckles on a standard PFD, even though they were highly trained and motivated and had a great deal of experience with these devices.

The shivering becomes more intense as body core temperature continues to fall, involving larger and larger groups of muscles. The shivering can be so strong as to even interfere with walking.

The victim at this point may show signs of confusion and a lack of responsiveness. Speech becomes slurred, and incoherent. If he is alone, or if there is no occasion to speak to companions, this change may go undetected.

As the body's temperature continues to fall and as resources are used up, the shivering diminishes, then stops. The victim becomes increasingly lethargic and uncoordinated, eventually passing into unconsciousness and death.

Prevention of Hypothermia

Prevention of hypothermia is relatively easy. Most of the things you can do to combat hypothermia are "common sense" things you would normally do anyway.

Avoid situations that promote loss of body heat. Essentially, this means keeping dry and out of the wind.

Of course, if you fall overboard, or if your boat capsizes, it is difficult to avoid getting wet. On the other hand, anything you can do to get out of the water, even though you are thoroughly soaked, helps reduce the rate at which you lose heat.

There are cases on record, for example, of capsizings in which the length of survival depended on the extent to which the victims were able to get out of the water. Those who were able to get out of the water reduced the rate of loss of body heat and survived longer, while those who stayed in the water died.

After avoiding getting wet, it is important to avoid the wind. Even a wet body in wet clothing can generate enough heat to maintain it's core temperature for a time if the heat it does make is kept close. Wet clothing can, under certain circumstances, even be dried by body heat. However, if the heat trapped in the clothing is carried away by wind, it must be replaced constantly. In addition, evaporation of water from the body and wet clothes carries more heat away with it, heat that comes from the body.

Wet clothing without wind is less effective than dry clothing, but it is far better than it would be if wind were present.

The type of clothing material also makes a significant difference in rate of heat loss when it is wet. Many synthetic fibers of the sort typically found in modern outdoor clothing are effective in reducing heat loss when dry, but afford virtually no protection to heat loss when wet. Wool, on the other hand, retains a higher percentage of its insulating properties than most other fibers. Wet wool clothing is a poorer insulator than dry wool clothing, or than dry synthetic clothing. But wet wool is far more effective than wet synthetic fabric.

If you have done all you can to reduce the rate of heat loss, the next concern is to increase the resources available to produce heat. This means food.

Since you seldom can eat after an accident dunks you in the water, and you cannot predict when an accident will occur, you should make it a practice never to go into a potential hypothermia situation without having eaten a good meal. This includes not only boating activities, but anything that involves working or playing out of doors.

A typical scenario has a sportsman skipping lunch to take advantage of good fishing conditions, or to get in some extra duck hunting before bad weather gets worse. Then when an incident does occur, he has no ready food reserves to be converted into heat, and a situation that is already bad gets worse more rapidly than it would have had the victim eaten properly.

Other physical conditions can also contribute to diminished capacity to maintain body heat. The elderly, the very young, and those who have recently been ill are particularly susceptible, as are those whose metabolism has been suppressed by drugs or alcohol.

Aftereffects of Hypothermia

Mild hypothermia, treated by the victim, will probably have no long-term effects. In fact, it is likely that you have experienced mild hypothermia at some time in your life and were not even aware of it.

More serious cases, those in whom the signs of hypothermia are obvious, should receive medical attention. Improperly managed treatment, especially that involving body rewarming, can cause worse damage than already exists. It can even cause death.

Summary

In conclusion, then, hypothermia is a condition which can turn a bad situation, or even only a mildly annoying one, into a life-threatening emergency. It is important to be aware of and sensitive to the conditions that favor the development of hypothermia, and to take prompt action to minimize risk to yourself and to others with you.

If hypothermia is suspected, seek prompt and competent medical attention.

Substance Abuse

A remarkable number of boating-related terms seem to be connected with alcohol use. Everybody knows what it means when the "sun is over the yardarm," and many even know that to "splice the mainbrace" means to take a drink.

Recreational boating is an activity that people engage in for fun: For many boaters, their entire social life revolves around boats, boating activity, and their boating friends. And some of these social activities include consumption of alcohol and other substances for the purpose of altering feelings, moods or perceptions. Some boaters have actually been heard to boast that, gallon for gallon, they consumed more beer, wine and liquor on their boat than they did fuel!

The moral and legal issues of drug and alcohol use and abuse aside, it is a simple fact that drugs and alcohol have no place on a boat underway, or in the operator or crew of a boat underway.

Operating a boat is usually a simple, relaxed affair. After all, we do it for fun and relaxation. But a single wrong choice, a single moment of inattention can turn a pleasant afternoon outing on the water into a disaster.

Over a thousand people a year die in boating accidents. Over half of those deaths involve the use of alcohol, either by the victim or by another party involved in the incident. Add to this number the thousands who each year receive serious injuries in boating accidents and you have a frightening picture of needless suffering and expense, much of which is directly attributable to unwise, and unnecessary use of alcohol and other drugs.

The fact is that boating, pleasant as it is, is a stressful activity. Studies have shown that after only a few hours on the water a normal, healthy, young boat operator's reactions, perceptions and judgment can be as impaired as if he were legally intoxicated, simply from the effects of unaccustomed exposure to fresh air, glare, ultraviolet light, motion, and noise.

If you doubt that these factors can alter behavior, spend a couple of hours at the launching ramps watching otherwise rational people trying to load their boats on trailers. Add the effects of a few drinks, and you have a truly explosive situation.

Alcohol and other drug use is not only a bad idea for the operator of a boat, but for passengers and guests, as well. It is often difficult enough to get about on the moving deck of a small boat when you are at your best. When you are unbalanced by the effects of a few beers, it is simply asking for a dunking.

If you survive the first few seconds of an automobile accident, the only additional pain you are likely to feel is in your pocketbook. In an accident on the water, on the other hand, even if you survive the initial accident, you may find your situation deteriorating rapidly. The aftermath can, in fact, be much worse than the accident itself.

If the victims of an accident have been ingesting drugs or alcohol, their chances of surviving are seriously reduced. Alcohol and depressant drugs lower the body's resistance to hypothermia (see Appendix A). An intoxicated person who falls into the water is much more likely than a sober one to become disoriented and swim downward rather than toward the surface. And finally, just when good judgment and mental sharpness is needed most, they are muddled by the intoxicants.

In summary, then, if you feel that you must serve or consume alcoholic beverages on your boat, do so after you are secured to a pier or ashore for the day. Even at that, it may be dangerous to negotiate along a pier after a few drinks.

Illegal drugs, on the other hand, are just that, illegal. If you or guests on your boat are found in possession of or using illegal drugs, the real consequences can be devastating for all involved. At the least you may stand to lose your boat and other personal assets, not to mention your freedom.

Note: Even legal drugs may impair physical ability and mental judgment (e.g., antihistamines, and other sedatives, tranquilizers, etc.).

To repeat, there is no place for alcohol or drug use, even in moderation, in boating. Don't do it, and don't tolerate it on your boat. You cannot afford the risk.

Appendix C

LISTING OF U. S. COAST GUARD DISTRICT OFFICES

FIRST COAST GUARD DISTRICT:

COMMANDER
U. S. Coast Guard
1st. Coast Guard District
Coast Guard Building
408 Atlantic Avenue
Boston, MA   02210-2209

SECOND COAST GUARD DISTRICT:

COMMANDER
U. S. Coast Guard
2nd. Coast Guard District
1430 Olive Street
St. Louis, MO   63101-2378

FIFTH COAST GUARD DISTRICT:

COMMANDER
U. S. Coast Guard
5th. Coast Guard District
Federal Building
431 Crawford Street
Portsmouth, VA   23704-5004

SEVENTH COAST GUARD DISTRICT:

COMMANDER
U. S. Coast Guard
7th. Coast Guard District
51 S. W. 1st Avenue
Miami, FL   33130-1608

EIGHTH COAST GUARD DISTRICT:

COMMANDER
U. S. Coast Guard
8th. Coast Guard District
Hale Boggs Federal Building
500 Camp Street
New Orleans, LA   70130-3396

NINTH COAST GUARD DISTRICT:

COMMANDER
U. S. Coast Guard
9th. Coast Guard District
1240 East 9th Street
Cleveland, OH 44199-2060

ELEVENTH COAST GUARD DISTRICT:

COMMANDER
U. S. Coast Guard
11th. Coast Guard District
Union Bank Building
400 Oceangate
Long Beach, CA 90822-5399

THIRTEENTH COAST GUARD DISTRICT:

COMMANDER
U. S. Coast Guard
13th. Coast Guard District
Jackson Federal Building
915 Second Avenue
Seattle, WA 98174-1067

FOURTEENTH COAST GUARD DISTRICT:

COMMANDER
U. S. Coast Guard
14th. Coast Guard District
Prince Kalanianaole Federal Building
300 Ala Moana Blvd, 9th Floor
Honolulu, HI 96850-4892

SEVENTEENTH COAST GUARD DISTRICT:

COMMANDER
U. S. Coast Guard
17th. Coast Guard District
P. O. Box 3-5000
Juneau, AK 99802-1217

Float Plan

When you go on an outing you plan as much as possible so that nothing goes wrong. You watch the weather, you carry enough fuel, and you carry spare parts for emergency repairs.

But if you were to have an accident, or be stranded with a disabled boat, or if the boat were to sink or be destroyed by fire, would anyone know where you were? Would they even know you were gone?

You can ensure that all the answers to these questions will be answered in your favor if you simply file a <u>float plan</u> with a responsible authority, family member, or friend before you leave.

A well thought-out float plan provides invaluable information that will help searchers locate you if you should be lost — information that others may simply not have, such as the sort of emergency equipment you have on board, the fuel capacity (useful in determining where you

<u>might</u> have decided to go for the day).

Most important, it will tell when you should be back, which in turn tells when you should be considered overdue, and where you intend to cruise. This helps focus search activities in areas where they will do the most good.

In this section is a sample form that you can copy or modify to suit your needs. Be sure to give it to a <u>responsible individual</u>, and be equally certain to notify them on your return or if you decide to change your plans.

You will probably never need it, but if you do become the object of a search, a good float plan will help you be found quicker, when the danger of permanent injury is less. In addition, your quick rescue will also help your fellow man, since it will free up search and rescue facilities to look for others who were not as far-sighted and well-prepared as you.

VESSEL INFORMATION DATA SHEET

When requesting assistance from the Coast Guard, you may be asked to furnish the following details. This list should, therefore, be filled out as completely as possible and posted alongside your transmitter with the *Distress Communications Form.*

1. *Description of Vessel Requiring Assistance.*

Hull markings _____

Home port _____

Draft _____

Sails: Color _____

        Markings _____

Bowsprit ? _____

Outriggers ? _____

Flying Bridge ? _____

Other prominent features _____

2. *Survival Gear Aboard (Circle Yes or No)*

Personal Flotation Devices	Yes	No
Flares	Yes	No
Flashlight	Yes	No
Raft	Yes	No
Dinghy or Tender	Yes	No
Anchor	Yes	No
Spotlight	Yes	No
Auxiliary power	Yes	No
Horn	Yes	No

3. *Electronic Equipment*

	VHF	MF	HF
Radiotelephone(s)			
Channels/Frequencies	22	Yes	No;
available	2670 kHz	Yes	No
Radar		Yes	No
Depth Finder		Yes	No
Loran		Yes	No
Direction Finder		Yes	No
EPIRB		Yes	No

4. *Vessel Owner/Operator*

Owner name _____

    Address _____

        _____

    Telephone number _____

Operator's name _____

    Address _____

        _____

    Telephone number _____

Is owner/operator an experienced sailor?   Yes No

5. *Miscellaneous*

Be prepared to describe local weather conditions.

FLOAT PLAN

Complete this plan, before going boating and leave it with a reliable person who can be depended upon to notify the Coast Guard, or other rescue organization, should you not return as scheduled. Do not file this plan with the Coast Guard.

TODAY'S DATE_____

1. NAME OF PERSON REPORTING _____

   TELEPHONE NUMBER_____

2. DESCRIPTION OF BOAT. TYPE_____COLOR_____

   TRIM_____REGISTRATION NO._____

   LENGTH_____NAME_____MAKE_____

   OTHER INFO._____

3. PERSONS ABOARD_____

NAME	AGE	ADDRESS & TELE. NO.
_____	____	_____
_____	____	_____
_____	____	_____

4. ENGINE TYPE_____H.P._____

   NO. OF ENGINES_____FUEL CAPACITY_____

5. SURVIVAL EQUIPMENT: (CHECK AS APPROPRIATE)

   PFDs_____FLARES_____MIRROR_____

   SMOKE SIGNALS_____FLASHLIGHT_____FOOD_____

   PADDLES_____WATER_____OTHERS_____

   ANCHOR_____RAFT OR DINGHY_____EPIRB_____

6. RADIO   YES/NO   TYPE_____FREQS._____

7. TRIP EXPECTATIONS: LEAVE AT_____(TIME)

   FROM_____GOING TO_____

   EXPECT TO RETURN BY_____(TIME) AND IN

   NO EVENT LATER THAN_____

8. ANY OTHER PERTINENT INFO._____

9. AUTOMOBILE LICENSE_____TYPE_____

   TRAILER LICENSE_____COLOR AND MAKE OF

   AUTO_____

   WHERE PARKED_____

10. IF NOT RETURNED BY_____(TIME) CALL THE

    COAST GUARD, OR_____(LOCAL AUTHORITY)

    TELEPHONE NUMBERS_____

Accident Reporting

If you have a boating accident that results in death or injury to a person, or in more than $200 in damage to vessels, you must file a report.

If someone dies as a result of the accident, or if a person is missing after an accident and it is reasonable to assume that that person is dead or injured, you must file the report within 48 hours of the accident. Otherwise, you must file within 10 days.

When someone dies or is missing, it is obvious that a report must be filed. Other cases may not be so obvious. If the worst injury is minor enough to need first aid only, you may not need to file a report. On the other hand, it does not take much damage to amount to $200 worth.

There are no penalties for filing a report that was not needed. There are, on the other hand, penalties for failing to report a reportable accident. You can be fined a few hundred dollars for failing to report an accident. If the case involves gross negligence and failure to file a proper report, criminal penalties up to and including a $1,000 fine and up to a year in jail may be assessed. So it is to your advantage to report all but the most trivial accidents.

If you are involved in an accident, you are expected to render whatever help you can to others who may need it. This humanitarian concern is supported by legal penalties (up to $1,000 in fines and/or two years in prison) for failure to render reasonable assistance.

Just remember that, while you are expected to help if you can, you are **NOT** expected to attempt rescues that are beyond your ability, or that are likely to result in additional injury or damage. No matter how noble the intentions, heroic efforts that result in additional victims only place an added burden on search and rescue resources. These attempts may be worse than no assistance at all.

Whom do you report to? In most cases, you should report to state conservation or department of natural resources officers. Occasionally, depending on the location and other factors, reports should go to the county sheriff, state police, or municipal police. On Federal waters, or in areas where other authorities are not available, report to the nearest Coast Guard office.

You should know who the responsible authority is in the area where you do your boating, but if you contact the wrong ones, they will direct you to the proper channels. The important thing is that you make the report.

The officers to whom you report will give you the necessary forms (Coast Guard form CG-3865 or equivalent.) These forms ensure that necessary information is provided, and that it is in a format that allows for consistent gathering of accident information. This information is compiled by the Coast

Guard, and is used to determine future directions for boating safety programs and activities.

The personal details of the report (name and address of owner, names of accident victims, etc.) are protected under Federal law. You need not worry that this information will be released to any other than appropriate law enforcement personnel.

STUDENT COURSE CRITIQUE and QUESTIONNAIRE

We are asking you for your comments on improving this course. Please comment on the entire course as you desire. We would like definite answers on the following questions:

1. I found out about this course through: (Check those that apply.)
   - (a) Newspaper feature article ( )   (e) Word of mouth ( )
   - (b) Newspaper classified ad ( )   (f) Posters ( )
   - (c) Radio broadcast ( )   (g) Other (Please ( )
   - (d) TV program or spot ( )   list below)

   _____

2. My impression of the course is that it has been:
   - (a) Very worthwhile ( )   (e) Too detailed ( )   (h) Too short ( )
   - (b) Good ( )   (f) Too skimpy ( )   (i) Too costly ( )
   - (c) Only fair ( )   (g) Too long ( )   (j) Other (Please
   - (d) Poor ( )   indicate below)

   _____

3. I feel that more time should have been spent on_____
   _____

4. I think that too much time was spent on_____
   _____

5. I feel the course should be improved by_____
   _____

6. What is your evaluation of the following training aids:
   - (a) Slides _____
   - (b) Films _____
   - (c) Instructor's training aids _____
   - (d) Student response_____

7. Additional comments:

After you have completed this questionnaire, please tear it out, fold it, tape it across the bottom, and mail it directly to the addressee. No postage is necessary. Thank you for your cooperation.

DEPARTMENT OF TRANSPORTATION
COMMANDANT, G-BAU
Washington, DC 20593

DC-E
_____

U. S. COAST GUARD AUXILIARY NATIONAL STORE
9449 Watson Industrial Park
St. Louis, MO 63126

 DC-E

STUDENT COURSE CRITIQUE and QUESTIONNAIRE

We are asking you for your comments on improving this course. Please comment on the entire course as you desire. We would like definite answers on the following questions:

1. I found out about this course through: (Check those that apply.)
   - (a) Newspaper feature article ( )   (e) Word of mouth ( )
   - (b) Newspaper classified ad ( )   (f) Posters ( )
   - (c) Radio broadcast ( )   (g) Other (Please ( )
   - (d) TV program or spot ( )   list below)

   _____

2. My impression of the course is that it has been:
   - (a) Very worthwhile ( )   (e) Too detailed ( )   (h) Too Short ( )
   - (b) Good ( )   (f) Too skimpy ( )   (i) Too costly ( )
   - (c) Only fair ( )   (g) Too long ( )   (j) Other (Please
   - (d) Poor ( )   indicate below)

   _____

3. I feel that more time should have been spent on _____

4. I think that too much time was spent on _____

5. I feel the course should be improved by _____

6. What is your evaluation of the following training aids:
   - (a) Slides _____
   - (b) Films _____
   - (c) Instructor's training aids _____
   - (d) Student response _____

7. Do you know of any group (Boating, industrial, church, scouts, fraternal, social, etc.) who would be interested in one of the following: (Check ones that apply.)
   - (a) Six Lesson - Boating Course ( )
   - (b) Thirteen Lesson - Boating Course ( )
   - (c) Fourteen Lesson - Sail Course ( )
   - (d) A Speaker from the USCG Auxiliary ( )

8. If any of the above are checked, whom should we contact?
   Name _____
   Address _____
   Phone Number _____

9. Are you interested in joining the United States Coast Guard Auxiliary? If so, please fill in the following:
   Name _____
   Address _____
   Phone Number _____

10. This course was sponsored by Flotilla _____ We meet at _____
   _____ on _____
   (Please make a note of the place and date. You will be most welcome to attend our next meeting and meet our other members.)

After you have completed this questionnaire, please tear it out and hand it to your Instructor or Course Supervisor. Thank you for your cooperation.

PRIVACY ACT STATEMENT

CG-2730 (REV 6-73) AUXILIARY - ENROLLMENT APPLICATION.

IN ACCORDANCE WITH 5 USC 552a(e)(3), THE FOLLOWING INFORMATION IS PROVIDED TO YOU WHEN SUPPLYING PERSONAL INFORMATION TO THE U. S. COAST GUARD.

1. AUTHORITY WHICH AUTHORIZED THE SOLICITATION OF THE INFORMATION: 14 USC SEC 821, 822, 826.

2. PRINCIPAL PURPOSE(S) FOR WHICH INFORMATION IS INTENDED TO BE USED: TO ESTABLISH A RECORD FOR THE INDIVIDUAL IN THE AUXILIARY MANAGEMENT INFORMATION SYSTEM.

3. THE ROUTINE USES WHICH MAY BE MADE OF THE INFORMATION: PROVIDE IDENTIFICATION AND ADDRESS INFORMATION TO THE FOLLOWING: (1) DIRECTORS OF AUXILIARY. (2) MEMBERS OF THE AUXILIARY. (3) COAST GUARD INSTITUTE. (4) NOAA.

4. WHETHER OR NOT DISCLOSURE OF SUCH INFORMATION IS MANDATORY OR VOLUNTARY (REQUIRED BY LAW OR OPTIONAL) AND THE EFFECTS ON THE INDIVIDUAL, IF ANY, OF NOT PROVIDING ALL OR ANY PART OF THE REQUESTED INFORMATION: DISCLOSURE OF THIS INFORMATION IS VOLUNTARY, BUT FAILURE TO PROVIDE INFORMATION CAN PREVENT ENROLLMENT OF THE PERSON IN THE AUXILIARY.

DEPARTMENT OF
TRANSPORTATION
U. S. COAST GUARD
CG-2730 (Rev. 6-73)

AUXILIARY-ENROLLMENT APPLICATION

SECTION I - PERSONAL DATA(All Blocks Not Shaded To Be Completed By Applicant)

MEMBER NUMBER (1-10) | Trans Code (11-13) | LAST NAME (14-25) | FIRST NAME & INITIAL (26-37)

Ø 1 1

Check (38-39) | (Area) HOME PHONE (40-49) | (Area) BUSINESS PHONE (50-59)

MR.

MS.

STREET OR P.O. BOX (60-79)

MEMBER NUMBER (1-10) | Trans Code (11-13) | NAME (14-17) | CITY (18-32) | State (33-34)

Keypunch from above | Ø 1 2

Zip Code (35-39) | Status (40-41) | Occ. (42-44) | Date of Birth (45-50) | Fac. (51-52, 55)

M M D D Y Y

U

SOCIAL SECURITY NO. (56-64) | Date of Enrl. (65-70) | Base Enrl. Date(71-76)

M M D D Y Y | M M D D Y Y

OCCUPATION:

FACILITY STATUS (Indicate Type & Percent Owned)

	%		%	Name and Address of Facility Co-Owner (if any)
BOAT		Radio Station		
ACFT		Non-Facility Owner		

List any Yacht, Motorboat, Aeronautical, or Radio organizations to which you belong.

Describe briefly any nautical, aeronautical, or communications experience and list certificates and/or licenses held. If applying for special membership (non-facility status), describe special qualifications.

U.S. Citizen ➤	CHECK	PRIOR AUXILIARY MEMBERSHIP DATA			
	YES	PRIOR MEMBER NO.	FROM (Date)	TO (Date)	HIGHEST OFFICE HELD
	NO				

I Pledge to support the U. S. Coast Guard Auxiliary and its purposes and abide by the governing policies established by the Commandant of the U. S. Coast Guard and the Auxiliary Manual, CG-305.

SIGNATURE OF APPLICANT | DATE SIGNED

SECTION II - AUXILIARY RECOMMENDATIONS

APPLICANT IS:	Reason for Non-Acceptability	BASIS FOR MEMBERSHIP
Acceptable		Facility Owner
Not Acceptable		Special Qualifications

ATTACHMENTS: ☐ CG-2736 ☐ CG-2746 ☐ CG-3616 ☐ OTHER

Date Fwd.	Signature of Flotilla Commander	Optional Endorsement	Flotilla Number

SECTION III - DIRAUX ENDORSEMENT

Applicant is:	accepted	Remarks:
	not accepted	
as a:	facility owning member	
	specially qualified member	
	flotilla member	Signature of DIRAUX	Date
with status as a:	member-at-large	

PREVIOUS EDITIONS ARE OBSOLETE

SECTION IV - MEMBERSHIP RECORD

DESIGNATION	DATE DESIGNATED & FORMS ISSUED	REMARKS
CONDITIONAL MEMBER		
BASICALLY QUALIFIED MEMBER		
AUXOP		
PERMANENT MEMBER		
OTHER *(Specify)*		
INSTRUCTOR		
COURTESY EXAMINER		
AVIATION INSPECTOR		
COMMUNICATIONS INSPECTOR		
MEMBER-AT-LARGE		

OFFICES HELD				AWARDS AND DECORATIONS	
ELECTED	DATE	APPOINTED	DATE	TITLE	DATE

SECTION V - OPERATIONAL SPECIALTY RECORD

SPECIALTY		DATE OSC EXAM PASSED	OSC EXAM GRADE	DATE PRACTICAL FACTORS COMPLETED	CG-2836 ISSUED
PATROLS					
SEARCH AND RESCUE					
COMMUNICATIONS					
SEAMANSHIP					
PILOTING	Part A				
	Part B				
WEATHER					
ADMINISTRATION					

SECTION VI - TRANSFER AND DISENROLLMENT RECORD

Transferred to *(List New Member No.)*	Date Transferred	Transferred to *(List New Member No.)*	Date Transferred

DISENROLLMENT	Date Disenrolled:	Reason for Disenrollment: ☐ INACTIVITY ☐ CAUSE ☐ DEATH ☐ OWN REQUEST ☐ OTHER *(Specify)*	CG-4949 submitted ☐
Signature of DIRAUX			Date

U.S. AIDS TO NAVIGATION SYSTEM
on navigable waters except Western Rivers and Intracoastal Waterway

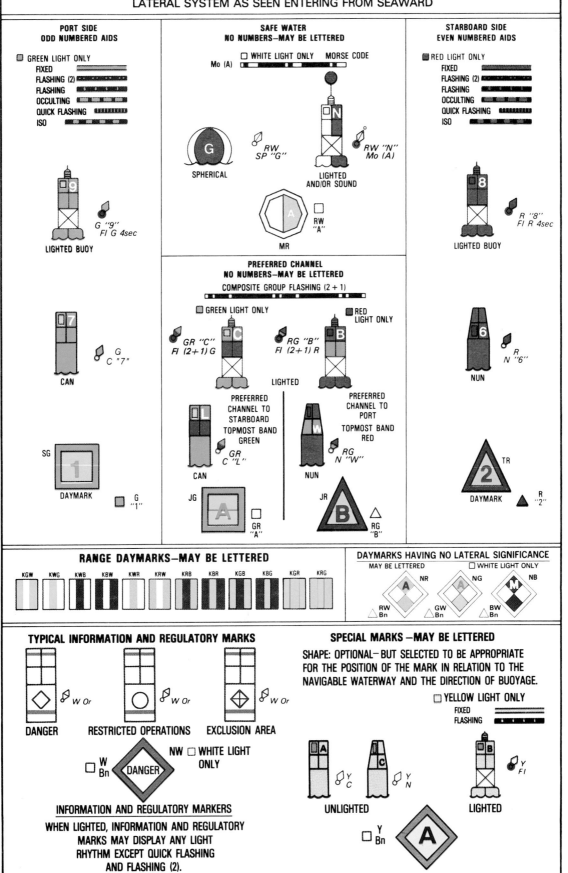

Plate 1

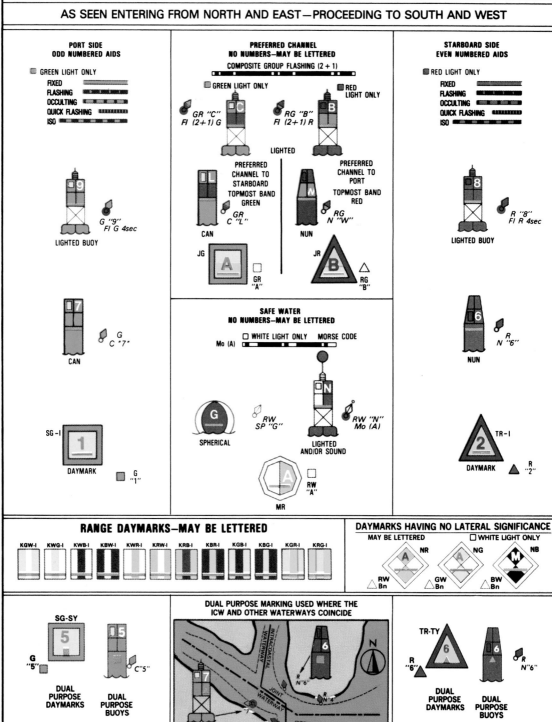

U.S. AIDS TO NAVIGATION SYSTEM
on the Intracoastal Waterway

AS SEEN ENTERING FROM NORTH AND EAST—PROCEEDING TO SOUTH AND WEST

PORT SIDE
ODD NUMBERED AIDS

GREEN LIGHT ONLY

FIXED	
FLASHING	
OCCULTING	
QUICK FLASHING	
ISO	

G "9"
Fl G 4sec

LIGHTED BUOY

CAN

G
C "7"

SG-I
1
DAYMARK

G "1"

PREFERRED CHANNEL
NO NUMBERS—MAY BE LETTERED
COMPOSITE GROUP FLASHING (2 + 1)

GREEN LIGHT ONLY

RED LIGHT ONLY

GR "C"
Fl (2+1) G

RG "B"
Fl (2+1) R

LIGHTED

PREFERRED CHANNEL TO STARBOARD
TOPMOST BAND GREEN

GR C "L"

CAN

PREFERRED CHANNEL TO PORT
TOPMOST BAND RED

RG N "W"

NUN

JG
A
GR "A"

JR
B
RG "B"

SAFE WATER
NO NUMBERS—MAY BE LETTERED

WHITE LIGHT ONLY   MORSE CODE
Mo (A)

G
RW SP "G"

SPHERICAL

N
RW "N"
Mo (A)

LIGHTED AND/OR SOUND

A
MR

RW "A"

STARBOARD SIDE
EVEN NUMBERED AIDS

RED LIGHT ONLY

FIXED	
FLASHING	
OCCULTING	
QUICK FLASHING	
ISO	

8
R "8"
Fl R 4sec

LIGHTED BUOY

6
R N "6"

NUN

2
TR-I
DAYMARK

R "2"

RANGE DAYMARKS—MAY BE LETTERED

KGW-I KWG-I KWB-I KBW-I KWR-I KRW-I KRB-I KBR-I KGB-I KBG-I KGR-I KRG-I

DAYMARKS HAVING NO LATERAL SIGNIFICANCE

MAY BE LETTERED   WHITE LIGHT ONLY

A NR   A NG   M NB

RW Bn   GW Bn   BW Bn

PORT SIDE DUAL PURPOSE

SG-SY
5

5

G "5"

DUAL PURPOSE DAYMARKS

C "5"

DUAL PURPOSE BUOYS

TR-SY
6

6

R "6"

R N "6"

JG-SY
A

JR-SY
D

RG "A"   RG "D"

DUAL PURPOSE MARKING USED WHERE THE ICW AND OTHER WATERWAYS COINCIDE

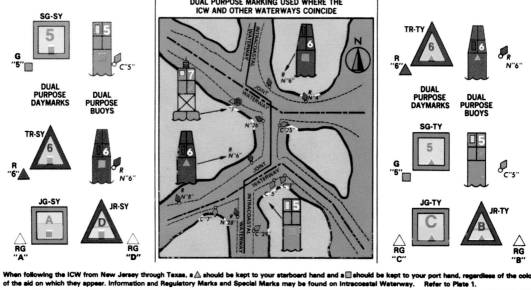

STARBOARD SIDE DUAL PURPOSE

TR-TY
6

6

R "6"

R N "6"

DUAL PURPOSE DAYMARKS

DUAL PURPOSE BUOYS

SG-TY
5

5

G "5"

C "5"

JG-TY
C

JR-TY
B

RG "C"   RG "B"

When following the ICW from New Jersey through Texas, a △ should be kept to your starboard hand and a ▢ should be kept to your port hand, regardless of the color of the aid on which they appear. Information and Regulatory Marks and Special Marks may be found on Intracoastal Waterway.   Refer to Plate 1.

Plate 2

AS SEEN ENTERING FROM SEAWARD

PORT SIDE OR RIGHT DESCENDING BANK

GREEN
FLASHING

ISO

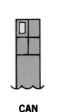

LIGHTED BUOY

CAN

SG

PASSING DAYMARK

CG

CROSSING DAYMARK

176.9

MILE BOARD

PREFERRED CHANNEL

MARK JUNCTIONS AND OBSTRUCTIONS
COMPOSITE GROUP FLASHING (2+1)

PREFERRED CHANNEL TO STARBOARD	PREFERRED CHANNEL TO PORT
TOPMOST BAND GREEN	TOPMOST BAND RED
Fl (2+1) G	Fl (2+1) R
☐ WHITE OR GREEN LIGHTS	☐ WHITE OR RED LIGHTS

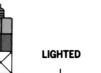

LIGHTED

CAN   **NUN**

JG   **JR**

STARBOARD SIDE OR LEFT DESCENDING BANK

RED
FLASHING (2)

ISO

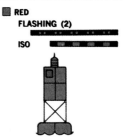

LIGHTED BUOY

NUN

TR

PASSING DAYMARK

CR

CROSSING DAYMARK

123.5

MILE BOARD

DAYMARKS HAVING NO LATERAL SIGNIFICANCE

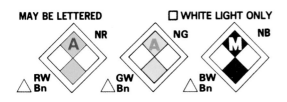

MAY BE LETTERED   ☐ WHITE LIGHT ONLY

NR   NG   NB

RW Bn   GW Bn   BW Bn

INFORMATION AND REGULATORY
MARKS, AND SPECIAL MARKS,
MAY BE FOUND ON THE
WESTERN RIVER SYSTEM.

Refer to Plate 1

Plate 3

UNIFORM STATE WATERWAY MARKING SYSTEM

STATE WATERS AND DESIGNATED STATE WATERS FOR PRIVATE AIDS TO NAVIGATION

REGULATORY MARKERS

BOAT EXCLUSION AREA

EXPLANATION MAY BE PLACED OUTSIDE THE CROSSED DIAMOND SHAPE, SUCH AS DAM, RAPIDS, SWIM AREA, ETC.

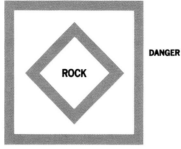

DANGER

THE NATURE OF DANGER MAY BE INDICATED INSIDE THE DIAMOND SHAPE, SUCH AS ROCK, WRECK, SHOAL, DAM, ETC.

CONTROLLED AREA

TYPE OF CONTROL IS INDICATED IN THE CIRCLE, SUCH AS SLOW, NO WAKE, ANCHORING, ETC.

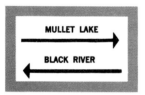

MULLET LAKE →

← BLACK RIVER

INFORMATION

FOR DISPLAYING INFORMATION SUCH AS DIRECTIONS, DISTANCES, LOCATIONS, ETC.

BUOY USED TO DISPLAY REGULATORY MARKERS

MAY SHOW WHITE LIGHT
MAY BE LETTERED

AIDS TO NAVIGATION

MAY SHOW WHITE REFLECTOR OR LIGHT

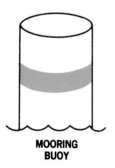

MOORING BUOY

WHITE WITH BLUE BAND

MAY SHOW WHITE REFLECTOR OR LIGHT

RED-STRIPED WHITE BUOY

MAY BE LETTERED
DO NOT PASS BETWEEN BUOY AND NEAREST SHORE

BLACK-TOPPED WHITE BUOY

MAY BE NUMBERED

PASS TO NORTH OR EAST OF BUOY

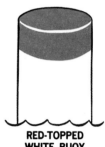

RED-TOPPED WHITE BUOY

PASS TO SOUTH OR WEST OF BUOY

CARDINAL SYSTEM

MAY SHOW GREEN REFLECTOR OR LIGHT

MAY SHOW RED REFLECTOR OR LIGHT

SOLID RED AND SOLID BLACK BUOYS

USUALLY FOUND IN PAIRS
PASS BETWEEN THESE BUOYS

PORT SIDE ————— LOOKING UPSTREAM ————— STARBOARD SIDE

LATERAL SYSTEM

Plate 4